Gail Duff's
COUNTRY SEASONS COOKBOOK

By the same author:
ORIENTAL VEGETARIAN COOKING

Gail Duff's
COUNTRY SEASONS COOKBOOK

Seasonal recipes for feasts throughout the year

THORSONS PUBLISHING GROUP

Text illustrations by Elaine Hill

First published 1988

© GAIL DUFF 1988

British Library Cataloguing in Publication Data

Duff, Gail
Gail Duff's country seasons cookbook.
1. Vegetarian cookery 2. Dinners and
dining
I. Title
641.5'636   TX837

ISBN 0-7225-1306-2

Published by Thorsons Publishers Limited,
Wellingborough, Northamptonshire, NN8 2RQ,
England.

Printed in Great Britain by Butler & Tanner Limited,
Frome, Somerset.

1 3 5 7 9 10 8 6 4 2

Contents

Introduction

One of the pleasures of life is to be able to entertain friends to a good meal in one's own home, to invite them for a few hours to share your food and your way of life.

Over the past few years, the food and lifestyle of many people have changed in that they have dropped meat from their diet and have become vegetarian. Nuts, pulses, eggs, cheese, fresh vegetables and fruits now form the basis of their everyday meals and many are the tasty dishes that appear on the family supper table. However, when it comes to entertaining guests, especially when some may not be vegetarian, the competent family cook may think that there is a problem. Will they enjoy what I cook? Will it be tasty enough? Will it be grand enough? These are all the questions that may go through his or her mind.

The best piece of advice that I ever heard was that, when you are entertaining, simply make the same meals as you would every day - but make more of them. Take this as the basis of all your vegetarian entertaining and work out from there. You and your family must have a favourite supper dish and, if you all like it, it must be tasty and others will enjoy it too.

Attractive presentation will help to make any dish more special. Arrange food on a serving dish instead of spooning it onto plates in a haphazard fashion. Garnish it with sprigs of fresh herbs, nut halves or chopped nuts, small twists of lemon or cucumber, or a sprinkling of spice, such as paprika. Desserts can be put into pretty glasses which you can stand on lacy paper mats or fresh green leaves for serving. Garnish the plates, if you wish, with fresh flowers. Appealing presentation will always add to the enjoyment of a dish and will give the impression that loving care and trouble have gone into making the meal.

There are many luxury vegetarian ingredients that are too expensive to be added to everyday meals, but which will make perfect dishes for entertaining. Just a few pine nuts or macadamia nuts, for example, will give special and unusual flavours to nut roasts or salads. Then think of all those exotic vegetables and fruits - mangoes, kiwi fruits, pawpaws, globe artichokes and avocados are just a few. These, combined with other seasonal vegetables and fruits, will help to make your dishes both delicious and impressive.

Very simple dishes, made with the best of ingredients and prettily garnished, will always be successful, but as you gain more confidence with your vegetarian entertaining, you may well wish to try more advanced techniques such as making soufflés, wrapping savoury fillings in fresh leaves, or deep frying small fritters in a light and crispy batter. Admittedly, some of these processes are time-consuming, but they are well worth the effort for the effect, flavour and subsequent pleasure that they give.

Never neglect the vegetables when you are entertaining. Make them as important as the main dish, cook them with wine or flavour them with herbs, make them into fresh and attractive salads and they will always turn an ordinary meal into a special one.

Something else which helps to set the scene for a successful dinner party is the look of your table. Use matching crockery and napkins and the best cutlery, put flowers on the table and perhaps a small spray of flowers by each plate.

Entertaining for me, however, does not always mean a grand occasion. It is simply enjoying myself with friends, whether it be in the dining room, round the kitchen table or sitting in the woods with a picnic. So in the Spring, Summer, Autumn and Winter sections, you will find recipes for all occasions, from informal picnics to elegant dinner parties and Sunday teas. They are meals made for sharing and I hope that they will all help with your vegetarian entertaining.

Entertaining in Spring

Where does spring begin and winter end? Although the weather is still cold and often damp, the feeling of spring starts for me on Shrove Tuesday. From then on, I can go out to look for pussy willows and the buds bursting on the other trees. I love keeping the old customs and many has been the time when I have had a pancake party.

Then, in the middle of Lent, comes Mothering Sunday. Originally a day when serving-girls working away went home to visit their mother church in their own parish, it also became a day when they visited their mothers. In our household, this tradition is kept up the other way round. My mother and father visit me, either for lunch or for tea, providing another excuse for me to invent a festival meal.

Over the four days which make up the Easter holiday, you may wish to go to church, dig the garden, go out for a picnic, or simply have a lazy time. You may be having guests to stay and so will have to think up suitable menus for everyone over the whole holiday, or you may wish to entertain only at Sunday tea-time. Whatever your plans, you should find a menu in the following pages that will suit.

The next spring holiday is May Day. In former centuries it was always held on May 1st, whichever day this happened to be, but now it is on the first Monday of the month. If the weather is good, why not go for a walk in the country, or go into the town or local village to watch the Morris Dancers or traditional May Day processions? Then come home to an informal buffet that you have prepared in advance.

The final holiday of Spring was once the Monday after Whitsunday. It has again been fixed, this time to the last Monday of the month called, less romantically, the Spring Bank Holiday. The three days off work provide time for families and friends to get together and look forward to summer, which should be only a few days away.

The moods and weathers of spring are many. With the last of the old vegetables and the first of the new we can prepare meals that will suit them all. In the middle of February, when I first start to think about spring, there are still winter carrots, swede and parsnips about, together with the winter cabbages. Leeks are a reliable vegetable that last well from winter until the end of April.

The true Spring vegetables are mainly green. First come the spring greens, also called collards or unhearted cabbage. They are full of vitamins and minerals and their rich flavour makes them suitable for cooking with strong-tasting ingredients, such as olives and wine. Depending of course on the weather, there should be cauliflowers in plenty in the spring followed by the purple-sprouting and white-sprouting broccoli with their delicate-flavoured sprouts and dark green leaves. Spring cabbages are conical-shaped, less dense than winter cabbages and with a light, fresh flavour that goes with your spring moods; and after the last snows, I eagerly await my spinach, a sure sign that summer is on the way.

Watercress grows best of all in the spring

and it can be accompanied in salads by radishes, greenhouse cucumbers and the first of the firm-hearted lettuces. Avocados are available all year but are particularly good in the spring. Large onions are poor in spring, so I use spring onions instead in both salads and cooked dishes. They look attractive and have a pleasing, mild flavour.

In the herb garden, the perennial herbs such as sage, thyme and marjoram are beginning to grow new, soft leaves and, about the end of March, out of the ground spring chives. Then in April come the parsley, chervil and, best of all, the sorrel. Use the herbs as much as you can to add both flavour and goodness to all your Spring dishes.

Home-grown fruit is not particularly abundant in May, since all the apple and pears put into cold store in the Autumn are now past their best. However, there is always rhubarb, and no matter how much you may take it for granted, it can be turned into some delicious dishes. Of the imported fruits, kiwi fruits, fresh dates, limes and mangoes are all available. You can also buy strawberries, but I would rather associate these with summer. If you are lucky, you may be able to buy the first of the new season's gooseberries at the end of May.

Dairy products are freely available to us all the year round, but at one time they were very seasonal. As soon as the cows went out to grass in May, milk was plentiful and cheese making began. These old traditions always seem to affect my style of cooking, and so in the spring I frequently tend to use modern dairy products such as curd and low-fat cheeses, soured cream, natural yogurt and, a relative newcomer to the supermarket shelves, creamed smetana. This is a fermented milk product which tastes like an exceptionally creamy yogurt and which is far more economical than double cream.

Eggs are another once seasonal but now readily available product. But goose eggs and even duck eggs are even now available only in the spring and early summer. These are always free-range since neither ducks nor geese adapt well to intensive systems, and so they are well worth buying. Some country shops and large London stores may also sell quail eggs at this time of year. You may feel that these are rather expensive for their size, but they can be so attractive when made into first courses.

If you combine all these ingredients with the vegetables, fruits, nuts, pulses, grains and dried fruits that are available all the year, you will see that there is no limit to the delicious meals that you can produce, both for your family and for entertaining your friends.

SPECIAL MENUS

The following menus have all been worked out to suit the particular holidays and festivals of spring. Of course, you do not have to stick with them rigidly, or serve them on the specific days, but they should help to show you how to plan special vegetarian meals.

Shrove Tuesday Pancake Party

If you are a traditionalist, you will like to have your pancakes sprinked with lemon juice and brown sugar or melted honey, rolled up and eaten as a dessert. Whenever I serve them this way I cook them at the last minute. Everyone gathers in the kitchen; I stand at the stove, frying and handing out the pancakes as fast as I can and everyone helps themselves to the honey and lemon wedges. Doing it this way is fun and it means that everyone will be eating their pancakes when they are at their best—hot and crisp and fresh.

However, if you would like to do the work beforehand, you can cook all the pancakes in advance and reheat them in the oven. This will give you the opportunity to roll them or fold them around fillings, or to stack them with a sauce in between.

Pancakes can be given sweet or savoury fillings and you can also flavour the batter with herbs and spices. The basic recipe overleaf will make 12 pancakes. If you are serving pancakes as a dessert, one quantity will be enough. If you are planning a pancake party for six with savoury pancakes, make two different types using double the quantity of the basic batter.

Basic Pancake (Crêpe) Batter

Imperial (Metric)

6 oz (170g) wholemeal
flour
Pinch fine sea salt
2 eggs, beaten
½ pint (285ml) milk
¼ pint (150ml) water
2 tablespoons oil
Vegetable oil for frying

American

1½ cups wholewheat flour
Pinch fine sea salt
2 eggs, beaten
1¼ cups milk
⅔ cup water
2 tablespoons oil
Vegetable oil for frying

1. Put the flour and salt into a bowl. Make a well in the centre.
2. Break in the eggs and gradually mix in a little flour from the sides of the well.
3. Mix together the milk and water. Gradually beat half the mixture into the flour.
4. Beat in the oil.
5. Beat in the rest of the milk and water. Beat until the batter is very smooth and bubbles appear on the surface.
6. Leave the batter for 30 minutes in a cool place.
7. To cook, heat 1 tablespoon oil in a 7-8 inch (18-20cm) omelette or crêpe pan on a high heat. Turn the heat to medium. Put in 3 tablespoons of the batter and tip the pan slightly to spread it out. If the batter is thicker than usual, as in some of the following recipes, spread it out carefully with the back of a tablespoon.
8. Fry the batter until it is golden brown on the underside and the top is beginning to set. Turn it over to brown the other side. Slip the pancake (crêpe) onto a plate.
9. Keeping the heat at medium, cook the other pancakes (crêpes) in the same way, adding more oil to the pan as and when necessary.

Note: This makes 12 pancakes (crêpes). They can be eaten immediately or cooled, filled and reheated in the oven. To keep pancakes (crêpes) for up to 24 hours, stack them on a plate, cover them with clingfilm and put them into the refrigerator. To freeze, stack them with greaseproof paper or clingfilm in between them. Freeze them on a tray and then put them into a polythene bag. Store for up to two months. Thaw at room temperature.

Mushroom and Haricot (Navy) Bean Pancakes (Crêpes)

*Basic pancake batter with
2 teaspoons paprika and
1 tablespoon dried thyme
added to the flour*
Filling:
*4 tablespoons vegetable oil
1 large onion, thinly
sliced
1 garlic clove, finely
chopped
6 oz (170g) mushrooms,
thinly sliced
4 oz (115g) haricot beans,
soaked and cooked
12 black olives, stoned
and quartered
6 oz (170g) Mozzarella
cheese*
Sauce:
*1 lb (455g) tomatoes
2 tablespoons vegetable oil
1 large onion, finely
chopped
1 garlic clove, finely
chopped
2 teaspoons dried basil*

1. Make the pancakes (crêpes) and cool them (see opposite).
2. Heat the oven to 400°F/200°C/Gas Mark 6.
3. Heat the vegetable oil in a frying pan (skillet) on a low heat. Put in the onion and garlic and soften them.
4. Raise the heat. Put in the mushrooms and stir them for 2 minutes, then mix in the beans and olives. Take the pan from the heat.
5. To make the sauce, scald, skin and chop the tomatoes. Heat the oil in a frying pan (skillet) on a low heat. Put in the onion and garlic and soften them. Add the tomatoes and basil. Simmer, uncovered, for 10 minutes or until the tomatoes are soft and pulpy. Take the pan from the heat.
6. Cut the Mozzarella into 12 strips about ½ inch (1.5cm) wide.
7. Lay a piece of Mozzarella on one side of each pancake (crêpe). Put a portion of the bean mixture on top. Roll up the pancake (crêpe) from that end.
8. Put the rolled pancakes (crêpes) into an ovenproof dish. Spoon the tomato sauce over the top.
9. Bake the pancakes (crêpes) in the oven for 20 minutes.

*Basic crêpe batter with 2
teaspoons paprika and 1
tablespoon dried thyme
added to the flour*
Filling:
*¼ cup vegetable oil
1 large onion, thinly
sliced
1 garlic clove, finely
chopped
6 ounces mushrooms,
thinly sliced
⅔ cup navy beans, soaked
and cooked
12 black olives, pitted and
quartered
6 ounces Mozzarella
cheese*
Sauce:
*1 pound tomatoes
2 tablespoons vegetable oil
1 large onion, finely
chopped
1 garlic clove, finely
chopped
2 teaspoons dried basil*

Courgette Pancakes (Zucchini Crêpes)

Imperial (Metric)

*Basic pancake batter with
2 tablespoons grated
Parmesan cheese added to
the flour*
Filling:
*1 lb (455g) courgettes
1 oz (30g) butter
2 tablespoons wholemeal
flour
½ pint (285ml) milk
4 oz (115g) Cheddar
cheese, grated
6 tablespoons chopped
parsley
1 garlic clove, crushed*
Topping:
*3 oz (85g) Cheddar
cheese, grated
2 tablespoons grated
Parmesan cheese*

1. Make the pancakes (crêpes) and cool them (see page 12).
2. Heat the oven to 400°F/200°C/Gas Mark 6.
3. Coarsely grate the courgettes (zucchini).
4. Melt the butter in a saucepan on a high heat. Put in the courgettes (zucchini) and stir them for 1 minute or until they are beginning to soften.
5. Stir in the flour and then the milk. Bring to the boil, stirring. Cook for 2 minutes, stirring frequently.
6. Take the pan from the heat and beat in the cheese, parsley and garlic. Leave the mixture until it is completely cold.
7. Put a portion of the courgette (zucchini) mixture onto one side of each pancake (crêpe) and roll it up from that side.
8. Lay the rolled pancakes (crêpes) in an ovenproof dish.
9. Mix together the Cheddar and Parmesan cheeses and scatter them over the top.
10. Bake the pancakes (crêpes) in the oven for 20 minutes.

American

*Basic pancake batter with
2 tablespoons grated
Parmesan cheese added to
the flour*
Filling:
*1 pound zucchini
2 tablespoons butter
2 tablespoons wholewheat
flour
1¼ cups milk
1 cup grated Cheddar
cheese
⅓ cup chopped parsley
1 garlic clove, crushed*
Topping:
*¾ cup grated Cheddar
cheese
2 tablespoons grated
Parmesan cheese*

Carrot and Walnut Pancakes (Crêpes)

Imperial (Metric)

Basic pancake mixture
Filling:
8 oz (225g) carrots
8 oz (225g) tomatoes
3 oz (85g) walnuts
3 tablespoons vegetable oil
1 medium onion, finely chopped
1 garlic clove, finely chopped
2 tablespoons chopped thyme
Sauce:
1 oz (30g) butter
2 tablespoons wholemeal flour
½ pint (285ml) milk
2 tablespoons tomato purée
3 oz (85g) Cheddar cheese, grated

1. Make the pancakes (crêpes) and cool them (see page 12).
2. Heat the oven to 400°F/200°C/Gas Mark 6.
3. Grate the carrots. Scald, skin and chop the tomatoes. Coarsely grind the walnuts.
4. Heat the oil in a frying pan (skillet) on a low heat. Put in the onion, garlic and carrots. Cook them until they are beginning to soften and the carrots turn to a more yellow colour. Take the pan from the heat. Mix in the tomatoes, walnuts and thyme.
5. Put a portion of the filling on one side of each pancake (crêpe). Roll up the pancake (crêpe) from that side. Lay the pancakes (crêpes) in an ovenproof dish.
6. To make the sauce, melt the butter in a saucepan on a medium heat. Stir in the flour and then the milk. Bring them to the boil, stirring for 2 minutes. Off the heat, beat in the tomato purée (paste) and two-thirds of the cheese.
7. Spoon the sauce over the pancakes (crêpes). Scatter the remaining cheese over the top.
8. Bake the pancakes (crêpes) in the oven for 20 minutes.

American

Basic pancake mixture
Filling:
½ pound carrots
½ pound tomatoes
1 cup English walnuts
3 tablespoons vegetable oil
1 medium onion, finely chopped
1 garlic clove, finely chopped
2 tablespoons chopped thyme
Sauce:
2 tablespoons butter
2 tablespoons wholewheat flour
1¼ cups milk
2 tablespoons tomato paste
¾ cup grated Cheddar cheese

Marmalade Pancakes (Crêpes)

Imperial (Metric)

Batter:
6 oz (170g) wholemeal
flour
Pinch fine sea salt
Grated rind and juice of
1 large orange
2 eggs, beaten
½ pint (285ml) milk
Up to ¼ pint (140ml)
water
2 tablespoons vegetable oil
Vegetable oil for frying
Filling:
12 oz (340g) low-fat soft
cheese
6 oz (170g) sugar-free
marmalade
Sauce:
4 oz (115g) sugar-free
marmalade
¼ pint (140ml) natural
orange juice

1. Make the batter as for the basic pancake (crêpe) mixture (see page 12), adding the orange rind to the flour and salt, and making up the orange juice to ¼ pint (150ml/⅔ cup) with cold water. Add this mixture as plain water. Leave the batter in a cool place for 30 minutes.
2. For the filling, cream the cheese in a bowl then beat in the marmalade.
3. For the sauce, warm together the marmalade and orange juice until the marmalade has melted.
4. Make the pancakes (crêpes) and keep them warm.
5. Just before serving, roll a portion of the cheese mixture in each pancake (crêpe).
6. Serve the sauce separately.

American

Batter:
1½ cups wholewheat flour
Pinch fine sea salt
Grated rind and juice of
1 large orange
2 eggs, beaten
1¼ cups milk
Up to ⅔ cup water
2 tablespoons vegetable oil
Vegetable oil for frying
Filling:
1½ cups low-fat soft
cheese
½ cup sugar-free
marmalade
Sauce:
⅔ cup sugar-free
marmalade
⅔ cup natural orange
juice

Pineapple Pancakes (Crêpes)

Imperial (Metric)

2 x 15 oz (425g) tins
pineapple in natural juice
6 oz (170g) wholemeal
flour
Pinch fine sea salt
2 eggs, beaten
½ pint (285ml) milk
2 tablespoons vegetable oil
12 oz (340g) cottage
cheese
4 tablespoons rum

1. Drain the tins of pineapple and measure off ¼ pint (140ml/⅔ cup) of the juice.
2. Make up a basic pancake (crêpe) batter according to the instructions on page 12, using the juice from the pineapple instead of water. Leave the batter in a cool place for 30 minutes.
3. Finely chop the pineapple from one of the tins. Mix it into the cheese.
4. Liquidize the remaining pineapple with 2 tablespoons of the juice. Warm the mixture and add the rum. Keep the resulting sauce warm.
5. Make the pancakes (crêpes) and keep them warm.
6. Place a portion of the filling in each pancake (crêpe) and roll it up.
7. Lay the filled pancakes (crêpes) on a serving dish. Spoon the sauce over the top.

American

2 x 1 pound tins
pineapple in natural juice
1½ cups wholewheat flour
Pinch fine sea salt
2 eggs, beaten
1¼ cups milk
2 tablespoons vegetable oil
1½ cups cottage cheese
¼ cup rum

Apricot Pancake (Crêpe) Stack

Imperial (Metric)

Basic pancake batter with pinch ground mace added to flour
Filling:
8 oz (225g) dried whole apricots
¾ pint (425ml) natural orange juice
4 tablespoons apricot liqueur
6 oz (170g) silken tofu
Topping:
10 oz (285g) silken tofu
3 tablespoons no-sugar-added apricot jam
Garnish (optional):
Flaked almonds, toasted

1. Before making the batter, put the apricots into a saucepan with the orange juice. Bring them to the boil. Take the pan from the heat and leave them to soak for 4 hours.
2. Drain the apricots. Put them into a blender with the liqueur and 4 tablespoons of the drained orange juice. Work them to a smooth purée. Add the first amount of tofu and blend again.
3. For the topping, beat the second amount of tofu with the jam (jelly).
4. Make the batter according to the instructions on page 12 and leave it in a cool place for 30 minutes.
5. Make the pancakes (crêpes) and keep them warm.
6. Warm the filling gently. Place a small portion of the filling in each of 4 pancakes (crêpes) and roll them up.
7. Lay one of the remaining pancakes (crêpes) on a serving plate and spread it with the filling. Continue layering, ending with a pancake and having used up all the filling.
8. Arrange the 4 rolled pancakes (crêpes) round the pancake (crêpe) stack.
9. Spoon the topping over both the stack and the rolled pancakes (crêpes).
10. Garnish, if wished, with the almonds.

American

Basic crêpe batter with pinch ground mace added to flour
Filling:
½ pound dried whole apricots
2 cups natural orange juice
4 tablespoons apricot liqueur
¾ cup silken tofu
Topping:
1¼ cups silken tofu
3 tablespoons no-sugar-added apricot jelly
Garnish (optional):
Slivered almonds, toasted

Curranty Pancakes (Crêpes)

Imperial (Metric)

6 oz (170g) wholemeal
flour
2 oz (55g) ground mixed
nuts
Pinch fine sea salt
¼ nutmeg, freshly grated
3 eggs, beaten
½ pint (285ml) milk
¼ pint (140ml) water
2 tablespoons vegetable oil
4 oz (115g) currants
Vegetable oil for frying
Sauce:
3 oz (85g) honey
1/8 nutmeg, freshly
grated
¾ pint (425ml) natural
yogurt
Garnish:
Thinly pared rind of 1
large orange

1. Put the flour into a bowl with the nuts, sea salt and nutmeg. Mix them together and make a well in the centre.
2. Pour in the eggs and gradually beat in flour from the sides of the well. Mix together the milk and water. Gradually beat half into the flour. Beat in the oil and then the remaining milk and water.
3. Mix in the currants.
4. Leave the batter in a cool place for 30 minutes.
5. Make the sauce by beating the honey and nutmeg into the yogurt.
6. For the garnish, cut the rind of the orange into matchstick pieces. Blanch them in boiling water for 2 minutes. Drain them.
7. Heat 1 tablespoon vegetable oil in a heavy frying pan (skillet) on a high heat.
8. When the oil is hot, turn the heat to medium. Pour in 1 tablespoon of the batter. Spread it out to make a small circle. Cook until the under side of the pancake (crêpe) is just brown. Turn it over and brown the other side. Remove the pancake (crêpe) from the pan and keep it warm. Cook the rest in the same way.
9. Place the pancakes (crêpes) in slightly overlapping layers, on a warm serving dish.
10. Serve the pancakes (crêpes) with a little of the sauce spooned over them, and the orange rind sprinkled over the top. Serve the remaining sauce separately.

American

1½ cups wholewheat flour
½ cup ground mixed nuts
Pinch fine sea salt
¼ nutmeg, freshly grated
3 eggs, beaten
1⅓ cups milk
⅔ cup water
2 tablespoons vegetable oil
⅔ cup currants
Vegetable oil for frying
Sauce:
¼ cup honey
1/8 nutmeg, freshly
grated
2 cups unflavored yogurt
Garnish:
Thinly pared rind of 1
large orange

Mothering Sunday Lunch

Avocado Filled with Black Grapes
Nut and Watercress Rounds with Sherry Sauce
Julienne of Leeks and Tarragon (page 62)
Fig and Orange Pudding

The light avocado salad makes a refreshing contrast to the richly flavoured nut rounds. The traditional dessert at a Mothering Sunday lunch was once a fig pudding, made with flour and breadcrumbs. This would be far too heavy to follow the nut rounds. Far better is a pudding-shaped jelly containing dried fruits and orange juice.

Avocados Filled with Black Grapes

Imperial (Metric)

3 ripe but firm avocados
18 black grapes
4 tablespoons olive oil
1½ teaspoons white wine
  vinegar
2 tablespoons chopped
  chives
1 garlic clove, crushed
Freshly ground black
  pepper

1. Halve and stone (pit) the avocados.
2. Halve and seed the grapes.
3. Put the avocado halves into individual dishes and fill them with the grapes.
4. Beat together the oil, vinegar, 1½ tablespoons chives, garlic and pepper, then spoon this dressing over the grapes.
5. Sprinkle a tiny amount of chives over the top and serve.

American

3 ripe but firm avocados
18 black grapes
¼ cup olive oil
1½ teaspoons white wine
  vinegar
2 tablespoons chopped
  chives
1 garlic clove, crushed
Freshly ground black
  pepper

Nut and Watercress Rounds with Sherry Sauce

Imperial (Metric)

6 oz (170g) Brazil nuts
4 oz (115g) hazelnuts
10 oz (285g) fresh
wholemeal breadcrumbs
3 oz (85g) watercress
3 tablespoons chopped
chervil or parsley
4 fl oz (115ml) vegetable
oil
2 medium onions, finely
chopped
1 garlic clove, finely
chopped
¼ pint (140ml) dry sherry
Sauce:
2 tablespoons vegetable oil
1 small onion, finely
chopped
1 small carrot, finely
chopped
1 small celery stick, finely
chopped
2 tablespoons wholemeal
flour
1 tablespoon tomato purée
¾ pint (425ml) vegetable
stock
Bouquet garni
¼ pint (140ml) dry sherry
Garnish:
Watercress sprigs

1. Finely grind the nuts. Put them into a large bowl with the breadcrumbs.
2. Finely chop the watercress and add it to the nuts with the chervil or parsley.
3. Heat half the oil in a frying pan (skillet) on a low heat. Put in the onions and garlic and soften them.
4. Tip the onions into the nuts. Add the sherry and mix well. Leave the mixture for 15 minutes for the crumbs to soak up the sherry.
5. Using a pastry cutter as a guide, form the mixture into round, flat cakes about 2 inches (5cm) across and 1 inch (2.5cm) deep. Leave them in a cool place for 1 hour to set into shape.
6. Brush them with the remaining oil.
7. To make the sauce, heat the oil in a saucepan on a low heat. Stir in the chopped vegetables and cook them gently, stirring occasionally, until they are just beginning to brown.
8. Stir in the flour, tomato purée (paste) and stock and add the bouquet garni. Bring to the boil, stirring.
9. Partially cover and simmer for 30 minutes or until the sauce has been reduced by about a quarter.
10. Strain the sauce. Return it to the cleaned pan. Add the sherry. Bring just to boiling point and simmer for 10 minutes.
11. To cook the nut cakes, heat the grill (broiler) to high and if you have a wire rack, cover it with foil. Grill (broil) the cakes for about 2 minutes on each side or until they are golden brown.
12. To serve, spoon a little of the sauce onto each of 6 dinner plates. Set the nut rounds on top. Garnish with watercress.
Note: To freeze, make the cakes and leave them to stand for 1 hour. Freeze them on a tray before packing them into

American

1 cup Brazil nuts
¾ cup hazelnuts
5 cups fresh wholewheat
breadcrumbs
3 ounces watercress
3 tablespoons chopped
chervil or parsley
½ cup vegetable oil
2 medium onions, finely
chopped
1 garlic clove, finely
chopped
⅔ cup dry sherry
Sauce:
2 tablespoons vegetable oil
1 small onion, finely
chopped
1 small carrot, finely
chopped
1 small celery stalk, finely
chopped
2 tablespoons wholewheat
flour
1 tablespoon tomato paste
2 cups vegetable stock
Bouquet garni
⅔ cup dry sherry
Garnish:
Watercress sprigs

a polythene bag. Thaw on a tray at
room temperature. Coat with oil and
grill (broil) as before.

Fig and Orange Pudding

Imperial (Metric)

10 oz (285g) dried figs
10 oz (285g) raisins
1 pint (570ml) orange
juice
2 inch (5cm) cinnamon
stick
4 tablespoons whisky,
optional
3 large oranges
Agar-agar for 1 pint
(575ml) liquid (see
manufacturer's
instructions)
½ pint (285ml) double
cream

1. Finely chop the figs. Put them into a
saucepan with the raisins, orange juice
and cinnamon stick. Bring them just to
boiling point and simmer for 10
minutes.
2. Drain them, reserving the juice. Add
the whisky to the juice if using.
3. Cut the rind and pith from the
oranges. Finely chop the flesh, removing
the pips.
4. Add the chopped orange to the figs
and raisins.
5. Return the juice to the saucepan.
Bring it just to boiling point. Stir in the
agar-agar and stir until it has dissolved.
Take the pan from the heat.
6. Mix in the figs, raisins and oranges.
7. Pour everything into a 2 pint (1.1
litre) pudding basin. Cool the jelly
completely and put it into the
refrigerator for 2 hours to set.
8. Whip the cream. Turn the jelly out of
the mould onto a serving plate. Either
surround it with the cream or pipe some
of the cream on the jelly as a decoration
and serve the rest separately.

American

10 ounces dried figs
1⅔ cups raisins
2½ cups orange juice
2 inch cinnamon stick
¼ cup whisky, optional
3 large oranges
Agar-agar for 2½ cups
liquid (see manufacturer's
instructions)
1¼ cups heavy cream

Easter Sunday Lunch

Cauliflower and Tomato Soup
Nut Roast with Sorrel Stuffing
Potato Cubes with Spring Onions (Scallions) and Mustard (see page 57)
Spring Greens with Parmesan (see page 59)
Rhubarb Vinegar Pie

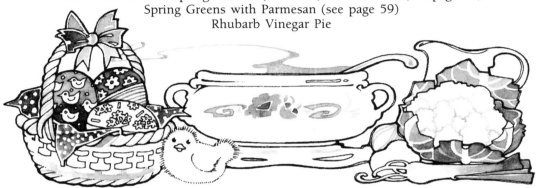

Bitter herbs such as sorrel and sage were once added to stuffings served at the Easter Day Dinner. Sorrel goes especially well in a roast made from the sweeter nuts, almonds, hazelnuts and Brazil nuts. Another tradition was to make the first rhubarb from the garden into a pie.

Cauliflowers to make the soup should be plentiful in April.

Cauliflower and Tomato Soup

Imperial (Metric)

1 large cauliflower
12 oz (340g) ripe tomatoes
1 large onion, thinly sliced
2 pints (1.1 litres) vegetable stock
1 bay leaf
Sea salt and freshly ground black pepper
4 fl oz (125ml) medium sherry or Marsala
3 fl oz (90ml) natural yogurt or soured cream
Approximately 1 tablespoon tomato purée

1. Chop the cauliflower.
2. If you are going to use a blender for the soup, scald and skin the tomatoes; if a vegetable mill, then just roughly chop them. This gives the best flavour.
3. Put the cauliflower and tomatoes into a saucepan with the onion, stock and bay leaf, and season.
4. Cover and bring to the boil and simmer for 20 minutes.
5. Remove the bay leaf and rub everything through the fine blade of a vegetable mill or liquidize in a blender.
6. Return the soup to the rinsed pan. Add the sherry or Marsala and reheat without boiling.
6. Pour the soup into individual soup bowls, swirl in the yogurt or soured cream and put a small blob of tomato purée (paste) on top.

American

1 large cauliflower
¾ pound ripe tomatoes
1 large onion, thinly sliced
5 cups vegetable stock
1 bay leaf
Sea salt and freshly ground black pepper
½ cup medium sherry or Marsala
⅓ cup unflavored yogurt or sour cream
Approximately 1 tablespoon tomato paste

Nut Roast with Sorrel Stuffing

Imperial (Metric)

8 oz (225g) mung beans
1 bay leaf
1 large onion, thinly sliced
4 oz (115g) hazelnuts
4 oz (115g) Brazil nuts
4 oz (115g) ground almonds
4 tablespoons dry white wine
4 sorrel leaves, chopped
2 tablespoons chopped thyme
2 tablespoons chopped parsley
Sea salt and freshly ground black pepper
Stuffing:
4 tablespoons vegetable oil
1 large onion, finely chopped
20 sorrel leaves
4 oz (115g) fresh wholemeal breadcrumbs
4 tablespoons chopped parsley
6 tablespoons dry white wine
Coating:
3 oz (85g) fresh wholemeal breadcrumbs
2 tablespoons sesame seeds
4 tablespoons vegetable oil

American

1 cup mung beans
1 bay leaf
1 large onion, thinly sliced
1 cup hazelnuts
1 cup Brazil nuts
1 cup ground almonds
¼ cup dry white wine
4 sorrel leaves, chopped
2 tablespoons chopped thyme
2 tablespoons chopped parsley
Sea salt and freshly ground black pepper
Stuffing:
¼ cup vegetable oil
1 large onion, finely chopped
20 sorrel leaves
2 cups fresh wholewheat breadcrumbs
¼ cup chopped parsley
6 tablespoons dry white wine
Coating:
1½ cups fresh wholewheat breadcrumbs
2 tablespoons sesame seeds
¼ cup vegetable oil

1. Soak the beans. Cook them with the bay leaf and onion for 40 minutes or until they are soft. Drain them. Remove the bay leaf. Mash the beans with the onion.

2. Heat the oven to 400°F/200°C/Gas Mark 6.

3. Grind the hazelnuts and Brazil nuts. Mix these and the almonds into the beans.

4. Mix in the wine, sorrel, thyme, parsley and seasoning.

5. To make the stuffing, heat the oil in a frying pan (skillet) on a low heat. Put in the onion and soften it. Add the sorrel and cook for 1 minute more.

6. Take the pan from the heat. Mix in the breadcrumbs, parsley and wine.

7. Lay a base of half the bean and nut mixture in a long, flat dish. Put all the stuffing on top, leaving a small space round the edge. Cover the stuffing with the remaining nut mixture. Smooth the surface so the stuffing is completely enclosed.

8. For the coating, mix together the breadcrumbs, sesame seeds and oil. Press the mixture evenly over the surface of the nut shape.

9. Bake the roast for 45 minutes or until the outside is crisp and brown.

Note: Freeze on a flat tray. Wrap securely in foil and put into a polythene bag. Store for up to 2 months. Thaw at room temperature and reheat on a baking sheet or ovenproof dish in a hot oven for 15 minutes.

Shortcrust Pastry

Imperial (Metric)

8 oz (225g) wholemeal
flour
Pinch fine sea salt
4 oz (115g) vegetable
margarine
Cold water to mix

1. Put the flour and salt into a bowl.
2. Rub in the margarine.
3. Mix to a dough with cold water.
4. Leave in a cool place for 30 minutes
   before using.

American

2 cups wholewheat flour
Pinch fine sea salt
1 cup vegetable margarine
Cold water to mix

Rhubarb Vinegar Pie

Imperial (Metric)

1 lb (455g) rhubarb
¼ pint (140ml) red grape
juice
6 oz (170g) honey
2 tablespoons wholemeal
flour
1 teaspoon ground mixed
spice
Pinch fine sea salt
Shortcrust pastry made
with 8 oz (225g)
wholemeal flour
(see above) .
4 egg yolks
8 fl oz (225ml) soured
cream
3 tablespoons cider
vinegar
8 oz (225g) raisins
2 egg whites

1. Cut the rhubarb into 1 inch (2.5cm)
pieces. Put them into a saucepan with
the grape juice and 2 oz (50g) honey.
Bring them to the boil. Cover and
simmer for 10 minutes or until the
pieces are soft but still whole. Cool
them.
2. Heat the oven to 450°F/250°C/Gas
Mark 8.
3. Mix the flour with the mixed spice
and salt.
4. Roll out the pastry and use it to line
a 10-inch (25cm) tart tin.
5. Put the egg yolks and remaining
honey into a bowl. Beat them with an
electric beater for about 10 minutes so
the mixture is light and thick and any
dropped from the beater will leave a
trail on the rest.
6. Mix in the flour, soured cream and
vinegar. When the mixture is smooth,
fold in the raisins.
7. Stiffly whip the egg whites and fold
them into the rest.
8. Lift the rhubarb pieces from their
liquid with a slotted spoon. Arrange
them in the bottom of the pastry shell.
9. Spoon the egg mixture over the top,
making sure that the raisins are evenly
distributed.
10. Put the pie into the oven for 10
minutes. Then turn the heat down to
350°F/180°C/Gas Mark 4 and cook for

American

1 pound rhubarb
⅔ cup red grape juice
½ cup honey
2 tablespoons wholewheat
flour
1 teaspoon ground mixed
spice
Pinch fine sea salt
Shortcrust pastry made
with 2 cups wholewheat
flour (see above).
4 egg yolks
1 cup sour cream
3 tablespoons cider
vinegar
1½ cups raisins
2 egg whites

24

a further 20 minutes so the filling is
firm and browned.
11. Serve the pie warm. No
accompaniment is needed.
Note: Unsuitable for freezing.

Easter Sunday Tea

Eggs with Green Mayonnaise
Wholemeal Bread
Easter Biscuits
Almond Cake

One meal on Easter Day must be based on eggs. If you did not have them for breakfast, serve them with green coats for tea. Make or buy wholemeal (wholewheat) bread to go with them and decorate a plate of biscuits and a special cake with Easter chicks and flowers.

Eggs with Green Mayonnaise

Imperial (Metric)		American
9 eggs	1. Hard-boil (cook) the eggs.	9 eggs
Mayonnaise:	2. To make the mayonnaise, put the egg yolks into a bowl and beat in the mustard powder and pepper. Gradually beat in 2 tablespoons of the oil and then 2 teaspoons of the lemon juice. Beat in the remaining oil about 1 tablespoon at a time. Add extra lemon juice to taste.	**Mayonnaise:**
2 egg yolks		2 egg yolks
1 teaspoon mustard powder		1 teaspoon mustard powder
Freshly ground black pepper		Freshly ground black pepper
8 fl oz (225ml) sunflower oil	3. Remove any tough stalks from the watercress and finely chop the rest.	1 cup sunflower oil
Juice of 1 lemon	4. Put the mayonnaise into a blender or food processor with the cress, parsley and chives. Liquidize until you have a smooth, green sauce.	Juice of 1 lemon
3 oz (85g) watercress		3 ounces watercress
8 tablespoons chopped parsley		½ cup chopped parsley
4 tablespoons chopped chives		¼ cup chopped chives
Salad:	5. Finely shred the lettuce. Make a bed of shredded lettuce on a large, flat serving plate, building it up slightly round the edges to make a border.	**Salad:**
1 iceberg lettuce		1 iceberg lettuce
5 oz (150g) radishes, sliced	6. Place the eggs, cut side down, on the lettuce. Spoon the mayonnaise over them. Put a parsley sprig on each one and garnish the plate with radish slices.	5 ounces radishes, sliced
18 tiny parsley sprigs		18 tiny parsley sprigs

Easter Biscuits

Imperial (Metric)

8 oz (225g) wholemeal
flour
½ teaspoon ground
cinnamon
½ teaspoon ground mixed
spice
4 oz (115g) butter
3 tablespoons brandy
1 egg, beaten
2 oz (55g) currants
1 oz (30g) candied peel,
chopped
4 oz (115g) Barbados
sugar

1. Heat the oven to 350°F/180°C/Gas Mark 4.
2. Put the flour and spices into a bowl. Rub in the butter. Make a well in the centre. Beat in the brandy and egg.
3. Fold in the currants, peel and sugar, mix everything to a stiff dough and knead it lightly. Roll it out to ¼ inch (6mm) thick. Cut it into rounds with a 2 ½ inch (6.5cm) biscuit cutter.
4. Lay the rounds on a floured baking sheet.
5. Bake the biscuits for 20 minutes. Lift them onto a wire rack to cool.
Note: Unsuitable for freezing.

American

2 cups wholewheat flour
½ teaspoon ground
cinnamon
½ teaspoon ground mixed
spice
½ cup butter
3 tablespoons brandy
1 egg, beaten
⅓ cup currants
2 tablespoons chopped
candied peel
⅔ cup Barbados sugar

Almond Cake

Imperial (Metric)

3 oz (85g) stoned dates
3 oz (85g) dried apple
rings
1 pint (570ml) apple juice
6 oz (170g) wholemeal
flour
1½ oz (40g) ground
almonds
1 teaspoon bicarbonate of
soda
½ teaspoon ground mixed
spice
3 fl oz (90ml) corn oil
3 eggs, beaten
6 oz (170g) sultanas
Filling:
8 oz (225g) curd or
cream cheese
6 tablespoons no-sugar-
added apricot jam
2 tablespoons brandy
2 tablespoons flaked
almonds, toasted

1. Put the dates, apple and juice into a saucepan. Bring to the boil, then remove the pan from the heat and leave to soak for 4 hours. Drain, reserving the juice. Liquidize the fruits with 3 fl oz (90ml/⅓ cup) of the reserved juice.
2. Heat the oven to 350°F/180°C/Gas Mark 4.
3. In a bowl, mix in the flour, almonds, bicarbonate of (baking) soda and mixed spice.
4. Make a well in the centre. Pour in the liquidized fruits, corn oil and eggs. Beat until you have a smooth batter.
5. Mix in the sultanas (golden seedless raisins).
6. Divide the mixture between two 7-inch (18cm) sponge tins and bake for 20 minutes or until firm.
7. Turn them onto wire racks to cool.
8. To make the filling, beat the cheese to a cream. Beat in half the jam (jelly) and all the brandy.
9. Sandwich the cakes together with half the cheese mixture and the remaining jam (jelly). Spread the remaining cheese

American

3 ounces pitted dates
3 ounces dried apple rings
2½ cups apple juice
1½ cups wholewheat flour
⅓ cup ground almonds
1 teaspoon baking soda
½ teaspoon ground mixed
spice
⅓ cup corn oil
3 eggs, beaten
1 cup golden seedless
raisins
Filling:
1 cup curd or cream
cheese
⅓ cup no-sugar-added
apricot jelly
2 tablespoons brandy
2 tablespoons slivered
almonds, toasted

mixture on top.

10. Scatter the toasted flaked (slivered) almonds over the top.

Note: To freeze the cake, cool it completely and wrap each sandwich cake in clingfilm. Freeze them flat. Store for up to 2 months. Thaw at room temperature. The filling is unsuitable for freezing.

Easter Monday Picnic

Lentil and Walnut Pasties
Radish, Spring Cabbage and Cheese Pittas
Eggs in Jackets
Fresh Date Loaf
Spiced Peanut Cake

If you are entertaining guests for the whole of the Easter weekend, you may well wish to take them out into the country or for a walk by the sea on Easter Monday, so pack up a picnic.

Because of the weather, long leisurely picnics are not suited to Spring so take food that can be easily eaten in the hand. Then, in case of downpours, you can eat in the car! This is not the height of elegant entertaining but a delicious meal that is fun to eat.

Lentil and Walnut Pasties

Imperial (Metric)

*Shortcrust pastry made
with 1 lb 4 oz (565g)
wholemeal flour (see
page 24)
6 oz (170g) green lentils,
soaked and cooked
3 oz (85g) shelled
walnuts, finely chopped
3 oz (85g) mushrooms
5 oz (140g) potato, peeled
1 small green pepper
1 medium carrot
1 medium onion
3 tablespoons tomato
purée
3 tablespoons chopped
parsley
2 tablespoons chopped
thyme
Sea salt and freshly
ground black pepper
1 egg, beaten*

1. Heat the oven to 350°F/180°C/Gas Mark 4.

2. Divide the pastry into eight portions and roll each into a circle.

3. Chop all the vegetables and mix together all the remaining ingredients except the egg.

4. Put a portion of the mixture onto one half of each pastry circle. Fold over the other half and seal the edges.

5. Lay the pasties on a floured baking sheet. Brush them with the beaten egg.

6. Bake the pasties for 45 minutes or until they are golden brown. Lift them onto wire racks to cool.

Note: To freeze, cool completely. Freeze the pasties on a flat tray and pack them into polythene bags. Store for up to 1 month. Reheat from frozen by laying them onto a baking sheet and putting them into a hot oven for 20 minutes.

American

*Shortcrust pastry made
with 5 cups wholewheat
flour (see page 24)
1 cup green lentils, soaked
and cooked
⅔ cup chopped English
walnuts
3 ounces mushrooms
5 ounces potato, peeled
1 small sweet green
pepper
1 medium carrot
1 medium onion
3 tablespoons tomato
paste
3 tablespoons chopped
parsley
2 tablespoons chopped
thyme
Sea salt and freshly
ground black pepper
1 egg, beaten*

Eggs in Jackets

Imperial (Metric)

4 tablespoons vegetable oil
1 large onion, finely
    chopped
1 garlic clove, finely
    chopped
6 oz (170g) split red
    lentils
4 oz (115g) millet
1¼ pints (710ml)
    vegetable stock
2 bay leaves
2 tablespoons tomato
    purée
Freshly ground black
    pepper
2 oz (55g) peanuts
2 tablespoons chopped
    thyme
4 tablespoons chopped
    parsley
6 eggs, hard-boiled
1 oz (30g) wholemeal
    flour
Vegetable oil for frying

1. Heat the oil in a saucepan on a low heat. Put in the onion and garlic and soften them.
2. Stir in the lentils and millet. Stir for 1 minute. Pour in the stock and bring it to the boil. Add the bay leaves and tomato purée (paste) and season with the pepper.
3. Cover and simmer for 45 minutes or until the lentils and millet are soft and all the liquid has been absorbed. Cool the mixture completely. Remove the bay leaves.
4. Finely grind the peanuts and mix them into the lentils. Mix in the herbs.
5. Coat each egg in the mixture then roll it in the flour.
6. Heat a deep pan of oil to 370°F/190°C. Deep-fry the eggs, two at a time, for about 1½ minutes on each side, so they become golden brown.
7. Drain the eggs on kitchen paper and cool them completely.
Note: Unsuitable for freezing.

American

¼ cup vegetable oil
1 large onion, finely
    chopped
1 garlic clove, finely
    chopped
¾ cup split red lentils
½ cup millet
3 cups vegetable stock
2 bay leaves
2 tablespoons tomato
    paste
Freshly ground black
    pepper
¼ cup peanuts
2 tablespoons chopped
    thyme
¼ cup chopped parsley
6 eggs, hard-cooked
¼ cup wholewheat flour
Vegetable oil for frying

Radish, Spring Cabbage and Cheese Pittas

Imperial (Metric)

5 oz (150g) radishes
1 small spring cabbage
6 spring onions
Dressing:
1 egg yolk
½ teaspoon mustard
    powder
2 tablespoons olive oil
4 fl oz (115ml) natural
    yogurt
4 oz (115g) Cheshire
    cheese, finely grated
6 wholemeal pitta breads

1. Thinly slice the radishes. Finely shred the cabbage and chop the spring onions (scallions). Mix all these in a bowl.
2. To make the dressing, put the egg yolk into a bowl with the mustard powder. Beat in the oil, drop by drop, as though you were making mayonnaise. Beat in the yogurt, 2 teaspoons at a time. Stir in the cheese.
3. Fold the dressing into the salad.
4. If eating the pittas at home, leave the salad for 15 minutes and serve it and the pittas separately. If the pittas are being taken to a picnic, slit the pittas before packing them in a polythene bag.

American

5 ounces radishes
1 small spring cabbage
6 scallions
Dressing:
1 egg yolk
½ teaspoon mustard
    powder
2 tablespoons olive oil
½ cup unflavored yogurt
¼ pound Cheshire cheese,
    finely grated
6 wholewheat pitta breads

Take the salad separately in a rigid plastic container. This will prevent the pittas from becoming soggy in transit.

Fresh Date Loaf

Imperial (Metric)

8 oz (225g) fresh dates
8 oz (225g) wholemeal flour
½ teaspoon fine sea salt
½ teaspoon bicarbonate of soda
1/8 nutmeg, grated
3 oz (85g) low-fat soft cheese
1 egg, beaten
¼ pint (140ml) natural yogurt

1. Heat the oven to 350°F/180°C/Gas Mark 4.
2. Skin, stone (pit) and chop the dates.
3. Put the flour into a bowl with the salt and bicarbonate of (baking) soda and add the nutmeg.
4. Cream the cheese in a separate bowl. Gradually beat in the egg.
5. Make a well in the centre of the flour and pour in the cheese mixture and yogurt. Mix everything to a moist dough.
6. Put the dough into a greased, 1 pound (455g) loaf tin and smooth the top.
7. Bake the loaf for 1 hour. Turn it onto a wire rack to cool.

Note: This is a semi-sweet loaf. It can be eaten plain, buttered, or with cheese. If it is to be buttered, do so before taking it on the picnic and sandwich the slices together.

To freeze, cool completely and seal in a polythene bag. Store for up to 1 month. Thaw on a rack at room temperature.

American

½ pound fresh dates
2 cups wholewheat flour
½ teaspoon fine sea salt
½ teaspoon baking soda
1/8 nutmeg, grated
¾ cup low-fat soft cheese
1 egg, beaten
⅔ cup unflavored yogurt

Spiced Peanut Cake

Imperial (Metric)

4 oz (115g) peanuts
8 oz (225g) butter,
softened, or vegetable
margarine
8 oz (225g) Barbados
sugar
8 oz (225g) wholemeal
flour
2 teaspoons baking
powder
2 teaspoons ground mixed
spice
4 eggs, beaten
4 tablespoons buttermilk
or milk

1. Heat the oven to 350°F/180°C/Gas Mark 4.
2. Finely grind the peanuts.
3. Cream the butter or margarine and beat in the sugar.
4. Mix the flour with the baking powder and spice.
5. Beat the eggs and flour alternately into the butter.
6. Mix in the buttermilk or milk and then the peanuts.
7. Put the mixture into a greased 8 by 11-inch (20 by 27cm) 2-inch (5cm) deep cake tin.
8. Bake the cake for 30 minutes or until it is firm and has shrunk slightly from the sides of the tin. Cool it in the tin for 10 minutes and then turn it onto a wire rack to cool completely.
9. Cut the cake into squares and pack them into a rigid plastic container.

Note: To freeze. cool completely. Wrap the cake in clingfilm and freeze it flat. Store for up to 2 months. Thaw on a rack at room temperature.

American

¾ cup peanuts
1 cup butter, softened, or
vegetable margarine
1⅓ cups Barbados sugar
2 cups wholewheat flour
2 teaspoons baking
powder
2 teaspoons ground mixed
spice
4 eggs, beaten
¼ cup buttermilk or milk

SOUPS

The soups of spring have light, fresh flavours to suit the new season, but are nevertheless warming enough to keep away the last of the wintry weather.

Make use of all the vegetables and herbs of the season. Begin with beetroot and leeks, and in May turn to sorrel, spinach and herbs such as chervil.

Spiced Beetroot Soup

Imperial (Metric)

1 lb 4 oz (565g) beetroot
1 large onion
2 pints (1.1 litres)
vegetable stock
10 allspice berries
6 cloves
2 blades mace
2-inch (5cm) cinnamon
stick
¼ pint (140ml) dry red
wine
¼ pint (140ml) soured
cream
3 tablespoons chopped
parsley

American

1¼ pounds beetroot
1 large onion
5 cups vegetable stock
10 allspice berries
6 cloves
2 blades mace
2-inch cinnamon stick
⅔ cup dry red wine
⅔ cup sour cream
3 tablespoons chopped
parsley

1. Peel and finely chop the beetroot. Finely chop the onion.
2. Put them into a saucepan with the stock and spices. Bring to the boil, cover and simmer for 30 minutes.
3. Strain the beetroot, reserving the stock. Pick out the spices from the beetroot.
4. Either liquidize the beetroot and stock in a blender or food processor until you have a smooth soup; or put the beetroot plus a little of the stock through the fine blade of a vegetable mill and then stir back the remaining stock.
5. Put the blended or sieved soup back into the saucepan. Add the wine and reheat without boiling.
6. Take the pan from the heat and stir in the soured cream.
7. Pour the soup into individual bowls and serve garnished with the parsley.
Note: Freeze after blending or sieving, but without adding the wine or cream.
Cool completely, pour into a rigid container and cover. Store for up to 2 months. Thaw at room temperature and reheat in a saucepan. Add the wine and heat to just below boiling point. Take the pan from the heat and add the cream.

31

Avocado, Watercress and Lime Soup

Imperial (Metric)

4 ripe avocados
3 oz (85g) watercress
Juice and thinly pared
    rind of 1 lime
1 pint (570ml) buttermilk
1 garlic clove, crushed
¼ teaspoon Tabasco sauce
1 pint (570ml) vegetable
    stock

1. Peel, stone (pit) and chop the avocados. Finely chop the watercress.
2. Reserve 2 tablespoons watercress and put the rest into a blender or food processor with the avocados, lime juice, buttermilk, garlic and Tabasco sauce. Liquidize to a smooth, thin purée containing small but distinguishable flecks of watercress.
3. Put the mixture into a saucepan and stir in the stock. Heat the soup gently to just below boiling point.
4. For the garnish, cut the strips of lime rind into very thin slices. Bring a small pan of water to the boil. Put in the strips of rind and boil them for 2 minutes. Drain them.
5. To serve, pour the soup into individual bowls. Float the reserved watercress and the strips of lime rind on top.

American

4 ripe avocados
3 ounces watercress
Juice and thinly pared
    rind of 1 lime
2½ cups buttermilk
1 garlic clove, crushed
¼ teaspoon Tabasco sauce
2½ cups vegetable stock

Pine Nut Soup

Imperial (Metric)

4 tablespoons vegetable oil
2 medium onions, finely
    chopped
1 garlic clove, finely
    chopped
2 tablespoons wholemeal
    flour
2¼ pints (1.3 litres)
    vegetable stock
Juice of up to 1 lemon
5 oz (150g) pine nuts
1 oz (25g) parsley, finely
    chopped

1. Heat the oil in a saucepan on a low heat. Put in the onions and garlic and soften them.
2. Stir in the flour and then the stock. Bring to the boil, stirring. Simmer, uncovered, for 5 minutes. Add most of the lemon juice and the pine nuts and simmer for a further 5 minutes.
3. Liquidize the contents of the pan in a blender or food processor until you have a smooth soup with the pine nuts finely ground. Taste and add extra lemon juice if required.
4. Return the soup to the saucepan. Add the parsley and reheat.
Note: Freeze before adding the parsley. Cool the soup completely. Freeze covered in a rigid plastic container. Store for up to 1 month. Thaw at room temperature and reheat in a saucepan.

American

¼ cup vegetable oil
2 medium onions, finely
    chopped
1 garlic clove, finely
    chopped
2 tablespoons wholewheat
    flour
5⅔ cups vegetable stock
Juice of up to 1 lemon
1¼ cups pine nuts
1 cup parsley, finely
    chopped

Sorrel and Tomato Soup

Imperial (Metric)

30 sorrel leaves
1½ lb (685g) tomatoes
1 large onion
1 oz (30g) butter
2 teaspoons paprika
1¼ pints (720ml)
vegetable stock
¼ pint (140ml) dry sherry

1. Finely chop the sorrel leaves.
2. Scald, skin and finely chop the tomatoes.
3. Finely chop the onion.
4. Melt the butter in a saucepan on a low heat, add the onion and paprika and cook until the onion is soft.
5. Mix in the sorrel and tomatoes. Cover and cook on a low heat for 10 minutes. Mash the tomatoes down well.
6. Pour in the stock and bring it to the boil. Cover and simmer for 10 minutes.
7. Pour in the sherry. Reheat the soup if necessary, but do not boil.
Note: To freeze, cool the soup completely after simmering. Pack into a covered container and store for up to 1 month. Thaw at room temperature. Reheat to just below boiling point and add the sherry.

American

30 sorrel leaves
1½ pounds tomatoes
1 large onion
2 tablespoons butter
2 teaspoons paprika
3¼ cups vegetable stock
⅔ cup dry sherry

Curried Leek Soup

Imperial (Metric)

1 lb 4 oz (565g) leeks
1 oz (30g) butter or
vegetable margarine
1½ tablespoons curry
powder
3 tablespoons wholemeal
flour
2 ¼ pints (1.3 litres)
vegetable stock
1 bay leaf
4 tablespoons chopped
parsley
Grated rind of ½ lemon
Juice of 1 lemon
2 tablespoons mango
chutney

1. Wash and finely chop the leeks.
2. Melt the butter or margarine in a saucepan on a low heat. Stir in the leeks. Cover and cook them gently for 10 minutes.
3. Stir in the curry powder, flour and stock. Bring to the boil, stirring, and put in the bay leaf, parsley and lemon rind and juice.
4. Simmer, uncovered, for 10 minutes, then remove the bay leaf.
5. Finely chop any large pieces in the mango chutney and stir the chutney into the soup before serving.
Note: To freeze, do not add the chutney but keep the bay leaf in the soup. Cool the soup completely. Pack it into a rigid container and cover. Store for up to 2 months. Thaw at room temperature, and reheat in a saucepan. Add the chutney.

American

1¼ pounds leeks
2 tablespoons butter or
vegetable margarine
1½ tablespoons curry
powder
3 tablespoons wholewheat
flour
5⅔ cups vegetable stock
1 bay leaf
¼ cup chopped parsley
Grated rind of ½ lemon
Juice of 1 lemon
2 tablespoons mango
chutney

33

Potato and Cucumber Soup

Imperial (Metric)

1½ lb (685g) potatoes
1½ large cucumbers
1½ pints (850ml)
vegetable stock
2 large onions, thinly
sliced
Sea salt and freshly
ground black pepper
Bouquet garni
1 garlic clove, crushed
1 teaspoon dill seeds
8 fl oz (230ml) natural
yogurt
3 tablespoons chopped
parsley

1. Peel and thinly slice the potatoes. Peel and thinly slice half the total amount of cucumber. Dice the rest, leaving it unpeeled.
2. Bring the stock to the boil in a large saucepan. Put in the potatoes, peeled sliced cucumber and onions. Season well and add the bouquet garni. Cover and simmer for 20 minutes. Remove the bouquet garni.
3. Put the soup through the fine blade of a vegetable mill or liquidize it in a blender or food processor until it is smooth.
4. Return the soup to the cleaned pan and bring it to the boil. Add the garlic, dill seeds and diced cucumber and simmer for 2 minutes.
5. Take the pan from the heat and stir in the yogurt. Reheat if necessary, without boiling.
6. Serve in individual bowls with the parsley sprinkled over the top.

American

1½ pounds potatoes
1½ large cucumbers
3¾ cups vegetable stock
2 large onions, thinly
sliced
Sea salt and freshly
ground black pepper
Bouquet garni
1 garlic clove, crushed
1 teaspoon dill seeds
1 cup unflavored yogurt
3 tablespoons chopped
parsley

Spinach, Leek and Barley Soup

Imperial (Metric)

1 lb (455g) spinach
8 oz (225g) leeks
4 tablespoons vegetable oil
1 large onion, finely
chopped
1 garlic clove, finely
chopped
3 oz (85g) pot barley
2¼ pints (1.3 litres)
vegetable stock
4 tablespoons chopped
parsley
1 tablespoon chopped
thyme
8 fl oz (225ml) natural
yogurt

1. Finely chop the spinach and leeks.
2. Heat 2 tablespoons oil in a large saucepan on a low heat, add the onion and garlic and soften them
3. Stir in the barley. Pour in the stock and bring it to the boil. Season and add the parsley and thyme. Cover and simmer for 20 minutes or until the barley is tender.
4. Heat the remaining oil in a very large frying pan (skillet) or paella pan on a high heat. Put in the spinach and leeks and stir-fry them for about 4 minutes or until they begin to soften.
5. Add the spinach and leeks to the soup. Continue to simmer for 2 minutes.
6. Take the pan from the heat and stir in the yogurt. Serve as soon as possible.

American

1 pound spinach
½ pound leeks
¼ cup vegetable oil
1 large onion, finely
chopped
1 garlic clove, finely
chopped
3 ounces pot barley
5⅔ cups vegetable stock
¼ cup chopped parsley
1 tablespoon chopped
thyme
1 cup unflavored yogurt

Note: The soup may be frozen before the yogurt is added. Cool it, pour it into a rigid container and cover. Store for up to 1 month. Thaw at room temperature and reheat in a saucepan before adding the yogurt.

Watercress, Onion and White Wine Soup

Imperial (Metric)

5 oz (150g) watercress
2 large onions
1 oz (30g) butter
2 tablespoons wholemeal
flour
1½ pints (850ml)
vegetable stock
¼ teaspoon ground mace
Sea salt and freshly
ground black pepper
2 bay leaves
¾ pint (425ml) dry white
wine
Six 2 inch (5cm) squares
wholemeal bread, toasted
4 oz (115g) Gruyère
cheese, finely grated

1. Trim the thicker stalks from the watercress. Finely chop the rest. Chop the onions.
2. Melt the butter in a saucepan on a low heat and cook the onions until they are golden, stirring occasionally.
3. Stir in the flour and gradually mix in the stock. Bring it to the boil, stirring. Add the mace, seasoning and the bay leaves.
4. Simmer, uncovered, for 10 minutes.
5. Add the wine and watercress. Bring the soup to just below boiling point and take it from the heat.
6. Put a square of toast into the bottom of each of six soup bowls. Top it with the cheese.
7. Pour the soup over the toast and serve.

Note: The soup can be frozen before adding the watercress and wine. Cool it completely and pack it into covered containers. Store it for up to 1 month. Thaw at room temperature. Reheat and add the wine and watercress as above.

American

5 ounces watercress
2 large onions
2 tablespoons butter
2 tablespoons wholewheat
flour
3¾ cups vegetable stock
¼ teaspoon ground mace
Sea salt and freshly
ground black pepper
2 bay leaves
2 cups dry white wine
Six 2 inch (5cm) squares
wholewheat bread, toasted
1 cup grated Gruyère
cheese

FIRST COURSES

Spring first courses can be hot or cold, depending on your mood and the weather. Make them small but delectable and present them prettily, then they will set the mood for the delicious main dish to come.

Spinach Leaves Stuffed with Rice and Aubergines (Eggplants)

Imperial (Metric)

18 large spinach leaves
10 oz (285g) aubergines
1 tablespoon sea salt
6 oz (170g) long-grain brown rice
8 oz (225g) tomatoes
1 teaspoon paprika
1 teaspoon ground cinnamon
¼ teaspoon cayenne pepper
¼ pint (140ml) vegetable stock
¼ pint (140ml) tomato juice

1. Break off the stalks of the spinach leaves at the point where they meet the leaves. Bring the pan of water to the boil, add the spinach leaves and cook for 1 minute. Drain.

2. Finely chop the aubergines (eggplants). Put them into a colander and sprinkle them with the salt. Leave them to drain for 20 minutes. Rinse them with cold water and dry them with kitchen paper.

3. Cook the rice in lightly salted water for 25 minutes. Drain it.

4. Heat the oven to 400°F/200°C/Gas Mark 6.

5. Scald, skin and finely chop the tomatoes.

6. In a bowl, mix together the aubergines (eggplants), rice, tomatoes, paprika, cinnamon and cayenne pepper.

7. Lay one spinach leaf on the table, stalk side up. Put 1 tablespoon of the rice mixture on the stalk end. Fold over the end, then the two sides and then roll up the leaf. Continue in the same way until all the leaves are used.

8. Lay the stuffed leaves, with the folded-over tips underneath, in a large, flat ovenproof dish.

9. Mix together the stock and tomato juice. Pour them over the stuffed leaves.

10. Bake the dish, uncovered, in the oven for 45 minutes.

American

18 large spinach leaves
10 ounces eggplants
1 tablespoon sea salt
¾ cup long-grain brown rice
½ pound tomatoes
1 teaspoon paprika
1 teaspoon ground cinnamon
¼ teaspoon cayenne pepper
⅔ cup vegetable stock
⅔ cup tomato juice

Surprise Avocado Vinaigrette

Imperial (Metric)

3 ripe avocados
4 oz (115g) watercress,
plus extra for garnish if
wished
6 firm tomatoes
3 fl oz (90ml) olive or
sunflower oil
2 tablespoons white wine
vinegar
1 garlic clove, crushed
Freshly ground black
pepper
3 tablespoons chopped
walnuts

1. Peel, stone (pit) and mash 2½ avocados. Press the purée into the bottom of 4 small soufflé dishes or ramekins.
2. Finely chop the watercress and fill the dishes with it, covering the avocados completely.
3. Finely chop the tomatoes and put them on top of the watercress.
4. Beat the oil, vinegar, garlic and pepper together to make the dressing and spoon it into the dishes.
5. Scatter the walnuts over the top.
6. Garnish with small strips from the reserved avocado.
7. Put the dishes onto small plates and surround them with extra watercress sprigs if wished.

American

3 ripe avocados
¼ pound watercress, plus
extra for garnish if wished
6 firm tomatoes
⅓ cup olive or sunflower
oil
2 tablespoons white wine
vinegar
1 garlic clove, crushed
Freshly ground black
pepper
3 tablespoons chopped
English walnuts

Cucumber and Blue Cheese Salad

Imperial (Metric)

1 large cucumber
6 oz (170g) blue cheese
6 spring onions
3 fl oz (90ml)
mayonnaise
Outer leaves from 2 small
round lettuces
24 small dandelion leaves
Approximately ½ teaspoon
paprika
24 walnut halves

1. Cut both the cucumber and the cheese into ⅜-inch (1cm) dice.
2. Finely chop the spring onions (scallions).
3. Mix the cucumber, cheese and onions into the mayonnaise.
4. Arrange the lettuce leaves on each of six small plates, the curved edges making the edge of a circle. Arrange the dandelion leaves on the lettuce to form a star.
6. Put a portion of the cucumber salad in the centre and sprinkle it lightly with paprika.
7. Put the walnut halves in between the dandelion leaves before serving.

American

1 large cucumber
6 ounces blue cheese
6 scallions
⅓ cup mayonnaise
Outer leaves from 2 small
round lettuces
24 small dandelion leaves
Approximately ½ teaspoon
paprika
24 English walnut halves

Watercress and Sesame Salad

Imperial (Metric)

4 oz (115g) watercress
2 red peppers
6 small tomatoes
1 tablespoon tahini
(sesame paste)
1 garlic clove, crushed
Freshly ground black
pepper
4 tablespoons sesame oil
2 tablespoons cider
vinegar
2 tablespoons sesame
seeds
2 oz (55g) stoned dates,
finely chopped
2 oz (55g) currants
6 walnut halves

1. Chop the watercress. Core, seed and chop the peppers. Chop the tomatoes. Mix them together in a bowl.
2. Put the tahini into a small bowl with the garlic and pepper. Gradually beat in first the oil and then the vinegar. Mix the resulting dressing into the watercress, peppers and tomatoes.
3. Put the sesame seeds into a heavy frying pan (skillet). Stir them on a medium heat until they brown and start to pop and jump about. Tip them onto a plate to cool. Mix them with the dates and currants.
4. Divide the salad between 6 small plates. Scatter the sesame seeds and dried fruits over the top. Garnish each salad with a walnut half.
Note: Unsuitable for freezing.

American

¼ pound watercress
2 sweet red peppers
6 small tomatoes
1 tablespoon tahini
(sesame paste)
1 garlic clove, crushed
Freshly ground black
pepper
¼ cup sesame oil
2 tablespoons cider
vinegar
2 tablespoons sesame
seeds
2 ounces pitted dates,
finely chopped
2 ounces currants
6 English walnut halves

Parsley Hummus

Imperial (Metric)

6 oz (170g) chick peas,
soaked and cooked
1½ oz (45g) sesame seeds
1 garlic clove, crushed
Juice of 1½ lemons
3 tablespoons tahini
(sesame paste)
3 fl oz (90ml) olive oil
1½ oz (45g) parsley,
finely chopped
¼ teaspoon cayenne
pepper
1 lb (455g) tomatoes
2 small onions, cut into
rings
3 black olives

1. Put the chick peas (garbanzos) through the fine blade of a vegetable mill; or rub them through a sieve; or purée them in a blender or food processor.
2. Put the sesame seeds into a heavy frying pan (skillet). Set them on a medium heat and stir them until they brown. Immediately tip them onto a plate to cool.
3. Mix the sesame seeds into the chick peas (garbanzos).
4. Beat in the garlic, lemon juice and tahini. Gradually add the oil.
5. Mix in the parsley and cayenne pepper.
6. Divide the hummus into six small portions and put one in the centre of each of six small plates. Using a flat knife, mould it into a round shape. Alternatively, the hummus can be pressed into small, oiled moulds or

American

1 cup garbanzo beans,
soaked and cooked
¼ cup sesame seeds
1 garlic clove, crushed
Juice of 1½ lemons
3 tablespoons tahini
(sesame paste)
⅓ cup olive oil
1½ cups chopped parsley
¼ teaspoon cayenne
pepper
1 pound tomatoes
2 small onions, cut into
rings
3 black olives

soufflé dishes and turned onto the plates. This will give a more even shape and will probably take less time in the long run.

7. Surround the hummus with tomato slices and onion rings and top with an olive half to serve.

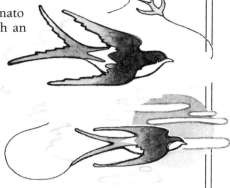

Cauliflower Fritters with Lemon and Caper Sauce

Imperial (Metric)

2 medium cauliflowers
2 thinly pared strips lemon rind
1 thyme sprig
Vegetable oil for deep frying
Batter:
6 oz (170g) wholemeal flour
1 teaspoon mustard powder
Pinch fine sea salt
4 tablespoons olive oil
7 fl oz (200ml) warm water
2 egg whites
Sauce:
4 fl oz (115ml) olive oil
Juice of 1 lemon
4 tablespoons chopped parsley
3 tablespoons chopped capers
Freshly ground black pepper
Garnish:
Parsley sprigs

1. Break the cauliflowers into small florets. Steam them with the lemon rind and thyme sprig for 15 minutes or until they are just tender. Cool them.

2. For the batter, put the flour into a bowl and toss in the mustard powder and salt. Make a well in the centre and pour in the oil. Beat in a small amount of flour from the sides of the well. Gradually beat in the water. Leave the batter to stand for 30 minutes. Stiffly whip the egg whites and fold them into the mixture just before serving.

3. For the sauce, beat together the oil and lemon juice. Stir in the parsley, capers and pepper.

4. Heat a deep pan of oil to 375°F/190°C.

5. Dip the cauliflower florets into the batter. Deep-fry them, about 5 at a time, until they are golden brown. Drain them on kitchen paper and keep warm while you cook the rest in the same way.

6. Divide the cauliflower between six small plates. Garnish with parsley sprigs. Serve the sauce separately.

Note: Unsuitable for freezing.

American

2 medium cauliflowers
2 thinly pared strips lemon rind
1 thyme sprig
Vegetable oil for deep frying
Batter:
1½ cups wholewheat flour
1 teaspoon mustard powder
Pinch fine sea salt
¼ cup olive oil
¾ cup warm water
2 egg whites
Sauce:
½ cup olive oil
Juice of 1 lemon
¼ cup chopped parsley
3 tablespoons chopped capers
Freshly ground black pepper
Garnish:
Parsley sprigs

Avocado and Almond Tartlets

Imperial (Metric)

*Shortcrust pastry made
with 4 oz (115g)
wholemeal flour (see
page 24)
2 ripe avocados
1 garlic clove, crushed
Juice of ½ lemon
2 oz (55g) ground
almonds
3 tablespoons chopped
parsley or chervil
2 tablespoons flaked
almonds
6 small parsley or chervil
sprigs
1 lb (455g) tomatoes
6 spring onions
4 tablespoons olive oil
1 tablespoon white wine
vinegar
Freshly ground black
pepper*

1. Heat the oven to 400°F/200°C/Gas
Mark 6. Roll out the pastry and use it to
line six 3½-inch (8cm) tartlet tins. Bake
blind for 15 minutes, then cool the
pastry shells and turn them out of the
tins.
2. For the filling, peel and stone (pit)
the avocados. Mash them to a purée.
Mix in the garlic, lemon juice, ground
almonds and parsley or chervil.
3. Put the avocado filling into the
tartlets. Scatter flaked (slivered) almonds
over the top. Garnish with a chervil or
parsley sprig.
4. Put one tartlet in the centre of each
of six small plates.
5. Thinly slice the tomatoes and arrange
the slices around the tartlets.
6. Finely chop the spring onions
(scallions) and scatter them over the
tomatoes.
7. Beat the oil, vinegar and pepper
together. Spoon a little of the resulting
dressing over the tomatoes.
Note: The tartlet cases can be frozen on
a flat tray and then packed in polythene
bags to be stored for up to 2 months.
Thaw them singly at room temperature.
The filling is unsuitable for freezing.

American

*Shortcrust pastry made
with 1 cup wholewheat
flour (see page 24)
2 ripe avocados
1 garlic clove, crushed
Juice of ½ lemon
1 cup ground almonds
3 tablespoons chopped
parsley or chervil
2 tablespoons slivered
almonds
6 small parsley or chervil
sprigs
1 pound tomatoes
6 scallions
¼ cup olive oil
1 tablespoon white wine
vinegar
Freshly ground black
pepper*

Stir-Fried Leeks and Cheese

Imperial (Metric)

*Thinly pared rind of 1
orange
1 lb (455g) leeks
3 tablespoons vegetable oil
4 tablespoons tarragon
vinegar
6 oz (170g) Cheddar
cheese, diced*

1. Cut the orange rind into matchstick
pieces. Put them into boiling water and
cook for 2 minutes. Drain them.
2. Cut the leeks in half lengthways.
Wash them well and cut them into
⅜-inch (1cm) slices.
3. Heat the oil in a large frying pan
(skillet) on a high heat. Put in the leeks
and stir-fry them for 2 minutes.
4. Add the vinegar and let it bubble.
5. Take the pan from the heat and mix
in the cheese.

American

*Thinly pared rind of 1
orange
1 pound leeks
3 tablespoons vegetable oil
¼ cup tarragon vinegar
6 ounces Cheddar cheese,
diced*

6. Immediately put the leeks and cheese into six small bowls and scatter the orange rind over the top to serve.
Note: The flavour and texture are spoiled if the dish is kept warm, so prepare it only just before serving. Unsuitable for freezing.

Grilled Mushrooms and Aubergines (Eggplants) with Chervil

Imperial (Metric)

1½ lbs (680g) aubergines
1 tablespoon sea salt
4 fl oz (115ml) olive oil
8 fl oz (250ml) natural yogurt
4 tablespoons chopped chervil
1 garlic clove, crushed
Freshly ground black pepper
12 oz (340g) open mushrooms
Tiny chervil sprigs for garnish

1. Cut the aubergines (eggplants) into ⅜-inch (1cm) slices. Put them into a colander, sprinkle with the salt and leave to drain for 30 minutes
2. In a large bowl, beat the oil into the yogurt and mix in the chervil, garlic and pepper.
3. Fold in the mushrooms and leave them to marinate for 30 minutes.
4. Rinse the aubergines (eggplants) under cold water and dry them with kitchen paper.
5. Heat the grill (broiler) to high.
6. Lift the mushrooms from the marinade. Lay them on the hot grill (broiler) rack.
7. Lay the aubergines (eggplants) beside them and brush them with half the remaining marinade.
8. Grill (broil) the vegetables for 2 minutes.
9. Turn the aubergines (eggplants) over and brush them with the remaining marinade.
10. Return the mushrooms and aubergines (eggplants) to the heat for a further 2 minutes.
11. Serve sizzling hot, garnished with the chervil sprigs.

American

1½ pounds eggplants
1 tablespoon sea salt
½ cup olive oil
1 cup unflavored yogurt
¼ cup chopped chervil
1 garlic clove, crushed
Freshly ground black pepper
¾ pound open mushrooms
Tiny chervil sprigs for garnish

MAIN DISHES

All the following main dishes are based on spring produce, such as fresh vegetables or goose and duck eggs. Their common characteristic is that they are warming and substantial enough for chilly days and yet their flavours are light. This makes them so suitable for this time of the year.

Nut Roast with Rhubarb

Imperial (Metric)

6 oz (170g) hazelnuts
4 oz (115g) sunflower seeds
4 tablespoons vegetable oil
1 large onion, finely chopped
8 oz (225g) rhubarb, finely chopped
8 oz (225g) wholemeal breadcrumbs
2 oz (55g) porridge oats
¼ pint (140ml) dry red wine
3 fl oz (90ml) vegetable stock
2 tablespoons chopped thyme
2 tablespoons chopped marjoram
Pinch ground allspice
Pinch ground cloves
Sauce:
2 tablespoons vegetable oil
1 small onion, finely chopped
1 small carrot, finely chopped
½ celery stick, finely chopped
2 tablespoons wholemeal flour
¾ pint (425ml) vegetable stock
4 oz (115g) rhubarb, finely chopped
3 fl oz (90ml) dry red wine

1. Heat the oven to 400°F/200°C/Gas Mark 6.
2. Coarsely grind the hazelnuts and sunflower seeds and put them into a large bowl.
3. Heat the oil in a frying pan (skillet) on a low heat. Put in the onion and rhubarb. Cook them, stirring frequently, until they are soft.
4. Add the onion and rhubarb to the nuts and seeds. Mix in the breadcrumbs, oats, wine, stock, herbs and spices.
5. Put the mixture into a deep, ovenproof dish. Bake the roast for 45 minutes or until it feels firm and the top is brown.
6. Make the sauce while the roast is cooking. Heat the oil in a saucepan on a low heat. Put in the onion, carrot and celery and cook them until they begin to brown. Stir in the flour and then the stock. Bring to the boil, stirring. Add the rhubarb, partially cover and simmer for 30 minutes. Strain the sauce and return it to the cleaned pan. Add the wine and simmer for 10 minutes, uncovered.
7. Either serve the roast straight from the dish with the sauce separately; or cut it into wedges, put a little sauce on each of six dinner plates and put a wedge of the roast on top. Garnish with parsley sprigs if wished.
Note: Unsuitable for freezing.

American

1⅓ cups hazelnuts
1 cup sunflower seeds
¼ cup vegetable oil
1 large onion, finely chopped
½ pound rhubarb, finely chopped
4 cups wholewheat breadcrumbs
½ cup rolled oats
⅔ cup dry red wine
⅓ cup vegetable stock
2 tablespoons chopped thyme
2 tablespoons chopped marjoram
Pinch ground allspice
Pinch ground cloves
Sauce:
2 tablespoons vegetable oil
1 small onion, finely chopped
1 small carrot, finely chopped
½ small celery stalk, finely chopped
2 tablespoons wholewheat flour
2 cups vegetable stock
¼ pound rhubarb, finely chopped
⅓ cup dry red wine

Chick Pea (Garbanzo) and Spinach Sausages

Imperial (Metric)

8 oz (225g) chick peas
4 oz (115g) burghul
    wheat
8 oz (225g) fresh spinach
4 tablespoons vegetable oil
1 large onion, finely
    chopped
1 garlic clove, finely
    chopped
4 tablespoons chopped
    parsley
½ teaspoon ground cumin
½ teaspoon ground
    cinnamon
Juice of 1 lemon
2 tablespoons tomato
    purée
Parsley sprigs
1 oz (30g) wholemeal
    flour
4 tablespoons vegetable oil
Sauce:
2 tablespoons vegetable oil
8 oz (225g) tomatoes,
    chopped
1 small onion, finely
    chopped
1 garlic clove, finely
    chopped
½ teaspoon ground cumin
½ teaspoon ground
    cinnamon
½ pint (285ml) natural
    yogurt

1. Soak the chick peas (garbanzos) and cook them until they are tender. Drain and wash them.
2. Soak the burghul wheat in warm water for 20 minutes. Drain and squeeze it dry.
3. Wash and finely chop the spinach.
4. Heat the oil in a large frying pan (skillet) on a low heat. Put in the onion and garlic and soften them. Raise the heat. Put in the spinach and stir-fry it until it has just wilted, about 3 minutes. Take the pan from the heat.
5. Mix the wheat and spinach into the chick peas (garbanzos). Add the parsley, cumin, cinnamon, lemon juice and tomato purée (paste).
6. Divide the mixture into 12 portions and mould them into sausage shapes. Chill for 30 minutes to firm them. Coat in the flour and brush them with oil.
7. To make the sauce, heat the oil in a saucepan on a low heat. Put in the tomatoes, onion, garlic and spices. Cover and cook gently for 10 minutes. Rub the mixture through a sieve and cool it. Mix in the yogurt.
8. To cook the sausages, heat the grill (broiler) to high and if you have an open wire rack cover it with foil. Lay the sausages on the hot rack and cook them for about 7 minutes, turning them several times, until they are brown all round.
9. Lay the sausages on a serving dish and garnish with parsley. Serve the sauce separately
Note: Unsuitable for freezing.

American

1 cup garbanzo beans
⅔ cup burghul wheat
½ pound fresh spinach
¼ cup vegetable oil
1 large onion, finely
    chopped
1 garlic clove, finely
    chopped
¼ cup chopped parsley
½ teaspoon ground cumin
½ teaspoon ground
    cinnamon
Juice of 1 lemon
2 tablespoons tomato
    paste
Parsley sprigs
¼ cup wholewheat flour
¼ cup vegetable oil
Sauce:
2 tablespoons vegetable oil
½ pound tomatoes,
    chopped
1 small onion, finely
    chopped
1 garlic clove, finely
    chopped
½ teaspoon ground cumin
½ teaspoon ground
    cinnamon
1⅓ cups unflavored
    yogurt

Stir-Braised Almonds with Cauliflower, Peppers and Beansprouts

Imperial (Metric)

1 medium cauliflower
2 green peppers
1 medium onion
8 oz (225g) beansprouts
2 tablespoons arrowroot
2 tablespoons tamari or
shoyu sauce
4 tablespoons dry sherry
1 tablespoon tomato purée
½ pint (285ml) vegetable
stock
Vegetable oil for frying
1 garlic clove, finely
chopped
½ oz (15g) fresh ginger
root, peeled and grated
12 oz (340g) blanched
almonds

1. Break the cauliflower into small florets. Core and seed the peppers and cut them into 1-inch (2.5cm) strips. Finely chop the onion. Rinse the beansprouts and drain them well.
2. Put the arrowroot into a bowl and gradually mix in the tamari or shoyu sauce, sherry and tomato purée (paste) to make a smooth paste. Gradually mix in the stock.
3. Heat the oil in a wok or large frying pan (skillet) on a high heat. Put in the garlic and ginger and stir them until they sizzle.
4. Put in the almonds, cauliflower, peppers and onion. Stir-fry for 2 minutes.
5. Add the beansprouts and stir for 1 minute more.
6. Give the stock mixture a stir and pour it into the pan. Cover and cook on a low heat for 10 minutes, stirring occasionally. Serve as soon as possible.

American

1 medium cauliflower
2 sweet green peppers
1 medium onion
4 cups beansprouts
2 tablespoons arrowroot
2 tablespoons tamari or
shoyu sauce
¼ cup dry sherry
1 tablespoon tomato paste
1⅓ cups vegetable stock
Vegetable oil for frying
1 garlic clove, finely
chopped
1 tablespoon grated fresh
ginger root
3 cups blanched almonds

Brie and Courgette (Zucchini) Lasagne

Imperial (Metric)

12 oz (340g) wholemeal
lasagne
1½ oz (45g) butter
2 lb (900g) courgettes,
coarsely grated
Juice of 1 lemon
1 oz (30g) parsley,
chopped
4 tablespoons chopped
chives
12 oz (340g) Brie cheese,
finely diced
2 eggs
8 fl oz (230ml) natural
yogurt
2 tablespoons grated
Parmesan cheese
3 tablespoons wheatgerm

1. Heat the oven to 400°F/200°C/Gas Mark 6.
2. Cook the lasagne in lightly salted boiling water for 15 minutes or until it is just tender. Drain it. Run cold water through it and drain it again.
3. Heat the butter in a large saucepan on a high heat. Put in the courgettes (zucchini) and stir them for 4 minutes or until they are just cooked through. Take the pan from the heat and mix in the lemon juice, parsley and chives.
4. Put one-third of the lasagne into a 2-inch (5cm) deep 10-inch (25cm) square ovenproof dish. Put in one-third of the Brie, then one-third of the courgettes (zucchini). Repeat the layers

American

¾ pound wholewheat
lasagne
3 tablespoons butter
2 pounds zucchini,
coarsely grated
Juice of 1 lemon
1 cup parsley, chopped
¼ cup chopped chives
¾ pound Brie cheese,
finely diced
2 eggs
1 cup unflavored yogurt
2 tablespoons grated
Parmesan cheese
3 tablespoons wheatgerm

twice more, finishing with the courgettes (zucchini).

5. Beat together the eggs, yogurt and Parmesan cheese. Pour them over the top layer of courgettes (zucchini).

6. Scatter the wheatgerm over the top.

7. Bake the lasagne for 20 minutes or until the top is just beginning to colour.

Note: Unsuitable for freezing.

Watercress Cream

Imperial (Metric)

8 oz (225g) haricot beans
3 oz (85g) watercress
2 oz (55g) butter
7 fl oz (200ml) milk
2 oz (55g) wholemeal flour
3 oz (85 g) Cheddar cheese, grated
¼ pint (140ml) soured cream
1 tablespoon Dijon mustard
4 eggs, beaten
Sauce:
4 oz (115g) curd cheese
½ pint (285ml) buttermilk
1 oz (30g) parsley, chopped
1 oz (30g) watercress, finely chopped
Watercress sprigs for garnish

American

1¼ cups navy beans
3 ounces watercress
¼ cup butter
1 cup milk
½ cup wholewheat flour
⅔ cup grated Cheddar cheese
⅔ cup sour cream
1 tablespoon Dijon mustard
4 eggs, beaten
Sauce:
½ cup curd cheese
1⅓ cups buttermilk
1 cup chopped parsley
1 cup watercress, finely chopped
Watercress sprigs for garnish

1. Soak and cook the haricot (navy) beans. Mash them well or purée them in a blender or food processor.

2. Finely chop the watercress and mix it into the beans.

3. Put the butter and milk into a saucepan. Bring them to the boil and boil them until the butter has melted. Take the pan from the heat and stir in all the flour at once. Beat until you have a smooth mixture. Mix it into the beans.

4. Add the cheese, soured cream and mustard and mix well.

5. Add the eggs a little at a time, beating after each addition.

6. Put the mixture into a large, deep, well-buttered ovenproof dish. Cover it with buttered greaseproof paper.

7. Bring some water to the boil in a large steamer. Put in the dish. Cover and steam for 50 minutes or until the bean mixture is set and firm.

8. While the cream is steaming, make the sauce. Put the cheese into a bowl and gradually beat in the buttermilk. Add the parsley and watercress. Put the sauce into a saucepan. Heat it gently, without boiling.

9. When the cream has set, run a knife round the edge and then turn it onto a large, flat plate.

10. Pour the sauce over the top.

11. Garnish with watercress sprigs.

Note: Unsuitable for freezing.

Herb Risotto with Two Cheeses

Imperial (Metric)

4 tablespoons olive oil
12 oz (340g) short-grain
brown rice
16 spring onions, finely
chopped
2½ pints (1.4 litres)
vegetable stock
Pinch sea salt
Pinch saffron
1 oz (30g) parsley,
chopped
2 tablespoons chopped
thyme
2 tablespoons chopped
marjoram
12 oz (340g) aubergines,
finely chopped
12 oz (340g) Gruyère
cheese, coarsely grated
4 tablespoons grated
Parmesan cheese

1. Heat the oil in a saucepan on a low heat. Stir in the rice and onions (scallions). Stir for 1 minute.
2. Pour in about one-third of the stock. Bring to the boil. Add the salt, saffron and herbs. Simmer, uncovered, until nearly all the stock has been absorbed, about 15 minutes.
3. Pour in a further third of the stock. Simmer, uncovered, for a further 15 minutes.
4. Add the remaining stock and the aubergines (eggplants) and simmer, uncovered, for a further 20 minutes or until the rice is tender and the liquid has reduced to a creamy textured glaze.
5. Fork in the two cheeses just before serving.

Note: The risotto can be frozen before the cheeses are added. Cool it completely. Pack it into a rigid plastic container and cover. Store for up to 1 month. Thaw at room temperature. Reheat by stirring in a saucepan on a low heat. Add the cheeses.

American

¼ cup olive oil
1½ cups short-grain
brown rice
16 scallions, finely
chopped
5½ cups vegetable stock
Pinch sea salt
Pinch saffron
1 cup parsley, chopped
2 tablespoons chopped
thyme
2 tablespoons chopped
marjoram
¾ pound eggplants, finely
chopped
¾ pound Gruyère cheese,
coarsely grated
¼ cup grated Parmesan
cheese

Duck Eggs Niçoise

Imperial (Metric)

1½ lb (680g) spinach
3 tablespoons olive oil
2 medium onions, thinly
sliced
1 garlic clove, finely
chopped
12 oz (340g) firm
tomatoes, skinned and
roughly chopped
12 black olives, stoned
and chopped
6 duck eggs
6 fl oz (170ml) double
cream
2 tablespoons grated
Parmesan cheese
2 oz (55g) Cheddar
cheese, grated

1. Break the stalks from the spinach where they meet the leaves. Put the spinach into a saucepan with only the water that clings to it after washing. Cover it and set it on a moderate heat for 15 minutes, stirring it twice. Drain if necessary and finely chop.
2. Heat the oven to 350°F/180°C/Gas Mark 4.
3. Heat the oil in a large frying pan (skillet) on a low heat. Put in the onion and garlic and cook until the onion is golden.
4. Take the pan from the heat and mix in the tomatoes, olives and spinach. Put the mixture into a flat, ovenproof dish.
5. Using a tablespoon, make six

American

1½ pounds spinach
3 tablespoons olive oil
2 medium onions, thinly
sliced
1 garlic clove, finely
chopped
¾ pound firm tomatoes,
skinned and roughly
chopped
12 black olives, pitted and
chopped
6 duck eggs
¾ cup heavy cream
2 tablespoons grated
Parmesan cheese
½ cup grated Cheddar
cheese

indentations in the top. Break an egg into each one.

6. Beat together the cream and Parmesan cheese. Spoon about 2 tablespoons of the mixture over each egg yolk.

7. Scatter the Cheddar cheese over the top.

8. Bake the eggs for 25 minutes or until they are just set. Duck eggs are best if they are firm rather than runny.

Note: This can also be made with hens' eggs. Unsuitable for freezing.

Leek and Pine Nut Pie

Imperial (Metric)

3 oz (85g) pine nuts
3 oz (85g) chopped mixed nuts
1 oz (30g) butter
1½ lb (680g) leeks, thinly sliced
4 tablespoons wholemeal flour
2 teaspoons curry powder
¾ pint (425ml) vegetable stock
4 tablespoons soured cream
4 tablespoons chopped parsley
6 eggs, hard-boiled and chopped
Shortcrust pastry made with 1 lb (455g) wholemeal flour (see page 24)
1 egg, beaten
1 tablespoon sesame seeds

1. Heat the oven to 400°F/200°C/Gas Mark 6.

2. Put the pine nuts and chopped mixed nuts into a heavy saucepan. Set them on a medium heat and stir them continually until they are golden brown. Tip them onto a plate to cool.

3. Melt the butter in a saucepan on a low heat. Put in the leeks, cover them and cook them gently for 15 minutes, turning them once.

4. Stir in the flour and curry powder. Pour in the stock and bring it to the boil, stirring. Simmer for 2 minutes.

5. Take the pan from the heat and stir in the soured cream, parsley, nuts and eggs. Cool the mixture to lukewarm.

6. Roll out about two-thirds of the pastry and use it to line a 10-11 inch (25-27.5cm) square by 2 inch (5cm) deep ovenproof dish. Put in the leek mixture. Cover it with the remaining pastry.

7. Brush the top with the beaten egg. Sprinkle the sesame seeds over the top.

8. Bake the pie for 30 minutes or until the top is golden brown.

Note: Chopped mixed nuts can be bought from many supermarkets and health food shops.

To freeze, cool completely. Freeze the pie in the dish. Thaw at room temperature. Reheat in a hot oven for 20 minutes.

American

⅔ cup pine nuts
⅔ cup chopped mixed nuts
2 tablespoons butter
1½ pounds leeks, thinly sliced
¼ cup wholewheat flour
2 teaspoons curry powder
2 cups vegetable stock
¼ cup sour cream
¼ cup chopped parsley
6 hard-cooked eggs, chopped
Shortcrust pastry made with 4 cups wholewheat flour (see page 24)
1 egg, beaten
1 tablespoon sesame seeds

Leek, Rice and Lentil Layer

Imperial (Metric)

1 lb (455g) leeks
4 fl oz (115ml) vegetable oil
12 oz (340g) long-grain brown rice
1 teaspoon paprika
3 pints (1.7 litres) vegetable stock
Pinch sea salt
1 lb (455g) tomatoes
1 large onion, finely chopped
2 teaspoons paprika
Pinch cayenne pepper
12 oz (340g) green lentils
¼ pint (150ml) dry white wine
2 tablespoons tomato purée
1 bay leaf
4 tablespoons dried wholemeal breadcrumbs

1. Thinly slice the leeks.
2. Heat half the oil in a saucepan on a low heat. Stir in the leeks. Cover and cook them on a low heat for 5 minutes.
3. Stir in the rice and paprika. Pour in half the stock and bring it to the boil. Add the salt. Cover and cook on a low heat for 40 minutes or until the rice is tender and all the liquid has been absorbed.
4. Scald, skin and chop 12 ounces (340g) of the tomatoes. Mix them into the rice when it is cooked.
5. Prepare the lentils while the rice is cooking. Heat the remaining oil in a saucepan on a low heat. Put in the onion and soften it. Add the paprika, cayenne pepper and lentils and stir for 1 minute. Pour in the remaining stock and bring it to the boil. Add the wine, the tomato purée (paste) and the bay leaf.
6. Cover and simmer for 45 minutes or until the lentils are soft and most of the liquid has been absorbed; extract the bay leaf and discard it.
7. Heat the oven to 350°F/180°C/Gas Mark 4.
8. Put one-third of the lentils into an oven-to-table casserole. Top them with one-third of the rice. Repeat the layers twice.
9. Thinly slice the remaining tomatoes and put them on top. Scatter them with the breadcrumbs.
10. Put the dish into the oven, uncovered and bake for 20 minutes.

American

1 pound leeks
½ cup vegetable oil
1½ cups long-grain brown rice
1 teaspoon paprika
7½ cups vegetable stock
Pinch sea salt
1 pound tomatoes
1 large onion, finely chopped
2 teaspoons paprika
Pinch cayenne pepper
1½ cups green lentils
⅔ cup dry white wine
2 tablespoons tomato paste
1 bay leaf
¼ cup dried wholewheat breadcrumbs

48

Curranty Pancakes (page 18), Carrot and Walnut Pancakes (page 15)
and Apricot Pancake Stack (page 17).
Overleaf A May Day Buffet: Potato and Cucumber Soup (page 34),
Chickpea and Macadamia Nut Salad (page 63), Nutty Spring Salad
(page 58), Leek and Pine Nut Pie (page 47) and Caraway Rolls (page 82).

Stuffed Fresh Dates (page 75).

Goose Eggs Baked in a Bed

Imperial (Metric)

1½ lb (680g) tomatoes
1 large cucumber
1 oz (30g) butter
2 medium onions, finely chopped
1 garlic clove, finely chopped
1 teaspoon dill seeds
6 oz (170g) low-fat soft cheese
6 oz (170g) Cheshire cheese, grated
1 oz (30g) parsley, finely chopped
½ pint (285ml) single cream
6 goose eggs

1. Heat the oven to 400°F/200°C/Gas Mark 6.
2. Scald, skin and finely chop the tomatoes. Finely chop the cucumber.
3. Melt the butter in a large frying pan (skillet) on a low heat. Put in the cucumber, onions and garlic. Cook them, stirring occasionally, until they are just beginning to brown.
4. Put in the tomatoes and dill seeds. Cook, uncovered, for 5 minutes, so the tomatoes begin to soften. Take the pan from the heat and cool the mixture.
5. Put the soft cheese into a bowl. Beat in the Cheshire cheese and parsley, and then the cream, a little at a time.
6. Since goose eggs are so large, it is best to use two ovenproof dishes about 8 by 10 inches (20 by 25 cm), and 2 inches (5cm) deep. Divide the tomato mixture between the two dishes. Make three large indentations in each one. Break in the goose eggs.
7. Cover the goose eggs with the cheese mixture. The best way to do this is to make a ring round each yolk first, using small pieces of mixture from a teaspoon. Then take more small pieces to cover the yolk completely. Use any remaining mixture to cover the spaces between the eggs. It will spread out to cover the whole surface during cooking.
8. Bake the eggs for 25 minutes or until they are set and the cheese mixture has browned lightly.
Note: Unsuitable for freezing.

American

1½ pounds tomatoes
1 large cucumber
2 tablespoons butter
2 medium onions, finely chopped
1 garlic clove, finely chopped
1 teaspoon dill seeds
¾ cup low-fat soft cheese
1½ cups grated Cheshire cheese
1 cup chopped parsley
1⅓ cups light cream
6 goose eggs

Eggs with Pine Nut and Sorrel Sauce

Imperial (Metric)

8 eggs
Rice:
4 tablespoons vegetable oil
1 large onion, finely
chopped
2 oz (55g) sorrel leaves,
finely chopped
12 oz (340g) long-grain
brown rice
1½ pints (850ml)
vegetable stock
Pinch sea salt
2 oz (55g) pine nuts
2 oz (55g) currants
Sauce:
4 oz (115g) sorrel leaves
3 oz (85g) pine nuts
2 tablespoons vegetable oil
1 large onion, finely
chopped
1 garlic clove, finely
chopped
¼ pint (140ml) vegetable
stock
½ pint (285ml) creamed
smetana or soured cream

1. Hard-boil (cook) the eggs and keep
them warm.
2. For the rice, heat the oil in a
saucepan on a low heat. Put in the
onion and soften it. Stir in the sorrel
and rice.
3. Pour in the stock and bring it to the
boil. Add the salt. Cover and simmer for
40 minutes or until the rice is tender
and all the liquid absorbed, then toss in
the pine nuts and currants. Cover and
leave off the heat for 10 minutes.
4. For the sauce, finely chop the sorrel
leaves and finely grind the pine nuts.
Heat the oil in a saucepan on a low
heat. Put in the onion and garlic and
soften them.
5. Stir in the sorrel and pine nuts. Pour
in the stock and bring it to the boil.
Simmer, uncovered, for 2 minutes. Take
the pan from the heat.
6. Liquidize in a blender or food
processor. Add the smetana and blend
again. Heat the sauce, without boiling.
7. To serve, make a bed of rice on a
large serving plate. Halve the eggs
lengthways and lay them on top. Pour
the sauce over the eggs.

American

8 eggs
Rice:
¼ cup vegetable oil
1 large onion, finely
chopped
2 ounces sorrel leaves,
finely chopped
1½ cups long-grain brown
rice
3¾ cups vegetable stock
Pinch sea salt
½ cup pine nuts
⅓ cup currants
Sauce:
¼ pound sorrel leaves
¾ cup pine nuts
2 tablespoons vegetable oil
1 large onion, finely
chopped
1 garlic clove, finely
chopped
⅔ cup vegetable stock
1⅓ cups creamed smetana
or sour cream

Green Rice Mould

2 lb (900g) spring greens
4 tablespoons olive oil
*12 oz (340g) long-grain
brown rice*
1 teaspoon dried oregano
*1½ pints (850ml)
vegetable stock*
12 spring onions
*12 oz (340g) Cotswold
cheese*
1 lb (455g) tomatoes

1. Heat the oven to 350°F/180°C/Gas Mark 4.
2. Reserve about 10 large outer leaves of the spring greens, enough to layer a 3 pint (1.7 litre/7½ cup) ovenproof dish. Break off the stalks where they meet the leaves. Finely chop the remaining leaves, after removing the tougher stalks.
3. Heat 2 teaspoons of the oil in a saucepan on a low heat and stir in the rice and oregano. Pour in the stock and bring it to the boil. Cover and simmer for 45 minutes or until the rice is tender and all the stock has been absorbed.
4. Bring a large pan of water to the boil. Put in the whole leaves of spring greens. Cook them for 2 minutes and drain them.
5. Heat the remaining oil in a saucepan on a high heat. Stir in the chopped spring greens and the spring onions (scallions). Pour in 8 fl oz (230ml/1 cup) water and bring it to the boil. Cover and cook on a medium heat for 15 minutes or until the spring greens are just tender. Drain them well.
6. Mix together the rice and the drained spring greens and onions (scallions).
7. Thinly slice the cheese and the tomatoes.
8. Line your dish with the whole blanched leaves. Put in one-quarter of the rice mixture, then one-third of the cheese and one-third of the tomatoes.
Repeat these layers twice more and finish with a layer of rice. Cover the top with oiled foil and weight it down with a flat plate.
9. Bake the mould for 20 minutes.
10. Turn the mould out onto a flat serving plate. Serve it cut into wedges.
Note: Unsuitable for freezing.

2 pounds spring greens
¼ cup olive oil
*1½ cups long-grain brown
rice*
1 teaspoon dried oregano
3¾ cups vegetable stock
12 scallions
¾ pound Cotswold cheese
1 pound tomatoes

Carling Pancakes (Crêpes)

Imperial (Metric)

6 oz (170g) borlotti beans
4 tablespoons vegetable oil
1 large onion, finely
chopped
4 oz (115g) walnuts,
finely chopped
2 tablespoons chopped
chives
4 tablespoons chopped
parsley
2 tablespoons chopped
thyme
1 tablespoon chopped
marjoram
6 eggs, beaten
Sunflower oil for frying
Sauce:
4 tablespoons chopped
chives
½ pint (285ml) creamed
smetana or soured cream
Garnish:
Parsley sprigs

1. Soak the beans and cook them until they are tender. Drain and mash them.
2. Heat the oil in a saucepan on a low heat. Put in the onion and soften it.
3. Mix the onion into the beans.
4. Add the walnuts, herbs and eggs and mix well.
5. To make the sauce, chop the chives finely and mix them into the smetana or soured cream. Liquidizing the sauce quickly in a blender or food processor will release more of the chive flavour.
6. To cook, heat 2 tablespoons sunflower oil in a frying pan (skillet) on a moderate heat. Place a 2½-3-inch (7-7.5cm) metal biscuit cutter on the frying pan (skillet). Spoon in enough of the bean mixture to make a small pancake (crêpe) ¼ inch (6mm) thick. Remove the biscuit cutter and make another pancake (crêpe). Fry the pancakes (crêpes) until they are brown on the underside and beginning to set. Turn them carefully. They will be quite soft at this point. Brown the other side. Remove the pancakes (crêpes), keep them warm and cook the rest in the same way.
7. To serve, place the pancakes (crêpes) on a serving plate. Sprinkle a little of the sauce over the top and serve the rest separately. Garnish the plate with parsley sprigs.
Note: Unsuitable for freezing.

American

1 cup pinto beans
¼ cup vegetable oil
1 large onion, finely
chopped
¾ cup chopped English
walnuts
2 tablespoons chopped
chives
¼ cup chopped parsley
2 tablespoons chopped
thyme
1 tablespoon chopped
marjoram
6 eggs, beaten
Sunflower oil for frying
Sauce:
¼ cup chopped chives
1⅓ cups creamed smetana
or sour cream
Garnish:
Parsley sprigs

Stuffed Spring Cabbage

Imperial (Metric)

3 medium-sized spring cabbages
4 tablespoons vegetable oil
12 oz (340g) small brown lentils
12 spring onions, finely chopped
½ pint (285ml) tomato and vegetable juice
1 pint (570ml) vegetable stock
¼ pint (140ml) dry white wine
10 chopped sage leaves
3 oz (85g) Cheddar cheese, grated

1. Remove the outer leaves from the cabbages. Trim the bases so they stand upright. Cut off the tops, leaving a base about 4 inches (10cm) high. Hollow out the bottom parts with a knife, leaving a shell of about ¾ inch (2cm) thick. Chop the tops and the hollowed out parts.
2. Heat the oil in a saucepan on a low heat. Mix in the lentils and spring onions (scallions) and stir for 1 minute.
3. Pour in the tomato and vegetable juice, ¾ pint (425ml/2 cups) vegetable stock and the wine. Bring them to the boil. Add the sage. Cover and simmer for 40 minutes or until the lentils are almost tender and most of the stock has been absorbed.
4. Fill the cabbage shells with the lentil mixture. Mix the chopped cabbage into any remaining lentils in the saucepan.
5. Set the stuffed cabbages on top of the lentil and cabbage mixture.
6. If the mixture looks dry, pour in the remaining stock.
7. Cover and simmer for 20 minutes or until the cabbage shells are tender.
8. To serve, make a bed of the lentils and chopped cabbage on a large flat serving dish. Set the stuffed cabbages on top. Scatter the cheese over the stuffed cabbages.
Note: Spring cabbages are bright green and conical-shaped. Unsuitable for freezing.

American

3 medium-sized spring cabbages
4 tablespoons vegetable oil
1½ cups small brown lentils
12 scallions, finely chopped
1⅓ cups tomato and vegetable juice
2½ cups vegetable stock
⅔ cup dry white wine
10 chopped sage leaves
¾ cup grated Cheddar cheese

Watercress Fritters

Imperial (Metric)

12 oz (340g) flageolets,
soaked and cooked
3 oz (85g) watercress
10 spring onions, finely
chopped
2 tablespoons chopped
capers
1 tablespoon Dijon
mustard
Sauce:
1½ oz (45g) butter
2 tablespoons wholemeal
flour
1 pint (570ml) vegetable
stock
Juice of 1 lemon
1 tablespoon Dijon
mustard
4 tablespoons chopped
parsley
Batter:
1 egg yolk
Pinch bicarbonate of soda
¾ pint (425ml) iced
water
7 oz (200g) wholemeal
flour
Garnish:
Watercress sprigs

1. Mash the flageolets to a purée. Finely chop the watercress and the spring onions (scallions).
2. Beat the mustard into the flageolets. Mix in the watercress, spring onions (scallions) and capers.
3. Form the mixture into 24 small balls. Cool them for 30 minutes so that they set into shape.
4. To make the sauce, melt the butter in a saucepan on a low heat. Stir in the flour and then the stock. Bring to the boil, stirring. Add the lemon juice and mustard. Simmer, uncovered, for 2 minutes. Add the parsley and keep the sauce warm.
5. For the batter, lightly beat the egg yolk in a bowl. Beat in the bicarbonate of (baking) soda and then the water. Scatter in the flour and mix well with a wooden spoon. Keep the batter standing for no longer than 10 minutes once it is made.
6. Heat a deep pan of oil to 375°F/190°C. Dip the watercress balls into the batter and deep-fry them for about 2 minutes or until they are golden brown. Drain them on kitchen paper.
7. Serve the fritters with watercress sprigs and serve the sauce separately.
Note: The watercress balls can be frozen before cooking. Freeze them separately on a tray and then pack them into a polythene bag. Store them for up to 2 months. The sauce can be frozen in a separate rigid container. The batter should not be stored.

American

2 cups flageolets, soaked
and cooked
3 ounces watercress
10 scallions, finely
chopped
2 tablespoons chopped
capers
1 tablespoon Dijon
mustard
Sauce:
3 tablespoons butter
2 tablespoons wholewheat
flour
2½ cups vegetable stock
Juice of 1 lemon
1 tablespoon Dijon
mustard
¼ cup chopped parsley
Batter:
1 egg yolk
Pinch baking soda
2 cups iced water
1¾ cups wholewheat flour
Garnish:
Watercress sprigs

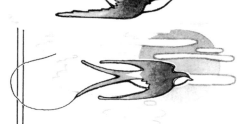

Spinach and Pasta Moulds

Imperial (Metric)

12 oz (340g) fresh spinach
12 oz (340g) small pasta shapes, cooked and drained
4 tablespoons olive oil plus extra for greasing
1 large onion, finely chopped
8 oz (225g) low-fat soft cheese
6 oz (170g) hazelnuts, finely chopped
2 eggs, beaten
Juice of 1 lemon
4 tablespoons chopped parsley
4 tablespoons chopped chives
2 tablespoons chopped thyme
6 oz (170g) carrots

1. Heat the oven to 350°F/180°C/Gas Mark 4.
2. Finely chop 6 oz (170g) spinach. Break the stems from the rest at the point where they reach the leaves.
3. Cook the pasta in lightly salted boiling water for 12 minutes or until it is tender. Drain it, run cold water through it and drain it again.
4. Heat the oil in a saucepan on a low heat. Put in the onion and soften it.
5. Raise the heat to high. Put in the chopped spinach and stir it for about 2 minutes or until it begins to wilt.
6. Off the heat, mix in the cheese, hazelnuts, eggs, lemon juice and herbs. Mix in the pasta.
7. Line 6 small bowls with spinach leaves, leaving some to cover the top. Put in the pasta mixture. Cover it with the remaining spinach leaves.
8. Cover each bowl with oiled foil. Stand the bowls in water to come three-quarters of the way up the sides, in a baking tin.
9. Put the moulds into the oven for 15 minutes.
10. Cut the carrots into very thin matchstick pieces. Bring a pan of water to the boil. Put in the carrots and cook them for 2 minutes, then drain them.
11. To serve, turn each mould onto an individual plate. Put a portion of the carrots on top.
Note: Unsuitable for freezing.

American

¾ pound fresh spinach
3 cups small pasta shapes
¼ cup olive oil plus extra for greasing
1 large onion, finely chopped
1 cup low-fat soft cheese
1⅓ cups hazelnuts, finely chopped
2 eggs, beaten
Juice of 1 lemon
¼ cup chopped parsley
¼ cup chopped chives
2 tablespoons chopped thyme
6 ounces carrots

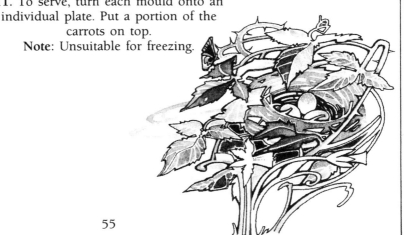

VEGETABLE DISHES

At the beginning of spring, the familiar winter vegetables need to be given a new look. Jacket potatoes, for example, are superb in the winter but for special spring meals, cook them with herbs or make them into a light soufflé; try spicing beetroot and cook thin slices of leeks with tarragon.

It will not be long before the real spring vegetables arrive: rich spring greens, light pointed cabbages and tender broccoli. Watercress will grow large-leaved and thick and delicate spring onions (scallions) will replace the tired, old winter ones.

For entertaining, make use of every vegetable available and give them a new look. Add herbs and spices, mustards and wines and make them a special feature of the meal.

Watercress and Potato Soufflé

Serve this as a side dish to replace plain potatoes.

Imperial (Metric)

2 lb (900g) potatoes
1 small onion, thinly sliced
4 oz (115g) watercress
1 oz (30g) butter, plus extra for greasing
Sea salt and freshly ground black pepper
3 fl oz (90ml) milk
2 eggs, separated

American

2 pounds potatoes
1 small onion, thinly sliced
¼ pound watercress
2 tablespoons butter, plus extra for greasing
Sea salt and freshly ground black pepper
⅓ cup milk
2 eggs, separated

1. Heat the oven to 400°F/200°C/Gas Mark 6.
2. Cut the potatoes into chunks. Boil them with the onion until they are soft. Drain and mash them with the onion as soon as they are cool enough to handle.
3. Chop the watercress. Melt the butter in a saucepan on a low heat and stir in the watercress. Stir it for 2 minutes or until it has wilted. Mix it into the potatoes and onion.
4. Put the potato, onion and watercress mixture through the fine blade of a vegetable mill or rub them through a sieve.
5. Season and beat in the milk and egg yolks.
6. Stiffly whip the egg whites and fold them into the potatoes.
7. Pile the mixture into a deep buttered ovenproof dish.
8. Bake the soufflé for 35 minutes so it is light and risen and the top is golden brown. Serve as soon as possible.
Note: Unsuitable for freezing.

Buttered Watercress and Capers

Imperial (Metric)

9 oz (255g) watercress
1 oz (30g) butter
*2 tablespoons chopped
caper*

1. Chop the watercress into pieces about 1 inch (2.5cm) long.
2. Melt the butter in a heavy saucepan on a high heat. When it stops bubbling, stir in the watercress and capers. Keep turning them over on the heat until the leaves begin to wilt, about 2 minutes.
3. Serve as soon as possible.

American

9 ounces watercress
2 tablespoons butter
*2 tablespoons chopped
capers*

Potato Cubes with Spring Onions (Scallions) and Mustard

Imperial (Metric)

2 lb (900g) potatoes
12 spring onions
1 oz (30g) butter
*1 tablespoon mustard
powder*
*¾ pint (425ml) vegetable
stock*
Pinch salt

1. Peel the potatoes and chop them into ¼-inch (5mm) cubes. Chop the spring onions (scallions).
2. Melt the butter in a heavy saucepan, on a low heat. Put in the potatoes, onions and mustard. Stir to coat the potatoes with butter and to incorporate the mustard.
3. Pour in the stock and add the salt. Bring the stock to the boil, cover the pan, and set on a very low heat for 30 minutes or until most of the stock has been absorbed.

American

2 pound potatoes
12 scallions
2 tablespoons butter
*1 tablespoon mustard
powder*
2 cups vegetable stock
Pinch salt

Spiced Beetroot with Horseradish Yogurt

Imperial (Metric)

1 lb (455g) beetroot
6 allspice berries, crushed
*Freshly ground black
pepper*
1 oz (30g) butter
½ pint (285ml) water
*¼ pint (140ml) natural
yogurt*
*2 tablespoons preserved
grated horseradish*

1. Peel the beetroot and cut it into ¼ inch (5mm) thick slices.
2. Put it into a saucepan with the allspice, pepper, butter and water.
3. Bring them to the boil on a high heat. Cover and simmer gently for 45 minutes or until the beetroot is tender and slightly glazed.
4. Mix the yogurt with the horseradish.
5. Put the beetroot into a serving dish and spoon over the yogurt while it is still piping hot.

American

1 pound beetroot
6 allspice berries, crushed
*Freshly ground black
pepper*
2 tablespoons butter
1⅓ cups water
⅔ cup unflavored yogurt
*2 tablespoons preserved
grated horseradish*

57

Nutty Spring Salad

Imperial (Metric)

4 oz (115g) watercress
4 oz (115g) radishes
12 dandelion leaves
½ small cucumber
1 oz (30g) parsley
1 tablespoon peanut
    butter
4 tablespoons vegetable oil
2 tablespoons white wine
    vinegar
1 garlic clove, crushed
Freshly ground black
    pepper
1 lb (455g) tomatoes

1. Break the watercress into small pieces. Thinly slice the radishes. Chop the dandelion leaves. Cut the cucumber into quarters lengthways. Chop them into ¼ inch (5mm) thick pieces. Finely chop the parsley.

2. Mix the watercress, radishes, dandelion leaves, cucumber and parsley in a bowl.

3. Put the peanut butter into another bowl. Gradually beat in the oil and then the vinegar. Mix in the garlic and pepper.

4. Fold the dressing into the salad.

5. Put the salad into the centre of a large serving plate.

6. Cut the tomatoes into rings or wedges and arrange them round the salad to serve.

American

¼ pound watercress
¼ pound radishes
12 dandelion leaves
½ small cucumber
1 ounce parsley
1 tablespoon peanut
    butter
¼ cup vegetable oil
2 tablespoons white wine
    vinegar
1 garlic clove, crushed
Freshly ground black
    pepper
1 pound tomatoes

Whole Spring Cabbage with Simple Tomato Sauce

Imperial (Metric)

1 large spring cabbage
¼ pint (140ml) stock
1 oz (30g) butter
8 oz (225g) ripe tomatoes,
    scalded, skinned and
    chopped
1 tablespoon chopped
    savory

1. Trim away the outer leaves of the cabbage and trim the base so that it will stand upright.

2. Put the stock into a large saucepan and bring it to the boil.

3. Put in the cabbage, cover the pan and keep it on a low heat for 25 minutes, turning the cabbage occasionally so it cooks evenly.

4. While the cabbage is cooking, melt the butter in a small frying pan (skillet) on a low heat. Put in the tomatoes and savory. Cover and simmer for 10 minutes so you have a thick pulpy sauce.

4. When the cabbage is done set it upright on a serving dish and slit the top in a cross about 3 inches (7.5cm) deep.

5. Pour the tomato sauce into the cut cabbage to serve.

American

1 large spring cabbage
⅔ cup stock
2 tablespoons butter
½ pound ripe tomatoes,
    scalded, skinned and
    chopped
1 tablespoon chopped
    savory

Stir-Fried Spinach with Nutmeg

Imperial (Metric)

1½ lb (680g) spinach
1 oz (30g) butter
*Freshly grated nutmeg,
about 1/8 nut*

1. Break the stalks from the spinach where they join the leaves.
2. Wash the leaves, drain them well and finely chop them.
3. Heat the butter in a large paella pan on a high heat. Put in the spinach and stir it about. Grate in the nutmeg. Cook briskly, stirring it about all the time, for about 7 minutes, or until the spinach is just tender and all the moisture has been driven away.

Note: Variation: Add 8–12 chopped spring onions (scallions) to the pan with the spinach.

American

1½ pounds spinach
2 tablespoons butter
*Freshly grated nutmeg,
about 1/8 nut*

Spring Greens with Parmesan

Imperial (Metric)

*1½ lb (680g) spring
greens*
1 oz (30g) butter
*1 large onion, thinly
sliced*
*1 garlic clove, finely
chopped*
*6 fl oz (170ml) vegetable
stock*
*2 tablespoons grated
Parmesan cheese*

1. Wash and chop the spring greens.
2. Melt the butter in a saucepan on a low heat, put in the onions and garlic and soften them.
3. Stir in the spring greens. Pour in the stock and bring it to the boil. Cover and cook on a medium heat for 20 minutes, or until all the water has evaporated and the leaves are bright and shiny.
4. Mix in the Parmesan cheese just before serving.

American

1½ pounds spring greens
2 tablespoons butter
*1 large onion, thinly
sliced*
*1 garlic clove, finely
chopped*
¾ cup vegetable stock
*2 tablespoons grated
Parmesan cheese*

Cauliflower with Pepper and Thyme

Imperial (Metric)

1 large cauliflower
1 green pepper
1 oz (30g) butter
*¼ pint (140ml) vegetable
stock or water*
*1 tablespoon chopped
thyme*

1. Break the cauliflower into florets. Cut the pepper into 1-inch (2.5cm) strips.
2. Put the butter and stock or water into a saucepan and set on a low heat for the butter to melt. Bring them to the boil.
3. Put in the cauliflower, pepper and thyme. Cook on a medium heat for 15 minutes or until most of the liquid has evaporated and the cauliflower is just tender.

American

1 large cauliflower
1 sweet green pepper
2 tablespoons butter
*⅔ cup vegetable stock or
water*
*1 tablespoon chopped
thyme*

Stir-Braised Leeks with Mustard

Imperial (Metric)

1½ lb (680g) leeks about
1 inch (2.5cm) in
diameter, and as closely
formed as possible at the
green ends
6 fl oz (175ml) vegetable
stock
1 teaspoon spiced
granular mustard
4 tablespoons vegetable oil

1. Wash the leeks well and cut them in half first crossways and then lengthways.
2. Mix the stock and mustard together.
3. Heat the oil in a large frying pan (skillet) on a high heat. Put in the leeks and cook them until they are just beginning to brown, keeping the pieces complete as far as possible.
4. Pour in the stock and mustard mixture and bring it to the boil.
5. Cover the pan and keep it on a medium heat for 10 minutes. All the stock should be absorbed and the leeks will be glossy and bright and dotted with small grains of mustard.

American

1½ pounds leeks about 1
inch in diameter, and as
closely formed as possible
at the green ends
¾ cup vegetable stock
1 teaspoon spiced
granular mustard
¼ cup vegetable oil

Purple Sprouting with Tomatoes and Olives

Imperial (Metric)

1½ lb (680g) purple
sprouting
12 oz (340g) tomatoes
6 green olives
1 oz (30g) butter
1 medium onion, thinly
sliced
1 garlic clove, finely
chopped

1. Trim the purple sprouting and remove some of the tougher leaves. Scald, skin, seed and chop the tomatoes. Quarter and stone (pit) the olives.
2. Melt the butter in a saucepan on a low heat. Put in the onion and garlic and soften them.
3. Raise the heat and turn the purple sprouting in the onion and butter. Pour in ½ pint (285ml/1⅓ cups) water and bring it to the boil. Cover and cook on a medium heat for 15 minutes.
4. Drain the purple sprouting only if necessary. Return it to the pan. Toss in the tomatoes and olives and heat them through before serving.

American

1½ pounds purple
sprouting
¾ pound tomatoes
6 green olives
2 tablespoons butter
1 medium onion, thinly
sliced
1 garlic clove, finely
chopped

Tomatoes Baked with Chervil

Imperial (Metric)

12 tomatoes
½ oz (15g) butter
4 tablespoons chopped
chervil

1. Scald and skin the tomatoes and leave them whole.
2. Use the butter to grease a small casserole.
3. Put in the tomatoes and scatter the chervil over the top. Cover them and bake for 15 minutes.
4. Serve them straight from the casserole, spooning any juices over the top.

Note: The chervil used with these tomatoes gives them a very special flavour. However, if none is available use 3 tablespoons chopped parsley and 1 tablespoon chopped thyme.

American

12 tomatoes
1 tablespoon butter
¼ cup chopped chervil

Carrot and Leek Salad

Imperial (Metric)

1 lb (455g) carrots
3 oz (85g) leeks
4 oz (115g) dates
1 tablespoon tahini
(sesame paste)
4 tablespoons sesame or
sunflower oil
2 tablespoons cider
vinegar
Freshly ground black
pepper
½ iceberg lettuce or small
Chinese cabbage
2 oz (55g) walnuts, finely
chopped

1. Grate the carrots.
2. If the leeks are on the small side, cut them in half lengthways. If large, cut them into quarters lengthways. Thinly slice them.
3. Finely chop the dates.
4. In a bowl, mix together the carrots, leeks and dates.
5. Put the tahini into a small bowl. Gradually beat in first the oil and then the vinegar. Season with the pepper. Mix the resulting dressing into the carrots.
6. Put the carrot salad into the centre of a flat serving dish.
7. Finely shred the lettuce or Chinese cabbage. Arrange it round the edge.
8. Scatter the walnuts over the carrots.

American

1 pound carrots
3 ounces leeks
¼ pound dates
1 tablespoon tahini
(sesame paste)
¼ cup sesame or
sunflower oil
2 tablespoons cider
vinegar
Freshly ground black
pepper
½ iceberg lettuce or small
Chinese cabbage
½ cup chopped English
walnuts

Cauliflower in a Garden

Imperial (Metric)

1 medium cauliflower
1 lb (455g) purple
  sprouting
2½ oz (70g) butter
1 bay leaf
Juice of ½ lemon
2 large pickled dill
cucumbers, finely chopped
1 tablespoon grated
  Parmesan cheese

1. Trim the cauliflower but leave it whole with some of its inner leaves in place. Cut the base so that the cauliflower will stand upright. Trim the purple sprouting and remove some of the tougher stalks.
2. Melt ½ oz (15g/1 tablespoon) butter in a saucepan on a high heat. Turn the purple sprouting in the butter. Pour in ½ pint (285ml/⅓ cup) water and bring it to the boil. Cover and cook on a medium heat for 15 minutes.
3. Steam the cauliflower with the bay leaf for 10 minutes or until it is just tender.
4. Put the cauliflower in the centre of a large, flat serving dish. Arrange the purple sprouting around the edge.
5. Melt the remaining butter in a saucepan on a high heat. When it is just beginning to brown, stir in the lemon juice and cucumbers.
6. Pour the sauce over the cauliflower.
7. Scatter the cheese over the purple sprouting.

American

1 medium cauliflower
1 pound purple sprouting
⅓ cup butter
1 bay leaf
Juice of ½ lemon
2 large pickled dill
cucumbers, finely chopped
1 tablespoon grated
  Parmesan cheese

Julienne of Leeks and Tarragon

Imperial (Metric)

1½ lb (680g) leeks
3 fl oz (90ml) vegetable
  stock
1½ tablespoons tarragon
  vinegar
4 tablespoons olive oil
1 teaspoon crumbled dried
tarragon or, if available,
  1 tablespoon fresh
  tarragon

1. Cut the leeks in half lengthways and then into 1½ inch (4cm) lengths. Cut each piece into strips about ¼ inch (5mm) wide.
2. Mix the stock and vinegar together.
3. Heat the oil in a large frying pan (skillet) on a low heat. Stir in the leeks and the dried tarragon. Cook them until they are wilted but not coloured, turning them frequently. If you are using fresh tarragon, add it at this point.
4. Raise the heat to medium. Pour in the stock and vinegar. Let the mixture bubble and boil it until it is reduced by half. Serve as soon as possible so the leeks stay firm.

American

1½ pounds leeks
⅓ cup vegetable stock
1½ tablespoons tarragon
  vinegar
¼ cup olive oil
1 teaspoon crumbled dried
tarragon or, if available,
  1 tablespoon fresh
  tarragon

62

Curried Cucumber Salad

Imperial (Metric)

1 large cucumber
3 fl oz (90ml) natural yogurt
2 tablespoons chopped mint
2 tablespoons chopped chives
2 tablespoons chopped parsley
½ teaspoon curry powder

1. Thinly slice half the cucumber. Cut the rest into ⅜ inch (1cm) dice.
2. Mix the yogurt with half the mint, chives and parsley and all the curry powder.
3. Mix the diced cucumber into the yogurt.
4. Put the mixture in the centre of a serving plate. Arrange the cucumber slices around the edge.
5. Scatter the remaining herbs over the cucumber slices.

American

1 large cucumber
⅓ cup unflavored yogurt
2 tablespoons chopped mint
2 tablespoons chopped chives
2 tablespoons chopped parsley
½ teaspoon curry powder

Chick Pea (Garbanzo) and Macadamia Nut Salad

Imperial (Metric)

Imperial (Metric)
8 oz (225g) chickpeas, soaked and cooked
4 oz (115g) macadamia nuts, chopped
1 oz (30g) parsley, chopped
1 lemon
1 tablespoon tahini (sesame paste)
4 tablespoons olive oil
juice ½ lemon
1 garlic clove, crushed

1. Mix the chickpeas, macadamia nuts and parsley in a bowl.
2. Cut the rind and pith from the lemon. Finely chop the flesh, discarding the pips. Mix the chopped flesh into the chickpeas.
3. Put the tahini into a bowl. Gradually beat in first the oil and then the lemon juice. Beat in the garlic.
4. Fold the dressing into the salad.
Note: The salad can be dressed in advance if wished. This will actually improve the flavour and will be less work prior to serving.

American

1 cup garbanzos, soaked and cooked
¾ cup chopped macadamia nuts
1 cup chopped parsley
1 lemon
1 tablespoon tahini (sesame paste)
¼ cup olive oil
juice ½ lemon
1 garlic clove, crushed

Hot Cucumber and Radish Salad

Imperial (Metric)

1 large cucumber
5 oz (140g) radishes
2 tablespoons white wine vinegar
1 tablespoon preserved grated horseradish
1 pickled cucumber, finely chopped
4 tablespoons vegetable oil
1 garlic clove, finely chopped

1. Slice the cucumber and the radishes.
2. Mix together the vinegar, horseradish and pickled cucumber.
3. Heat the oil in a large frying pan (skillet) on a high heat. Put in the cucumber, radishes and garlic and stir-fry them for 2 minutes or until they are just beginning to brown
4. Pour in the vinegar mixture and let it bubble. Then serve as soon as possible.

American

1 large cucumber
5 ounces radishes
2 tablespoons white wine vinegar
1 tablespoon preserved grated horseradish
1 pickled cucumber, finely chopped
4 tablespoons vegetable oil
1 garlic clove, finely chopped

GRAIN ACCOMPANIMENTS

When you are basing a meal on pulses or nuts you will need to serve a grain dish to complement the proteins. All the following grain dishes are lifted out of the ordinary by the use of Spring vegetables and herbs.

Spiced Burghul with Yogurt Sauce

Imperial (Metric)

12 oz (340g) aubergines
1 tablespoon plus 1 pinch fine sea salt
3 tablespoons vegetable oil
1 large onion, finely chopped
12 oz (340g) burghul wheat
½ teaspoon ground paprika
½ teaspoon ground cinnamon
1½ pints (850ml) vegetable stock
4 tablespoons chopped parsley
8 fl oz (230ml) natural yogurt
4 tablespoons chopped chervil
1 garlic clove, crushed, optional

1. Finely dice the aubergines (eggplants). Put them into a colander and sprinkle them with 1 tablespoon of the salt. Leave them to drain for 15 minutes. Run cold water through them and dry them with kitchen paper.
2. Heat the oil in a saucepan on a low heat. Put in the onion and soften it. Raise the heat and put in the aubergines (eggplants). Stir them for 1 minute.
3. Mix in the burghul, paprika and cinnamon.
4. Pour in the stock and bring it to the boil. Add the pinch of sea salt and the parsley. Cover and simmer for 20 minutes or until the wheat is soft and all the stock has been absorbed.
5. While the wheat is cooking, mix the yogurt with the chervil and garlic if using.
6. Put the wheat into a warmed serving dish and spoon the yogurt over the top.
Note: If chervil is not available, chives or mint, or a mixture, may be used instead.
Freeze without the yogurt. Pack into a rigid container and cover. Store for up to 1 month. Thaw at room temperature. Reheat by tossing in 2 tablespoons hot oil in a saucepan. The yogurt dressing is unsuitable for freezing.

American

¾ pound eggplants
1 tablespoon plus 1 pinch fine sea salt
3 tablespoons vegetable oil
1 large onion, finely chopped
2 cups burghul wheat
½ teaspoon ground paprika
½ teaspoon ground cinnamon
3¾ cups vegetable stock
¼ cup chopped parsley
1 cup unflavored yogurt
¼ cup chopped chervil
1 garlic clove, crushed, optional

Spiced Rice with Leeks

Imperial (Metric)

1 lb (445g) leeks
4 tablespoons vegetable oil
1 teaspoon ground cumin
1 teaspoon ground
coriander
12 oz (340g) long-grain
brown rice
1½ pints (850ml)
vegetable stock
Juice of ½ lemon
2 oz (55g) flaked
almonds, toasted

1. Thinly slice the leeks.
2. Heat the oil on a low heat. Put in the leeks. Stir in the cumin and coriander. Cover and cook gently for 5 minutes.
3. Stir in the rice and cook it for 1 minute.
4. Pour in the stock and bring it to the boil. Add the lemon juice.
5. Cover and simmer for 40 minutes or until the rice is tender and all the stock is absorbed.
6. Mix in the almonds. Cover and leave off the heat for 10 minutes before serving.

Note: Freeze before adding the almonds. Cool completely and pack into a rigid container. Cover. Store for up to 1 month. Thaw at room temperature. Reheat gently in a saucepan. Stir in the almonds just before serving.

American

1 pound leeks
¼ cup vegetable oil
1 teaspoon ground cumin
1 teaspoon ground
coriander
1½ cups long-grain brown
rice
3¾ cups vegetable stock
Juice of ½ lemon
½ cup slivered almonds,
toasted

Kasha with Yogurt and Cucumber

Imperial (Metric)

10 oz (285g) buckwheat
groats
1 egg, beaten
1¼ pints (710ml)
vegetable stock, boiling
12 spring onions, finely
chopped
1 medium cucumber
¼ pint (140ml) natural
yogurt

1. Put the buckwheat into a large frying pan (skillet) and stir it on a medium heat until it browns and begins to smell nutty.
2. Pour in the egg and stir until it sets and coats the buckwheat grains.
3. Pour in the stock and bring it to the boil.
4. Put in the onions (scallions).
5. Cover and cook on a low heat for 20 minutes or until all the stock has been absorbed and the buckwheat is soft.
6. Finely chop the cucumber. Mix it into the buckwheat. Cover again and leave the pan on a low heat for 2 minutes for the cucumber to heat through.
7. Take the pan from the heat. Add the yogurt and stir until it 'disappears' into the buckwheat.
8. Serve as soon as possible so the cucumber stays crisp.

Note: Unsuitable for freezing.

American

1¼ cups buckwheat groats
1 egg, beaten
3 cups vegetable stock,
boiling
12 scallions, finely
chopped
1 medium cucumber
⅔ cup unflavored yogurt

Green Barley

1 lb (455g) spring greens
12 spring onions
4 tablespoons vegetable oil
12 oz (340g) pot barley
1½ pints (850ml)
vegetable stock
2 teaspoons chopped
rosemary
¼ teaspoon sea salt
Freshly ground black
pepper

1. Finely chop the greens and the spring onions (scallions). Heat the oil in a large saucepan on a low heat.
2. Stir in the onions and barley and cook them for 1 minute. Pour in the stock and bring it to the boil. Add the rosemary and seasonings.
3. Cover and simmer for 20 minutes. Add the greens.
4. Cover and simmer for a further 20 minutes or until the barley is soft and all the stock has been absorbed.
Note: Unsuitable for freezing.

American

1 pound spring greens
12 scallions
¼ cup vegetable oil
1½ cups pot barley
3¾ cups vegetable stock
2 teaspoons chopped
rosemary
¼ teaspoon sea salt
Freshly ground black
pepper

Pasta with Spinach

Imperial (Metric)

12 oz (340g) wholemeal
pasta spirals or shells
12 oz (340g) spinach
8 spring onions
12 oz (340g) tomatoes
1 oz (30g) butter or
vegetable margarine
Freshly grated nutmeg

1. Cook the pasta in lightly salted boiling water for 10 minutes or until tender. Drain it. Run cold water through it and drain it again.
2. Finely chop the spinach and the spring onions (scallions). Scald, skin and chop the tomatoes.
3. Melt the butter or margarine in a large frying pan (skillet) on a low heat. Put in the spinach and spring onions (scallions) and stir-fry them for about 3 minutes or until the spinach is soft. Grate in about 1/8 of a nutmeg.
4. Mix in the pasta and tomatoes and toss on the heat for them to heat through.
Note: Unsuitable for freezing.

American

¾ pound wholewheat
pasta spirals or shells
¾ pound spinach
8 scallions
¾ pound tomatoes
2 tablespoons butter or
vegetable margarine
Freshly grated nutmeg

Brown Rice and Sorrel

Imperial (Metric)

12 oz (340g) long-grain
brown rice
2 oz (55g) butter or
vegetable margarine
20 sorrel leaves, finely
chopped

1. Cook the rice in lightly salted boiling water for 40 minutes or until it is tender. Drain it, run cold water through it and drain it again.
2. Melt the butter or margarine in a saucepan on a low heat. Put in the sorrel and stir it for 1 minute or until it begins to wilt and look dull green.

American

1½ cups long-grain brown
rice
¼ cup butter or vegetable
margarine
20 sorrel leaves, finely
chopped

3. Stir in the rice. Cover and keep the pan on a low heat for 5 minutes.
Note: To freeze, cool completely. Pack into a rigid container and cover. Store for up to 1 month. Thaw at room temperature. Reheat by putting into a covered saucepan and setting on a low heat for about 10 minutes.

Pasta with Chive Sauce

Imperial (Metric)

12 oz (340g) wholemeal pasta (any shape, including spaghetti)
¼ pint (140ml) creamed smetana or soured cream
6 tablespoons chopped chives
Juice of ½ lemon
Freshly ground black pepper

1. Cook the pasta in lightly salted boiling water for 10 minutes or until tender. Drain it, run cold water through it and drain it again.
2. Put the smetana or soured cream, chives and lemon juice into a saucepan. Bring them to just below boiling point.
3. Mix in the pasta and season with the pepper. Stir on a low heat for the pasta to heat through.
Note: Unsuitable for freezing.
As a variation, replace half the chives with chopped fresh chervil.

American

¾ pound wholewheat pasta (any shape, including spaghetti)
⅔ cup creamed smetana or sour cream
⅓ cup chopped chives
Juice of ½ lemon
Freshly ground black pepper

Millet with Avocados

Imperial (Metric)

4 tablespoons vegetable oil
12 spring onions, chopped
12 oz (340g) millet
1 pint (570ml) vegetable stock
½ pint (285ml) tomato juice
2 ripe avocados
4 tablespoons chopped parsley

1. Heat the oil in a saucepan on a low heat. Mix in the spring onions (scallions) and millet and stir them for 1 minute.
2. Pour in the stock and tomato juice and bring them to the boil. Cover and simmer for 20 minutes or until the millet is soft and all the liquid has been absorbed.
3. Peel, stone (pit) and chop the avocados. Just before serving, toss them into the millet with the parsley.
Note: Freeze before adding the avocados and parsley. Cool completely. Pack into a rigid container and cover. Store for up to 2 months. Thaw at room temperature and reheat by tossing in 2 tablespoons oil in a saucepan on a low heat. Add the avocados and parsley just before serving.

American

¼ cup vegetable oil
12 scallions, chopped
3 cups millet
2½ cups vegetable stock
1⅓ cups tomato juice
2 ripe avocados
¼ cup chopped parsley

Rice Fried with Spring Onions (Scallions)

Imperial (Metric)

12 oz (340g) long-grain
brown rice
4 tablespoons vegetable oil
16 spring onions, chopped
1 teaspoon ground ginger
3 fl oz (90ml) tamari or
shoyu sauce

1. Cook the rice in lightly salted boiling water for 40 minutes or until tender. Drain it, run cold water through it and drain it again.
2. Heat the oil in a wok or large frying pan (skillet) on a high heat. Put in the spring onions (scallions) and stir-fry them for ½ minute.
3. Put in the rice and ginger. Stir them for 1 minute or until the rice has heated through and the ginger is well distributed.
4. Pour in the tamari or shoyu sauce. Stir for a further minute or until the rice no longer looks wet.

Note: To freeze, cool completely. Pack into a rigid container and cover. Store for up to 1 month. Thaw at room temperature. Reheat in a wok or frying pan (skillet) on a high heat, adding 1 tablespoon oil to the pan if necessary.

American

1½ cups long-grain brown
rice
¼ cup vegetable oil
16 scallions, chopped
1 teaspoon ground ginger
⅓ cup tamari or shoyu
sauce

Pasta with Walnut, Parsley and Lemon Sauce

Imperial (Metric)

12 oz (340g) wholemeal
pasta (any shape,
including spaghetti)
3 oz (85g) shelled walnuts
4 tablespoons olive oil
1 garlic clove, crushed
Juice of 1 lemon
1 oz (30g) parsley, finely
chopped

1. Cook the pasta in lightly salted boiling water for 10 minutes or until tender. Drain it, run cold water through it and drain it again.
2. Grind the walnuts.
3. Heat the oil in a saucepan on a medium heat. Put in the garlic and cook it for ½ minute. Pour in the lemon juice and bring it to the boil. Mix in the walnuts and parsley.
4. Gently fold in the pasta and reheat it.

Note: To freeze, cool completely. Pack into a rigid container and cover. Store for up to 1 months. Thaw at room temperature. Reheat by tossing in a saucepan on a low heat.

American

¾ pound wholewheat
pasta (any shape,
including spaghetti)
⅔ cup shelled English
walnuts
¼ cup olive oil
1 garlic clove, crushed
Juice of 1 lemon
2 tablespoons chopped
parsley

DESSERTS

These desserts are combinations of the traditional and the new, and most are based on the fruits that are available in spring.

The doughnuts are included since in parts of England these were once an Ash Wednesday Speciality. Pudding Pies were little curd tarts made in Kent throughout Lent. The recipe on page 74 is a large variation and the addition of coconut was my daughter's idea.

Desserts do not have to be complicated to make perfect conclusions to a meal. Nothing could be simpler than the fresh date and mango salads but how welcome they are after a rich meal. The stuffed dates are more of a sweetmeat and can be eaten in place of a dessert or handed round when everyone has left the table for more comfortable chairs.

Kiwi Fruit and Cheese Mousse

Imperial (Metric)

6 kiwi fruits
3 oz (85g) honey
3 eggs, separated
¼ pint (140ml) orange juice
Agar-agar for 1 pint (275ml) liquid (see manufacturer's instructions)
12 oz (340g) curd cheese, or other low-fat soft cheese

American

6 kiwi fruits
¼ cup honey
3 eggs, separated
⅔ cup orange juice
Agar-agar for 2½ cups liquid (see manufacturer's instructions)
1½ cups curd cheese, or other low-fat soft cheese

1. Peel the kiwi fruits. Finely chop five. Liquidize them to a purée in a blender and then rub them through a sieve.
2. Put them into a saucepan with the honey and stir on a low heat for the honey to dissolve.
3. Beat in the egg yolks, one at a time. Stir on a low heat, without boiling, until the mixture begins to thicken and coat the back of a wooden spoon. Take the pan from the heat.
4. Put the orange juice into a saucepan and bring it just to boiling point. Stir in the agar-agar and boil it until it dissolves.
5. Take the pan from the heat. As soon as the mixture has come off the boil, stir it quickly into the kiwi fruit purée. Leave the mixture until it is cool but not set.
6. Cream the cheese in a bowl or liquidize it lightly in a blender or food processor. Beat in the kiwi fruit purée.
7. Stiffly whip the egg whites and fold them into the mixture.
8. Pour the mousse into six individual glasses and leave it in a cool place for 2 hours to set.
9. Thinly slice the remaining kiwi fruit and use as a garnish.

Rhubarb and Almond Jelly

Imperial (Metric)

1½ lb (680g) rhubarb
3-inch (7.5cm) cinnamon
stick
1 blade mace
4 tablespoons water
½ pint (285ml) dry red
wine
4 oz (115g) honey
Agar-agar to set 1 pint
(570ml) liquid (see
manufacturer's
instructions)
6 oz (170g) ground
almonds
Blanched almonds for
garnish

1. Chop the rhubarb. Put it into a saucepan with the cinnamon, mace and water. Cover it and set it on a low heat for 20 minutes or until it is very soft. Remove the spices.
2. Rub the rhubarb through a sieve or put it through the fine blade of a vegetable mill.
3. Return the rhubarb to the cleaned saucepan. Pour in the wine and add the honey. Stir on a low heat for the honey to dissolve.
4. Bring the mixture to just below boiling point. Sprinkle in the agar-agar. Stir at the same temperature until the agar-agar has dissolved.
5. Take the pan from the heat and mix in the almonds.
6. Pour the mixture into six glass dishes or open wine glasses, or into one large dish.
7. Chill for at least 2 hours to set.
8. Garnish with the blanched almonds before serving.

American

1½ pounds rhubarb
3-inch cinnamon stick
1 blade mace
4 tablespoons water
1⅓ cups dry red wine
⅓ cup honey
Agar-agar to set 2½ cups
liquid (see manufacturer's
instructions)
1½ cups ground almonds
Blanched almonds for
garnish

Kiwi Fruit Sherbet

Imperial (Metric)

7 kiwi fruits
4 oz (115g) honey
16 fl oz (455ml) natural
yogurt
2 egg whites

1. Peel and finely chop six of the kiwi fruits. Purée them in a blender or food processor. Rub them through a sieve to remove the seeds.
2. Return the purée to the cleaned blender or food processor. Add the honey and yogurt and mix well. Turn the mixture into a bowl.
3. Stiffly whip the egg whites. Fold them into the kiwi fruit mixture.
4. Put the mixture into a freezing tray. Put the tray into the freezing compartment of the refrigerator (set at the lowest temperature) or into the coldest part of the freezer. Freeze to a slush, about 2 hours.
5. Take out the tray and turn the sherbet mixture into a bowl. Whip it to

American

7 kiwi fruits
⅓ cup honey
2 cups unflavored yogurt
2 egg whites

break up the ice particles.

6. Return the sherbet to the freezing tray. Put it back into the freezing compartment of the refrigerator or into the freezer for 4 hours to freeze completely.

7. To serve, put the sherbet into the refrigerator (now at a normal setting and not in the freezing compartment). Leave it for 20 minutes. Using an ice-cream scoop take out portions of the sherbet and put them onto a flat tray. Put them into the freezer or the freezing compartment of the refrigerator for 1 hour, or until they have re-frozen.

8. Put the frozen portions into dishes or glasses. Garnish with the remaining kiwi fruit, sliced or chopped.

Note: The frozen portions can be put into a polythene bag and stored in the freezer for up to 1 month or in the freezing compartment of the refrigerator for up to 1 week.

Rhubarb Fool

Imperial (Metric)

1½ lb (680g) rhubarb
4 tablespoons honey
3 fl oz (90ml) water
3 egg yolks
½ pint (285ml) milk
½ pint (285ml) double
cream
Chopped toasted hazelnuts

American

1½ pounds rhubarb
¼ cup honey
⅓ cup water
3 egg yolks
1¼ cups milk
1¼ cups heavy cream
Chopped toasted hazelnuts

1. Chop the rhubarb. Put it into a saucepan with the honey and water. Cover it and cook it on a low heat for 15 minutes, so it is soft but the pieces are still intact.

2. Lift out the pieces with a perforated spoon. Put them into a blender or food processor. Liquidize to a purée and cool.

3. Put the egg yolks into a double saucepan (or into a bowl standing in a saucepan of water). Stir in the milk. Stir on a low heat, without letting the water boil, until you have a thick custard.

4. Cool it completely.

5. Stiffly whip the cream.

6. Whip in the custard and then the rhubarb purée.

7. Pour the fool into 6 individual glass dishes or into one large bowl. Chill it for 2 hours.

8. Serve scattered with chopped toasted hazelnuts.

Apricot Jam (Jelly) Doughnuts

Imperial (Metric)

½ oz (15g) fresh yeast or
2 teaspoons dried yeast
¼ pint (140ml) milk,
warmed
3 oz (85g) honey
14 oz (395g) wholemeal
flour
½ teaspoon fine sea salt
2 eggs, beaten
5 tablespoons sunflower or
corn oil
3 fl oz (90ml) no-sugar-
added apricot jam
Vegetable oil for deep
frying
Syrup:
3 oz (85g) honey
3 fl oz (90ml) sugar-free
apricot jam, sieved
¼ pint (140ml) water
3 fl oz (90ml) medium
sherry

American

1 tablespoon fresh yeast
or 2 teaspoons dried yeast
⅔ cup milk, warmed
¼ cup honey
3½ cups wholewheat flour
½ teaspoon fine sea salt
2 eggs, beaten
5 tablespoons sunflower or
corn oil
⅓ cup no-sugar-added
apricot jelly
Vegetable oil for deep
frying
Syrup:
¼ cup honey
⅓ cup sugar-free apricot
jelly, sieved
⅔ cup water
⅓ cup medium sherry

1. If you are using fresh yeast, crumble it into a bowl and pour in the milk. If you are using dried, dissolve 1 teaspoon of the honey in the milk and sprinkle in the yeast. Leave the yeast in a warm place until it is frothy.

2. Put the flour and salt into a bowl and make a well in the centre. Put in the honey, eggs, oil and yeast mixture. Gradually beat in the flour from the sides of the well. Form the mixture into a moist dough with your fingers. Turn it onto a floured work surface and knead it until it is smooth.

3. Return the dough to the bowl. Cover it with a clean tea cloth and leave it in a warm place for 1 hour to double in size.

4. Heat the oven to 200°F/70°C/Gas Mark under ¼.

5. Knead the dough again. Divide it into eighteen pieces. Flatten out each piece and put 1 teaspoon apricot jam (jelly) in the centre. Bring the sides together and seal them to form each piece of dough into a ball.

6. Lay the doughnuts on a floured baking sheet. Put them into the oven for 10 minutes to double in size.

7. Heat a deep pan of oil to 375°F/190°C. Put in 4 doughnuts at a time and cook them for 5 minutes, turning them once, so they are a rich brown all over. Lift them out with a slotted spoon and drain them on kitchen paper. Cook the remaining doughnuts in the same way.

8. To make the syrup, put the honey, sieved jam (jelly) and water into a saucepan. Set them on a low heat for the honey and jam (jelly) to melt. Take the pan from the heat and stir in the sherry.

9. Put the doughnuts into a large, flat dish and spoon the syrup over them. Leave them for 2 hours, turning them

several times so they soak up the syrup evenly.

10. Serve with any remaining syrup poured over them and accompanied by whipped cream or natural (unflavored) yogurt.

Rum and Lime Jellies

Imperial (Metric)

5 egg yolks
Juice of 5 limes and grated rind of 1½ limes
5 tablespoons dark rum
1¼ pints (710ml) hot water
4 oz (115g) honey
Agar-agar to set 1½ pints (850ml) liquid (see manufacturer's instructions)
1 lime for garnish

1. In a bowl, beat together the egg yolks, lime juice and rind and rum.
2. Put the water and honey into a bowl and stir on a low heat for the honey to melt. Bring the syrup to the boil. Sprinkle in the agar-agar. Boil, stirring, until it has dissolved.
3. Gradually beat 6 tablespoons of the hot liquid into the egg yolks. Stir all the mixture back into the saucepan. Cook on a very low heat, stirring until the mixture begins to thicken. Do not let it boil or it will curdle.
4. Pour the jelly into six small pots or glasses.
5. Put the jellies into a refrigerator or into a cool cupboard for 2 hours to set.
6. Garnish with twists of lime to serve.
Note: Unsuitable for freezing.

American

5 egg yolks
Juice of 5 limes and grated rind of 1½ limes
⅓ cup dark rum
3 cups hot water
⅓ cup honey
Agar-agar to set 3½ cups liquid (see manufacturer's instructions)
1 lime for garnish

Fresh Dates and Mangoes

Imperial (Metric)

3 mangoes
36 fresh dates
6 fl oz (170ml) natural yogurt
Freshly grated nutmeg
6 walnut or pecan nut halves

1. To prepare the mangoes, cut a thick slice from each flat side. Scoop out and chop the flesh. Cut away the skin from the remaining pieces. Cut away the flesh from the stone and chop it. Divide the mango flesh between six small plates, piling it up in the centre.
2. Halve and stone (pit) the dates. Arrange them round the mango, radiating from the centre.
3. Spoon the yogurt over the mango only and grate over a little nutmeg.
4. Top each plate with a walnut or pecan half and serve as soon as possible.
Note: Unsuitable for freezing.

American

3 mangoes
36 fresh dates
¾ cup unflavored yogurt
Freshly grated nutmeg
6 English walnut or pecan nut halves

Coconut Pudding Pie

Imperial (Metric)

*Shortcrust pastry made
with 8 oz (225g)
wholemeal flour (see page
24)
3 oz (85g) brown rice
flour
1½ pints (850ml) milk
4 eggs, beaten
3 oz (85g) honey
12 maraschino cherries
6 oz (170g) sultanas
3 oz (85g) flaked coconut
Freshly grated nutmeg*

American

*Shortcrust pastry made
with 2 cups wholewheat
flour (see page 24)
¾ cup brown rice flour
3¾ cups milk
4 eggs, beaten
¼ cup honey
12 maraschino cherries
1 cup golden seedless
raisins
1 cup slivered coconut
Freshly grated nutmeg*

1. Heat the oven to 350°F/180°C/Gas Mark 4.
2. Use the pastry to line a 10-inch (25cm) square, 2-inch (5cm) deep ovenproof dish.
3. Put the rice flour into a saucepan and gradually stir in the milk. Set it on a low heat and bring it to the boil, stirring. Simmer, uncovered, for 15 minutes, stirring occasionally.
4. Take the pan from the heat and beat in the eggs and honey.
5. Quarter the cherries and scatter them in the bottom of the pastry shell. Put in the sultanas (golden seedless raisins) and coconut.
6. Pour in the rice mixture. Sprinkle the grated nutmeg on the top.
7. Bake the pie for 40 minutes or until the filling is set and beginning to brown.
8. Serve warm, decorated if wished with daffodils.

Kiwi Fruit and Avocado Whip

Imperial (Metric)

*4 kiwi fruits
2 small avocados
2 large bananas
1¼ lb (565g) silken tofu
Juice of 1 lime or ½
lemon
2 tablespoons sunflower
seeds*

American

*4 kiwi fruits
2 small avocados
2 large bananas
1¼ pounds silken tofu
Juice of 1 lime or ½
lemon
2 tablespoons sunflower
seeds*

1. Peel the kiwi fruits. Reserve one and finely chop the rest.
2. Peel, stone (pit) and chop the avocados. Peel and chop the bananas.
3. Put the kiwi fruits, avocados and bananas into a blender or food processor. Liquidize them to a purée.
4. Add the tofu. Liquidize to a smooth, pale green whip. Add the lime or lemon juice and whip again.
5. Pour the whip into a serving bowl. Thinly slice the remaining kiwi fruit and use it as a garnish. Scatter the sunflower seeds between the slices of kiwi fruits.
Note: The texture of this whip will be like a thick custard. Do not leave it standing for more than 1 hour before serving or the top may start to discolour. Should you wish to make it up to 2 hours in advance, leave the

mixture in the blender or food processor. Then whip it again before pouring it into a serving bowl, garnishing and serving immediately. This dessert is unsuitable for freezing.

Mango Ice

Imperial (Metric)

American

4 ripe mangoes
Juice of 2 limes
2 egg whites
Angelica

4 ripe mangoes
Juice of 2 limes
2 egg whites
Angelica

1. Set the refrigerator to its lowest temperature or clear a space in the coldest part of the freezer.
2. Cut a thick slice from each side of the mangoes. Scoop out and chop the flesh. Cut the skin away from the remaining pieces. Cut away the flesh from the stone and chop it.
3. Put the mango flesh and lime juice into a blender or food processor and liquidize them to a purée. Alternatively, they can be mashed together.
4. Put the purée into an ice tray and freeze it for 2 hours.
5. Stiffly whip the egg whites.
6. Whip the frozen purée to break up the ice particles. Fold it into the egg whites.
7. Return the frozen purée to the ice tray, and freeze it for a further 2 hours, breaking up the crystals every 30 minutes.
8. Using an ice-cream scoop, put the portions of the mango ice onto a tray. Freeze them completely.
9. Serve garnished with small pieces of angelica.

Stuffed Fresh Dates

Imperial (Metric)

American

1 lb (455g) fresh dates
12 oz (340g) Philadelphia cream cheese or curd cheese
10 pieces preserved stem ginger
2 tablespoons syrup from the ginger jar

1 pound fresh dates
1½ cups Philadelphia cream cheese or curd cheese
10 pieces preserved stem ginger
2 tablespoons syrup from the ginger jar

1. Slit the dates open and remove the stones.
2. Cream the cheese in a bowl.
3. Finely chop the ginger and mix it into the cheese with the syrup.
4. Use the mixture to stuff the dates.
5. Serve as a sweetmeat, on a bed of fresh fern or ivy leaves.

Pineapple Layer

¾ pint (425ml) soured
cream
3 oz (85g) toasted oat
cereal or granola
2 medium pineapples
4 tablespoons Kirsch
2 tablespoons flaked
almonds, toasted

1. Mix the soured cream with the oat
cereal. Put the mixture into the
refrigerator for 2 hours.
2. Cut the husk from the pineapples.
Slice the flesh, stamp out the cores and
cut each slice into quarters.
3. Put one-third of the pineapple into a
serving dish (a glass one will look
attractive). Sprinkle on a little Kirsch.
Top it with one-third of the oat cereal
mixture. Repeat the layers twice.
4. Scatter the toasted almond flakes
(slivers) over the top.
5. Serve as soon as possible.
Note: Unsuitable for freezing.

2 cups sour cream
3 ounces toasted oat
cereal or granola
2 medium pineapples
¼ cup Kirsch
2 tablespoons slivered
almonds, toasted

Rhubarb Strudel

Pastry:
12 oz (340g) wholemeal
flour
Pinch fine sea salt
8 fl oz (230ml) water
4 fl oz (115ml) corn oil
Filling:
2 lb (900g) rhubarb
4 oz (115g) sultanas
2 oz (55g) sunflower
seeds
2 oz (55g) pear and
apple spread
1 teaspoon cinnamon
Grated rind and juice of
1 large orange

1 egg, beaten
2 tablespoons ground
almonds

1. Put the flour and salt into a bowl. Put
the water into a small saucepan and
bring it to the boil. Add the oil and boil
until the mixture begins to look opaque
and the oil and water are well mixed.
2. Pour the mixture into the flour and
beat it in with a wooden spoon.
3. Knead the mixture in the bowl to
make it smooth and shiny.
4. Put the dough into a polythene bag
and put it into a refrigerator for 30
minutes.
5. Heat the oven to 400°F/200°C/Gas
Mark 6.
6. Chop the rhubarb. Put it into a bowl
and mix in the sultanas (golden seedless
raisins), sunflower seeds, pear and apple
spread, cinnamon and orange rind and
juice.
7. Divide the dough into two. Roll out
one piece to a very thin rectangle. Trim
the ends if necessary. Spread it with half
the rhubarb mixture. Roll up the dough
from one narrow end. Lay the roll on a
floured baking sheet with the end on
the underside. Make a second roll in the
same way.

Pastry:
3 cups wholewheat flour
Pinch fine sea salt
1 cup water
½ cup corn oil
Filling:
2 pounds rhubarb
⅔ cup golden seedless
raisins
½ cup sunflower seeds
3 tablespoons pear and
apple spread
1 teaspoon cinnamon
Grated rind and juice of
1 large orange

1 egg, beaten
2 tablespoons ground
almonds

8. Brush the rolls with beaten egg and sprinkle them with the ground almonds.

9. Bake the strudel for 25 minutes or until golden brown.

10. Cool them a little on the baking sheet. Serve them warm with single (light) cream, creamed smetana or natural (unflavored) yogurt.

Note: To freeze, cool the strudels completely. Freeze them on a flat tray and put into a polythene bag. Store for up to 1 month. Thaw by putting them onto a baking tray and into a hot oven for 20 minutes.

Wholemeal (Wholewheat) Eclairs

Imperial (Metric)

3 oz (85g) butter or vegetable margarine
8 fl oz (230ml) water
4 oz (115g) wholemeal flour
3 eggs, beaten
Filling:
8oz (225g) curd cheese
3 tablespoons honey
Topping:
3 tablespoons clear honey
3 tablespoons smooth peanut butter

1. Heat the oven to 400°F/200°C/Gas Mark 6.

2. Put the butter or margarine and water into a saucepan. Set them on a high heat until the fat has melted and the mixture is bubbling.

3. Stir in the flour all at once. Take the pan from the heat and beat until the mixture is smooth.

4. Leave to cool for 5 minutes. Gradually beat in the eggs. Beat well so the mixture is smooth and glossy.

5. Put the mixture into a piping bag fitted with a wide, smooth nozzle. Lightly wet a baking tray. Pipe the mixture onto it in eight long shapes.

6. Put the eclairs into the oven for 25 minutes, raising the temperature to 425°F/230°C/Gas Mark 7 after 10 minutes.

7. Lift the eclairs onto a rack to cool. Make a small slit in each one for the steam to escape.

8. To make the filling, mix the cheese with the honey.

9. For the topping, mix the clear honey with the peanut butter.

10. Slit the eclairs in half lengthways. Fill them with the cheese mixture. Spread the peanut butter mixture over the top.

American

¼ cup butter or vegetable margarine
1 cup water
1 cup wholewheat flour
3 eggs, beaten
Filling:
1 cup curd cheese
3 tablespoons honey
Topping:
3 tablespoons clear honey
3 tablespoons smooth peanut butter

BREADS AND SCONES

Wholemeal (wholewheat) bread can be served with all the soups and first courses in the previous pages, and wholemeal (wholewheat) biscuits at the end with the cheese. However, you may wish to serve a completely home-made meal and even bake the bread yourself.

The following recipes make use of spring herbs for flavour and interest.

Spring Onion (Scallion) Bread

Imperial (Metric)

1 oz (30g) fresh yeast or
½ oz (15g) dried yeast
12 fl oz (340ml) warm water
1 teaspoon honey, if using dried yeast
2 teaspoons sea salt
1 lb 4 oz (565g) wholemeal flour
4 tablespoons olive oil
20 spring onions, finely chopped
1 egg, beaten

1. If you are using fresh yeast, crumble it into a bowl and pour on half the warm water; if using dried, dissolve the honey into half the water and sprinkle in the yeast. Leave the yeast in a warm place to froth.
2. Dissolve the salt in the remaining water.
3. Put the flour into a bowl. Make a well in the centre. Pour in the yeast mixture and mix in a little of the flour from the sides of the well. Add the salted water and oil and mix everything to a dough.
4. Turn the dough onto a floured work surface and knead it until it is smooth and elastic.
5. Return it to the bowl, cover it with a clean tea cloth and leave it in a warm place for 1 hour to double in size.
6. Heat the oven to 425°F/220°C/Gas Mark 7.
7. Knead the dough again. Roll it out to a rectangle 12 by 15 inches (30 by 37.5cm) and about ½ inch (1cm) thick.
8. Scatter the spring onions (scallions) over the dough, then roll up the dough from one long side.
9. Lay the loaf on a floured baking tray. Brush it with the beaten egg.
10. Bake the loaf for 35 minutes or until it is golden brown and sounds hollow when tapped. Lift the loaf onto a wire rack to cool completely.

American

2 tablespoons fresh yeast or 1 tablespoon dried yeast
1½ cups warm water
1 teaspoon honey, if using dried yeast
2 teaspoons sea salt
5 cups wholewheat flour
¼ cup olive oil
20 scallions, finely chopped
1 egg, beaten

Note: To freeze, cool completely. Seal the loaf in a polythene bag. Freeze it flat. Store for up to 2 months. Thaw on a rack at room temperature.

Cheese and Parsley Bread

Imperial (Metric)

2 tablespoons skimmed milk powder
½ pint (285ml) water
1 oz (30g) fresh yeast or
½ oz (15g) dried yeast
1 teaspoon honey, for dried yeast only
1 oz (30g) butter or vegetable margarine
1 lb (455g) wholemeal flour
2 teaspoons fine sea salt
4 oz (115g) Cheddar cheese, grated
8 tablespoons chopped parsley
Vegetable oil for greasing
Beaten egg for glaze

American

2 tablespoons skimmed milk powder
1⅓ cups water
2 tablespoons fresh yeast or 1 tablespoon dried yeast
1 teaspoon honey, for dried yeast only
2 tablespoons butter or vegetable margarine
4 cups wholewheat flour
2 teaspoons fine sea salt
1 cup grated Cheddar cheese
⅓ cup chopped parsley
Vegetable oil for greasing
Beaten egg for glaze

1. Dissolve the milk powder in the water. Put the mixture into a saucepan and very gently warm it.
2. If you are using fresh yeast, crumble it into a bowl and pour on half the milk powder mixture. If you are using dried, pour half the mixture into a bowl, mix in the honey and add the yeast. Leave the yeast in a warm place until it is frothy.
3. Put the butter or margarine into the saucepan with the remaining milk powder mixture. Set the pan on a low heat for it to melt. Take the pan from the heat and cool the mixture to lukewarm.
4. Put the flour into a bowl. Add the salt, cheese and parsley. Toss them in with your fingers.
5. Make a well in the centre of the flour. Pour in the yeast and the milk and fat mixture. Mix everything to a dough.
6. Turn the dough onto a floured work surface and knead it until it is no longer sticky. Return it to the bowl and make a cross-cut on the surface. Cover the dough with a clean tea cloth and leave it in a warm place for 1 hour or until it has doubled in size.
7. Heat the oven to 400°F/200°C/Gas Mark 6. Oil a 2 pound (900g) loaf tin.
8. Knead the dough again. Form it into a loaf shape and put it into the tin. Brush the top with beaten egg. Cover the loaf with the cloth again and leave it in a warm place for 20 minutes or until it has risen ½ inch (1cm) above the top of the tin.
9. Bake the loaf for 50 minutes. Turn it onto a wire rack to cool.

Savoury Bannocks

Imperial (Metric)

8 oz (225g) medium
oatmeal
8 oz (225g) wholemeal
flour
1 teaspoon fine sea salt
4 teaspoons baking
powder
2 teaspoons dried mixed
herbs
2 oz (55g) butter or
vegetable margarine
½ pint (285ml) buttermilk
Vegetable oil or butter for
greasing griddle

American

2 cups medium oatmeal
2 cups wholewheat flour
1 teaspoon fine sea salt
4 teaspoons baking
powder
2 teaspoons dried mixed
herbs
¼ cup butter or vegetable
margarine
1⅓ cups buttermilk
Vegetable oil or butter for
greasing griddle

1. Put the oatmeal, flour, salt, baking powder and herbs into a bowl. Rub in the butter or margarine.
2. Make a well in the centre and mix in the buttermilk.
3. Mix everything to a smooth dough.
4. Roll out the dough to a thickness of about ¼ inch (5mm) and stamp it into 2-inch (5cm) rounds with a biscuit cutter.
5. Lightly grease a griddle or a flat, heavy frying pan (skillet). Set it on a moderate heat.
6. Cook the bannocks for about 5 minutes each side or until they are just beginning to brown and sound slightly hollow when tapped.
7. Serve straight from the griddle or cool on wire racks and serve lightly toasted.
Note: Freeze on a tray and pack into polythene bags. Store for up to 2 months. Thaw at room temperature and lightly toast before serving.

Chive Scone Rounds

Imperial (Metric)

1 lb (455g) wholemeal
flour
1 teaspoon fine sea salt
1 teaspoon bicarbonate of
soda
2 teaspoons mustard
powder
3 oz (85g) butter or
vegetable margarine
6 tablespoons chopped
chives
½ pint (285ml) buttermilk

American

1 pound wholewheat flour
1 teaspoon fine sea salt
1 teaspoon baking soda
2 teaspoons mustard
powder
⅓ cup butter or vegetable
margarine
⅓ cup chopped chives
1⅓ cups buttermilk

1. Heat the oven to 400°F/200°C/Gas Mark 6.
2. Put the flour into a bowl. Add the salt, soda and mustard powder and toss them in with your fingers.
3. Rub in the butter or vegetable margarine.
4. Toss in the chives.
5. Make a well in the centre. Pour in the buttermilk. Mix everything to a dough. Turn it onto a floured work surface and knead it lightly to make it smooth.
6. Divide the dough into two. Roll each one into a 7-inch (18cm) round.
7. Lightly dust two 7-inch (18cm) sponge tins or skillets with flour. Put in the rounds of dough.
8. Score the top of each round into triangles.

9. Bake the rounds for 20 minutes. Lift them onto wire racks to cool completely.

Note: To freeze, cool completely. Wrap in clingfilm and freeze flat. Put into polythene bags. Store for up to 2 months. Thaw at room temperature.

Herb Twists

Imperial (Metric)

*1 oz (30g) fresh yeast or
½ oz (15g) dried yeast
¼ pint (140ml) warm water
1 teaspoon honey, if using dried yeast
1 lb (455g) wholemeal flour
2 teaspoons fine sea salt
1 tablespoon chopped thyme
1 tablespoon chopped marjoram
4 sage leaves, finely chopped
1½ oz (45g) butter or vegetable margarine
¼ pint (140ml) buttermilk
1 egg, beaten
2 tablespoons poppy seeds*

1. If you are using fresh yeast, crumble it into a bowl and pour in the water; if dried, dissolve the honey in the water and sprinkle in the yeast. Leave the yeast in a warm place to froth.
2. Put the flour, salt and herbs into a bowl. Rub in the butter or margarine.
3. Make a well in the centre. Pour in the yeast mixture and buttermilk. Mix everything to a dough.
4. Turn the dough onto a floured board and knead it until it is smooth and elastic.
5. Return it to the bowl. Make a cross-cut in the top. Cover it with a clean tea cloth. Leave it in a warm place for 1 hour or until it has doubled in size.
6. Heat the oven to 400°F/200°C/Gas Mark 6.
7. Knead the dough again. Divide it into sixteen pieces. Roll them into sausage shapes and then make them into spirals and lay them on a floured baking sheet.
8. Brush the tops with beaten egg and scatter them with poppy seeds.
9. Leave the rolls in a warm place for 20 minutes to prove.
10. Bake them for 20 minutes or until they are golden brown. Cool them on a wire rack.

Note: To freeze, cool completely. Freeze on a tray, then pack into polythene bags. Store for up to 2 months. Thaw on a rack at room temperature.

American

*2 tablespoons fresh yeast or 1 tablespoon dried yeast
⅔ cup warm water
1 teaspoon honey, if using dried yeast
4 cups wholewheat flour
2 teaspoons fine sea salt
1 tablespoon chopped thyme
1 tablespoon chopped marjoram
4 sage leaves, finely chopped
3 tablespoons butter or vegetable margarine
⅔ cup buttermilk
1 egg, beaten
2 tablespoons poppy seeds*

Caraway Rolls

*1 oz (30g) fresh yeast or
½ oz dried yeast
8 fl oz (230ml) milk,
warmed
1 tablespoon honey
1 lb (455g) wholemeal
flour
1 teaspoon fine sea salt
1 tablespoon caraway
seeds
1 oz (30g) butter or
vegetable margarine
1 egg, beaten*

1. If you are using fresh yeast, crumble it into a bowl and pour in the milk. If dried, dissolve 1 teaspoon of the honey in the milk and sprinkle in the yeast. Leave the yeast in a warm place until it is frothy.

2. Put the flour into a bowl. Toss in the salt and caraway seeds and rub in the butter or margarine.

3. Make a well in the flour. Put in the yeast mixture, egg and remaining honey. Mix everything to a dough.

4. Turn the dough onto a floured board and knead it until it is smooth and not sticky.

5. Return the dough to the bowl. Make a cross-cut in the top. Cover it with a clean tea cloth and leave it in a warm place for 1 hour or until it has doubled in size.

6. Heat the oven to 400°F/200°C/Gas Mark 6.

7. Knead the dough again. Shape it into sixteen small rolls. Lay them on a floured baking sheet. Put them into a warm place for 15 minutes to prove.

8. Bake the rolls for 20 minutes or until they are golden brown and risen. Then lift them onto wire racks to cool completely.

Note: To freeze, cool completely. Freeze the rolls on a tray and pack them into polythene bags. Store for up to 2 months. Thaw on a rack at room temperature.

American

*2 tablespoons fresh yeast
or 1 tablespoon dried
yeast
1 cup milk, warmed
1 tablespoon honey
4 cups wholewheat flour
1 teaspoon fine sea salt
1 tablespoon caraway
seeds
2 tablespoons butter or
vegetable margarine
1 egg, beaten*

Entertaining in Summer

Summer is a special season for a cook. Its fruits and vegetables are unique to that season and for the first few brief weeks that they are available they are a special treat. We can buy many of them frozen or imported throughout the rest of the year but there is nothing like those that are home-grown.

The first truly summer vegetable to arrive in the shops is also the most luxurious. Asparagus can be bought from the middle of May until the end of June. The first of the season should always be appreciated on its own, boiled quite plainly and served with melted butter or with a light sauce as a first course. It is, however, surprisingly versatile. It can be made into soups, salads, quiches and hot main meals, many very simple but made special by this very special vegetable.

Early broad beans are the next of summer's bounty, and oh how delicious they are when they are young and tender. They are even sweet enough to add raw to salads. Broad beans are a fairly extravagant vegetable. You need heaps of them to provide a vegetable dish for six people, but they can also be added to main dishes, combined with grains or used for soups.

The peas come next, so different from the frozen kinds that it does not seem possible that they are the same vegetable. Like the beans, they do not have to be used only as a side vegetable but can be used as a base for main meals and soups. I grow mange-tout snow peas and these are ready at the same time. They are crisp and light and just right for stir-frying.

Only summer has new potatoes and what a treat they are. All you really need to do with them is give them a wash and boil them in their skins and they will still taste superb. Toss them with butter and summer herbs or mix in a simple vinaigrette to make a salad.

Summer cabbages are lighter and crisper than any other cabbages and can be cooked with only a little oil or butter and no water at all. They are not as suitable for salads as the winter kinds but there are so many other salad vegetables that this does not matter at all.

Many of my summer salads are based on lettuce. I grow about five different kinds and mix fruits, summer herbs and other vegetables with them. You should be able to find Webbs and Cos lettuces in the shops besides the more usual, floppier kinds.

Home-grown tomatoes get cheaper as the season progresses. You can be really extravagant with these, using four or more pounds at a time to make soups and sauces. Keep them simple and rely on summer herbs for flavouring. With the tomatoes come the courgettes (zucchini), so much sweeter than the aging imported ones that can be bought for the rest of the year.

Runner beans in the shops signify that autumn is coming, but the days during the runner bean season can be the hottest of the year. French beans are around at the same time, fatter and juicier than the thin imported types and with far more flavour.

The soft fruits of summer will provide endless desserts, from a simple fruit salad to ice-creams, mousses and fruit pies. Like the vegetables, they taste far better fresh than frozen and, with the popularity of the pick-your-own system, strawberries, raspberries, gooseberries and currants are available in abundance to everyone at very reasonable prices. Cherries have a short season so make the most of them while they are available. Then there are peaches, nectarines and juicy watermelons to complete the summer fruit bowl, and later plums and sweet greengages.

One of the extra delights of summer cooking is the variety of scents and flavours that is provided by the herb garden. All the perennial herbs, thyme, sage and marjoram, are so much more prolific in summer than in winter and their leaves are soft and highly scented. Besides these there are the summer herbs, basil, dill, coriander, summer savory and lovage, to name only a few, and flowers such as marigolds and nasturtiums which make such an attractive garnish.

Summer is also special because of the weather. Even in the worst of years there are at least a few days in which we can sit lazily at the garden table with a spread of cold food and a bottle of chilled white wine. It is called eating 'al fresco' and it is ideally suited to weekend and bank holiday lunches.

On most warm summer evenings, even when it is only the family that are at home, I am to be seen with tongs in hand assessing the temperature of the burning charcoal in the barbecue. Barbecue cooking is great fun for the family and yet can still be suitable for entertaining. You can cook a wide variety of vegetarian foods on the barbecue and most people enjoy sitting near the fire listening to the sound of their food being cooked and being tantalized by the various delicious smells.

Another great love of mine is picnics, by the sea, in the country or anywhere there is a special event going on, and what better than to ask friends to share it?

And if the weather is not quite what you would like? Well, don't worry. Take everything back indoors again. Summer food will always be the same, whatever the weather.

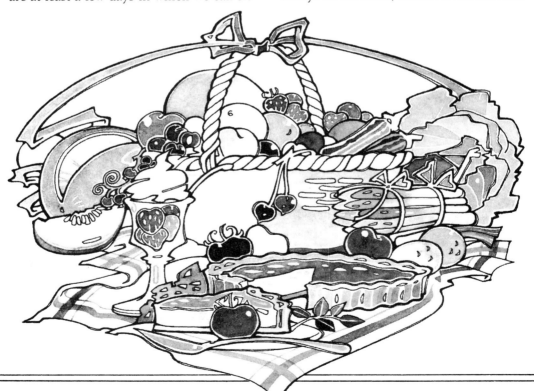

SPECIAL MENUS

There are no special feast days in the summer such as Christmas or Easter, but you can make any day special by asking guests for an outdoor meal. Al fresco meals are perfect for lazy, hot summer days, barbecues for warm evenings and picnics for simple outings or trips to shows and fairs.

All the meals below are adaptable in that you can just as easily eat them indoors should the weather turn against you. If you have to do this, make one hot dish such as soup, potatoes or a grain or pasta accompaniment. This will make the meal more welcoming.

Al Fresco Meal for Early Summer

Avocado, Apricot and Cashew Nut Salad
Asparagus, Egg and Cheese Salad
Mushroom Salad
Pasta Shell Salad
Gooseberries in a Cloud

Avocado, Apricot and Cashew Nut Salad

Imperial (Metric)

3 ripe avocados
12 ripe apricots
4 oz (115g) cashew nut pieces
2 tablespoons chopped fennel
2 tablespoons chopped chives
4 tablespoons olive oil
2 tablespoons white wine vinegar
1 garlic clove, crushed
Freshly ground black pepper
6 chive flowers

1. Peel and stone (pit) the avocados and chop them into ½ inch (1cm) dice. Stone (pit) and thinly slice the apricots.
2. In a bowl, mix the avocados, apricots, cashew nut pieces and herbs.
3. Beat together the oil, vinegar, garlic and pepper. Fold the resulting dressing into the salad.
4. Divide the salad between six small bowls. Garnish each one with a chive flower.

Note: Unsuitable for freezing.

American

3 ripe avocados
12 ripe apricots
¾ cup cashew nut pieces
2 tablespoons chopped fennel
2 tablespoons chopped chives
¼ cup olive oil
2 tablespoons white wine vinegar
1 garlic clove, crushed
Freshly ground black pepper
6 chive flowers

Asparagus, Egg and Cheese Salad

Imperial (Metric)

1½ lb (680g) asparagus
3 fl oz (90ml) olive oil
2 tablespoons white wine
  vinegar
4 tablespoons chopped
  parsley
Freshly ground black
  pepper
12 oz (340g) Cheddar
  cheese
8 eggs, hard-boiled

1. Trim the asparagus. Using either an asparagus boiler or a tall saucepan, bring some water to the boil. Stand the asparagus in the saucepan with the tips above the water. Cover with a lid or a dome of foil. Boil for 15 minutes or until tender. Drain carefully.
2. Beat together the oil, vinegar, parsley and pepper.
3. Finely grate the cheese and fold it into the dressing.
4. Mix the dressing into the asparagus.
5. Put the salad into a large, flat serving dish. Garnish with quarters and slices of hard-boiled (cooked) egg.
Note: Unsuitable for freezing.

American

1½ pounds asparagus
⅓ cup olive oil
2 tablespoons white wine
  vinegar
¼ cup chopped parsley
Freshly ground black
  pepper
¾ pound Cheddar cheese
8 eggs, hard-cooked

Mushroom Salad

Imperial (Metric)

1¼ lb (565g) button
  mushrooms
4 tablespoons olive oil
3 fl oz (90ml) dry red
  wine
1 tablespoon Dijon
  mustard

1. Thinly slice the mushrooms.
2. Heat the oil in a large frying pan (skillet) on a medium heat. Put in the mushrooms and stir them for 2 minutes. Pour in the wine. Raise the heat to high and cook until the wine has reduced by half. Take the pan from the heat and stir in the mustard.
3. Turn the salad into a bowl to cool completely.
Note: Unsuitable for freezing.

American

1¼ pounds button
  mushrooms
¼ cup olive oil
⅓ cup dry red wine
1 tablespoon Dijon
  mustard

Pasta Shell Salad

Imperial (Metric)

12 oz (340g) pasta shells
1 tablespoon chopped
capers
4 tablespoons olive oil
1 tablespoon white wine
vinegar
1 tablespoon vinegar from
caper jar
Freshly ground black
pepper
6 tablespoons chopped
parsley
4 tablespoons chopped
chives

1. Cook the pasta in lightly salted boiling water for 12 minutes or until tender. Drain it.
2. Crush the capers to a paste. Put them into a bowl and mix in the oil, vinegars and pepper.
3. Use this mixture to coat the pasta while it is still warm. Leave the pasta to cool.
4. Fold in the parsley and chives just before serving.
Note: Unsuitable for freezing.

American

6 cups pasta shells
1 tablespoon chopped
capers
¼ cup olive oil
1 tablespoon white wine
vinegar
1 tablespoon vinegar from
caper jar
Freshly ground black
pepper
⅓ cup chopped parsley
4 tablespoons chopped
chives

Gooseberries in a Cloud

Imperial (Metric)

8 oz (225g) gooseberries
8 fl oz (225ml) medium
sweet white wine
3 tablespoons honey
8 fl oz (225ml) double
cream
8 fl oz (225ml) natural
yogurt
Agar-agar to set 1 pint
(570ml) liquid (see
manufacturer's
instructions)
3 egg whites

1. Top and tail the gooseberries. Put them into a saucepan with the wine and honey. Cover them and set them on a low heat for 10 minutes or until they are soft but still hold their shape. Drain them carefully and reserve the liquid.
2. Whip the cream and whip in the yogurt. Put 6 fl oz (175ml/¾ cup) of the cooking liquid into a saucepan. Bring it to just below boiling point. Stir in the agar-agar and stir until it has melted. Cool the mixture only very slightly. Beat it into the cream and yogurt. Stiffly whip the egg whites and fold them into the cream mixture.
3. Put the mixture into a shallow, 10 inch (25cm) diameter dish. Very gently, one at a time, put the gooseberries on top. They should half sink into the cloud.
4. Leave the cloud in a cool place to set. It should be light and fluffy.
Note: Unsuitable for freezing.

American

½ pound gooseberries
1 cup medium sweet
white wine
3 tablespoons honey
1 cup heavy cream
1 cup unflavored yogurt
Agar-agar to set 2½ cups
liquid (see manufacturer's
instructions)
3 egg whites

Al Fresco Meal for Mid Summer

Tomato and Bread Salad
Beetroot and Blue Cheese Salad
Green Pea Ring Mould
Potato and Redcurrant Salad
Strawberry and Walnut Shortcake

Tomato and Bread Salad

Imperial (Metric)

1 lb (455g) tomatoes
1 lemon
1 medium-sized mild onion
12 green olives
3 oz (85g) fresh wholemeal breadcrumbs
3 tablespoons chopped parsley
1 tablespoon chopped basil
4 tablespoons olive oil
2 tablespoons white wine vinegar
Freshly ground black pepper
3 oz (85g) sunflower seeds

1. Chop the tomatoes. Cut the rind and pith from the lemon and finely chop the flesh. Finely chop the onion. Stone (pit) and quarter the olives.

2. Put the tomatoes, lemon, onion, olives, breadcrumbs and herbs into a bowl.

3. Beat together the oil, vinegar and pepper. Fold the resulting dressing into the salad.

4. Divide the salad between six small bowls. Scatter the sunflower seeds over the top.

Note: Unsuitable for freezing.

American

1 pound tomatoes
1 lemon
1 medium-sized mild onion
12 green olives
1½ cups fresh wholewheat breadcrumbs
3 tablespoons chopped parsley
1 tablespoon chopped basil
¼ cup olive oil
2 tablespoons white wine vinegar
Freshly ground black pepper
¾ cup sunflower seeds

Beetroot and Blue Cheese Salad

Imperial (Metric)

1½ lb (680g) beetroot
¼ cucumber
2 oz (55g) soft blue cheese
3 tablespoons soured cream
2 tablespoons chopped dill

1. Boil the beetroot until tender. Drain and peel it. Cut it into ½ inch (1 cm) dice.

2. Finely grate the cucumber. Grate or cream the cheese. Mix it with the cucumber. Mix in the soured cream and dill.

3. Fold the mixture into the beetroot.

Note: Unsuitable for freezing.

American

1½ pounds beetroot
¼ cucumber
2 ounces soft blue cheese
3 tablespoons sour cream
2 tablespoons chopped dill

88

Green Pea Ring Mould

Imperial (Metric)

2 lb (900g) peas in pods
1 pint (570ml) soya milk
Juice of 1 lemon
3 tablespoons chopped
    mint
Agar-agar to set 1½ pints
    (850ml) liquid
    (see manufacturer's
    instructions)
Filling:
1 lb (455g) peas,
    unshelled weight
8 oz (225g) haricot beans,
    soaked and cooked
4 tablespoons olive oil
2 tablespoons white wine
    vinegar
Freshly ground black
    pepper
4 tablespoons chopped
    mint

1. Shell the peas. Steam them for 20 minutes. Liquidize them in a blender or food processor with ¼ pint (140ml/⅔ cup) soya milk mint, and the lemon juice.
2. Heat the remaining soya milk to just below boiling point. Stir in the agar-agar until it dissolves. Mix the milk into the green pea purée.
3. Put the mixture into a 10 inch (25cm) ring mould. Leave it for 2 hours in a cool place to set.
4. For the filling, shell and steam the peas. Mix them with the haricot (navy) beans. Beat together the oil, vinegar and pepper. Fold the resulting dressing into the peas and beans together with half the mint.
5. Turn the mould onto a plate. Fill it with the pea and bean salad. Scatter the remaining mint over the top of the salad.
Note: Unsuitable for freezing.

American

2 pounds peas in pods
2½ cups soya milk
Juice of 1 lemon
3 tablespoons chopped
    mint
Agar-agar to set 3¾ cups
    liquid
    (see manufacturer's
    instructions)
Filling:
1 pound peas, unshelled
    weight
1 cup navy beans, soaked
    and cooked
¼ cup olive oil
2 tablespoons white wine
    vinegar
Freshly ground black
    pepper
¼ cup chopped mint

Potato and Redcurrant Salad

Imperial (Metric)

2¼ lb (1.15kg) new
    potatoes
1 mint sprig
3 fl oz (90ml) olive oil
2 tablespoons white wine
    vinegar
Freshly ground black
    pepper
6 oz (170g) redcurrants
2 tablespoons chopped
    savory
2 tablespoons chopped
    mint

1. Wash the potatoes but do not scrape them. Boil them in lightly salted water with the mint sprig until tender. Drain them and discard the mint sprig. Slice them.
2. In a large bowl, beat together the oil, vinegar and pepper. Mix in the redcurrants and herbs.
3. Fold in the potatoes while they are still warm. Cool before serving.
Note: Unsuitable for freezing.

American

2¼ pounds new potatoes
1 mint sprig
⅓ cup olive oil
2 tablespoons white wine
    vinegar
Freshly ground black
    pepper
1 cup redcurrants
2 tablespoons chopped
    savory
2 tablespoons chopped
    mint

Strawberry and Walnut Shortcake

Imperial (Metric)

4 oz (115g) butter
4 oz (115g) pear and
apple spread
12 oz (340g) wholemeal
flour
4 oz (115g) walnuts,
chopped
½ pint (285ml) double
cream
8 oz (225g) low-fat soft
cheese
4 oz (115g) honey
12 oz (340g) strawberries
8-10 walnut halves

American

½ cup butter
⅓ cup pear and apple
spread
3 cups wholewheat flour
¾ cup chopped English
walnuts
1¼ cups heavy cream
1 cup low-fat soft cheese
⅓ cup honey
¾ pound strawberries
8-10 English walnut
halves

1. Heat the oven to 350°F/180°C/Gas Mark 4.
2. Cream the butter and beat in the pear and apple spread. Mix together the flour and walnuts. Beat them into the butter mixture to form a workable dough. Knead the dough lightly if necessary to bring it together and make it smooth.
3. Divide the dough into two. Roll each piece to a 10 inch (25cm) diameter circle and use it to line the base only of a 10 inch (25cm) flan tin.
4. Bake the shortbread rounds for 20 minutes, or until firm but not coloured. Turn them onto wire racks to cool. Lay one of the rounds on a serving platter.
5. Stiffly whip the cream. Beat in the cheese, a little at a time. Then beat in the honey.
6. Spread half the cream and cheese mixture over the shortbread round that is on the platter.
7. Chop half of the strawberries. Arrange them over the cheese mixture.
8. Place the second shortbread round on top. Spread over the remaining cheese mixture.
9. Garnish with the remaining strawberries, either whole or in halves, and the walnut halves.
Note: Unsuitable for freezing.

Al Fresco Meal for Late Summer

Cucumber and Egg Salad
Mushroom and Nut Rolls
Courgette (Zucchini) and Cheese Salad
Potato and French Bean Salad
Plum Ice-Cream with Hot Spiced Sauce

Cucumber and Egg Salad

Imperial (Metric)

1 cucumber
2 tablespoons chopped dill
4 tablespoons chopped parsley
3 hard-boiled eggs
4 tablespoons olive oil
2 tablespoons white wine vinegar
1 garlic clove, crushed
1 teaspoon mustard powder

1. Cut the cucumber in half lengthways and thinly slice it. Put it into a bowl with the dill and parsley.
2. Cut the eggs in half. Remove and reserve the yolks. Finely chop the whites and mix them into the cucumber.
3. Beat the oil, vinegar, garlic and mustard powder together. Fold the resulting dressing into the salad.
4. Put the salad into a serving dish.
5. Hold a sieve over the dish and rub the yolks through it onto the salad.
Note: Unsuitable for freezing.

American

1 cucumber
2 tablespoons chopped dill
¼ cup chopped parsley
3 hard-cooked eggs
¼ cup olive oil
2 tablespoons white wine vinegar
1 garlic clove, crushed
1 teaspoon mustard powder

Mushroom and Nut Rolls

Imperial (Metric)

6 oz (170g) open mushrooms
1 oz (30g) butter
3 tablespoons potato flour
1 pint (570ml) vegetable stock
4 oz (115g) cashew nuts
2 oz (55g) walnuts
4 oz (115g) buckwheat
Coating:
4 oz (115g) walnuts, ground
Garnish:
Parsley sprigs

1. Finely chop the mushrooms. Melt the butter in a frying pan (skillet) on a medium heat. Put in the mushrooms and cook them for 3 minutes, stirring.
2. Stir in the potato flour (powder) and half the stock. Cook, stirring, until they make a thick sauce. Take the pan (skillet) from the heat. Leave until cool.
3. Grind the cashew nuts and walnuts. Mix them into the mushrooms.
4. Heat a heavy frying pan (skillet) on a medium heat without fat. Put in the buckwheat and stir until it browns. Add the remaining stock. Cover and simmer for 20 minutes or until the buckwheat is soft and all the stock has been absorbed.
5. Mix the buckwheat into the mushroom mixture. Chill the mixture for 2 hours or until it is firm.
6. Form the mixture into three rolls, each about 1½ inches (4cm) in diameter. Roll them in the ground walnuts. Put the rolls on a flat tray and chill them for 1 hour.
7. Cut the rolls into ½ inch (1cm) thick slices. Arrange them on a serving plate and garnish with the parsley sprigs.
Note: Unsuitable for freezing.

American

6 ounces open mushrooms
2 tablespoons butter
3 tablespoons potato powder
2½ cups vegetable stock
¾ cup cashew nuts
⅓ cup English walnuts
½ cup buckwheat
Coating
1 cup ground English walnuts
Garnish:
Parsley sprigs

Courgette (Zucchini) and Cheese Salad

Imperial (Metric)

2 lb (900g) courgettes
4 tablespoons olive oil
2 medium onions, thinly sliced
1 garlic clove, finely chopped
3 tablespoons white wine vinegar
2 tablespoons chopped lemon thyme
4 oz (115g) Cheddar cheese, grated
6 nasturtium flowers

1. Thinly slice the courgettes (zucchini). Heat the oil in a frying pan (skillet) on a low heat. Mix in the courgettes (zucchini), onion and garlic. Cover them and cook them gently for 10 minutes. Mix the vinegar and lemon thyme together.
2. Take the pan from the heat and add the vinegar. Turn the mixture into a bowl to cool completely.
3. Just before serving, fold in about three quarters of the cheese.
4. Put the salad into a serving dish and scatter the remaining cheese on top. Garnish with the nasturtium flowers.
Note: Unsuitable for freezing.

American

2 pounds zucchini
¼ cup olive oil
2 medium onions, thinly sliced
1 garlic clove, finely chopped
3 tablespoons white wine vinegar
2 tablespoons chopped lemon thyme
1 cup grated Cheddar cheese
6 nasturtium flowers

Potato and French Bean Salad

Imperial (Metric)

2 lb (900g) new potatoes
1 lb (450g) French beans
3 fl oz (90m) olive oil
2 tablespoons white wine vinegar
Freshly ground black pepper
4 sage leaves, chopped
1½ tablespoons chopped thyme
Petals from 8 marigold heads

1. Wash the potatoes but do not scrape them. Boil them until tender. Drain and slice them.
2. Top and tail the beans and break them into 1 inch (2.5cm) lengths. Steam them for 20 minutes or until tender.
3. Beat together the oil, vinegar and pepper. Mix in the beans and potatoes while they are still warm. Add the sage and thyme and cool completely.
4. Just before serving, mix in the petals from 6 of the marigold heads. Put the salad into a serving dish. Scatter the remaining marigold petals over the top.
Note: Unsuitable for freezing.

American

2 pounds new potatoes
1 pound French beans
⅓ cup olive oil
2 tablespoons white wine vinegar
Freshly ground black pepper
4 sage leaves, chopped
1½ tablespoons chopped thyme
Petals from 8 marigold heads

Plum Ice-Cream with Hot Spiced Sauce

Imperial (Metric)

8 oz (225g) plums
4 oz (115g) honey
Two 3-inch (7.5cm)
cinnamon sticks
3 fl oz (90ml) red grape
juice
¾ pint (425ml) double
cream
¾ pint (425ml) natural
yogurt
Sauce:
1 lb (455g) plums
3-inch (7.5cm) cinnamon
stick
1 blade mace
3 fl oz (90ml)
concentrated apple juice
1 tablespoon arrowroot
4 tablespoons red grape
juice

1. Stone (pit) and slice the plums. Put them into a saucepan with the honey, cinnamon sticks and grape juice. Cover and simmer until soft. Cool the plums completely. Remove the cinnamon sticks. Liquidize the plums in a blender or food processor.

2. Whip the cream. Whip in the yogurt and then the puréed plums.

3. Put the mixture into a freezing tray. Put it either into the coldest part of the freezer or into the freezing compartment of the refrigerator, set at the lowest temperature. Freeze for 2 hours. Take out the mixture and whip it to break up the ice particles. Put the mixture into a rigid plastic container and cover it. Freeze it for a further 4 hours.

4. Before serving, put the ice-cream into the refrigerator and leave it for 45 minutes

5. To make the sauce, stone (pit) and slice the plums. Put them into a saucepan with the cinnamon stick, mace and concentrated apple juice. Bring them to the boil and simmer for 20 minutes. Remove the cinnamon and mace and rub the plums and liquid through a sieve.

6. Put the arrowroot into a bowl. Mix in the grape juice.

7. Put the sieved plums into a saucepan and bring them to just below boiling point. Stir in the arrowroot. Bring the sauce to the boil and stir until it is thick.

8. Serve the sauce hot, from a warmed bowl.

Note: The ice-cream may be stored for up to three months in the freezer or up to two weeks or according to the star rating in the freezer compartment of the refrigerator, at a normal setting.

American

½ pound plums
¾ cup honey
Two 3-inch cinnamon
sticks
⅓ cup red grape juice
2 cups heavy cream
2 cups unflavored yogurt
Sauce:
1 pound plums
3-inch cinnamon stick
1 blade mace
⅓ cup concentrated apple
juice
1 tablespoon arrowroot
¼ cup red grape juice

Barbecue Meals

Barbecue Meal One

Barbecued Mushrooms with Cheese Filling
Spiced Vegetable Kebabs
Lentil and Split Pea Koftas
Mixed Green Salad
Blackcurrant and Mint Cheesecake

Barbecued Mushrooms with Cheese Filling

Imperial (Metric)

24 open mushrooms
4 tablespoons sunflower oil
4 oz (115g) Cheshire cheese, grated
4 tablespoons soured cream
2 tablespoons chopped parsley
1 tablespoon chopped thyme
2 sage leaves, chopped

1. Remove the stalks from the mushrooms. Brush the caps with oil.
2. Mix together the cheese, cream and herbs.
3. Cook the mushrooms, underside down, 4-6 inches (10-15cm) over hot coals for 2 minutes. Turn them and fill them with the cheese mixture.
4. Continue cooking for 5-7 minutes or until the mushrooms are heated through and the cheese is beginning to melt.

American

24 open mushrooms
¼ cup sunflower oil
1 cup grated Cheshire cheese
¼ cup sour cream
2 tablespoons chopped parsley
1 tablespoon chopped thyme
2 sage leaves, chopped

Spiced Vegetable Kebabs

Imperial (Metric)

1 lb (455g) aubergines
1 tablespoon sea salt
1 lb (455g) courgettes
Marinade:
3 fl oz (90ml) olive oil
Juice of 1 lemon
1 tablespoon tomato purée
½ teaspoon ground cinnamon
½ teaspoon ground cumin
Pinch chilli powder
1 garlic clove, crushed

1. Cut the aubergines (eggplants) into 1 inch (2.5cm) dice. Put them into a colander and sprinkle them with salt. Leave them to drain for 15 minutes. Rinse them with cold water and dry them with kitchen paper.
2. Cut the courgettes (zucchini) into 1 inch (2.5cm) pieces.
3. Mix together all the marinade ingredients. Turn the vegetable pieces in the marinade and leave them for 15 minutes.

American

1 pound eggplants
1 tablespoon sea salt
1 pound zucchini
Marinade:
⅓ cup olive oil
Juice of 1 lemon
1 tablespoon tomato paste
½ teaspoon ground cinnamon
½ teaspoon ground cumin
Pinch chili powder
1 garlic clove, crushed

4. Alternate pieces of aubergine (eggplant) and courgette (zucchini) onto six kebab skewers.
5. Grill the kebabs 4-6 inches (10-15cm) over medium hot coals for 20 minutes, turning them several times so they cook through evenly.
Note: Unsuitable for freezing.

Lentil and Split Pea Koftas

Imperial (Metric)

6 oz (170g) split red lentils
4 oz (115g) green split peas
1¼ pints (710ml) vegetable stock
1 bay leaf
Salt and freshly ground black pepper
8 oz (225g) burghul wheat
7 fl oz (220ml) natural yogurt
4 tablespoons chopped mint
8 spring onions, chopped
Sauce:
1 lb (455g) ripe tomatoes
¼ pint (140ml) creamed smetana or natural yogurt

American

¾ cup split red lentils
½ cup green split peas
3 cups vegetable stock
1 bay leaf
Salt and freshly ground black pepper
1⅓ cups burghul wheat
1 cup unflavored yogurt
¼ cup chopped mint
8 scallions, chopped
Sauce:
1 pound ripe tomatoes
⅔ cup creamed smetana or unflavored yogurt

1. Put the lentils and split peas into a saucepan with the stock. Add the bay leaf and season. Bring them to the boil. Cover and simmer for 50 minutes or until all the stock has been absorbed and the mixture can be beaten to a purée. Cool the mixture completely.
2. Soak the burghul in warm water for 20 minutes. Drain it and squeeze it dry.
3. Mix the burghul into the lentil and split pea mixture.
4. Beat in the yogurt, mint and onions (scallions).
5. Form the mixture into eighteen sausage shapes. Chill them for 30 minutes so they set into shape.
6. To make the sauce, scald, skin and chop the tomatoes. Put them into a saucepan. Cover them and set them on a low heat. Simmer them for 15 minutes and then mash them to a thick purée. Cool the purée to lukewarm and mix in the smetana or yogurt. The sauce can be served cold or reheated, gently, without boiling.
7. Grill the koftas 4-6 inches (10-15cm) over hot coals, for about 15 minutes, turning them several times so they brown evenly.
Note: The koftas may be frozen before cooking. Freeze them on a tray and then pack them in a polythene bag. Store for up to three months. Thaw at room temperature before cooking.

Mixed Green Salad

1 large lettuce
1 green pepper
½ large cucumber
2 oz (50g) corn salad (if
available)
1 box mustard and cress
1 lemon
2 sorrel leaves, chopped
1 tablespoon chopped
thyme
1 tablespoon chopped
basil
4 tablespoons olive oil
Freshly ground black
pepper

1. Shred the lettuce. Core and seed the
pepper. Cut it into quarters, lengthways.
Thinly slice the quarters crossways. Cut
the cucumber in half lengthways. Thinly
slice it. Chop the corn salad. Cut the
cress from the box. Mix all these in a
salad bowl.
2. Cut the lemon in half crossways. Cut
the rind and pith from one of the
halves. Finely chop the flesh. Add it to
the salad.
3. Add the herbs.
4. Squeeze the juice from the remaining
lemon half. Beat it with the oil and
pepper.
5. Fold the resulting dressing into the
salad.
Note: Unsuitable for freezing.

American

1 large lettuce
1 sweet green pepper
½ large cucumber
2 ounces corn salad (if
available)
1 box mustard and cress
1 lemon
2 sorrel leaves, chopped
1 tablespoon chopped
thyme
1 tablespoon chopped
basil
¼ cup olive oil
Freshly ground black
pepper

Blackcurrant and Mint Cheesecake

Imperial (Metric)

Base:
8 oz (225g) plain
oatcakes
4 oz (115g) butter
½ teaspoon vanilla
essence
Topping:
12 oz (340g)
blackcurrants
1 mint sprig
7 fl oz (200ml) black
grape juice
4 oz (115g) honey
6 oz (170g) low-fat soft
cheese
2 eggs, separated
7 fl oz (200ml) double
cream
Agar-agar to set 1½ pints
(850ml) liquid (see
manufacturer's
instructions)
2 teaspoons arrowroot
2 tablespoons chopped
mint
Mint leaves to decorate

1. For the base, heat the oven to
400°F/200°C/Gas Mark 6.
2. Reduce the oatcakes to crumbs, either
by putting them in a blender or food
processor or by rolling them in a
polythene bag. Put the crumbs into a
bowl.
3. Melt the butter and mix it into the
crumbs, together with the vanilla
essence.
4. Press the mixture into the base only
(not the sides) of an 8 inch (20cm)
diameter spring-clip cake tin. Bake the
crumb base for 15 minutes. Cool it
completely, still in the tin.
5. String the blackcurrants. Put them
into a saucepan with the mint sprig,
grape juice and half the honey. Cover
them and set them on a low heat until
they are soft and juicy, about 15
minutes. Drain them, reserving the juice.
Cool them completely.
6. Put the cheese into a bowl. Beat in
the egg yolks and the remaining honey.

American

Base:
½ pound plain oatcakes
½ cup butter
½ teaspoon vanilla
essence
Topping:
2 cups blackcurrants
1 mint sprig
¾ cup black grape juice
⅓ cup honey
¾ cup low-fat soft cheese
2 eggs, separated
¾ cup heavy cream
Agar-agar to set 3¾ cups
liquid (see manufacturer's
instructions)
2 teaspoons arrowroot
2 tablespoons chopped
mint
Mint leaves to decorate

Lightly whip the cream. Beat it into the cheese mixture.

7. Put half the reserved juice into a saucepan and bring it to just below boiling point. Add the agar-agar and stir for about 2 minutes or until it has dissolved. Take the pan from the heat and cool the juice slightly. Beat it into the cheese mixture.

8. Fold in half the blackcurrants.

9. Stiffly whip the egg whites and fold them into the mixture.

10. With the biscuit base still in the tin, line the sides of the tin with greaseproof paper that you have oiled on both sides.

11. Pour the cheese mixture into the tin and put it into the refrigerator for 2 hours to set.

12. Mix the arrowroot with 2 tablespoons of the reserved juice. Put the rest of the juice into a saucepan and bring it to the boil. Stir in the arrowroot and cook, stirring, until the juice is thick and transparent. Take it from the heat. Stir in the remaining blackcurrants and chopped mint and cool it completely.

13. Just before serving, remove the sides of the tin and carefully peel away the greaseproof paper. Transfer the cheesecake to a serving plate, carefully removing the base of the tin as you do so. Decorate the top of the cheesecake with the blackcurrants in the thickened juice and the mint leaves.

Note: Unsuitable for freezing

Barbecue Meal Two

Haricot (Navy) Bean and Blue Cheese Dip with Crudités
Nut Burgers with Dill
French Beans in Foil
Barbecued Whole Potatoes
Apricot and Cherry Tarts

Haricot (Navy) Bean and Blue Cheese Dip with Crudités

Imperial (Metric)

8 oz (225g) haricot beans
2 oz (55g) blue cheese,
    grated or crumbled
Juice of 1 lemon
2 tablespoons mayonnaise
¼ pint (140ml) natural
    yogurt
2 tablespoons chopped
    parsley
3 tablespoons chopped
    chives
Pinch cayenne pepper
Crudités:
Fingers of crisp raw
vegetables of choice

1. Soak and cook the haricot (navy) beans. Drain and cool them.
2. Put the beans into a blender or food processor with the cheese, lemon juice, mayonnaise, yogurt, herbs and cayenne pepper. Liquidize to a purée.
3. Put the dip into a dish and cover it with clingfilm to prevent a skin from forming. Chill for 1 hour before serving.
4. Put the dish onto a large platter and surround it with the fingers of vegetables.

American

1 cup navy beans
½ cup blue cheese, grated
    or crumbled
Juice of 1 lemon
2 tablespoons mayonnaise
⅔ cup unflavored yogurt
2 tablespoons chopped
    parsley
3 tablespoons chopped
    chives
Pinch cayenne pepper
Crudités:
Fingers of crisp raw
vegetables of choice

Nut Burgers with Dill

Imperial (Metric)

6 oz (170g) almonds
3 oz (85g) pine nuts
6 oz (170g) Brazil nuts
12 oz (340g) fresh
wholemeal breadcrumbs
1½ tablespoons chopped
    coriander
2 tablespoons chopped dill
7 fl oz (200ml) buttermilk
7 fl oz (200ml) tomato
    juice
Sauce:
½ cucumber
½ pint (285ml) Greek-
style natural yogurt
1 tablespoon chopped dill
1 tablespoon chopped
    coriander

1. Grind the nuts. Mix them with the breadcrumbs and herbs. Bind the mixture with the buttermilk and tomato juice.
2. Form the mixture into twelve flat burger shapes. Using a burger press will very much help. Refrigerate them for 30 minutes on a flat tray so they set into shape.
3. To make the sauce, finely chop the cucumber. Mix it into the yogurt. Mix in the herbs.
4. Cook the burgers 4-6 inches (10-15cm) over hot coals for 4 minutes on each side.
5. Serve the sauce separately.
Note: The burgers can be frozen uncooked. Place a round of waxed paper

American

1½ cups almonds
⅔ cup pine nuts
1½ cup Brazil nuts
6 cups fresh wholewheat
    breadcrumbs
1½ tablespoons chopped
    coriander
2 tablespoons chopped dill
¾ cup buttermilk
¾ cup tomato juice
Sauce:
½ cucumber
1¼ cups Greek-style
    unflavored yogurt
1 tablespoon chopped dill
1 tablespoon chopped
    coriander

above and below each one. Freeze them separately and then pack in stacks of six in polythene bags. Store for up to 2 months. Thaw separately at room temperature before cooking.

French Beans in Foil

Imperial (Metric)

1½ lb (680g) French beans
Butter for greasing
3 fl oz (90ml) vegetable stock
3 fl oz (90ml) dry white wine
1 tablespoon chopped marjoram
1 tablespoon chopped thyme

1. Top and tail the beans but leave them whole.
2. Grease six pieces of foil about 12 inches (28cm) square. (Note: heavy duty foil is best. If this is not available, use a double layer of standard weight.)
3. Divide the beans between the pieces of foil.
4. Mix together the stock and wine. Sprinkle 2 tablespoons liquid over each portion of beans.
5. Mix together the herbs. Sprinkle 1 tablespoon of the mixed herbs over each portion of beans.
6. Bring the sides of the foil together and seal them. Fold the ends over.
7. Place the packets of beans 4-6 inches (10-15cm) over hot coals and cook, turning frequently, for 30 minutes. Put the packets to the side of the barbecue while you cook the burgers.
Note: Unsuitable for freezing.

American

1½ pounds French beans
Butter for greasing
⅓ cup vegetable stock
⅓ cup dry white wine
1 tablespoon chopped marjoram
1 tablespoon chopped thyme

Barbecued Whole Potatoes

Imperial (Metric)

12 large new potatoes, each about 3 inches (7.5cm) long
3 fl oz (90ml) sunflower or olive oil

1. Wash the potatoes. Prick them twice on both sides with a fork.
2. Brush them all over with oil.
3. Lay the potatoes on the barbecue rack 4-6 inches (10-15cm) over hot coals. Cook them for 10 minutes, turning them several times.
4. Move them to the side of the barbecue where the heat is lower. Continue cooking for a further 15 minutes or until the skins are crisp and the middles soft. The skins will be slightly charred but have an excellent flavour and should not be thrown away.
Note: Unsuitable for freezing.

American

12 large new potatoes, each about 3 inches (7.5cm) long
½ cup sunflower or olive oil

Apricot and Cherry Tarts

Imperial (Metric)

*10 oz (285g) wholemeal
flour
Pinch sea salt
7 oz (200g) butter,
softened, or vegetable
margarine
2 egg yolks
2 tablespoons honey
Filling:
12 apricots
24 cherries
12 almonds
4 tablespoons honey*

1. Heat the oven to 400°F/200°C/Gas Mark 6.
2. To make the pastry, put the flour and salt onto a clean work surface. Make a well in the centre and put in the butter or margarine, egg yolks and honey. Work the mixture together with your finger tips, gradually bringing in flour from the edges to make eventually a smooth ball of dough.
3. Wrap the dough in a clean tea cloth and leave it in a cool place for 30 minutes.
4. Put the apricots into a bowl and pour boiling water over them. Leave them for 2-3 minutes so the skins slip off easily. Drain and peel them. Carefully halve them by running a knife around the indentation and easing them apart. Remove the stones.
5. Stone (pit) the cherries.
6. Blanch and split the almonds.
7. Roll out the pastry and stamp it into 24 3 inch (7.5cm) rounds. Use the rounds to line 24 tartlet tins.
8. Put a cherry into each tart and cover it with an apricot half.
9. Spoon ½ teaspoon honey over each apricot half and top it with a piece of almond.
10. Bake the tarts for 20 minutes. Cool them completely in the tins.
11. When lifting the tarts out of the tins, handle them with extreme care as the honey softens the pastry slightly.
Note: Unsuitable for freezing.

American

*2½ cups wholewheat flour
Pinch sea salt
1¾ cups butter, softened,
or vegetable margarine
2 egg yolks
2 tablespoons honey
Filling:
12 apricots
24 cherries
12 almonds
¼ cup honey*

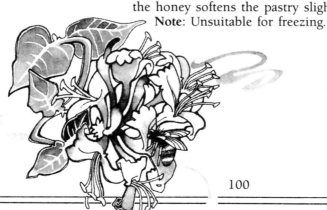

Barbecue Meal Three

Globe Artichokes with White Wine Vinaigrette
Browned Almond Paella
Spicy Cucumber Salad
Banana and Nectarine Kebabs
with Fondue Sauce

Globe Artichokes with White Wine Vinaigrette

Imperial (Metric)

6 globe artichokes
7 fl oz (200ml) dry white wine
7 fl oz (200ml) olive oil
Water
Juice of 1 lemon
Freshly ground black pepper
6 tablespoons chopped parsley
1 egg, hard-boiled

American

6 globe artichokes
¾ cup dry white wine
¾ cup olive oil
Water
Juice of 1 lemon
Freshly ground black pepper
⅓ cup chopped parsley
1 hard-cooked egg

1. Trim the tops and stems of the artichokes. Put ¼ pint (140ml/⅔ cup) of the wine and 4 fl oz (125ml/½ cup) of the oil into a saucepan with enough water to cover the artichokes. Bring the liquid to the boil. Put in the artichokes. Cover and simmer for 45 minutes.
2. Drain the artichokes well by holding them upside down with tongs. Gently prize the leaves apart and remove the hairy chokes in the middle. Put each artichoke onto a separate plate, big enough to hold all the discarded leaves as the tender pieces are eaten.
3. Put the remaining wine and oil into a saucepan with the lemon juice. Heat them to just under simmering point. Take the pan from the heat. Season with the pepper and stir in the parsley.
4. Spoon the dressing into the artichokes. Finely chop the egg and scatter the pieces over the top.

Browned Almond Paella

Imperial (Metric)

8 oz (225g) shelled
almonds
1½ lb (680g) aubergines
1 tablespoon fine sea salt
12 oz (340g) tomatoes
4 tablespoons olive oil
2 oz (50g) pine nuts
1 large onion, thinly
sliced
1 garlic clove, finely
chopped
2 green peppers, cored,
seeded and cut into strips
1 inch by ¼ inch (2.5cm
by 6mm) thick
2 red peppers, cored,
seeded and cut into strips
1 inch by ¼ inch (2.5cm
by 6mm) thick
12 oz (340g) long-grain
brown rice
2 teaspoons paprika
1½ pints (850ml)
vegetable stock

1. Put the almonds into a saucepan and cover them with cold water. Bring them to the boil. Drain them and squeeze them from their skins. (Alternatively ready-blanched almonds may be used.)
2. Cut the aubergines (eggplants) into ¾ inch (2cm) dice. Put them into a colander and sprinkle them with the salt. Leave them to drain for 15 minutes. Rinse them with cold water and dry them with kitchen paper.
3. Scald and skin the tomatoes and cut them, lengthways into thin wedges.
4. Heat the oil in a paella pan on a barbecue rack 4-6 inches (10-15cm) over hot coals. Put in the almonds and pine nuts and stir them until they become an even, golden brown. Remove them.
5. Put in the onion and garlic and cook them for 2 minutes.
6. Put in the peppers and aubergines (eggplants) and stir for 1 minute.
7. Put in the rice and sprinkle in the paprika. Stir for a further minute.
8. Pour in the stock and bring it to the boil. Cover the pan with foil and cook for 35 minutes, moving the pan to the side of the barbecue if the stock boils too rapidly.
9. Mix in the almonds and pine nuts, cover again and cook for a further 10 minutes, or until the rice is soft and all the stock has been absorbed.
10. Mix in the tomatoes and leave the pan over the charcoal for 1 minute more to heat them through.
Note: This may be frozen after the first 35 minutes' cooking time, before the nuts and tomatoes are added. Store it in a covered container for up to three months. However, the beauty of this dish is that it can be cooked completely on the barbecue just before it is to be eaten.

American

2 cups shelled almonds
1½ pounds eggplants
1 tablespoon fine sea salt
¾ pound tomatoes
¼ cup olive oil
½ cup pine nuts
1 large onion, finely sliced
1 garlic clove, finely
chopped
2 sweet green peppers,
cored, seeded and cut into
strips 1 inch by ¼ inch
thick
2 sweet red peppers,
cored, seeded and cut into
strips 1 inch by ¼ inch
thick
1½ cups long-grain brown
rice
2 teaspoons paprika
3¾ cups vegetable stock

Spicy Cucumber Salad

Imperial (Metric)

1½ large cucumbers
¼ pint (140ml) natural
   yogurt
1 garlic clove, crushed
¼ teaspoon Tabasco sauce
1 teaspoon paprika
2 tablespoons chopped
   fennel
2 tablespoons chopped
   chives

1. Wipe and thinly slice the cucumbers and put into a bowl.
2. Mix the remaining ingredients together.
3. Fold the resulting dressing into the cucumber.
4. Chill for 10 minutes before serving.
Note: The salad should be chilled immediately it is made and then not allowed to stand for longer than a further 10 minutes. Otherwise the dressing may become slightly watery.
Unsuitable for freezing.

American

1½ large cucumbers
⅔ cups unflavored yogurt
1 garlic clove, crushed
¼ teaspoon Tabasco sauce
1 teaspoon paprika
2 tablespoons chopped
   fennel
2 tablespoons chopped
   chives

Banana and Nectarine Kebabs with Fondue Sauce

Imperial (Metric)

Sauce:
6 oz (170g) no-sugar-
   added raspberry jam
2 tablespoons arrowroot
½ pint (285ml) natural
   orange juice
¼ pint (140ml) sweet
   white wine
¼ pint (140ml) soured
   cream

6 nectarines, scalded,
skinned, stoned and cut
into 1 inch (2.5cm) cubes
3 large bananas, cut into
1 inch (2.5cm) pieces
3 tablespoons no-sugar-
added raspberry jam
3 tablespoons sweet white
   wine

1. Melt the jam (jelly) in a saucepan.
2. Mix the arrowroot with 3 fl oz (90ml/⅓ cup) orange juice.
3. Stir the remaining juice and the wine into the jam (jelly) and warm on a low heat.
4. Stir in the arrowroot. Bring the mixture to the boil and stir until you have a thick, transparent sauce.
5. Take the pan from the heat and cool the sauce slightly. Stir in the soured cream.
6. Alternate pieces of nectarine and banana on six kebab skewers.
7. Put the jam (jelly) and wine into a small pan and stir for the jam (jelly) to melt. This can be done either in advance or on the barbecue just before cooking the kebabs.
8. Brush the mixture over the kebabs.
9. Cook the kebabs 4-6 inches (10-15cm) over the hot coals for 10 minutes, turning them several times.
10. Serve the sauce separately.
Note: Unsuitable for freezing.

American

Sauce:
½ cup no-sugar-added
   raspberry jelly
2 tablespoons arrowroot
1¼ cups natural orange
   juice
⅔ cup sweet white wine
⅔ cup sour cream

6 nectarines, scalded,
skinned, stoned and cut
   into 1 inch cubes
3 large bananas, cut into
   1 inch pieces
3 tablespoons no-sugar-
added raspberry jelly
3 tablespoons sweet white
   wine

Three Picnic Menus

Picnic One

Feta Cheese and French Bean Salad
Potato and Herb Vinaigrette
Spiced Ratatouille
Mushroom Koulibiac
Yogurt and Redcurrant Trifles

Feta Cheese and French Bean Salad

Imperial (Metric)

1½ lb (680g) French
beans
1 sprig thyme
4 tablespoons olive oil
2 tablespoons white wine
vinegar
1 tablespoon tomato purée
1 garlic clove, crushed
2 tablespoons chopped
thyme
1 tablespoon chopped
marjoram
Freshly ground black
pepper
18 black olives
10 oz (285g) Feta cheese

1. Top and tail the beans. Cut them into 1 inch (2.5cm) lengths. Steam them with the thyme sprig for 20 minutes or until they are just tender.
2. Beat together the oil, vinegar, tomato purée (paste), garlic, thyme, marjoram and pepper.
3. Fold them into the beans while the beans are still warm.
4. Halve and stone (pit) the olives and mix them into the salad when the beans have cooled.
5. Dice the cheese.
6. Carry the salad and the cheese in two separate containers. Mix the cheese into the salad just before serving.

American

1½ pounds French beans
1 sprig thyme
¼ cup olive oil
2 tablespoons white wine
vinegar
1 tablespoon tomato paste
1 garlic clove, crushed
2 tablespoons chopped
thyme
1 tablespoon chopped
marjoram
Freshly ground black
pepper
18 black olives
10 ounces Feta cheese

104

Potato and Herb Vinaigrette

Imperial (Metric)

2¼ lb (1 kg) new potatoes
3 fl oz (90ml) olive oil
3 tablespoons white wine vinegar
Freshly ground black pepper
4 tablespoons chopped parsley
3 tablespoons chopped chives
2 tablespoons chopped mint

1. Boil the potatoes in their skins until they are just tender. Drain them and slice them while they are still hot.
2. While the potatoes are cooking, beat together the oil, vinegar and pepper in a large bowl. Fold in the potatoes while they are still hot and leave them to cool.
3. Fold in the herbs just before packing.
Note: Unsuitable for freezing.

American

2¼ pounds new potatoes
⅓ cup olive oil
3 tablespoons white wine vinegar
Freshly ground black pepper
¼ cup chopped parsley
3 tablespoons chopped chives
2 tablespoons chopped mint

Spiced Ratatouille

Imperial (Metric)

12 oz (340g) aubergines
1 tablespoon sea salt
1 lb (455g) tomatoes
1 lb (455g) courgettes
1 red pepper
2 green peppers
2 medium onions
4 tablespoons olive oil
2 garlic cloves, chopped
1 teaspoon ground coriander
1 teaspoon ground cumin
2 tablespoons white wine vinegar

1. Dice the aubergines (eggplants). Put them into a colander and sprinkle them with the salt. Leave them to drain for 15 minutes. Rinse them under cold water and dry them with kitchen paper.
2. Scald, skin and chop the tomatoes.
3. Thinly slice the courgettes (zucchini).
4. Core and seed the peppers and cut them into strips 1 by ¼ inch (2.5cm by 6mm).
5. Thinly slice the onions.
6. Heat the oil in a frying pan (skillet) on a low heat. Put in the onions and garlic and cook them for 2 minutes.
7. Mix in the aubergines (eggplants), courgettes (zucchini) and peppers. Cover and cook gently for 10 minutes.
8. Add the tomatoes, coriander, cumin and vinegar. Cover again and simmer for 20 minutes, or until the tomatoes are reduced to a thick sauce.
9. Cool completely and chill.
Note: This can be made several days in advance and stored in the refrigerator in the rigid container in which it is to be carried. Freeze in the container. Store for up to three months. Thaw at room temperature.

American

¾ pound eggplants
1 tablespoon sea salt
1 pond tomatoes
1 pound zucchini
1 sweet red pepper
2 sweet green peppers
2 medium onions
¼ cup olive oil
2 garlic cloves, chopped
1 teaspoon ground coriander
1 teaspoon ground cumin
2 tablespoons white wine vinegar

Mushroom Koulibiac

Imperial (Metric)

Yeast Pastry:
1 oz (30g) fresh yeast or
½ oz (15g) dried yeast
6 fl oz (175ml) milk,
warmed
1 teaspoon honey (for
dried yeast only)
1 lb (455g) wholemeal
flour
1 teaspoon fine sea salt
2 eggs, beaten
2 oz (55g) butter, melted
and cooled
Filling:
2 tablespoons sunflower
oil
2 medium onions, thinly
sliced
4 oz (115g) long-grain
brown rice
½ pint (285ml) vegetable
stock
Pinch sea salt
8 oz (225g) button
mushrooms
1 oz (30g) butter
6 eggs, hard-boiled
Sauce:
1 oz (30g) butter
2 tablespons wholemeal
flour
1 teaspoon mustard
powder
8 fl oz (25ml) vegetable
stock
1 tablespoon Dijon
mustard
1 oz (30g) parsley,
chopped
Glaze:
1 egg, beaten

1. If you are using fresh yeast, crumble it into a bowl and pour in the milk; if dried, pour the milk into a bowl, stir in the honey and scatter the yeast on top. Leave the yeast in a warm place until it is frothy.
2. Put the flour and salt into a bowl. Make a well in the centre. Pour in the yeast mixture, eggs and butter. Mix everything to a dough. Turn it onto a floured work surface and knead it well. Return it to the bowl. Cover it with a clean tea cloth and leave it in a warm place for 1½-2 hours or until it has doubled in size.
3. For the filling, heat the oil in a saucepan on a low heat. Put in one of the onions and soften it. Stir in the rice. Pour in the stock and bring it to the boil. Add the salt. Cover and simmer for 40 minutes or until the rice is tender and all the stock has been absorbed.
4. Thinly slice the mushrooms. Melt the butter in a frying pan (skillet) on a low heat. Put in the remaining onion and soften it. Raise the heat. Put in the mushrooms and cook them, stirring, for 2 minutes. Take them from the heat.
5. Slice the eggs.
6. For the sauce, melt the butter in a saucepan on a medium heat. Stir in the flour and mustard powder and then the stock. Bring them to the boil, stirring. Simmer gently for 2 minutes. Stir in the Dijon mustard and parsley. Take the pan from the heat.
7. Heat the oven to 400°F/200°C/Gas Mark 6.
8. Knead the dough again and divide it into two pieces, one slightly bigger than the other.
9. Roll the smaller piece into a large rectangle and lay it on a baking sheet.
10. Put on half the rice, leaving a gap of about 1½ inches (4cm) round the edge. Put on half the mushrooms, half the

American

Yeast Pastry:
2 tablespoons fresh yeast
or 1 tablespoon dried
yeast
¾ cup milk, warmed
1 teaspoon honey (for
dried yeast only)
4 cups wholewheat flour
1 teaspoon fine sea salt
2 eggs, beaten
¼ cup butter, melted and
cooled
Filling:
2 tablespoons sunflower
oil
2 medium onions, thinly
sliced
½ cup long-grain brown
rice
1¼ cups vegetable stock
Pinch sea salt
½ pound button
mushrooms
2 tablespoons butter
6 hard-cooked eggs
Sauce:
2 tablespoons butter
2 tablespoons wholewheat
flour
1 teaspoon mustard
powder
1 cup vegetable stock
1 tablespoon Dijon
mustard
1 cup chopped parsley
Glaze:
1 egg, beaten

eggs and half the sauce. Repeat the layers again. Roll out the remaining pastry. Cover the filling and seal the edges.
11. Brush the pastry with beaten egg.
12. Leave the koulibiac in a warm place for 20 minutes.
13. Bake it for 30 minutes, or until golden brown.
14. Cool the koulibiac on a wire rack.

Yogurt and Redcurrant Trifles

Imperial (Metric)

6 oz (170g) wholemeal cake crumbs
4 tablespoons sweet sherry
8 oz (225g) redcurrants
3 tablespoons honey
Agar-agar to set ¾ pint (425ml) liquid (see manufacturer's instructions)
4 oz (115g) low-fat soft cheese
3 fl oz (90ml) natural yogurt
3 fl oz (90ml) natural apple juice
3 glacé cherries

1. Soak the cake crumbs in the sherry.
2. String the redcurrants. Put them into a saucepan with 2 tablespoons of the honey. Cover them and set them on a low heat for 10 minutes, or until they are soft and juicy. Rub them through a sieve.
3. Return the redcurrant purée to the saucepan. Bring it to just below boiling point. Sprinkle in half the agar-agar and stir on the heat until it has dissolved.
4. Take the pan from the heat and mix in the cake crumbs.
5. Divide the cake crumb mixture between six small plastic pots. Pour over the redcurrant purée and leave it to set.
6. Beat the cheese to soften it. Beat in the remaining honey. Gradually beat in the yogurt.
7. In a small pan, heat the apple juice to just below boiling point. Stir in the remaining agar-agar. Stir on the heat until it has dissolved. Cool slightly.
8. Beat the apple juice and agar-agar into the cheese mixture.
9. Spoon the mixture over the jelly and crumbs.
10. Top each small trifle with half a glacé cherry.
Note: Unsuitable for freezing. Cover for carrying.

American

3 cups wholewheat cake crumbs
¼ cup sweet sherry
½ pound redcurrants
3 tablespoons honey
Agar-agar to set 2 cups liquid (see manufacturer's instructions)
½ cup low-fat soft cheese
⅓ cup unflavored yogurt
⅓ cup natural apple juice
3 glacé cherries

Picnic Two

Melon Wedges with Tahini and Ginger Sauce
Flageolets Salad
Lettuce and Spring Onion (Scallion) Salad
Asparagus and Burghul Salad
Gooseberry and Hazelnut Slice

Melon Wedges with Tahini and Ginger Sauce

Imperial (Metric)

1 large honeydew melon
4 oz (115g) silken tofu
2 tablespoons tahini (sesame paste)
1 teaspoon ground ginger

1. Cut the melon into six wedges. Wrap each separately in clingfilm and put them into a rigid container for carriage.
2. Put the tofu, tahini and ginger into a blender and cream them together. Take the mixture separately.
3. To serve, spoon a portion of the sauce onto each melon wedge.
Note: Unsuitable for freezing.

American

1 large honeydew melon
½ cup silken tofu
2 tablespoons tahini (sesame paste)
1 teaspoon ground ginger

Flageolets Salad

Imperial (Metric)

4 tablespoons creamed smetana
Juice of ½ lemon
8 oz (225g) flageolet beans, soaked and cooked
4 tablespoons chopped parsley
1 tablespoon chopped thyme

1. Beat together the smetana and lemon juice to make the dressing.
2. While the beans are still hot, mix in the dressing.
3. Leave the beans to cool.
4. Mix in the herbs before packing into a rigid container for carriage.

American

¼ cup creamed smetana
Juice of ½ lemon
1 cup flageolet beans, soaked and cooked
¼ cup chopped parsley
1 tablespoon chopped thyme

Lettuce and Spring Onion (Scallion) Salad

Imperial (Metric)

2 round lettuces
8 spring onions
4 tablespoons olive oil
2 tablespoons white wine vinegar
1 tablespoon chopped thyme
1 teaspoon Dijon mustard

1. Shred the lettuces and chop the onions. Pack them together in a polythene bag, sprinkling them with a little water if they are dry.
2. Beat together the remaining ingredients. Put the resulting dressing in a tightly sealed plastic pot for carriage.
3. Dress the salad just before serving.

American

2 round lettuces
8 scallions
¼ cup olive oil
2 tablespoons white wine vinegar
1 tablespoon chopped thyme
1 teaspoon Dijon mustard

Asparagus and Burghul Salad

Imperial (Metric)

2 lb (900g) asparagus
12 oz (340g) burghul
    wheat
2 large avocados
8 oz (225g) black grapes
12 oz (340g) Edam
    cheese
4 tablespoons chopped
    parsley
4 fl oz (125ml) buttermilk
4 tablespoons olive oil

1. Cut the asparagus into 1 inch (2.5cm) lengths. Cook it in lightly salted boiling water for 15 minutes or until it is tender. Drain and cool it.
2. Soak the wheat in warm water for 20 minutes. Drain it and squeeze it dry.
3. Peel, stone (pit) and dice the avocados. Halve and stone (pit) the grapes. Dice the cheese.
4. Mix the asparagus, avocados, grapes and parsley into the wheat. Beat together the buttermilk and oil and fold them into the salad.
Note: The salad may be completely assembled and placed into a rigid container. Unsuitable for freezing.

American

2 pounds asparagus
2 cups burghul wheat
2 large avocados
½ pound black grapes
¾ pound Edam cheese
¼ cup chopped parsley
½ cup buttermilk
¼ cup olive oil

Gooseberry and Hazelnut Slice

Imperial (Metric)

1 lb (455g) gooseberries
2 oz (55g) sultanas
2 oz (55g) light Barbados
    sugar
3 oz (85g) hazelnuts
8 oz (225g) wholemeal
    flour
Pinch fine sea salt
4 oz (115g) butter, plus
    extra for greasing
3 eggs, two beaten
together, one separately

1. Heat the oven to 400°F/200°C/Gas Mark 6.
2. Top and tail and thinly slice the gooseberries. Mix them with the sultanas (golden seedless raisins) and sugar.
3. Finely grind the hazelnuts. Mix them with the flour and salt. Rub in the butter and mix to a dough with the two eggs.
4. Butter a 10-inch (25cm) square shallow tin.
5. Divide the dough into two. Roll out each piece 10 inches (25cm) square.
6. Put one piece into the tin. Put in the gooseberry mixture in an even layer. Cover it with the second square.
7. Brush the top with the remaining egg.
8. Bake the slice for 25 minutes, or until the top is golden brown.
9. While still warm, cut it into fingers or squares while it is still in the tin. Remove from the tin when completely cold.
10. Pack into a rigid container for carriage.

American

1 pound gooseberries
⅓ cup golden seedless
    raisins
⅓ cup light Barbados
    sugar
⅔ cup hazelnuts
2 cups wholewheat flour
Pinch fine sea salt
½ cup butter, plus extra
    for greasing
3 eggs, two beaten
together, one separately

109

Picnic Three

Mushroom and Sorrel Ramekins
Minted Pasta Salad
Green Pea and Broad Bean Strudel
Tomato Salad with Parsley and Basil Dressing
Summer Fruit Pies

Mushroom and Sorrel Ramekins

Imperial (Metric)

6 oz (170g) open
mushrooms
8 sorrel leaves
1 oz (30g) butter
8 oz (225g) curd cheese
4 tablespoons chopped
chervil
4 tablespoons chopped
chives
Oatcakes for serving

1. Finely chop the mushrooms and the sorrel leaves.
2. Melt the butter in a frying pan (skillet) on a medium heat. Put in the mushrooms and sorrel and cook them for 2 minutes, stirring. Take the pan from the heat and cool them.
3. Put the cheese, mushrooms and sorrel, chervil and chives into a blender or food processor. Liquidize them until you have a smooth purée.
4. Divide the purée between four small pots or ramekins, smoothing the tops. Cover with foil or lids and chill for 30 minutes. Serve with the oatcakes.
Note: Carry in the pots. Unsuitable for freezing.

American

6 ounces open mushrooms
8 sorrel leaves
2 tablespoons butter
1 cup curd cheese
¼ cup chopped chervil
¼ cup chopped chives
Oatcakes for serving

Minted Pasta Salad

Imperial (Metric)

12 oz (340g) pasta shapes
2 tablespoons olive oil
¼ pint (140ml) natural
yogurt
4 tablespoons chopped
mint
3 tablespoons chopped
chives
Freshly ground black
pepper

1. Cook the pasta in lightly salted boiling water until tender. Drain and cool it.
2. Beat the oil into the yogurt. Stir in the herbs and pepper.
3. Before packing, mix the resulting dressing into the salad.
Note: Unsuitable for freezing.

American

¾ pound pasta shapes
2 tablespoons olive oil
⅔ cup unflavored yogurt
4 tablespoons chopped
mint
3 tablespoons chopped
chives
Freshly ground black
pepper

Green Pea and Broad Bean Strudel

Imperial (Metric)

1 lb (455g) fresh peas in pods
2 lb (900g) broad beans in pods
1 oz (30g) vegetable margarine
1 large onion
4 tablespoons wholemeal flour
½ pint (285ml) soya milk
2 teaspoons Dijon mustard
2 tablespoons chopped parsley
2 tablespoons chopped mint
1 tablespoon chopped savory
1 tablespoon chopped marjoram
8 oz (225g) ground almonds
Grated rind of 1 lemon
Strudel Pastry:
8 oz (225g) wholemeal flour
Pinch fine sea salt
¼ pint (140ml) water
3 fl oz (90ml) corn oil
Beaten egg for glaze

American

1 pound fresh peas in pods
2 pounds broad beans in pods
2 tablespoons vegetable margarine
1 large onion
¼ cup wholewheat flour
1¼ cups soya milk
2 teaspoons Dijon mustard
2 tablespoons chopped parsley
2 tablespoons chopped mint
1 tablespoon chopped savory
1 tablespoon chopped marjoram
2 cups ground almonds
Grated rind of 1 lemon
Strudel Pastry:
2 cups wholewheat flour
Pinch fine sea salt
⅔ cup water
⅓ cup corn oil
Beaten egg for glaze

1. Shell the peas and beans. Steam or boil them until tender. Drain them.
2. Melt the margarine in a saucepan on a low heat. Put in the onion and soften.
3. Raise the heat to medium. Stir in the flour and soya milk. Bring to the boil and stir until you have a thick sauce.
4. Take the pan from the heat and beat in the mustard.
5. Stir in the herbs, ground almonds and lemon rind. Mix in the peas and beans. Cool the mixture completely.
6. Place the mixture on a sheet of oiled greaseproof paper and form it into a roll by rolling it in the paper. Chill the roll for at least 4 hours to set it into shape.
7. For the pastry, put the flour and salt into a bowl.
8. Bring the water to the boil in a saucepan and add the oil. Boil until the mixture begins to look opaque and the oil and water are well incorporated. Pour the mixture into the flour and beat it in with a wooden spoon until it forms a soft dough.
9. Knead the dough to make it smooth and shiny. Wrap it in foil and chill it for at least 30 minutes.
10. Heat the oven to 400°F/200°C/Gas Mark 6.
11. Roll out the dough to a very thin rectangle, large enough to cover the bean and pea roll.
12. Put the roll on one long side of the dough. Roll it in the dough and seal the ends.
13. Carefully transfer the roll to a floured baking sheet.
14. Brush it with beaten egg.
15. Bake the strudel for 25 minutes or until it is golden brown. Cool it on the baking sheet.

Note: For carriage, use two fish slices or palette knives to transfer the strudel to a rigid container. Unsuitable for freezing.

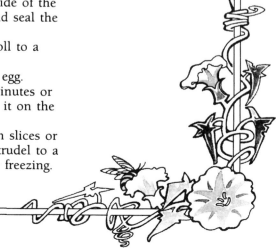

Tomato Salad with Parsley and Basil Dressing

Imperial (Metric)

1½ lb (680g) tomatoes
5 tablespoons olive oil
2 tablespoons white wine
vinegar
1 garlic clove, crushed
Freshly ground black
pepper
2 tablespoons chopped
basil
2 tablespoons chopped
parsley
2 tablespoons finely
grated Cheddar cheese

1. Slice the tomatoes and pack them into a rigid plastic container.
2. Beat together the oil, vinegar, garlic and pepper. Mix in the herbs and finally the cheese. Take this dressing separately and add it to the tomatoes just before serving.
Note: Unsuitable for freezing.

American

1½ pounds tomatoes
⅓ cup olive oil
2 tablespoons white wine
vinegar
1 garlic clove, crushed
Freshly ground black
pepper
2 tablespoons chopped
basil
2 tablespoons chopped
parsley
2 tablespoons finely
grated Cheddar cheese

Summer Fruit Pies

Imperial (Metric)

Shortcrust pastry made
with 10 oz (285g)
wholemeal flour
(see page 24)
4 oz (115g) raspberries
4 oz (115g) redcurrants
4 oz (115g) blackcurrants
2 bananas, chopped
3 oz (85g) honey
4 tablespoons chopped
lemon balm
1 egg, beaten

1. Heat the oven to 400°F/200°C/Gas Mark 6.
2. Divide the pastry into six equal pieces. Divide each piece into two thirds and one third. Roll out the larger pieces to line six individual foil tartlet cases, 3 inches (7.5cm) across and 2 inches (5cm) deep.
3. Mix together the soft fruits, bananas, honey and lemon balm. Use the mixture to fill the pies.
4. Roll out the remaining pieces of pastry. Cover the pies. Seal the edges and brush the tops with the beaten egg.
5. Put the pies on a baking sheet. Bake them for 25 minutes or until they are golden brown. Leave them in the foil cases and cool them completely.
Note: To freeze, place on a tray until frozen. Then pack into polythene bags. Store for up to three months. Thaw at room temperature.

American

Shortcrust pastry made
with 2½ cups wholewheat
flour (see page 24)
¼ pound raspberries
¼ pound redcurrants
¼ pound blackcurrants
2 bananas, chopped
¼ cup honey
4 tablespoons chopped
lemon balm
1 egg, beaten

Artichokes in Red Wine with Mushroom Vinaigrette (page 118).
Overleaf An Alfresco Meal for Early Summer (pages 85-7).

Cherry Tart (page 140).

SOUPS

Soups based on summer vegetables can be made hot or chilled to suit the weather and the occasion. It is best not to have both a chilled soup and a cold meal, but hot soups can be served at any time such as before one of the hot meals or as the start to an al fresco meal which has to be brought indoors.

Chilled Broad Bean and Pea Soup

Imperial (Metric)

3 lb (1.3kg) broad beans in pods
1½ lb (680g) peas in pods
1 oz (30g) butter
2 medium onions, finely chopped
2¼ pints (1.5 litres) vegetable stock
Sea salt and freshly ground black pepper
Bouquet of mint and savory
8 fl oz (225ml) natural yogurt
½ teaspoon curry paste
1 garlic clove, crushed
6 small mint leaves

1. Shell the beans and peas.
2. Melt the butter in a saucepan on a low heat. Put in the onions and soften them.
3. Pour in the stock and bring it to the boil. Season and put in the beans, peas and bouquet of mint and savory. Cover and simmer for 20 minutes.
4. Remove the bouquet of herbs. Liquidize the rest in a blender or food processor until you have a smooth, green purée. Add the yogurt, curry paste and garlic and blend again.
5. Pour the soup into a bowl and chill it.
6. Serve in individual bowls with a mint leaf floating on each one.
Note: Freeze without adding the yogurt, curry paste and garlic. Cool completely. Pour into a rigid container and cover. Store for up to two months. Thaw at room temperature, blend with the yogurt etc. and chill.

American

3 pounds broad beans in pods
1½ pounds peas in pods
2 tablespoons butter
2 medium onions, finely chopped
6 cups vegetable stock
Sea salt and freshly ground black pepper
Bouquet of mint and savory
1 cup unflavored yogurt
½ teaspoon curry paste
1 garlic clove, crushed
6 small mint leaves

Chilled Yogurt and Tomato Soup

Imperial (Metric)

3 lb (1.3kg) tomatoes
¾ pint (425ml) Greek-style natural yogurt
1 garlic clove, crushed
½ teaspoon Tabasco sauce
3 tablespoons chopped basil
4 tablespoons chopped parsley

1. Scald, skin and roughly chop the tomatoes. Put them into a blender with the yogurt, garlic, Tabasco sauce, basil and half the parsley. Liquidize to make a smooth soup.
2. Chill the soup for 30 minutes
3. Pour it into six small bowls and garnish with the remaining parsley.
Note: Unsuitable for freezing.

American

3 pounds tomatoes
2 cups Greek-style unflavored yogurt
1 garlic clove, crushed
½ teaspoon Tabasco sauce
3 tablespoons chopped basil
¼ cup chopped parsley

A Thick Soup of Summer Vegetables

Imperial (Metric)

1 lb (455g) peas in pods
1 lb (455g) broad beans
   in pods
8 oz (225g) new carrots
8 oz (225g) white turnips
8 large spring onions
½ Webbs lettuce
1 oz (30g) butter
2½ pints (1.4 litres)
   vegetable stock
Pinch sea salt
Freshly ground black
   pepper
Bouquet of savory, parsley
   and mint
2 tablespoons chopped
   mint
1 tablespoon chopped
   parsley

1. Shell the peas and the beans. Reserve two each of the best pods.
2. Scrub and thinly slice the carrots and turnips.
3. Chop the spring onions (scallions) and lettuce.
4. Melt the butter in a large frying pan (skillet) on a low heat. Stir in all the vegetables and the reserved pods. Cover and cook gently for 10 minutes.
5. Pour in the stock and bring it to the boil. Season and add the bouquet garni. Cover and simmer for 20 minutes.
6. Remove the bouquet garni and pods. Either liquidize the soup in a blender or food processor or rub it through the medium blade of a vegetable mill.
7. Serve hot, scattered with the mint and parsley.
Note: To freeze, cool completely. Put into a rigid container and cover. Store for up to two months. Thaw at room temperature and reheat in a saucepan.

American

1 pound peas in pods
1 pound broad beans in
   pods.
½ pound new carrots
½ pound white turnips
8 large scallions
½ Webbs lettuce
2 tablespoons butter
6½ cups vegetable stock
Pinch sea salt
Freshly ground black
   pepper
Bouquet of savory, parsley
   and mint
2 tablespoons chopped
   mint
1 tablespoon chopped
   parsley

Summer Herb Soup

Imperial (Metric)

1 oz (30g) butter
8 spring onions, chopped
2 pints (1.15 litres)
   vegetable stock
Bouquet of chervil,
parsley, thyme, marjoram,
fennel, summer savory,
   lemon balm
2 oz (55g) burghul wheat
2 eggs
1 tablespoon wholemeal
   flour
8 fl oz (225ml) natural
   yogurt
1 tablespoon each of
above herbs, chopped
2 sorrel leaves, chopped
Juice of ½ lemon

1. Melt the butter in a large saucepan on a low heat. Put in the spring onions (scallions) and cook them for 1 minute.
2. Pour in the stock and bring it to the boil. Add the bouquet of herbs and the burghul. Cover and simmer for 15 minutes. Cool for 5 minutes. Remove the bouquet of herbs.
3. Beat the eggs together. Scatter in the flour and beat well. Mix in the yogurt.
4. Stir the egg and yogurt mixture into the soup.
5. Set the soup on a low heat and stir until it comes to just below boiling point. Keep at this temperature, stirring, until the soup is thick.
6. Stir in the chopped herbs and the lemon juice just before serving.
Note: Unsuitable for freezing.

American

2 tablespoons butter
8 scallions, chopped
5 cups vegetable stock
Bouquet of chervil,
parsley, thyme, marjoram,
fennel, summer savory,
   lemon balm
¼ cup burghul wheat
2 eggs
1 tablespoon wholewheat
   flour
1 cup unflavored yogurt
1 tablespoon each of
above herbs, chopped
2 sorrel leaves, chopped
Juice of ½ lemon

Tomato and Pepper Soup

Imperial (Metric)

4 lb (1.8kg) tomatoes
2 green peppers
2 red peppers
3 fl oz (90ml) olive oil
2 garlic cloves, chopped
3 tablespoons chopped
thyme
2 tablespoons chopped
basil
2 tablespoons chopped
oregano
½ pint (285ml) dry sherry

1. Scald, skin and chop the tomatoes.
2. Core, seed and chop the peppers.
3. Heat the oil in a saucepan on a low heat. Put in the peppers and garlic. Cover and cook for 5 minutes.
4. Stir in the tomatoes and herbs. Cover and simmer for 30 minutes or until the tomatoes can be mashed to a liquid purée.
5. Add the sherry and reheat if necessary, without boiling.

Note: Freeze without the sherry. Cool completely. Put into a rigid container and cover. Store for up to two months. Thaw at room temperature. Reheat before adding the sherry

American

4 pounds tomatoes
2 sweet green peppers
2 sweet red peppers
⅓ cup olive oil
2 garlic cloves, chopped
3 tablespoons chopped
thyme
2 tablespoons chopped
basil
2 tablespoons chopped
oregano
1¼ cups dry sherry

Cucumber, Courgette (Zucchini) and Lettuce Soup

Imperial (Metric)

½ large cucumber,
chopped
12 oz (340g) courgettes,
chopped
1 large Webbs lettuce,
finely chopped
8 spring onions, chopped
4 tablespoons sunflower
oil
2 pints (1.15 litres)
vegetable stock
1 fennel sprig
½ pint (285ml) soured
cream
Juice of ½ lemon
4 tablespoons chopped
fennel

1. Heat the oil in a large saucepan on a low heat. Put in the cucumber, courgettes (zucchini) and spring onions (scallions.) Cover and cook for 10 minutes.
2. Pour in the stock and bring it to the boil. Add half the lettuce and the fennel sprig. Cover and simmer for 15 minutes.
3. Remove the fennel sprig. Either liquidize the soup in a blender or food processor or put it through the fine blade of a vegetable mill.
4. Stir in the soured cream and half the lemon juice. Taste and add more lemon juice if required. Stir in the remaining lettuce and the chopped fennel.
5. Reheat gently, without boiling.

Note: The soup should be frozen without adding the soured cream, raw lettuce and chopped fennel. Cool it completely. Pour it into a rigid container and cover. Store for up to two months. Thaw at room temperature. Reheat gently in a saucepan. Stir in the remaining ingredients.

American

½ large cucumber,
chopped
¾ pound zucchini,
chopped
1 large Webbs lettuce,
finely chopped
8 scallions, chopped
¼ cup sunflower oil
5 cups vegetable stock
1 fennel sprig
1¼ cups sour cream
Juice of ½ lemon
4 tablespoons chopped
fennel

FIRST COURSES

Summer vegetables are so delicious, that they can easily stand alone to make attractive and appetizing first courses. Who would want to do any more with asparagus than serve it with a creamy sauce on the side, or with artichokes than to give them a tasty vinaigrette?

Even a simple salad vegetable such as lettuce can be made into a pâté and an egg salad can be transformed by summer flowers.

Lettuce and Sorrel Cheese

Imperial (Metric)

Hearts of two round lettuces
12 sorrel leaves
10 spring onions
½ oz (15g) butter
6 oz (170g) curd cheese
6 radishes, sliced
Fingers of wholemeal toast

1. Finely chop the lettuce, sorrel and onions (scallions).
2. Melt the butter in a frying pan (skillet) on a low heat. Put in the onions and let them soften for 2 minutes.
3. Mix in the lettuce and sorrel. Stir them for 1 minute, or until they wilt. Take the pan from the heat.
4. Cream the cheese in a bowl. Mix in the contents of the pan.
5. Divide the mixture between six small ramekins and chill it for 2 hours.
6. Garnish the cheese with the radish slices and accompany it with the toast.

American

Hearts of two round lettuces
12 sorrel leaves
10 scallions
1 tablespoon butter
¾ cup curd cheese
6 radishes, sliced
Fingers of wholewheat toast

Broad Bean and Grapefruit Salad

Imperial (Metric)

2½ lb (1.15kg) broad beans in pods
3 fl oz (90ml) olive oil
Juice of 1 lemon
3 large grapefruit
2 tablespoons chopped mint
6 chive flowers
12 mint leaves

1. Shell the beans.
2. Put the oil into a saucepan and warm it on a low heat. Stir in the beans, cover and cook gently for 15 minutes.
3. Add the lemon juice. Take the pan from the heat and cool completely.
4. Cut the rind and pith from the grapefruit. Cut out and chop the segments.
5. Mix the grapefruit and mint into the beans.
6. Divide the salad between six small bowls. Garnish with the chive flowers and mint leaves.

American

2½ pounds broad beans in pods
⅓ cup olive oil
Juice of 1 lemon
3 large grapefruit
2 tablespoons chopped mint
6 chive flowers
12 mint leaves

Apricot and Curd Cheese Salad with Tarragon

Imperial (Metric)

1 round lettuce
1 small cucumber
12 apricots, ripe but firm
3 fl oz (90ml) olive oil
3 tablespoons white wine
vinegar
1½ tablespoons chopped
tarragon
1 garlic clove, crushed
Freshly ground black
pepper
8 oz (225g) low-fat soft
cheese
6 walnut halves

1. Shred the lettuce and arrange it over six small plates.
2. Finely dice the cucumber and arrange the dice in a circle over the edges of the lettuce.
3. Halve and stone (pit) the apricots and cut them into quarters lengthways. Arrange them in a circle on top of the cucumber.
4. Mix the oil, vinegar, tarragon, garlic and pepper to make the dressing and spoon it over the salads.
5. Put a portion of the cheese in the centre of each salad. Top it with a walnut half.
Note: Unsuitable for freezing.

American

1 round lettuce
1 small cucumber
12 apricots, ripe but firm
⅓ cup olive oil
3 tablespoons white wine
vinegar
1½ tablespoons chopped
tarragon
1 garlic clove, crushed
Freshly ground black
pepper
1 cup low-fat soft cheese
6 English walnut halves

Asparagus with Egg and Parsley Sauce

Imperial (Metric)

1½ lb (680g) asparagus
4 eggs, hard-boiled
4 tablespoons chopped
parsley
4 tablespoons Greek-style
natural yogurt
2 tablespoons double
cream

1. Trim the asparagus. Bring a tall, narrow saucepan of lightly salted water to the boil. Put in the asparagus, stems downwards with the tips about 1 inch (2.5cm) above the water. Cover with a lid or a dome of foil. Boil for 15 minutes. Drain.
2. While the asparagus is cooking, mash the eggs and mix in the parsley, yogurt and cream.
3. Divide the asparagus between six separate plates. Put a portion of the egg sauce beside it.
Note: Wholemeal (wholewheat) rolls, warmed in the oven, make a good accompaniment. Unsuitable for freezing.

American

1½ pounds asparagus
4 hard-cooked eggs
¼ cup chopped parsley
¼ cup Greek-style
unflavored yogurt
2 tablespoons heavy
cream

Artichokes in Red Wine with Mushroom Vinaigrette

Imperial (Metric)

6 globe artichokes
For cooking:
¼ pint (140ml) dry red wine
3 fl oz (90ml) olive oil
Vinaigrette:
3 fl oz (90ml) olive oil
3 tablespoons red wine vinegar
6 oz (170g) button mushrooms, finely chopped
2 tablespoons chopped thyme

1. Trim the stalks and tops of the artichokes.
2. Put the wine and oil into a large saucepan with enough water to cover the artichokes. Bring them to the boil. Put in the the artichokes. Cover and simmer for 30 minutes.
3. While the artichokes are cooking, make the vinaigrette. Beat together the oil and vinegar and fold in the mushrooms and thyme.
4. Lift the artichokes from the cooking liquid and drain them. Open the leaves and remove the chokes.
5. Put each artichoke onto a separate plate, big enough to take the leaves as they are discarded.
6. Spoon a portion of the mushroom vinaigrette into the centre of each artichoke.
Note: Unsuitable for freezing.

American

6 globe artichokes
For cooking:
⅔ cup dry red wine
⅓ cup olive oil
Vinaigrette:
⅓ cup olive oil
3 tablespoons red wine vinegar
6 ounces button mushrooms, finely chopped
2 tablespoons chopped thyme

Egg and Flower Salad

Imperial (Metric)

6 eggs, hard-boiled
3 fl oz (90ml) mayonnaise
Petals from 12 marigold heads
3 tablespoons chopped chives
1 large round lettuce
12 chive or 6 nasturtium flowers

1. Finely chop the eggs and mix with the mayonnaise, marigold petals and chives.
2. Shred the lettuce and arrange a base on each of six small plates.
3. Put a portion of the egg salad on top.
4. Decorate with the chive or nasturtium flowers.

American

6 hard-cooked eggs
⅓ cup mayonnaise
Petals from 12 marigold heads
3 tablespoons chopped chives
1 large round lettuce
12 chive or 6 nasturtium flowers

MAIN COURSES

The following main courses are all designed to be served hot and yet they are all light in texture and flavour to suit summer's moods.

New Potato Casserole

Imperial (Metric)

2¼ lb (1kg) small new potatoes
12 spring onions
4 tablespoons olive oil
1 pint (570ml) vegetable stock
¼ pint (140ml) dry white wine
2 tablespoons white wine vinegar
1 teaspoon coriander seeds, crushed
4 tablespoons chopped mint
12 oz (340g) red kidney beans, soaked and cooked
Accompaniment:
1 lb (455g) new carrots
½ pint (285ml) vegetable stock
2 tablespoons chopped marjoram
1 lb (455g) French beans
2 tablespoons sunflower oil
2 tablespoons chopped thyme

1. Wash the potatoes. If they are very small cut them in half, if larger, in quarters. If large potatoes are used cut them into 1 inch (2.5cm) pieces. Cut the spring onions (scallions) into 1 inch (2.5cm) lengths.
2. Heat the oil in a large saucepan on a high heat. Put in the potatoes and onions (scallions) and stir them for 2 minutes.
3. Pour in the stock and wine and bring them to the boil. Add the vinegar, coriander seeds, mint and kidney beans. Cover and keep on a medium heat for 20 minutes, by which time the potatoes should be tender and most of the liquid evaporated.
4. Scrub the carrots. Leave them whole if they are very small, otherwise cut them into 1 inch (2.5cm) pieces. Bring the stock to the boil in a saucepan. Put in the carrots and marjoram. Cover and cook on a medium heat for 15 minutes or until the carrots are just tender.
5. Top and tail the beans. Heat the oil in a saucepan on a high heat. Put in the beans and thyme. Pour in ¼ pint (140ml/⅔ cup) water and bring it to the boil. Cover and cook on a medium heat for 15 minutes, or until the beans are just tender.
6. Serve the potato casserole in the centre of a large serving plate, surrounded by the carrots and beans.
Note: Prepare the carrots and beans before you start to cook the potatoes. They should all be cooked at around the same time.
Unsuitable for freezing.

American

2¼ pounds small new potatoes
12 scallions
¼ cup olive oil
2½ cups vegetable stock
⅔ cup dry white wine
2 tablespoons white wine vinegar
1 teaspoon coriander seeds, crushed
¼ cup chopped mint
2 cups red kidney beans, soaked and cooked
Accompaniment:
1 pound new carrots
1¼ cups vegetable stock
2 tablespoons chopped marjoram
1 pound French beans
2 tablespoons sunflower oil
2 tablespoons chopped thyme

Minted Nut Roast with Redcurrant Sauce

Imperial (Metric)

3 oz (85g) pine nuts
5 oz (140g) hazelnuts
4 tablespoons sunflower oil
1 large onion, finely chopped
8 oz (225g) fresh wholemeal breadcrumbs
6 tablespoons chopped mint
2 teaspoons ground cumin
2 teaspoons ground coriander
¼ pint (140ml) natural yogurt
Sauce:
1 lb (455g) redcurrants
2 tablespoons sunflower oil
1 medium onion
4 tablespoons honey
6 tablespoons chopped mint
4 tablespoons chopped chives

1. Heat the oven to 400°F/200°C/Gas Mark 6.
2. Finely grate the pine nuts and hazelnuts.
3. Heat the oil in a frying pan (skillet) on a low heat. Put in the onion and soften it.
4. Off the heat, mix in the breadcrumbs, nuts, mint, cumin, coriander and yogurt.
5. Put the mixture into a large pie dish and bake it for 45 minutes or until the top is golden brown. Serve straight from the dish.
6. For the sauce, string the redcurrants if necessary.
7. Heat the oil in a saucepan on a low heat. Put in the onion and soften it.
8. Put in the redcurrants and honey. Cover and simmer for 20 minutes or until the redcurrants are very soft.
9. Rub everything through a sieve. Reheat and mix in the chopped mint and chives. Serve separately.

Note: The sauce can be frozen, without the herbs, for up to 2 months. The roast is unsuitable for freezing.

American

¾ cup pine nuts
1 cup hazelnuts
¼ cup sunflower oil
1 large onion, finely chopped
4 cups fresh wholewheat breadcrumbs
⅓ cup chopped mint
2 teaspoons ground cumin
2 teaspoons ground coriander
⅔ cup unflavored yogurt
Sauce:
1 pound redcurrants
2 tablespoons sunflower oil
1 medium onion
¼ cup honey
⅓ cup chopped mint
¼ cup chopped chives

Tomato Tart with Two Cheeses

Imperial (Metric)

Shortcrust pastry made with 8 oz (225g) wholemeal flour (see page 24)
1 lb (455g) tomatoes
6 spring onions, chopped
2 tablespoons chopped basil
4 oz (115g) Cheddar cheese, grated
4 oz (115g) Stilton cheese, grated
4 eggs
½ pint (285ml) milk

1. Heat the oven to 400°F/200°C/Gas Mark 6.
2. Use the pastry to line a 10 inch (25cm) diameter tart tin.
3. Thinly slice the tomatoes and put them into the bottom of the pastry case.
4. Scatter the spring onions (scallions) and basil and then the cheeses over the top.
5. Beat the eggs with the milk. Pour them over the tomatoes and cheese.
6. Bake the tart for 30 minutes or until the filling is set and beginning to brown.

Note: Unsuitable for freezing.

American

Shortcrust pastry made with 2 cups wholewheat flour (see page 24)
1 pound tomatoes
6 scallions, chopped
2 tablespoons chopped basil
1 cup grated Cheddar cheese
1 cup grated Stilton cheese
4 eggs
1¼ cups milk

Hot Runner Bean, Lentil and Egg Salad

Imperial (Metric)

8 oz (225g) green lentils
1½ lb (685g) runner
beans
8 eggs, hard-boiled
4 tablespoons sunflower
oil
2 medium onions, thinly
sliced
1 garlic clove, finely
chopped
2 teaspoons curry powder
3 tablespoons white wine
vinegar

1. Cook and drain the lentils.
2. Slice the beans.
3. Chop six of the eggs and quarter the other two.
4. Heat the oil in a large saucepan on a low heat. Put in the onions and garlic and soften them.
5. Mix in the beans and curry powder. Cover and cook on a low heat for 20 minutes.
6. Mix in the lentils.
7. Add the vinegar and let it bubble. Mix well and take the pan from the heat.
8. Mix in the chopped eggs.
9. Put the salad into a warmed serving dish and garnish with the quartered eggs.

Note: Unsuitable for freezing.

American

1 cup green lentils
1½ pounds runner beans
8 hard-cooked eggs
¼ cup sunflower oil
2 medium onions, thinly
sliced
1 garlic clove, finely
chopped
2 teaspoons curry powder
3 tablespoons white wine
vinegar

Asparagus and Sunflower Quiche

Imperial (Metric)

Pastry:
2 oz (55g) sunflower
seeds
6 oz (170g) wholemeal
flour
Pinch fine sea salt
4 oz (115g) butter or
vegetable margarine
4 tablespoons cold water
Filling:
1 lb (455g) asparagus
8 oz (225g) curd cheese
4 eggs, beaten
3 tablespoons grated
Parmesan cheese
3 oz (85g) sunflower
seeds

1. Heat the oven to 400°F/200°C/Gas Mark 6.
2. For the pastry, finely grind the sunflower seeds. In a bowl, mix them with the flour and salt. Rub in the butter or margarine. Mix to a dough with the water.
3. Trim away the tough ends of the asparagus stalks. Cut the rest into 1 inch (2.5cm) lengths. Boil them in lightly salted water for 15 minutes. Drain them well and cool them.
4. Line a 10 inch (25cm) diameter tart tin with the pastry. Arrange the asparagus in the bottom.
5. Beat the cream cheese in a bowl to cream it. Gradually beat in the eggs. Stir in the Parmesan cheese and sunflower seeds. Pour the mixture over the asparagus.
6. Bake the quiche for 25 minutes or until the filling is set and golden brown on top. Serve hot or warm.

Note: Unsuitable for freezing.

American

Pastry:
½ cup sunflower seeds
1½ cups wholewheat flour
Pinch fine sea salt
½ cup butter or vegetable
margarine
4 tablespoons cold water
Filling:
1 pound asparagus
1 cup curd cheese
4 eggs, beaten
3 tablespoons grated
Parmesan cheese
⅔ cup sunflower seeds

121

Flageolets with Asparagus and Pasta

Imperial (Metric)

12 oz (340g) flageolet
beans
1½ lb (680g) asparagus
10 spring onions
12 oz (340g) pasta shapes
1 oz (30g) butter or
vegetable margarine
8 oz (225g) low-fat soft
cheese
Grated rind and juice of
1 lemon
4 tablespoons chopped
parsley

1. Soak, cook and drain the flageolets.
2. Trim the asparagus. Cut it into 1 inch (2.5cm) lengths. Boil it in lightly salted water for 15 minutes. Drain it.
3. Cut the spring onions (scallions) into 1 inch (2.5cm) lengths.
4. Cook the pasta in lightly salted boiling water for 12 minutes, or until it is just tender. Drain it.
5. Melt the butter or margarine in a saucepan on a low heat. Put in the spring onions (scallions) and cook them for 1 minute.
6. Gently mix in the cheese and then the lemon rind and juice and parsley.
7. Mix in the beans and pasta. Fold in the asparagus.
8. Gently stir until all the ingredients have heated through.
9. Transfer to a warmed serving dish.
Note: Unsuitable for freezing.

American

1½ cups flageolet beans
1½ pounds asparagus
10 scallions
¾ pound pasta shapes
2 tablespoons butter or
vegetable margarine
1 cup low-fat soft cheese
Grated rind and juice of
1 lemon
¼ cup chopped parsley

Grilled Courgette (Zucchini) Rolls

Imperial (Metric)

9 medium-sized courgettes
8 oz (225g) carrots
6 oz (170g) fresh
wholemeal breadcrumbs
1½ oz (45g) butter
6 spring onions
8 oz (225g) Cheddar
cheese, grated
2 tablespoons chopped
marjoram
2 tablespoons chopped
parsley

1. Holding each courgette (zucchini) lengthways, cut away two thin slices from the sides and discard them. Cut the remaining part into four thin slices lengthways.
2. Blanch the courgette (zucchini) slices in boiling water for 3 minutes. Drain them well and cool them.
3. Boil or steam the carrots until they are just tender. Drain and mash them. Mix them with the breadcrumbs.
4. Melt ½ oz (15g/1 tablespoon) of the butter in a small frying pan (skillet) on a low heat. Put in the spring onions (scallions) and soften them. Mix them into the carrots and breadcrumbs.
5. Mix in the cheese and herbs.
6. Roll a small portion of the stuffing mixture in a courgette (zucchini) slice. Skewer six rolls on each of six kebab skewers.

American

9 medium-sized zucchini
½ pound carrots
3 cups fresh wholewheat
breadcrumbs
3 tablespoons butter
6 scallions
2 cups grated Cheddar
cheese
2 tablespoons chopped
marjoram
2 tablespoons chopped
parsley

7. Melt the remaining butter and brush it over the rolls.
8. Heat the grill (broiler) to high and if you have an open wire rack, cover it with foil.
9. Lay the courgette (zucchini) rolls on the hot rack and grill (broil) them for ½ minute only on each side to just heat them through. Too long a cooking time will cause the cheese to melt too much.

Note: Unsuitable for freezing.

Falafel with Tomato and Basil Sauce

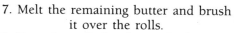

Imperial (Metric)

12 oz (340g) chick peas, soaked and cooked
3 fl oz (90ml) water
3 tablespoons tahini (sesame paste)
Grated rind of 1 lemon
Juice of 1½ lemons
3 tablespoons tomato purée
1½ oz (45g) fresh wholemeal breadcrumbs
6 tablespoons chopped parsley
2 teaspoons ground cumin
1 teaspoon ground coriander
¼ teaspoon cayenne pepper
1 garlic clove, crushed
2 oz (55g) wholemeal flour
Vegetable oil for deep frying
Sauce:
2 lb (900g) tomatoes
4 tablespoons olive oil
2 garlic cloves, crushed
4 tablespoons chopped basil
Garnish:
Parsley sprigs

1. Either mash the chick peas (garbanzos), or mince them twice, or liquidize them in a blender or food processor.
2. Beat in the water, tahini, lemon rind and juice and tomato purée (paste).
3. Mix in the breadcrumbs, parsley, spices and garlic.
4. Form the mixture into small balls about 1 inch (2.5cm) in diameter. Roll them in the flour.
5. To make the sauce, scald, skin and finely chop the tomatoes.
6. Heat the oil in a saucepan on a low heat. Put in the tomatoes, garlic and basil. Cover and simmer for 30 minutes. The sauce can either be served as it is or rubbed through a sieve and reheated.
7. To cook the falafel, heat a deep pan of oil to 360°F/185°C. Fry the falafel five or six at a time, for about 2½ minutes or until they are lightly browned. Drain them on kitchen paper and keep them warm.
8. Serve hot, garnished with parsley sprigs. Serve the sauce separately.

Note: The falafel can be frozen before they are cooked. Freeze them on a tray and then pack them into a polythene bag. Store for up to three months. Thaw at room temperature before cooking. The sauce can be frozen in a rigid container for up to three months.

American

1½ cups garbanzo beans, soaked and cooked
⅓ cup water
3 tablespoons tahini (sesame paste)
Grated rind of 1 lemon
Juice of 1½ lemons
3 tablespoons tomato paste
¾ cup fresh wholewheat breadcrumbs
⅓ cup chopped parsley
2 teaspoons ground cumin
1 teaspoon ground coriander
¼ teaspoon cayenne pepper
1 garlic clove, crushed
½ cup wholewheat flour
Vegetable oil for deep frying
Sauce:
2 pounds tomatoes
¼ cup olive oil
2 garlic cloves, crushed
4 tablespoons chopped basil
Garnish:
Parsley sprigs

Asparagus and Almond Risotto

Imperial (Metric)

2 lb (900g) asparagus
12 large spring onions
4 tablespoons sunflower oil
12 oz (340g) long-grain brown rice
¼ teaspoon saffron
1½ pints (850ml) vegetable stock
8 oz (225g) shelled almonds
4 tablespoons chopped parsley
3 tablespoons grated Parmesan cheese

1. Trim the tough pieces from the asparagus stems. Cut the rest into 1 inch (2.5cm) lengths. Cut the spring onions (scallions) into 1 inch (2.5cm) lengths.
2. Heat the oil in a large saucepan on a low heat. Stir in the rice and spring onions (scallions) and stir for 1 minute. Add the saffron and the vegetable stock. Bring the stock to the boil. Cover and simmer for 25 minutes.
3. Put in the asparagus. Cover again and simmer for 20 minutes.
4. Mix in the almonds, parsley and Parmesan cheese Take the pan from the heat. Leave the risotto, covered, for 5 minutes before serving.
Note: Freeze before adding the almonds, parsley and cheese. Pack into a rigid container and cover. Store for up to 2 months. Thaw at room temperature. Reheat in an oiled dish covered with oiled foil, in a medium oven for 15 minutes. Add the remaining ingredients just before serving.

American

2 pounds asparagus
12 large scallions
¼ cup sunflower oil
1½ cups long-grain brown rice
¼ teaspoon saffron
3¾ cups vegetable stock
2 cups shelled almonds
¼ cup chopped parsley
3 tablespoons Parmesan cheese

Summer Cabbage with Chick Peas (Garbanzo Beans) and Cashew Nuts

Imperial (Metric)

2 medium-sized summer cabbages
1½ oz (45g) butter or vegetable margarine
¼ pint (140ml) soured cream
4 tablespoons chopped fennel
1 cucumber, chopped
6 oz chick peas, soaked and cooked
6 oz (170g) cashew nuts

1. Shred the cabbages.
2. Melt the butter or margarine in a saucepan on a medium heat. Stir in the cabbage. Cover, lower the heat and simmer for 15 minutes or until the cabbage is just tender. (Summer cabbages are crisp and watery and no other water should be necessary.)
3. Stir in the soured cream, fennel, cucumber, chick peas (garbanzo beans) and cashew nuts. Cover and simmer for 2 minutes to heat through.
Note: Unsuitable for freezing.

American

2 medium-sized summer cabbages
3 tablespoons butter or vegetable margarine
⅔ cup sour cream
¼ cup chopped fennel
1 cucumber, chopped
¾ cup garbanzo beans, soaked and cooked
1 cup cashew nuts

Summer Vegetables with Cashew Nuts

Imperial (Metric)

2 lb (900g) broad beans
in pods
2½ lb (1.15kg) peas in
pods
1 lb (455g) ripe tomatoes
1 oz (30g) butter
2 tablespoons chopped
savory
2 tablespoons chopped
basil
6 spring onions, chopped
8 oz (225g) cashew nuts
8 oz (225g) Double
Gloucester cheese, grated
2 tablespoons wheatgerm

1. Shell the beans and peas.
2. Scald, skin and chop the tomatoes.
3. Melt the butter in a large saucepan on a low heat. Put in the tomatoes, herbs and spring onions (scallions). Cover and simmer for 2 minutes.
4. Put in the beans and peas. Cover and simmer for 20 minutes.
5. Heat the oven to 400°F/200°C/Gas Mark 6.
6. Take the beans and peas from the heat. Mix in the cashew nuts.
7. Put the mixture into a large ovenproof dish.
8. Scatter first the cheese and then the wheatgerm over the top.
9. Bake for 20 minutes for the cheese to melt.
Note: Unsuitable for freezing.

American

2 pound broad beans in
pods
2½ pounds peas in pods
1 pound ripe tomatoes
2 tablespoons butter
2 tablespoons chopped
savory
2 tablespoons chopped
basil
6 scallions, chopped
1⅔ cups cashew nuts
2 cups grated Double
Gloucester cheese
2 tablespoons wheatgerm

Burghul, Summer Vegetable and Feta Cheese Bake

Imperial (Metric)

12 oz (340g) burghul
wheat
2 lb (900g) broad beans
in pods
2 lb (900g) peas in pods
6 spring onions
12 oz (340g) Feta cheese
4 oz (115g) walnuts,
chopped
4 tablespoons chopped
parsley
2 tablespoons chopped
oregano
2 tablespoons chopped
thyme
4 eggs, beaten

1. Heat the oven to 400°F/200°C/Gas Mark 6.
2. Soak the wheat in warm water for 20 minutes. Drain it and squeeze it dry.
3. Shell the beans and peas. Boil them together for 12 minutes. Drain them.
4. Chop the spring onions (scallions). Chop the cheese.
5. Mix together the wheat, beans and peas, spring onions (scallions), cheese, walnuts and herbs. Mix in the eggs.
6. Put the mixture into a large, ovenproof dish.
7. Bake for 30 minutes or until the eggs are set and the top is golden brown.
Note: Unsuitable for freezing.

American

1½ cups burghul wheat
2 pounds broad beans in
pods
2 pounds peas in pods
6 scallions
¾ pound Feta cheese
¾ cup chopped English
walnuts
¼ cup chopped parsley
2 tablespoons chopped
oregano
2 tablespoons chopped
thyme
4 eggs, beaten

Stuffed Lettuce Leaves

Imperial (Metric)

8 eggs, hard-boiled
8 oz (225g) fresh
wholemeal breadcrumbs
8 spring onions, chopped
2 tablespoons chopped
thyme
2 tablespoons chopped
marjoram
Grated rind and juice of
1 lemon
7 fl oz (200ml) dry white
wine
18 large, soft lettuce
leaves
¾ pint (425ml) vegetable
stock

1. Heat the oven to 400°F/200°C/Gas Mark 6.
2. Finely chop the eggs.
3. Mix them with the breadcrumbs, spring onions (scallions), herbs, lemon rind and juice and 4 tablespoons (¼ cup) dry white wine.
4. Put a portion of the mixture on the bottom of each lettuce leaf. Roll the leaf over once, fold in the sides and then finish rolling it up.
5. Lay the stuffed leaves in a large, shallow, ovenproof dish (or two dishes if one is not large enough). Pour in the remaining wine and the stock.
6. Cover the dish with foil and put it into the oven for 20 minutes.
Note: Unsuitable for freezing.

American

8 hard-cooked eggs
4 cups fresh wholewheat
breadcrumbs
8 scallions, chopped
2 tablespoons chopped
thyme
2 tablespoons chopped
marjoram
Grated rind and juice of
1 lemon
¾ cup dry white wine
18 large, soft lettuce
leaves
2 cups vegetable stock

Tagliatelle, Beans and Mushrooms with Pine Nut Sauce

Imperial (Metric)

Sauce:
3 fl oz (90ml) olive oil
1½ lb (680g) onions,
thinly sliced
2 garlic cloves, finely
chopped
1 pint (570ml) tomato
juice
4 tablespoons chopped
basil
4 oz (115g) pine nuts
1 lb (455g) French beans
8 oz (225g) button
mushrooms
12 oz (340g) wholemeal
tagliatelle
3 tablespoons olive oil
1 oz (30g) parsley,
chopped
4 oz (115g) chopped
mixed nuts

1. Make the sauce first. Heat the oil in a saucepan on a low heat. Mix in the onions and garlic. Cover and cook very gently for 30 minutes, stirring occasionally, so they soften but do not colour.
2. Pour in the tomato juice and bring it to the boil. Add the basil. Simmer, uncovered, for 5 minutes.
3. Finely grind the pine nuts. Mix them into the sauce just before serving.
4. For the pasta, first top and tail the beans and break them into short lengths. Thinly slice the mushrooms.
5. Bring a large pan of lightly salted water to the boil. Put in the tagliatelle and beans. Cover and simmer for 10 minutes or until both are just tender. Drain.
6. Heat the oil in a saucepan on a low heat. Mix in the mushrooms and cook

American

Sauce:
⅓ cup olive oil
1½ pounds onions, thinly
sliced
2 garlic cloves, finely
chopped
2½ cups tomato juice
4 tablespoons chopped
basil
1 cup pine nuts
1 pound French beans
½ pound button
mushrooms
¾ pound wholewheat
tagliatelle
3 tablespoons olive oil
1 cup chopped parsley
1⅔ cups chopped mixed
nuts

them for 2 minutes. Add the pasta, beans, parsley and mixed nuts. Take the pan from the heat and gently fold everything together.

7. Put the pasta onto a large serving dish and pour the sauce over the top. Garnish with extra parsley if wished.

Note: The sauce and the pasta can be frozen separately for up to two months. Thaw both at room temperature. Reheat them separately in saucepans, adding a little extra oil to the pasta if necessary.

Courgette (Zucchini) and Walnut Layer

Imperial (Metric)

2 lb (900g) courgettes
1 large onion
4 tablespoons olive oil
1 garlic clove, finely chopped
1 lb (455g) tomatoes
6 spring onions
8 oz (225g) shelled walnuts
2 tablespoons chopped thyme
1lb 4 oz (565g) silken tofu
2 teaspoons paprika
¼ teaspoon cayenne pepper
1 teaspoon mustard powder
2 tablespoons pine nuts

1. Heat the oven to 400°F/200°C/Gas Mark 6.

2. Wipe and thinly slice the courgettes (zucchini). Thinly slice the onion.

3. Heat the oil in a saucepan on a low heat. Put in the courgettes (zucchini), onion and garlic. Cover and cook gently for 10 minutes. Take them from the heat and cool them.

4. Thinly slice the tomatoes. Chop the spring onions (scallions).

5. Finely chop 6 oz (170g/1¼ cups) walnuts. Finely grind the rest.

6. Put one third of the courgettes (zucchini) into a deep, ovenproof dish. Scatter in one third of the chopped walnuts and one third of the thyme and spring onions (scallions). Put in one third of the tomatoes. Repeat the layers twice.

7. Put the tofu into a blender or food processor with the paprika, cayenne pepper, mustard powder and ground walnuts. Liquidize it to a smooth purée.

8. Spoon the purée over the top layer in the dish. Scatter the pine nuts over the top.

9. Bake for 30 minutes or until the pine nuts are browned.

Note: Unsuitable for freezing.

American

2 pounds zucchini
1 large onion
¼ cup olive oil
1 garlic clove, finely chopped
1 pound tomatoes
6 scallions
1⅔ cups shelled English walnuts
2 tablespoons chopped thyme
2½ cups silken tofu
2 teaspoons paprika
¼ teaspoon cayenne pepper
1 teaspoon mustard powder
2 tablespoons pine nuts

VEGETABLES AND SALADS

There are so many superb vegetables available in the summer that it is often more difficult to decide what to leave out of a menu than what to add to it. The following recipes are a selection of my favourite ways of turning summer vegetables into accompaniments that will more than match the main dish.

Hot Potato and Lettuce Salad

Imperial (Metric)

2¼ lb (1kg) new potatoes
3 fl oz (90ml) olive oil
2 teaspoons mustard seeds
2 teaspoons mustard powder
3 tablespoons white wine vinegar
1 large, crisp lettuce

1. Boil the potatoes in their skins until they are just tender. Drain and halve or slice them (depending on their size) while they are still hot.
2. Heat the oil in a saucepan on a low heat. Put in the mustard seeds and simmer them gently for 2 minutes.
3. Mix in the potatoes. Sprinkle in the mustard powder and vinegar. Let the vinegar boil and give the potatoes a stir to heat them through. If the potatoes are to stand for a time, keep them warm.
4. Shred the lettuce and mix it in just before serving.
Note: Unsuitable for freezing.

American

2¼ pounds new potatoes
⅓ cup olive oil
2 teaspoons mustard seeds
2 teaspoons mustard powder
3 tablespoons white wine vinegar
1 large, crisp lettuce

New Potatoes with Fennel and Bay

Imperial (Metric)

2¼ lb (1kg) small new potatoes
1 oz (30g) butter
8 spring onions, chopped
1 pint (570ml) vegetable stock
4 tablespoons chopped fennel
2 bay leaves

1. Wash the potatoes
2. Melt the butter in a large saucepan or flameproof casserole on a low heat. Put in the spring onions (scallions) and cook them for 1 minute.
3. Pour in the stock and bring it to the boil
4. Add the potatoes, fennel and bay leaves. Cover and simmer for 30 minutes, by which time the stock should be reduced and the potatoes slightly glazed.
5. Remove the bay leaves before serving.
Note: Unsuitable for freezing.

American

2¼ pounds small new potatoes
2 tablespoons butter
8 scallions, chopped
2½ cups vegetable stock
¼ cup chopped fennel
2 bay leaves

128

Asparagus with Grated Courgettes (Zucchini)

Imperial (Metric)

1 lb (455g) asparagus
1 lb (455g) courgettes
1 oz (30g) butter or
vegetable margarine
Juice of 1 lemon
4 tablespoons chopped
parsley

1. Trim any tough parts from the asparagus stems. Cut the rest into 1 inch (2.5cm) pieces. Boil them for 15 minutes. Drain them well.
2. Coursely grate the courgettes (zucchini).
3. Melt the butter or margarine in a saucepan on a high heat. Put in the courgettes (zucchini) and stir them for 2 minutes. Pour in the lemon juice and let it boil.
4. Mix in the parsley and asparagus.
Note: Unsuitable for freezing.

American

1 pound asparagus
1 pound zucchini
2 tablespoons butter or
vegetable margarine
Juice of 1 lemon
¼ cup chopped parsley

New Carrots with Tarragon

Imperial (Metric)

1½ lb (685g) new carrots
¾ pint (425ml) vegetable
stock
1 oz butter or vegetable
margarine
2 tablespoons tarragon
vinegar
2 tablespoons chopped
tarragon
2 tablespoons chopped
parsley

1. Scrub and trim the carrots. Leave them whole.
2. Put the stock into a saucepan and bring it to the boil. Put in the butter or margarine and carrots. Cover and cook on a medium heat for 15 minutes.
3. Uncover the pan and cook on a high heat until the liquid is almost completely reduced and the carrots are glazed.
4. Add the vinegar and herbs and heat through.
Note: Unsuitable for freezing.

American

1½ pounds new carrots
2 cups vegetable stock
2 tablespoons butter or
vegetable margarine
2 tablespoons tarragon
vinegar
2 tablespoons chopped
tarragon
2 tablespoons chopped
parsley

Broad Beans with Apricots

Imperial (Metric)

4 lb (1.8kg) broad beans
in pods
2 mint sprigs
6 apricots
¼ pint (140ml) natural
yogurt
1 teaspoon mild granular
mustard

1. Shell the beans and steam them with the mint sprigs for 20 minutes or until they are just tender.
2. While the beans are cooking, stone (pit) and slice the apricots and mix the yogurt with the mustard.
3. As soon as the beans are cooked, mix them into the yogurt.
4. Mix in the apricots.
Note: Unsuitable for freezing.

American

4 pounds broad beans in
pods
2 mint sprigs
6 apricots
⅔ cup unflavored yogurt
1 teaspoon mild granular
mustard

New Carrot and Basil Salad

Imperial (Metric)

1 lb (455g) new carrots
2 tablespoons chopped
basil
1 crisp lettuce
Petals from 6 marigold
heads
4 tablespoons chopped
parsley
3 fl oz (90ml) olive oil
3 tablespoons cider
vinegar
2 teaspoons clear honey
6 apricots (if available)

1. Very thinly slice the carrots and mix them with the basil.
2. Shred the lettuce and mix it with the marigold petals and parsley.
3. Beat together the oil, vinegar and honey.
4. Spoon half the dressing into the carrots and the rest over the lettuce.
5. Arrange the carrots in the centre of a serving plate with the lettuce around the edge.
6. Halve, stone (pit) and slice the apricots. Arrange them on the lettuce.
Note: Unsuitable for freezing.

American

1 pound new carrots
2 tablespoons chopped
basil
1 crisp lettuce
Petals from 6 marigold
heads
¼ cup chopped parsley
⅓ cup olive oil
3 tablespoons cider
vinegar
2 teaspoons clear honey
6 apricots (if available)

Stir-Fried Mange-Tout with Carrot Strips

Imperial (Metric)

1 lb (455g) mange-tout
peas
8 oz (225g) carrots
4 tablespoons sunflower
oil
1 garlic clove, finely
chopped
3 fl oz (90ml) sweet
sherry

1. Top and tail the peas. Cut the carrots into matchstick pieces.
2. Heat the oil in a large frying pan (skillet) or wok on a high heat. Put in the peas, carrots and garlic and stir-fry them for 3 minutes.
3. Pour in the sherry and boil it until it has reduced to a glaze.
4. Serve immediately.
Note: Unsuitable for freezing.

American

1 pound snow peas
½ pound carrots
¼ cup sunflower oil
1 garlic clove, finely
chopped
⅓ cup sweet sherry

Redcurrant Salad

Imperial (Metric)

6 oz (170g) redcurrants
1 large lettuce
2 small ridge cucumbers
(or 1 small greenhouse
cucumber)
10 sage leaves, chopped
2 tablespoons chopped
tarragon
2 tablespoons chopped
chives
4 tablespoons olive oil
2 tablespoons tarragon
vinegar

1. String the redcurrants.
2. Shred the lettuce. Cut the cucumbers into quarters lengthways. Thinly slice the quarters.
3. Mix the currants, lettuce, cucumber and herbs in a salad bowl.
4. Beat together the oil and vinegar and fold them into the salad.
Note: Unsuitable for freezing.

American

6 ounces redcurrants
1 large lettuce
2 small ridge cucumbers
(or 1 small greenhouse
cucumber)
10 sage leaves, chopped
2 tablespoons chopped
tarragon
2 tablespoons chopped
chives
¼ cup olive oil
2 tablespoon tarragon
vinegar

Courgettes (Zucchini) Stuffed with Onions

Imperial (Metric)

9 small courgettes
3 tablespoons olive oil
plus extra for greasing
3 medium onions, finely
chopped
2 garlic cloves, finely
chopped
2 tablespoons chopped
thyme
2 tablespoons chopped
parsley

1. Heat the oven to 350°F/180°C/Gas Mark 4.
2. Wipe the courgettes (zucchini) and leave them whole. Wrap them in threes in lightly oiled foil and put them into the oven for 25 minutes.
3. Heat the 3 tablespoons oil in a frying pan (skillet). Put in the onions and garlic and cook them until they are just beginning to brown. Take the pan from the heat.
4. Halve the courgettes lengthways. Scoop out the middles, leaving the shells about ⅛ inch (3mm) thick. Lay the shells in a lightly oiled, ovenproof dish.
5. Discard the larger seeds from the scooped out parts and chop the rest. Mix the chopped parts with the onions, thyme and parsley.
6. Spoon the mixture into the shells.
7. Cover the dish with foil and put it into the oven for 20 minutes.
Note: Unsuitable for freezing.

American

9 small zucchini
3 tablespoons olive oil
plus extra for greasing
3 medium onions, finely
chopped
2 garlic cloves, finely
chopped
2 tablespoons chopped
thyme
2 tablespoons chopped
parsley

Mushrooms and Tomatoes in White Wine

Imperial (Metric)

8 oz (225g) button
mushrooms
1 lb (455g) tomatoes
4 tablespoons olive oil
1 large onion, thinly
sliced
1 garlic clove, finely
chopped
3 fl oz (90ml) dry white
wine
1 tablespoon tomato purée
3 tablespoons chopped
fresh coriander

1. Thinly slice the mushrooms. Scald, skin, seed and slice the tomatoes.
2. Heat the oil in a frying pan (skillet) on a low heat. Put in the onion and garlic and soften them.
3. Raise the heat to medium. Put in the mushrooms and stir them for 2 minutes.
4. Pour in the wine and stir in the tomato purée (paste) and coriander.
5. Boil until the liquid is reduced by half.
6. Mix in the tomatoes and heat them through.
Note: If no coriander is available use 6 tablespoons (⅓ cup) chopped parsley. Unsuitable for freezing.

American

½ pound button
mushrooms
1 pound tomatoes
¼ cup olive oil
1 large onion, thinly
sliced
1 garlic clove, finely
chopped
⅓ cup dry white wine
1 tablespoon tomato paste
3 tablespoons chopped
fresh coriander

French Beans with Almonds

Imperial (Metric)

1½ lb (685g) French beans
4 tablespoons sunflower oil
3 oz (85g) flaked almonds
1 garlic clove, finely chopped
2 tablespoons chopped thyme

1. Top and tail the beans. Boil them in lightly salted water for 12 minutes or until they are just tender.
2. Heat the oil in a frying pan (skillet) on a medium heat. Put in the almonds and stir until they are a golden brown. Remove them.
3. Raise the heat. Put in the beans and garlic and stir until the garlic is beginning to brown.
4. Mix in the almonds and thyme and take the pan from the heat.
Note: Unsuitable for freezing.

American

1½ pounds French beans
¼ cup sunflower oil
¾ cup slivered almonds
1 garlic clove, finely chopped
2 tablespoons chopped thyme

Spiced Summer Cabbage with Marigold Petals

Imperial (Metric)

1 large summer cabbage
4 tablespoons olive oil
8 allspice berries, crushed
8 black peppercorns, crushed
4 tablespoons dry white wine
Petals from 6 marigold heads

1. Shred the cabbage.
2. Heat the oil in a saucepan on a high heat. Stir in the cabbage and spices.
3. Lower the heat and add the wine.
4. Cover and cook gently for 10 minutes.
5. Toss in the marigold petals just before serving.
Note: Unsuitable for freezing.

American

1 large summer cabbage
¼ cup olive oil
8 allspice berries, crushed
8 black peppercorns, crushed
¼ cup dry white wine
Petals from 6 marigold heads

Runner Beans with Green Peppers

Imperial (Metric)

1 lb (455g) runner beans
3 green peppers
1 large onion
3 tablespoons olive oil
1 garlic clove, chopped
1 tablespoon chopped marjoram
1 tablespoon chopped thyme

1. Trim and slice the beans.
2. Core and seed the peppers. Cut them into strips 1 by ¼ inch (2.5cm by 6mm).
3. Thinly slice the onion.
4. Heat the oil in a saucepan on a low heat. Put in the onion and garlic and soften them.
5. Mix in the beans, peppers and herbs. Cover and cook gently for 15 minutes, stirring occasionally.
Note: Unsuitable for freezing.

American

1 pound runner beans
3 sweet green peppers
1 large onion
3 tablespoons olive oil
1 garlic clove, chopped
1 tablespoon chopped marjoram
1 tablespoon chopped thyme

Mixed Salad with Dill

Imperial (Metric)

2 eggs, hard-boiled
4 fl oz (125ml) olive oil
2 tablespoons white wine
vinegar
1 garlic clove, crushed
1 large, crisp lettuce
2 ridge cucumbers (or 1
medium glasshouse
cucumber)
1 lb (455g) tomatoes
3 tablespoons chopped
fresh dill

1. Cut the eggs in half. Take out the yolks and rub them through a sieve into a bowl.
2. Gradually beat in 3 tablespoons of the oil and then all the vinegar and the garlic. Beat in the rest of the oil, a little at a time.
3. Shred the lettuce and arrange it as a base on a large serving plate.
4. Thinly slice the cucumbers and arrange the slices over the centre of the lettuce.
5. Slice the tomatoes and arrange them round the edge.
6. Pour the dressing only over the cucumber.
7. Finely chop the egg whites and scatter it over the cucumber.
8. Sprinkle the dill over the cucumber and tomatoes.
Note: Unsuitable for freezing.

American

2 hard-cooked eggs
½ cup olive oil
2 tablespoons white wine
vinegar
1 garlic clove, crushed
1 large, crisp lettuce
2 ridge cucumbers (or 1
medium glasshouse
cucumber)
1 pound tomatoes
3 tablespoons chopped
fresh dill

Runner Beans with Spiced Mustard

Imperial (Metric)

1½ lb (685g) young
runner beans
3 fl oz (90ml) vegetable
stock
1½ teaspoons spiced
granular mustard
1 tablespoon tomato purée

1. Trim the beans and cut each one in half crossways.
2. In a saucepan, mix together the stock, mustard and tomato purée (paste). Bring them to the boil.
3. Put in the beans, cover and cook on a medium heat for 20 minutes, turning the beans half way through.
Note: Unsuitable for freezing.

American

1½ pounds young runner
beans
⅓ cup vegetable stock
1½ teaspoons spiced
granular mustard
1 tablespoon tomato paste

Green Peas and Summer Cabbage

Imperial (Metric)

2 lb (900g) peas in pods
1 summer cabbage
1 oz (30g) butter or
vegetable margarine
¼ pint (140ml) vegetable
stock
4 tablespoons chopped
mint

1. Shell the peas. Shred the cabbage.
2. Melt the butter or margarine in a large saucepan on a high heat. Stir in the cabbage.
3. Pour in the stock and bring it to the boil. Lower the heat and mix in the peas and mint.
4. Cover and cook gently for 15 minutes, stirring once.
Note: Unsuitable for freezing.

American

2 pounds peas in pods
1 summer cabbage
2 tablespoons butter or
vegetable margarine
⅔ cup vegetable stock
¼ cup chopped mint

GRAINS AND PASTA

Summer vegetables, herbs and even fruits will lighten the flavours and textures of grain accompaniments, making them more suitable for the warmer weather.

Brown Rice with Early Plums

Imperial (Metric)

12 oz (340g) long-grain brown rice
8 oz (225g) early red or purple plums
1 oz (30g) butter
1 medium onion, thinly sliced
3 tablespoons chopped fennel

1. Boil the rice in lightly salted water for 45 minutes or until it is tender. Drain it, run cold water through it and drain it again.
2. Halve, stone (pit) and slice the plums.
3. Melt the butter in a frying pan (skillet) on a low heat. Put in the onion and cook it until it is golden.
4. Raise the heat to high and mix in the rice.
5. When the rice has heated through, mix in the plums and fennel. Stir until the plums begin to stain the rice red. Take the pan from the heat.
Note: Unsuitable for freezing.

American

1½ cups long-grain brown rice
½ pound early red or purple plums
2 tablespoons butter
1 medium onion, thinly sliced
3 tablespoons chopped fennel

Millet with Peaches

Imperial (Metric)

4 tablespoons sunflower oil
1 large onion, finely chopped
1 garlic clove, finely chopped
12 oz (340g) millet
1¾ pints (1 litre) vegetable stock
2 large peaches
¼ pint (140ml) natural yogurt
4 tablespoons chopped fennel

1. Heat the oil in a saucepan on a low heat. Put in the onion and garlic and soften them.
2. Put in the millet and stir it for 1 minute.
3. Pour in the stock and bring it to the boil. Cover and simmer for 25 minutes or until all the stock is absorbed and the millet is soft and fluffy.
4. Stone (pit) and dice the peaches while the millet is cooking.
5. Take the pan from the heat and stir in the yogurt, peaches and fennel. Cover and leave to stand for 5 minutes before serving.
Note: Unsuitable for freezing.

American

¼ cup sunflower oil
1 large onion, finely chopped
1 garlic clove, finely chopped
1½ cups millet
4 cups vegetable stock
2 large peaches
⅔ cup unflavored yogurt
4 tablespoons chopped fennel

Pasta Shells with Broad Beans

Imperial (Metric)

2 lb (900g) broad beans
in pods
12 oz (340g) wholemeal
pasta shells
½ oz (15g) butter
6 spring onions, chopped
¼ pint (140ml) vegetable
stock
4 oz (115g) curd cheese
1 tablespoon chopped
savory
4 tablespoons chopped
parsley

1. Shell the beans. Cook them in lightly salted boiling water for 10 minutes. Drain them.
2. Cook the pasta in lightly salted boiling water for 12 minutes or until it is tender. Drain it.
3. Melt the butter in a saucepan on a low heat. Put in the spring onions (scallions) and cook them for 2 minutes.
4. Pour in the stock and bring it to the boil. Take the pan from the heat and add the cheese. Mix well to make a creamy sauce.
5. Fold in the pasta, broad beans and herbs. Gently heat them through.
Note: Unsuitable for freezing.

American

2 pounds broad beans in
pods
¾ pound wholewheat
pasta shells
1 tablespoon butter
6 scallions, chopped
⅔ cup vegetable stock
½ cup curd cheese
1 tablespoon chopped
savory
¼ cup chopped parsley

Rice with Peas and Tarragon

Imperial (Metric)

1½ lb (685g) peas in
pods
4 tablespoons sunflower
oil
12 spring onions, chopped
12 oz (340g) long-grain
brown rice
3 tablespoons chopped
tarragon
1½ pints (850ml)
vegetable stock

1. Shell the peas and reserve two of the best pods.
2. Heat the oil in a saucepan on a low heat. Stir in the spring onions (scallions), rice and tarragon.
3. Pour in the stock and bring it to the boil. Add the two reserved pea pods. Cover and simmer for 30 minutes.
4. Remove the pods and put in the peas. Cover and simmer for a further 15 minutes, or until the rice is tender and all the stock has been absorbed.
Note: To freeze, cool completely. Pack into a rigid container and cover. Store for up to three months. Thaw at room temperature and reheat gently in a saucepan, with a little extra oil if necessary.

American

1½ pounds peas in pods
¼ cup sunflower oil
12 scallions, chopped
1½ cups long-grain brown
rice
3 tablespoons chopped
tarragon
3¾ cups vegetable stock

Rice with Asparagus and Spinach

Imperial (Metric)

12 oz (340g) long-grain
  brown rice
1 lb (455g) asparagus
8 oz (225g) spinach
6 large spring onions
4 tablespoons sunflower
  oil
4 tablespoons chopped
  parsley

1. Cook the rice in lightly salted boiling water for 45 minutes or until it is tender. Drain it, run cold water through it and drain it again.
2. Trim the asparagus. Chop it into 1 inch (2.5cm) lengths. Cook it in gently boiling water for 15 minutes. Drain it.
3. Finely chop the spinach and spring onions (scallions).
4. Heat the oil in a large frying pan (skillet) or paella pan on a high heat. Put in the spinach and spring onions (scallions) and stir-fry them for about 3 minutes, or until the spinach begins to wilt.
5. Quickly mix in the rice, asparagus and parsley and keep stirring to heat them through. Take the pan from the heat.

Note: To freeze, cool completely and pack in a rigid container. Store for up to three months. Thaw at room temperature and reheat by stir-frying in a little more oil.

American

1½ cups long-grain brown
  rice
1 pound asparagus
½ pound spinach
6 large scallions
¼ cup sunflower oil
¼ cup chopped parsley

Buckwheat with Redcurrants

Imperial (Metric)

5 oz (150g) redcurrants
12 oz (340g) buckwheat
1½ pints (850ml)
  vegetable stock
3 tablespoons chopped
  chives
3 tablespoons chopped
  mint

1. String the redcurrants.
2. Put the buckwheat into a heavy frying pan (skillet) or sauté pan. Set it on a medium heat and stir it until it begins to brown and smell nutty. Pour in the stock and bring it to the boil. Cover and simmer for 20 minutes or until all the stock has been absorbed and the buckwheat is light and fluffy.
3. Take the pan from the heat. Stir in the redcurrants and herbs. Cover and leave to stand for 5 minutes.

Note: To freeze, cool completely and pack into a rigid container. Cover. Store for up to 2 months. Thaw at room temperature. Reheat in a saucepan, adding a little oil if necessary.

American

5 ounces redcurrants
1½ cups buckwheat
3¾ cups vegetable stock
3 tablespoons chopped
  chives
3 tablespoons chopped
  mint

Pasta with Basil and Pine Nuts

Imperial (Metric)

12 oz (340g) wholemeal
pasta shapes
4 oz (115g) pine nuts
4 tablespoons olive oil
1 garlic clove, crushed
2 tablespoons chopped
basil
Juice of ½ lemon

1. Cook the pasta in lightly salted boiling water for 12 minutes or until it is tender. Drain it.
2. Finely grind the pine nuts.
3. Heat the oil in a saucepan on a high heat. Stir in the garlic. Let it bubble for a few seconds without browning
4. Lower the heat. Stir in the pine nuts and basil.
5. Fold in the pasta and add the lemon juice. Stir gently to coat the pasta and to heat it through.
Note: To freeze, cool completely. Pack into a rigid container and cover. Store for up to six weeks. Thaw at room temperature. Reheat gently in a saucepan, adding a little more oil if necessary.

American

¾ pound wholewheat
pasta shapes
¾ cup pine nuts
¼ cup olive oil
1 garlic clove, crushed
2 tablespoons chopped
basil
Juice of ½ lemon

Pasta with Runner Beans

Imperial (Metric)

12 oz (340g) wholemeal
pasta shapes
1 lb (455g) runner beans
4 tablespoons olive oil
1 large onion, finely
chopped
1 garlic clove, finely
chopped
4 tablespoons dry white
wine
2 tablespoons chopped
savory

1. Cook the pasta in lightly salted boiling water for 12 minutes or until tender. Drain it.
2. Trim and slice the runner beans.
3. Heat the oil in a saucepan on a low heat. Put in the onion and garlic and soften them.
4. Raise the heat to medium. Stir in the beans. Pour in the wine and bring it to the boil. Add the savory.
5. Cover and cook on a low heat for 15 minutes or until the beans are just tender.
6. Mix the pasta into the beans.
Note: For a sharper flavour, 8 stoned (pitted) and quartered olives may be added with the pasta. 8 oz (225g) scalded, skinned and chopped tomatoes may also be added.
Unsuitable for freezing.

American

¾ pound wholewheat
pasta shapes
1 pound runner beans
¼ cup olive oil
1 large onion, finely
chopped
1 garlic clove, finely
chopped
¼ cup dry white wine
2 tablespoons chopped
savory

DESSERTS

If you enjoy making desserts, then summer is the season for you. Who could fail to be tempted by the delicious array of summer fruits that last from the first gooseberries in early June to the early plums in August. In between there are strawberries and raspberries, black and red currants, cherries, peaches and nectarines, and watermelons.

A simple bowl of strawberries and cream is a treat in itself, or a sliced peach accompanied by a slice of creamy goat's cheese. You can concoct all manner of fruit salads, or use one or more of the recipes that follow.

Strawberry and Cherry Ice-Cream

Imperial (Metric)

12 oz (340g) strawberries
¾ pint (425ml) double cream
8 fl oz (225ml) natural yogurt
3 oz (85g) no-sugar-added strawberry jam
1 lb (455g) red cherries
4 fl oz (125ml) red grape juice
2 tablespoons honey

1. Chop and sieve the strawberries.
2. Lightly whip the cream. Whip in the yogurt and jam (jelly) and then the strawberry purée.
3. Freeze as for Gooseberry and Elderflower Ice (see page 142).
4. Stone (pit) the cherries. Put them into a saucepan with the grape juice and honey. Simmer them for 15 minutes, or until they are soft but still whole. Drain them, reserving the juice, and cool.
5. Chop three quarters of the cherries.
6. After whipping the ice-cream for the last time, mix in the chopped cherries.
7. Put the ice-cream into a rigid container and cover. Put it into the freezer or the ice compartment of the refrigerator for 12 hours.
8. Before serving, put the ice-cream into the refrigerator for 45 minutes.
9. Serve in scoops sprinkled with a little of the cherry juice and garnished with the remaining cherries.
Note: The ice-cream will keep for up to three months in the freezer or up to 2 weeks or according to the star rating in the ice compartment of the refrigerator. The extra cherries do not keep well, so if the ice-cream is to be stored it is best not to use the extra 4 oz (115g).

American

¾ pound strawberries
2 cups heavy cream
1 cup unflavored yogurt
4 tablespoons no-sugar-added strawberry jelly
1 pound red cherries
½ cup red grape juice
2 tablespoons honey

Strawberry Trifle

Imperial (Metric)

12 oz (340g) firm
strawberries
8 oz (225g) wholemeal
cake crumbs
8 oz (225g) ripe
strawberries
¼ pint (140ml) natural
orange juice
Agar-agar to set 1 pint
(570ml) liquid (see
manufacturer's
instructions)
1 teaspoon arrowroot
3 eggs, beaten
3 tablespoons
concentrated apple juice
¾ pint (425ml) milk
1 vanilla pod
½ pint (285ml) double
cream
Decoration:
Glacé cherries, pieces of
angelica, blanched or
flaked almonds

1. If the firm strawberries are small, leave them whole. If larger, halve or quarter them.
2. Put the cake crumbs into a serving dish. Put the firm strawberries on top.
3. Chop and sieve the ripe strawberries.
4. Mix the strawberry purée with the orange juice in a saucepan. Bring the mixture to just below boiling point. Stir in the agar-agar until it has dissolved.
5. Pour the purée mixture over the firm strawberries and cake crumbs.
6. Chill for 1 hour for the jelly to set.
7. Put the arrowroot into a bowl. Beat the eggs and apple juice together and gradually stir into the arrowroot.
8. Put the milk into a saucepan with the vanilla pod and bring it to the boil. Remove the vanilla pod.
9. Stir the milk into the eggs.
10. Pour the custard mixture back into the pan and stir it on a very low heat, without letting it boil, until it becomes thick. Take the pan from the heat and dip the base in cold water to stop the cooking process. Leave the custard to cool completely.
11. Pour the custard over the jelly and put the trifle into the refrigerator for 1 hour.
12. Whip the cream and pipe it over the custard.
13. Decorate with glacé cherries, angelica and almonds.

Note: The amount of cream used is optional. It can either be piped on in small rosettes or more lavishly in circles or a lattice pattern. It could even be omitted altogether if wished.
Unsuitable for freezing.

American

¾ pound firm strawberries
4 cups wholewheat cake
crumbs
½ pound ripe strawberries
⅔ cup natural orange
juice
Agar-agar to set 2½ cups
liquid (see manufacturer's
instructions)
1 teaspoon arrowroot
3 eggs, beaten
3 tablespoons
concentrated apple juice
2 cups milk
1 vanilla pod
1¼ cups heavy cream
Decoration:
Glacé cherries, pieces of
angelica, blanched or
slivered almonds

Cherry Tart

Imperial (Metric)

Pastry:
2 oz (55g) almonds (not blanched)
6 oz (170g) wholemeal flour
Pinch fine sea salt
4 oz (115g) vegetable margarine
Cold water to mix
Filling:
1 lb 4 oz (565g) silken tofu
6 oz (170g) no-sugar-added black cherry jam
1 lb (455g) black or red cherries

1. Heat the oven to 400°F/200°C/Gas Mark 6.
2. Finely grind the almonds. Mix them with the flour and salt. Rub in the margarine and mix to a dough with cold water. Leave the dough in a cool place for 30 minutes.
3. Roll out the dough and use it to line a 10 inch (25cm) tart tin. Line the pastry with greaseproof paper and fill it with beans or screwed-up foil.
4. Bake the pastry case for 10 minutes. Remove the paper and beans or foil. Bake for a further 10 minutes. Cool completely.
5. Put the tofu into a blender or food processor and whip it until it is smooth. Add the jam (jelly) and whip again. Alternatively, rub both tofu and jam (jelly) through a sieve.
6. Put the whipped tofu into the tart case and spread it out evenly.
6. Stone (pit) the cherries and arrange them on top.
Note: If the tart is to stand for longer than 45 minutes, toss the cherries with the juice of a lemon before placing them into the tart.
Unsuitable for freezing.

American

Pastry:
½ cup almonds (not blanched)
1½ cups wholewheat flour
Pinch fine sea salt
½ cup vegetable margarine
Cold water to mix
Filling:
2½ cups silken tofu
½ cup no-sugar-added black cherry jelly
1 pound black or red cherries

Redcurrant and Raspberry Sherbet

Imperial (Metric)

4 oz (115g) redcurrants
4 oz (115g) raspberries, plus extra for garnish
2 tablespoons red grape juice
1 pint (570ml) water
6 oz (170g) honey
¼ pint (140ml) natural yogurt

1. String the redcurrants and put them into a saucepan with the raspberries and grape juice. Cover them and set them on a low heat for 10 minutes, or until the fruits are very juicy.
2. Rub the fruits through a sieve.
3. Boil the water and honey for 5 minutes to make a syrup. Skim it if necessary and stir it into the fruit purée. Cool and chill.
4. Pour the mixture into a freezing tray and freeze it to a slush, about 2 hours.
5. Whip the mixture well and whip in the yogurt.

American

¼ pound redcurrants
¼ pound raspberries, plus extra for garnish
2 tablespoons red grape wine
2½ cups water
½ cup honey
⅔ cup unflavored yogurt

6. Freeze for a further hour and whip again.
7. Put the sherbet into a rigid plastic container. Cover and freeze completely. This will take about 3 hours.
8. Before serving, put the sherbet into the refrigerator for 30 minutes to make it soft enough to scoop.
9. Serve garnished with extra raspberries.
Note: The sherbet will keep for up to three months in the freezer and up to two weeks or according to the star rating for ice-cream, in the ice compartment of the refrigerator.

Watermelon Water Ice

Imperial (Metric)

1 watermelon (about 6 lb/2.5kg)
½ pint (285ml) natural orange juice
4 oz (115g) raisins
¼ pint (140ml) white rum
4 tablespoons chopped mint

American

1 watermelon (about 6 pounds)
1½ cups natural orange juice
⅔ cup raisins
⅔ cup (140ml) white rum
¼ cup chopped mint

1. Take half the watermelon. Slice it and cut away the rind. Dice it and remove the pips. Liquidize the chopped watermelon to a purée in a blender or food processor.
2. Add the orange juice and blend again.
3. Put the purée into a freezing tray. Freeze it for 4 hours, beating it every hour.
4. Put the slushy beaten purée into a rigid container, cover it and freeze it for at least 4 hours.
5. Dice, seed and chill the other half of the watermelon.
6. Soak the raisins in the rum for at least four hours.
7. Before serving, put the water ice into the refrigerator for 30 minutes.
8. Put the diced watermelon into a chilled serving dish. Put scoops of the water ice on top.
9. Sprinkle the raisins and mint over the water ice.
10. Serve as soon as possible.
Note: The water ice will keep for up to two months in the freezer or up to two weeks, or according to the star rating for ice-cream in the ice compartment of the refrigerator.

141

Gooseberry and Elderflower Ice

Imperial (Metric)

1½ lb (685g) gooseberries
2 sprigs elderflowers
5 fl oz (150ml)
elderflower wine (or any
sweet white wine)
3 oz (85g) honey
8 fl oz (225ml) double
cream
8 fl oz (225ml) natural
yogurt
Sauce:
1 lb (455g) gooseberries
2 sprigs elderflowers
3 oz (85g) honey
3 fl oz (90ml) wine as
above
Garnish:
Crystallized violets

1. Put the gooseberries into a saucepan with the elderflower sprigs and wine. Cover and set them on a low heat for 15 minutes, or until they are soft and juicy.
2. Rub them through a sieve.
3. Return the purée to the cleaned pan. Put in the honey. Stir on a low heat for the honey to dissolve. Cool completely.
4. Lightly whip the cream. Whip in the yogurt.
5. Fold the mixture into the gooseberry purée.
6. Pour the mixture into a freezing tray and put it either into the coldest part of the freezer or into the ice compartment of the refrigerator (set at the lowest temperature). Freeze the ice-cream for 1 hour, or until it is slushy
7. Whip the ice-cream to break up the ice particles.
8. Freeze for a further 4 hours, whipping every hour.
9. Whip for a final time. Put the ice-cream into a rigid plastic container and cover.
10. Put the ice-cream into the freezer or ice compartment of the refrigerator (now at a normal setting) and leave it for at least 12 hours.
11. For the sauce, put the gooseberries, elderflower sprigs, honey and wine into a saucepan. Cover and set them on a low heat for 15 minutes. Rub the gooseberries and liquid through a sieve. Cool completely.
12. Before serving, put the ice-cream into the refrigerator for 45 minutes so it becomes soft enough to scoop.
13. Serve with a little of the sauce spooned over the top, garnished with crystallized violets. Any extra sauce may be served separately.

Note: The ice-cream will keep for up to three months in the freezer or for up to

American

1½ pounds gooseberries
2 sprigs elderflowers
⅔ cup elderflower wine
(or any sweet white wine)
¼ cup honey
1 cup heavy cream
1 cup unflavored yogurt
Sauce:
1 pound gooseberries
2 sprigs elderflowers
¼ cup honey
⅓ cup wine as above
Garnish:
Crystallized violets

two weeks, or according to the star rating, in the ice compartment of the refrigerator. The sauce may be frozen in a rigid plastic container for up to three months.

Strawberry Whip Flan

Imperial (Metric)

Base:
6 oz (170g) wholemeal flour
¼ teaspoon bicarbonate of soda
4 oz (115g) clear honey
3 fl oz (90ml) corn oil
3 fl oz (90ml) natural orange juice
3 eggs beaten
Topping:
12 oz (340g) ripe strawberries
12 oz (340g) curd cheese
4 oz (100g) cream cheese
3 tablespoons no-sugar-added strawberry jam
2 tablespoons chopped mixed nuts

1. Heat the oven to 350°F/180°C/Gas Mark 4.
2. Line a 10 inch (25cm) tart tin with oiled greaseproof paper.
3. Put the flour into a bowl with the bicarbonate of (baking) soda. Make a well in the centre. Put in the remaining base ingredients and beat until you have a smooth, thick batter. Alternatively, put all the ingredients into a food processor or blender.
4. Pour the batter into the prepared flan tin. Bake it for 15 minutes or until firm but not coloured. Turn the base onto a wire rack to cool. If wished, once cool, the edge can be trimmed to an even circle.
5. Rub the strawberries through a sieve.
6. Cream the cheeses together until soft. Beat in the jam (jelly). Gradually mix in the strawberries and beat until smooth.
Alternatively put the cheeses and strawberry purée into a blender or food processor.
7. Lay the base on a large serving plate. Spread the strawberry mixture on top in a thick layer. Scatter the chopped mixed nuts over the top.
Note: Extra firm strawberries may be used as a garnish as well as the nuts.
The base may be frozen. Wrap it in clingfilm and freeze it flat. Store for up to 3 months. Thaw on a tray at room temperature. The topping is unsuitable for freezing, although strawberry purée may be frozen for up to 2 months when unsweetened.

American

Base:
1½ cups wholewheat flour
¼ teaspoon baking soda
⅓ cup clear honey
⅓ cup corn oil
⅓ cup natural orange juice
3 eggs beaten
Topping:
¾ pound ripe strawberries
1½ cups curd cheese
½ cup cream cheese
3 tablespoons no-sugar-added strawberry jelly
2 tablespoons chopped mixed nuts

Apricot and Pine Nut Pie

Imperial (Metric)

Pastry:
12 oz (340g) wholemeal flour
1 teaspoon bicarbonate of soda
Pinch fine sea salt
8 oz (225g) butter or vegetable margarine
4 tablespoons cold water
Beaten egg for glaze
Filling:
1½ lb (685g) apricots
1½ oz pine nuts
3 oz (85g) clear honey
4 oz (115g) sultanas
½ teaspoon ground mace

1. Heat the oven to 400°F/200°C/Gas Mark 6.
2. For the pastry, put the flour into a bowl with the bicarbonate of (baking) soda and salt. Rub in the butter or margarine. Mix to a dough with the cold water. Leave the pastry in a warm place for 30 minutes.
3. Stone (pit) and slice the apricots.
4. Mix them in a bowl with the pine nuts, honey, sultanas (golden seedless raisins) and mace.
5. Roll out two thirds of the pastry and line a 10 inch (25cm) tart tin.
6. Put in the apricot mixture.
7. Cover with the remaining pastry. Seal the edges and brush the top with beaten egg.
8. Bake the pie for 30 minutes, or until it is golden brown.
9. Serve warm.

Note: Greek-style natural (unflavored) yogurt makes an ideal accompaniment. Freeze in the tin, sealed in a polythene bag. Store for up to three months. Reheat by putting directly from the freezer into a hot oven for 20 minutes.

American

Pastry:
3 cups wholewheat flour
1 teaspoon baking soda
Pinch fine sea salt
1 cup butter or vegetable margarine
4 tablespoons cold water
Beaten egg for glaze
Filling:
1½ pounds apricots
4 tablespoons pine nuts
4 tablespoons clear honey
⅔ cup golden seedless raisins
½ teaspoon ground mace

Cherry Brûlée

1 lb (455g) red cherries
Juice of 1 lemon
2 teaspoons arrowroot
4 tablespoons milk
4 eggs, beaten
½ pint (285ml) double cream
3 tablespoons no-sugar-added black cherry jam
½ pint (285ml) natural yogurt
4 tablespoons Barbados sugar

1 pound red cherries
Juice of 1 lemon
2 teaspoons arrowroot
4 tablespoons milk
4 eggs, beaten
1¼ cups heavy cream
3 tablespoons no-sugar-added black cherry jelly
1¼ cups unflavored yogurt
4 tablespoons Barbados sugar

1. Stone (pit) the cherries. Put them into a large soufflé dish and sprinkle them with the lemon juice.
2. Mix the arrowroot with the milk.
3. Put the eggs into the top of a double boiler.
4. Bring the cream to just below boiling point and stir it into the eggs.
5. Stir in the arrowroot and milk mixture.
6. Stir the mixture over water on a low heat until it is thick. Do not let the water boil. Cool completely.
7. Stir the jam (jelly) and the yogurt into the custard mixture.
8. Pour the mixture into the cherries.
9. Chill for 1 hour.
10. Just before serving, heat the grill (broiler) to high. Sprinkle the sugar over the top of the custard.
11. Put the dish under the grill (broiler), 2-3 inches (5-7.5cm) away from the heat, for 2-3 minutes, watching carefully to prevent burning. The sugar should melt and caramelize.
12. Chill the brûlée again so the sugar sets.
13. Break the sugar with the back of a spoon before serving.

Note: If no double boiler is available, use a bowl standing in a saucepan of water, on a trivet if possible.

Unsuitable for freezing.

145

Gooseberry Mousse Tart

Imperial (Metric)

Shortcrust pastry made with 8 oz (225g) wholemeal flour (see page 24)
1½ (685g) gooseberries
¼ pint (140ml) sweet white wine
8 oz (225g) pear and apple spread
Agar-agar to set 1½ pints (850ml) liquid (see manufacturer's instructions)
2 eggs, separated
½ pint (285ml) Greek-style natural yogurt
Almonds for garnish

1. Heat the oven to 400°F/200°C/Gas Mark 6.
2. Line a 10 inch (25cm) tart tin with the pastry. Line the pastry with greaseproof paper and fill it with either beans or screwed-up foil. Bake the tart shell for 10 minutes. Remove the paper and beans or foil. Bake for a further 10 minutes. Cool the shell completely.
3. Top and tail the gooseberries. Put them into a saucepan with the wine and pear and apple spread. Cover them and cook them gently for 15 minutes or until they are soft but still whole.
4. Reserve 12 of the best looking gooseberries for garnish. Either purée the rest in a blender or food processor, or rub them through a sieve.
5. Return the purée to the cleaned pan and bring it to just below boiling point. Stir in the agar-agar until it dissolves. Take the pan from the heat.
6. Beat in the egg yolks, one at a time. Leave the mixture to cool a little.
7. Stiffly whip the egg whites. Fold them into the gooseberry purée.
8. Fold in the yogurt.
9. Pour the mixture into the pastry shell.
10. Leave the tart in a cool place or in the refrigerator for 2 hours to set.
11. Before serving, garnish with the whole gooseberries and the almonds.
Note: Unsuitable for freezing.

American

Shortcrust pastry made with 2 cups wholewheat flour (see page 24)
1½ pounds gooseberries
⅔ cup sweet white wine
⅔ cup pear and apple spread
Agar-agar to set 3¾ cups liquid (see manufacturer's instructions)
2 eggs, separated
1¼ cups Greek-style unflavored yogurt
Almonds for garnish

Raspberry and Peach Syllabub

Imperial (Metric)

1½ lb (685g) raspberries
2 medium peaches
2 oz (55g) honey
10 oz (285g) silken tofu
3 tablespoons toasted
flaked coconut

1. Sieve 8 oz (225g) of the raspberries.
2. Put the peaches into a bowl. Pour boiling water over them and leave them for 2 minutes. Skin, stone (pit) and chop them. Either rub them through a sieve or purée them in a blender or food processor.
3. Either, put both purées into a blender or food processor with the honey and tofu and liquidize to a smooth purée; or, rub the tofu through a sieve and beat in the fruit purées and the honey.
4. Put half the remaining raspberries into a large serving bowl. Spoon half the tofu mixture on top.
5. Repeat the layers.
6. Scatter the toasted coconut on top.
7. Chill slightly before serving.

American

1½ pounds raspberries
2 medium peaches
3 tablespoons honey
1¼ cups silken tofu
3 tablespoons toasted
slivered coconut

Gooseberry Cream Pie

Imperial (Metric)

Pastry:
12 oz (340g) wholemeal
flour
1 teaspoon bicarbonate of
soda
Pinch fine sea salt
6 oz (170g) vegetable
margarine
Cold water to mix
Beaten egg for glaze
Filling:
1½ lb (685g) gooseberries
4 oz (115g) clear honey
¼ teaspoon ground mace
1 teaspoon ground
cinnamon
3 fl oz (90ml) double
cream

1. Heat the oven to 400°F/200°C/Gas Mark 6.
2. Put the flour, bicarbonate of (baking) soda and salt into a bowl. Rub in the vegetable margarine. Mix to a dough with cold water. Leave the dough in a cool place for 30 minutes.
3. Top and tail the gooseberries and mix them with the honey, mace and cinnamon.
4. Roll out two thirds of the pastry and use it to line a 10 inch (25cm) tart tin.
5. Put in the gooseberries. Spoon the cream over the top.
6. Cover with the remaining pastry. Seal the edges and brush the top with beaten egg.
7. Bake the pie for 45 minutes or until the top is golden brown.
8. Serve hot.
Note: No accompaniment is needed as the filling is so rich.
Unsuitable for freezing.

American

Pastry:
3 cups wholewheat flour
1 teaspoon baking soda
Pinch fine sea salt
¾ cup vegetable
margarine
Cold water to mix
Beaten egg for glaze
Filling:
1½ pounds gooseberries
⅔ cup clear honey
¼ teaspoon ground mace
1 teaspoon ground
cinnamon
⅓ cup heavy cream

Stuffed Nectarines

Imperial (Metric)

12 nectarines
4 oz (115g) stoned dates
4 oz (115g) almonds (not blanched)
4 oz (115g) hazelnuts
4 fl oz (125ml) Cointreau
¼ pint (140ml) natural orange juice
½ pint (285ml) double cream
6 glacé cherries

1. Heat the oven to 350°F/180°C/Gas Mark 4.
2. Put the nectarines into a bowl. Pour the boiling water over them and leave them for 2 minutes. Skin, halve and stone (pit) them.
3. Put the nectarine halves, cut side up, into a large, shallow, ovenproof dish.
4. Finely chop the dates. Either mince them with the nuts and mix in half the Cointreau; or put the dates, nuts and half the Cointreau into a food processor and finely chop them to a minced consistency.
5. Fill the nectarines with the date and nut mixture.
6. Pour the orange juice round the nectarines.
7. Bake for 10 minutes. Cool completely, in the dish. Remove the nectarines to a serving plate.
8. Whip the cream. Whip in the rest of the Cointreau. Pipe the mixture on top of the nectarines.
9. Top with the cherries, cut into quarters.

Note: This can also be made with small peaches. Unsuitable for freezing.

American

12 nectarines
¼ pound pitted dates
1 cup almonds (not blanched)
1 cup hazelnuts
½ cup Cointreau
⅔ cup natural orange juice
1¼ cups heavy cream
6 glacé cherries

Summer Fruit Mould

Imperial (Metric)

8 oz (225g) blackcurrants
8 oz (225g) redcurrants
12 oz (340g) raspberries
6 oz (170g) honey
Agar-agar to set 1½ pints (850ml) liquid (see manufacturer's instructions)
8 oz (225g) strawberries
8 fl oz (225ml) double cream
Hazelnuts for garnish

1. String the blackcurrants and redcurrants.
2. Put the black and redcurrants and raspberries into a saucepan with the honey. Cover them and set them on a low heat for 15 minutes, or until they are soft and juicy.
3. Stir in the agar-agar and stir until it has dissolved. Take the pan from the heat.
4. Quarter the strawberries and mix them into the rest.

American

½ pound blackcurrants
½ pound redcurrants
¾ pound raspberries
½ cup honey
Agar-agar to set 3¾ cups liquid (see manufacturer's instructions)
½ pound strawberries
1 cup heavy cream
Hazelnuts for garnish

148

5. Pour the fruits and liquid into a serving bowl.

6. Put the mould into a cool place or into the refrigerator to set.

7. Whip the cream and pipe it in rosettes on top of the mould.

8. Put a hazelnut on top of each rosette of cream.

Note: Unsuitable for freezing.

Raspberry Cake

Imperial (Metric)

4 oz (115g) dried whole apricots
2 oz (55g) dried apple rings
½ pint (285ml) natural orange juice
6 oz (170g) wholemeal flour
1 teaspoon bicarbonate of soda
3 fl oz (90ml) corn oil, plus extra for greasing
3 eggs, beaten
8 oz (225g) curd cheese
3 tablespoons no-sugar-added raspberry jam
8 oz (225g) raspberries

American

¼ pound dried whole apricots
2 ounces dried apple rings
1¼ cups natural orange juice
1½ cups wholewheat flour
1 teaspoon baking soda
⅓ cup corn oil, plus extra for greasing
3 eggs, beaten
1 cup curd cheese
3 tablespoons no-sugar-added raspberry jelly
½ pound raspberries

1. Put the apricots and apple rings into a saucepan with the orange juice. Bring them to the boil, take them from the heat and leave them for 4 hours.

2. Drain the fruits, reserving the juice. Liquidize them with 3 fl oz (90ml/⅓ cup) of the juice.

3. Heat the oven to 350°F/180°C/Gas Mark 4.

4. Put the flour into a mixing bowl. Toss in the bicarbonate of (baking) soda. Make a well in the centre.

5. Put in the oil and begin to beat in the flour from the sides of the well. Beat in the eggs and then the liquidized fruits.

6. Divide the mixture between two 7 inch (18cm) diameter sponge tins.

7. Bake the cakes for 20 minutes, or until they are firm and springy. Turn them onto wire racks to cool.

8. Cream the cheese in a bowl and beat in the jam (jelly).

9. Spread half the cheese mixture on one cake and put on half the raspberries.

10. Sandwich the cakes together.

11. Spread the top with the remaining cheese and garnish with the remaining raspberries.

Note: The cakes may be frozen. Wrap them in clingfilm and freeze on trays. Store for up to three months. Thaw on a rack at room temperature. The filling is unsuitable for freezing.

Cherry Batter

Imperial (Metric)

1½ lb (685g) sweet black cherries
Butter for greasing
1½ teaspoons vanilla essence
4 oz (115g) wholemeal flour
Pinch fine sea salt
3 oz (85g) clear honey
5 eggs
¾ pint (425ml) milk

1. Heat the oven to 350°F/180°C/Gas Mark 4.
2. Stone (pit) the cherries. Put them into a large, greased 2 inch (5cm) deep, ovenproof dish. Sprinkle in half the vanilla essence.
3. Put the flour and salt into a mixing bowl. Make a well in the centre. Put in the honey and break in the eggs.
4. Add 3 fl oz (90ml/⅓ cup) of the milk.
5. Beat the eggs and milk together with a wire whisk and then gradually beat in the flour from the sides of the bowl.
6. Add the remaining vanilla essence to the rest of the milk. Beat them into the flour mixture. Beat until you have a smooth batter.
7. Pour the batter over the cherries.
8. Bake for 1 hour. Serve warm.
Note: Unsuitable for freezing.

American

1½ pounds sweet black cherries
Butter for greasing
1½ teaspoons vanilla essence
1 cup wholewheat flour
Pinch fine sea salt
¼ cup clear honey
5 eggs
2 cups milk

Variations:

Peach and/or Nectarine Batter

Make as above, using six peaches or nectarines or three of each.

Plum Batter

Make as above, using 1½ lb (680g/1½ pounds) plums, stoned (pitted) and sliced.

Entertaining in Autumn

Autumn comes gradually, its weather and its produce overlapping with those of summer. The warm days of the past few months continue for a while, but suddenly, some time in the first two weeks of September, there is a chill in the evening air, a light mist in the morning and a thick dew hanging on the cobwebs on the garden gate. Autumn has arrived. As the season goes on, it becomes colder and damper and the food that we prepare should in some way match the weather.

In the early, warmer days, there are still runner beans, marrows, plums and tomatoes to be picked together with basil, chervil and parsley which still flourish in the herb garden. Courgettes (zucchini) and red and green peppers are at their best after the long hours of summer sun. I always associate mushrooms with autumn, although now they are cultivated in sheds and are with us all the year round. Regulations forbid greengrocers to sell field mushrooms nowadays, but I still have recent memories of going out with a basket and knife in hand to search the dewy grass in local orchards. Mushrooms should always feature in autumn cookery.

I always grow pumpkins, and they are becoming increasingly available in the shops. One plant can spread all over the garden and produce anything up to ten 'golden coaches', more than enough to supply our culinary needs and lanterns for Hallowe'en as well. The pumpkin is an amazingly versatile vegetable. Its flavour is bland but deliciously creamy which enables it to be turned into both sweet and savoury dishes. Its texture is creamy, too, so it is ideal for soups.

Sweetcorn is another vegetable peculiar to autumn. It reminds me of those tantalizing Indian summers, when we are hoodwinked into believing that winter is still far away. It is best in the spicy dishes typical of its South American home.

Many homes are pervaded by the sharp smell of pickles and chutneys in the autumn, brought about by housewives anxious to preserve as much of the season's abundant produce as possible. Jars of green tomato chutney and pickled onions will grace many a larder shelf by the end of October, but don't pickle them all. Button onions make a delightful vegetable, either as a side dish or in casseroles, and green tomatoes can be made into soups and added to vegetable dishes.

Watercress has a growth spurt in the autumn and is generally cut until the worst of the winter's frosts arrive. It is often more associated with spring, but it makes superb salads with autumn fruits and vegetables, and can also give flavour to cooked dishes.

Potatoes are probably at their best in the autumn, very firm and with no black 'eyes'. When baked in their jackets they are absolutely delicious. Green autumn cabbages and calabrese add a green freshness to the autumn dinner table and maincrop carrots are crisp and firm.

The fruits of autumn are many. In the early part of the season you can buy a wide variety of plums and greengages and later damsons have their own short season. Summer apples are sharp, but autumn apples are mellow and at their best in the shops since they have been freshly picked instead of coming out of the cold store. It is also better to wait for the real autumn days before you buy cooking apples. Only then will they cook down to a soft, fluffy purée.

Blackberrying is one of my favourite autumn occupations. After an hour's picking, you can come home scratched, red fingered, but exceedingly pleased with yourself for having gathered, on a good day, maybe nearly three pounds of the juicy black fruits. Mix them with apples or use them, rather extravagantly, alone.

There is nothing like the taste of a pear, freshly picked from the tree on a frosty autumn morning, and whether you buy pears or pick them, they will never be better than in October. Then you can buy the short-seasoned, impossible to store, dessert pears, besides the cooking varieties such as Conference, which are put into store for the winter.

With all this home-grown produce, there is little need to look for imported fruits, but there are two that have such a short season that they are well worth buying to enjoy in one or two unusual dishes. These are fresh figs and pomegranates.

Nuts always seem to be the most typical main ingredient for autumn main dishes. Whether they are ground to make nut roasts and patties, stir-fried with vegetables or put into a pie, they are always most welcome. Grains, too, whether as side-dishes or combined with other ingredients in a main dish, seem to have the right flavour and texture for this time of the year. There are no bank holidays in autumn, just two traditional festivals which I always love to keep. First comes Hallowe'en, with its lanterns made from pumpkins and placed in windows to keep witches and evil spirits away. Young girls once named hazelnuts after their suitors and lined them up in front of the fire. The first one to crack and jump would bear the name of the one they would marry. Games played on this night include Bob-Apples (attempting to bite apples that are floating in a bucket of water) and Snap-dragons, in which burning brandy is poured over raisins which have to be pulled out of the pile without too many burned fingers. Whether you plan to have a buffet or an informal dinner party on that night, all these games will help to set the scene.

There is something about bonfires and fireworks that for me is pure magic and a carefully organized bonfire at home will always to me be more enjoyable than a large event in a playing field. Bonfire Night is an outdoor party and so your food must be warming, even though you may be serving it inside. After the fireworks, give everyone a mug of hot soup while you stand by the barbecue or the indoor grill putting finishing touches to burgers and sausages, watching the guy burn to ashes and the sparklers drawing pictures in the air. However, if you would rather go to a large event, why not enjoy the food at home afterwards?

After bonfire night, the cold weather really sets in; pumpkins and sweetcorn disappear. We are looking forward to winter.

SPECIAL MENUS

Three of the following special menus are intended to be served on one or other of the festivals of late autumn: Hallowe'en and Bonfire Night.

At any Hallowe'en party, be it formal or informal, you can follow in the old traditions by including pumpkin, apples and hazelnuts in your menu. Combine these with other seasonal vegetables such as green cabbage and baby onions and you have a wide variety of recipes with which to please everyone.

For the Bonfire Night menu, the dip, salads and barbecue sauce can all be made in advance so that you do not have too much work to do.

When the winter evenings draw in, there is nothing like Sunday tea round the fire. The tea-time menu is easy to serve and can quite easily be eaten on laps as well as at the tea table.

Hallowe'en Dinner Party (for 6 people)

Stuffed Mushrooms
Macaroni with Tomato and Hazelnut Sauce
Cauldron Stew
Snapdragon Pudding

Stuffed Mushrooms

Imperial (Metric)

6 large, open mushrooms, about 2½ inches (6cm) across
1 oz (30g) butter
1 small onion, finely chopped
2 oz (55g) fresh wholemeal breadcrumbs
2 oz (55g) Edam cheese, grated
4 tablespoons chopped parsley
1 tablespoon capers
Watercress sprigs
3 tomatoes, cut into small wedges

1. Heat the oven to 400°F/200°C/Gas Mark 6.
2. Trim the stalks from the mushrooms and finely chop them.
3. Use half the butter to grease a large, 2 inch (5cm) deep, ovenproof dish. Put in the mushroom caps, top side down.
4. Melt the remaining butter in a frying pan (skillet) on a low heat. Put in the onion and soften it. Raise the heat to moderate. Mix in the chopped mushroom stalks and cook them for 1 minute, stirring.
5. Take the pan from heat. Mix in the breadcrumbs, cheese, parsley and capers.
6. Fill the mushroom caps with the mixture.
7. Bake the mushrooms for 15 minutes or until the crumbs on top are brown.
8. Serve garnished with watercress sprigs and tomato wedges.
Note: Unsuitable for freezing.

American

6 large, open mushrooms, about 2½ inches across
2 tablespoons butter
1 small onion, finely chopped
1 cup fresh wholewheat breadcrumbs
½ cup grated Edam cheese
¼ cup chopped parsley
1 tablespoon capers
Watercress sprigs
3 tomatoes, cut into small wedges

Macaroni with Tomato and Hazelnut Sauce

Imperial (Metric)

12 oz (340g) wholemeal
macaroni
3 oz (85g) hazelnuts
1 lb (455g) ripe tomatoes
4 tablespoons olive oil
1 medium onion, finely
chopped
1 garlic clove, finely
chopped
1 tablespoon chopped
fresh basil or 1 teaspoon
dried basil
1 tablespoon chopped
thyme

1. Cook the macaroni in lightly salted boiling water for 12 minutes or until it is just tender. Drain it, refresh it with cold water and drain it again.
2. Finely grind the hazelnuts. Scald, seed and finely chop the tomatoes.
3. Heat the oil in a saucepan on a low heat. Put in the onions and garlic to soften them.
4. Put in the tomatoes and herbs, cover and cook for 10 minutes. Stir in the ground nuts.
5. Mix in the pasta and heat it through gently.
Note: To freeze, cool completely. Pack into a rigid container and cover. Store for up to 1 month. Thaw at room temperature and reheat in a saucepan.

American

3 cups wholewheat
macaroni
⅔ cups hazelnuts
1 pound ripe tomatoes
¼ cup olive oil
1 medium onion, finely
chopped
1 garlic clove, finely
chopped
1 tablespoon chopped
fresh basil or 1 teaspoon
dried basil
1 tablespoon chopped
thyme

Cauldron Stew

Imperial (Metric)

1 large pumpkin, about
10 lb (5.5kg)
1 lb (455g) carrots
1 lb (455g) green cabbage
4 tablespoons sunflower
oil
2 large onions, thinly
sliced
2 garlic cloves, finely
chopped
1 tablespoon paprika
½ teaspoon chilli powder
1 pint (570ml) vegetable
stock
12 oz (340 g) butter
beans, soaked and cooked
for 1 hour
½ pint (285ml) soured
cream

1. Heat the oven to 350°F/180°C/Gas Mark 4.
2. Slice the top off the pumpkin. Scoop out all the seeds and pith from both the cap and the main part. Put the pumpkin on an ovenproof dish.
3. Thinly slice the carrots. Shred the cabbage.
4. Heat the oil in a large saucepan on a low heat. Put in the carrots, onions and garlic. Cover and cook gently for 10 minutes. Stir in the paprika and chilli powder and cabbage.
5. Pour in the stock and bring it to the boil.
6. Add the butter (Lima) beans and stir in half the soured cream.
7. Ladle the contents of the pan into the pumpkin. Put in the bay leaf. Put on the cap.
8. Bake the pumpkin for 1 hour 30 minutes.

American

1 large pumpkin, about
10 pounds
1 pound carrots
1 pound green cabbage
¼ cup sunflower oil
2 large onions, thinly
sliced
2 garlic cloves, finely
chopped
1 tablespoon paprika
½ teaspoon chili powder
2½ cups vegetable stock
2 cups Lima beans,
soaked and cooked for 1
hour
1¼ cups sour cream

9. Take off the cap. Spoon the remaining soured cream over the top of the stew.
10. Serve either straight from the dish or carefully transfer the pumpkin to another dish. Spoon out the stew, together with some of the pumpkin flesh which should be soft and creamy.
Note: Unsuitable for freezing.

Snapdragon Pudding

Imperial (Metric)

12 oz (340g) raisins
6 fl oz (175ml) brandy
6 oz (170g) wholemeal flour
1 teaspoon bicarbonate of soda
3 eggs, beaten
6 oz (170g) honey, melted
3 fl oz (90ml) corn oil
3 fl oz (90ml) orange juice
Sauce:
¼ pint (140ml) natural yogurt
8 oz (225g) low-fat soft cheese
2 tablespoons honey

1. Soak the raisins overnight in the brandy. Drain them, reserving the brandy.
2. Put the flour and bicarbonate of (baking) soda into a mixing bowl. Make a well in the centre and gradually beat in the eggs, taking in flour from the sides of the well. Beat in the honey, corn oil and orange juice in the same way.
3. Fold in three-quarters of the raisins.
4. Put the mixture into a greased, 1½ pint (850ml/3¾ cup) pudding basin. Cover it with a layer of greased greaseproof paper and one of foil. Tie them down securely.
5. Bring a saucepan of water to the boil. Lower in the pudding. Steam it for 1 hour 30 minutes, never letting it come off the boil and adding more water as and when necessary.
6. Beat first the yogurt and then the reserved brandy into the cheese. Whip the honey into this mixture. Fold in the reserved raisins.
7. Turn the pudding onto a warm serving plate. Spoon a little of the sauce over the top and serve the rest separately.
Note: To freeze, the cooled pudding, wrap in clingfilm and put it into a polythene bag. Freeze it on a plate or tray so that it keeps its shape. Store for up to three months. Once thawed, return the pudding to its bowl, cover with greaseproof and foil and steam for 20 minutes.
Sauce is unsuitable for freezing.

American

3 cups raisins
¾ cup brandy
1½ cups wholewheat flour
1 teaspoon baking soda
3 eggs, beaten
½ cup honey, melted
⅓ cup corn oil
⅓ cup orange juice
Sauce:
⅔ cup unflavored yogurt
1 cup low-fat soft cheese
2 tablespoons honey

Hallowe'en Buffet Party (for 6-8 people)

Pumpkin, Cheese and Tomato Tart
Baby Onion Pie
Potato and Celery Salad
Cabbage, Carrot and Picked Walnut Salad
Apple and Hazelnut Layers
Bob-Apple Jelly

Pumpkin, Cheese and Tomato Tart

Imperial (Metric)

1½ lb (685g) pumpkin
Shortcrust pastry made
  with 8 oz (225g)
  wholemeal flour
  (see page 24)
12 oz (340g) tomatoes
1 oz (30g) butter or
  vegetable margarine
1 large onion, thinly
  sliced
4 eggs, beaten
¼ pint (140ml) milk
4 oz (115g) Cheddar
  cheese, grated
2 tablespoons tomato
  purée
1 teaspoon paprika
Pinch cayenne pepper
2 tablespoons chopped
  parsley
1 tablespoon chopped
  thyme
Pinch fine sea salt

American

1½ pounds pumpkin
Shortcrust pastry made
with 2 cups wholewheat
  flour
  (see page 24)
¾ pound tomatoes
2 tablespoons butter or
  vegetable margarine
1 large onion, thinly
  sliced
4 eggs, beaten
⅔ cup milk
1 cup Cheddar cheese,
  grated
2 tablespoons tomato
  paste
1 teaspoon paprika
Pinch cayenne pepper
2 tablespoons chopped
  parsley
1 tablespoon chopped
  thyme
Pinch fine sea salt

1. Heat the oven to 400°F/200°C/Gas Mark 6.
2. Cut the rind, pith and seeds from the pumpkin. Cut the flesh into ¾ inch (2cm) dice. Wrap it in lightly oiled foil and bake it for 40 minutes. Mash it and rub it through a sieve.
3. Turn the oven to 350°F/180°C/Gas Mark 4.
4. Roll out the pastry and use it to line a 10 inch (25cm) tart tin.
5. Thinly slice the tomatoes and lay them in the base.
6. Melt the butter or margarine in a frying pan (skillet) on a low heat. Put in the onion and soften it. Take it from the heat.
7. In a bowl, mix the eggs, milk, cheese, tomato purée (paste), paprika, cayenne pepper and herbs. Season lightly with salt. Stir in the onion and the pumpkin.
8. Pour the mixture over the tomatoes. The pastry shell will be very full.
9. Bake the pie for 45 minutes or until the filling is set and golden brown.
10. Serve warm or cold.

Note: To freeze, cool completely. Either remove the tin and place the tart on a tray and freeze flat; or freeze in the tin. Seal in a polythene bag. Store for up to 1 month. Reheat from frozen by placing in a hot oven for 20 minutes.

Baby Onion Pie

Imperial (Metric)

12 oz (340g) button
onions
Shortcrust pastry made
with 12 oz (340g)
wholemeal flour
(see page 24)
8 oz (225g) Lancashire
cheese
1½ oz (45g) butter or
vegetable margarine
1 oz (30g) wholemeal
flour
½ pint (285ml) milk
¼ pint (140ml) vegetable
stock
2 teaspoons made English
mustard
1 garlic clove, crushed
2 eggs, separated
4 tablespoons chopped
parsley

1. Heat the oven to 400°F/200°C/Gas Mark 6.
2. Peel the onions. Put them into a pan of boiling water and cook them for 10 minutes. Drain them.
3. Roll out two thirds of the pastry and use it to line a 10 inch (25cm) tart tin.
4. Cut the cheese into thin shavings. Put them into the tart tin. Put the onions on top.
5. Melt the butter or margarine in a saucepan on a medium heat. Stir in the flour, milk and stock. Bring them to the boil, stirring. Simmer for 2 minutes.
6. Take the pan from the heat. Beat in the mustard, garlic, egg yolks and parsley. Pour the mixture over the onions.
7. Cover the pie with the remaining pastry and brush the top with the egg whites.
8. Bake the pie for 30 minutes or until the top is golden brown. Serve warm or cold.

Note: To freeze, cool completely. Freeze either in the tin or on a tray. Wrap in a polythene bag. Reheat by putting into a preheated 400°F/200°C/Gas Mark 6 oven for 20 minutes.

American

¾ pound button onions
Shortcrust pastry made
with 3 cups wholewheat
flour
(see page 24)
½ pound mild white
cheese
1½ oz (45g) butter or
vegetable margarine
¼ cup wholewheat flour
1¼ cups milk
⅔ cup vegetable stock
2 teaspoons made English
mustard
1 garlic clove, crushed
2 eggs, separated
¼ cup chopped parsley

Potato and Celery Salad

Imperial (Metric)

2½ lb (1.15kg) potatoes
1 head celery
3 fl oz (90ml)
mayonnaise
2 teaspoons Dijon
mustard
¼ pint (140ml) dry white
wine
6 sage leaves, chopped

1. Scrub the potatoes and boil them in their skins until they are just tender. Skin them as soon as they are cool enough to handle. Dice them.
2. Chop the celery. Mix together the mayonnaise and mustard.
3. Return the potatoes to the saucepan. Set them on a high heat. Pour in the wine and bring to the boil.
4. Take the pan from the heat. Fold in the mayonnaise mixture and the sage.
5. Cool completely. Mix in the celery.
Note: Unsuitable for freezing.

American

2½ lb pounds potatoes
1 head celery
⅓ cup mayonnaise
2 teaspoons Dijon
mustard
⅔ cup dry white wine
6 sage leaves, chopped

Cabbage, Carrot and Pickled Walnut Salad

Imperial (Metric)

1 medium white cabbage
8 oz (225g) carrots
6 pickled walnuts
3 fl oz (90ml) olive oil
2 tablespoons cider
    vinegar
1 garlic clove, crushed
Freshly ground black
    pepper

1. Shred the cabbage. Finely grate the carrots. Finely chop the pickled walnuts. Put all these into a salad bowl.
2. Beat together the remaining ingredients to make the dressing.
3. Fold the dressing into the salad.
4. Leave the salad to stand for 15 minutes before serving.

American

1 medium white cabbage
½ pound carrots
6 pickled English walnuts
⅓ cup olive oil
2 tablespoons cider
    vinegar
1 garlic clove, crushed
Freshly ground black
    pepper

Bob-Apple Jelly

Imperial (Metric)

1½ lb (685g) dessert
    apples
1 pint (570ml) apple juice
2-inch (5cm) cinnamon
    stick
4 cloves
½ pint (285ml) dry cider
2 tablespoons honey
Agar-agar to set 1 pint
    (570ml) liquid
    (see manufacturer's
    instructions)
Filling:
8 oz (225g) silken tofu
2 tablespoons honey
Freshly grated nutmeg

1. Peel and core the apples. Cut them in half lengthways and then into thin slices, crossways.
2. Put the apple juice into a saucepan with the cinnamon stick and cloves. Bring it to the boil and put in the apples. Poach them gently for 10-15 minutes, or until they are soft but still intact. Drain the apples, reserving the juice and the cinnamon stick.
3. Arrange the apples in the base of a 2 pint (1.1 litre/5 cup) ring mould.
4. Return the apple juice to the saucepan with the cinnamon stick. Add the cider and honey. Stir on a low heat for the honey to dissolve.
5. Bring to the liquid to just below boiling point. Stir in the agar-agar and keep stirring on the heat until it has dissolved.
6. Cool the jelly slightly and pour it over the apples in the mould. Leave the jelly in a cool place for 2 hours to set.
7. Drain the tofu and whip it in a blender or food processor. Beat in the honey and about one eighth of a nutmeg.
8. Turn the jelly out of the mould. Fill it with the tofu. Grate a little extra nutmeg over the top.
Note: Unsuitable for freezing.

American

1½ pounds dessert apples
2½ cups apple juice
2-inch cinnamon stick
4 cloves
1¼ cups dry cider
2 tablespoons honey
Agar-agar to set 2½ cups
    liquid
    (see manufacturer's
    instructions)
Filling:
1 cup silken tofu
2 tablespoons honey
Freshly grated nutmeg

158

Apple and Hazelnut Layers

Imperial (Metric)

2 lb (900g) cooking
apples
2 thinly pared strips
lemon rind
2 oz (55g) butter
4 oz (115g) no-sugar-
added apricot jam
4 oz (115g) hazelnuts
8 oz (225g) Danish rye
bread
3 tablespoons no-sugar-
added mixed berry jam
¼ pint (140ml) double
cream
4 oz (115g) low-fat soft
cheese
Angelica and extra
hazelnuts for garnish

1. Core and chop the apples, without peeling them. Put them into a saucepan with the lemon rind, half the butter and the apricot jam (jelly). Cover them and set them on a low heat for 15 minutes or until they can be beaten to a thick purée. Rub them through a sieve and cool them completely.

2. Finely grind the hazelnuts. Make the rye bread into crumbs.

3. Melt the remaining butter in a frying pan (skillet) on a low heat. Stir in the crumbs, raise the heat to medium and cook, stirring, until the crumbs are crisp.

4. Take the pan from the heat and mix the berry jam (jelly) and ground hazelnuts into the crumbs. Cool the mixture completely.

5. Put one third of the crumbs into a 1½ pint (3¾ cups) soufflé dish (or other suitable high-sided dish). Put in half the apple purée, another third of the crumbs, remaining purée and remaining crumbs. Chill the pudding for 1 hour.

6. Whip the cream and beat in the cheese. Pile the mixture on top of the top layer of crumbs.

7. Decorate with pieces of angelica and extra hazelnuts.

Note: Unsuitable for freezing.

American

2 pounds cooking apples
2 thinly pared strips
lemon rind
¼ cup butter
⅔ cup no-sugar-added
apricot jelly
¾ cup hazelnuts
½ pound Danish rye
bread
3 tablespoons no-sugar-
added mixed berry jelly
⅔ cup heavy cream
½ cup low-fat soft cheese
Angelica and extra
hazelnuts for garnish

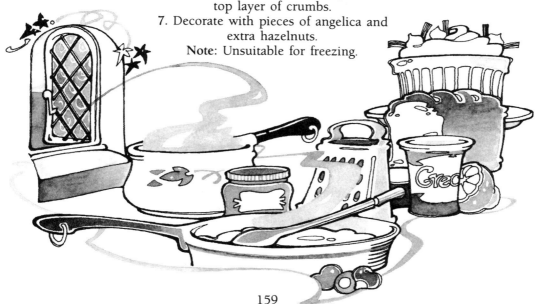

Bonfire Night Barbecue Party (for 12 people)

Tomato and Lentil Soup
Choice of three jacket potatoes
Sweetcorn Barbecue Sauce
Carrot and Sunflower Burgers
Nut Sausages
Hot Cider and Date Cake
Choice of Salads

Tomato and Lentil Soup

Imperial (Metric)

2 lb (900g) tomatoes
1 lb (445g) carrots
6 large celery sticks
3 large onions
4 tablespoons sunflower oil
2 garlic cloves, finely chopped
1 lb (445g) split red lentils
2 teaspoons paprika
3 pints (1.7 litres) vegetable stock
Bouquet garni

1. Scald, skin and finely chop the tomatoes. Finely chop the carrots, celery and onions.
2. Heat the oil in a saucepan on a low heat. Stir in the carrots, celery, onions and garlic. Cover and cook gently for 10 minutes.
3. Stir in the lentils and paprika. Add the tomatoes. Pour in the stock and bring it to the boil. Add the bouquet garni. Cover and simmer for 40 minutes or until the lentils are soft.
4. Remove the bouquet garni. Liquidize half the soup in a blender or food processor. Mix it back into the rest. Reheat if necessary.
Note: To freeze, cool the soup completely. Pour it into a rigid container and cover. Store for up to 2 months. Thaw at room temperature and reheat in a saucepan.

American

2 pounds tomatoes
1 pound carrots
6 large celery stalks
3 large onions
¼ cup sunflower oil
2 garlic cloves, finely chopped
4 cups split red lentils
2 teaspoons paprika
7½ cups vegetable stock
Bouquet garni

Potatoes Filled with Avocado and Almonds

Imperial (Metric)

6 large potatoes
2 ripe avocados
2 oz (55g) ground almonds
2 tablespoons tomato purée
Tomato slices for garnish

1. Cook and prepare the potatoes as in Cheesy Jacket Potatoes recipe (see below).
2. Peel, stone (pit) and mash the avocados. Mix these, the almonds and tomato purée (paste) into the mashed potato.
3. Fill the potato shells with the mixture. Lay two tomato slices on top of each potato half.
4. Return the potatoes to the oven for 15 minutes.

Note: Unsuitable for freezing. Do not prepare these more than 1 hour in advance or the avocados will discolour.

American

6 large potatoes
2 ripe avocados
½ cup ground almonds
2 tablespoons tomato purée
Tomato slices for garnish

Cheesy Jacket Potatoes

Imperial (Metric)

6 large potatoes
4 oz (115g) curd cheese
4 oz (115) Cheddar cheese, grated
2 tablespoons tomato purée

1. Heat the oven to 400°F/200°C/Gas Mark 6
2. Scrub the potatoes and prick them on each side with a fork. Put them into the oven, directly on the rack, for 1 hour 15 minutes.
3. Cut the potatoes in half lengthways. Scoop out and mash the middles.
4. Mix in the two cheeses and the tomato purée (paste).
5. Place the potato shells on a large, flat baking dish. Fill them with the cheese mixture. Make ridged patterns on the top with a fork.
6. Return the potatoes to the oven for 15 minutes or until the tops begin to brown.

Note: To freeze, before cooking, cool completely. Freeze on a tray and pack into polythene bags. Store them for up to 1 month. Reheat from frozen by putting the potatoes on a baking sheet and then into the oven for 30 minutes.

American

6 large potatoes
½ cup curd cheese
1 cup Cheddar cheese, grated
2 tablespoons tomato paste

Potatoes Filled with Cannellini Beans, Mozzarella and Olives

Imperial (Metric)

6 large potatoes
6 oz (170g) cannellini beans, soaked and cooked
4 oz (115g) Mozzarella cheese
6 black olives
4 tablespoons chopped parsley

1. Prepare and cook the potatoes as in previous recipe.
2. Mash the beans. Finely chop the cheese. Stone (pit) and finely chop the olives.
3. Mix the beans, cheese, olives and parsley into the mashed potato.
4. Fill the potato shells with the mixture.
5. Return them to the oven for 15 minutes or until the tops begin to brown.

Note: Freeze before returning the potatoes to the oven. Thaw and reheat as above.

American

6 large potatoes
1 cup cannellini beans, soaked and cooked
¼ pound Mozzarella cheese
6 black olives
¼ cup chopped parsley

Carrot and Sunflower Burgers

Imperial (Metric)

1 lb (445g) tofu
12 oz (340g) burghul wheat
8 oz (225g) carrots
2 oz (55g) sunflower seeds
1 medium onion
1 tablespoon chopped thyme
6 sage leaves, chopped
4 tablespoons chopped parsley
1 tablespoon German mustard
1 tablespoon grated horseradish
2 tablespoons white wine vinegar
3 tablespoons tamari or shoyu sauce
2 eggs, beaten
Vegetable oil for greasing

1. Wrap the tofu in a tea cloth. Lay it between two boards or flat plates and press it with a weight for 30 minutes. Twist the tea cloth to remove any remaining moisture, kneading the tofu slightly. Turn the tofu into a bowl. The texture should resemble that of cottage cheese.
2. Soak the burghul wheat in warm water for 20 minutes. Drain it and squeeze it dry.
3. Finely grate the carrots. Grind the sunflower seeds. Finely grate the onion.
4. Mix together all the ingredients except the eggs. Squeeze them together and add the eggs, a little at a time, to bind them.
5. Form the mixture into sixteen round, flat burger shapes. Chill them on a baking sheet to set them into shape.
6. To cook the burgers, place a sheet of foil over the barbecue grill. Oil it well and pierce small holes in it with a skewer. Get it hot. Cook the burgers for

American

1 pound tofu
2 cups burghul wheat
½ pound carrots
½ cup sunflower seeds
1 medium onion
1 tablespoon chopped thyme
6 sage leaves, chopped
¼ cup chopped parsley
1 tablespoon German mustard
1 tablespoon grated horseradish
2 tablespoons white wine vinegar
3 tablespoons tamari or shoyu sauce
2 eggs, beaten
Vegetable oil for greasing

about 5 minutes each side, or until they are browned and heated through.
Note: Freeze before cooking. Stack the burgers in threes with sheets of greaseproof paper between them. After freezing, pack in polythene bags. Store for up to 1 month. Thaw at room temperature.

Nut Sausages

Imperial (Metric)

2 oz (55g) hazelnuts
2 oz (55g) Brazil nuts
4 tablespoons sunflower oil
2 medium onions, finely chopped
3 oz (85g) yellow split peas
3 oz (85g) green split peas
¾ pint (425ml) vegetable stock
2 teaspoons dried mixed herbs
2 tablespoons tomato purée
1 bay leaf
1 egg, beaten
1 oz (30g) wholemeal flour
Vegetable oil for cooking

1. Grind the nuts.
2. Heat the oil in a saucepan on a low heat. Put in the onions and soften them.
3. Stir in the split peas. Pour in the stock and bring it to the boil. Add the mixed herbs, tomato purée (paste) and bay leaf. Cover and simmer for 45 minutes or until the split peas are soft and all the stock has been absorbed.
4. Beat the peas to a thick purée. Mix in the nuts and leave the mixture until it is completely cold.
5. Divide the mixture into 12-14 portions and form each into a sausage shape. Coat the sausages in egg and dip in the flour.
6. To cook, brush the sausages lightly with oil. Lay them on the barbecue grill about 4 inches (10cm) above hot coals. Cook them for about 3 minutes on each side or until they are browned and heated through.
Note: Freeze before cooking. Lay the floured sausages on a baking sheet or tray and freeze them separately. Pack them into a polythene bag. Store for up to 2 months. To thaw, take them from the bag and place them on a tray. Leave them at room temperature.

American

⅓ cup hazelnuts
⅓ cup Brazil nuts
¼ cup sunflower oil
2 medium onions, finely chopped
⅔ cup yellow split peas
⅔ cup green split peas
2 cups vegetable stock
2 teaspoons dried mixed herbs
2 tablespoons tomato paste
1 bay leaf
1 egg, beaten
¼ cup wholemeal flour
Vegetable oil for cooking

Sweetcorn Barbecue Sauce

Imperial (Metric)

2 lb (900g) ripe tomatoes
3 large onions
2 garlic cloves
4 tablespoons
concentrated apple juice
4 fl oz (125ml) tamari or
shoyu sauce
4 tablespoons Yorkshire
Relish
1 teaspoon ground black
pepper
½ teaspoon ground
allspice
½ teaspoon ground cloves
4 tablespoons sunflower
oil
12 oz (340g) tin
sweetcorn kernels

1. Roughly chop the tomatoes. Put these and all the rest of the ingredients except the sweetcorn into a saucepan. Bring them to the boil and simmer them for 1 hour or until the tomatoes are reduced to a thick pulp.
2. Rub the mixture through a sieve or put it through the fine blade of a vegetable mill.
3. Return the sauce to the cleaned pan. Add the sweetcorn. Bring the sauce to the boil and simmer it for 15 minutes.
Note: To freeze, cool completely and pour into a rigid container. Cover. Store for up to 1 month. Thaw at room temperature.

American

2 pounds ripe tomatoes
3 large onions
2 garlic cloves
¼ cup concentrated apple
juice
½ cup tamari or shoyu
sauce
¼ cup Yorkshire Relish
1 teaspoon ground black
pepper
½ teaspoon ground
allspice
½ teaspoon ground cloves
¼ cup sunflower oil
12 ounce tin sweetcorn
kernels

Hot Cider and Date Cake

Imperial (Metric)

8 oz (225g) butter or
vegetable margarine
8 oz (225g) Barbados
sugar
4 eggs, beaten
1 lb (455g) wholemeal
flour
2 teaspoons bicarbonate
of soda
1 nutmeg, grated
½ pint (285ml) dry cider
12 oz (340g) stoned
dates, chopped
butter or vegetable
margarine for greasing

1. Heat the oven to 350°F/180°C/Gas Mark 4.
2. Cream the butter or margarine. Beat in the sugar.
3. Beat in the eggs, a little at a time.
4. Mix the flour with the bicarbonate of (baking) soda and nutmeg. Beat half this mixture into the butter mixture.
5. Thoroughly mix in the cider. Fold in the remaining flour and then the dates.
6. Put the mixture into a greased, 8 by 11 inch (20 by 28cm), 2 inch (5cm) deep cake tin.
7. Bake the cake for 45 minutes.
8. Turn it onto a wire rack. Cool it for 10 minutes before cutting into squares.
Note: To freeze, cool completely and wrap in clingfilm. Store for up to two months. Thaw at room temperature. Reheat by placing on a baking sheet and putting into a moderate oven for 10-15 minutes.

American

1 cup butter or vegetable
margarine
1⅓ cups Barbados sugar
4 eggs, beaten
4 cups wholewheat flour
2 teaspoons baking soda
1 nutmeg, grated
1¼ cups dry cider
¾ pounds pitted dates,
chopped
butter or vegetable
margarine for greasing

Autumn Sunday Tea

Sunday Salad
Hazelnut Scones with Watercress Butter
Apple Tea Bread
Walnut and Cherry Cake

Sunday Salad

Imperial (Metric)

1 lb (455g) fresh 'wet'
walnuts, or 4 oz (115g)
chopped walnuts
8 oz (225g) Cheshire
cheese
3 large Russet apples
1 head celery
1 small onion
6 oz (170g) haricot beans,
soaked and cooked
6 sage leaves, chopped
3 fl oz (90ml) olive oil
2 tablespoons cider
vinegar
1 teaspoon mustard
powder
3 boxes mustard and cress

1. Shell and chop the walnuts.
2. Dice the cheese. Core and chop the apples. Chop the celery. Very thinly slice the onion. Put the apples, celery and onion into a bowl with the haricot (navy) beans and sage.
3. Beat together the oil, vinegar and mustard powder and fold them into the salad.
4. Put a ring of mustard and cress round the edge of a large serving plate. Arrange the salad in the middle. Scatter the walnuts over the top.

American

1 pound freshly picked
English walnuts, or ¾ cup
chopped English walnuts
½ pound Cheshire cheese
3 large Russet apples
1 head celery
1 small onion
1 cup navy beans, soaked
and cooked
6 sage leaves, chopped
⅓ cup olive oil
2 tablespoons cider
vinegar
1 teaspoon mustard
powder
3 boxes mustard and cress

165

Hazelnut Scones with Watercress Butter

Imperial (Metric)

12 oz (340g) fresh hazel
or cob nuts in their shell;
or 6 oz (170g) shelled
hazelnuts
1 lb (455g) wholemeal
flour
1 teaspoon fine sea salt
1 teaspoon bicarbonate of
soda
2 tablespoons chopped
thyme
½ pint (285ml) buttermilk
or natural yogurt
Butter:
6 oz (170g) butter,
softened
2 oz (55g) watercress
Grated rind and juice of
½ lemon
Watercress leaves for
garnish

1. Shell and grind the hazelnuts.
2. Heat the oven to 400°F/200°C/Gas
   Mark 6.
3. Put the flour into a bowl with the salt
   and bicarbonate of (baking) soda. Mix in
   the hazelnuts and thyme. Make a well in
   the centre and add the buttermilk or
   yogurt. Mix everything to a dough.
   Knead it lightly until it is smooth.
4. Roll out the dough to a thickness of
   about ¾ inch (2cm). Stamp it into 2
   inch (5cm) rounds with a biscuit cutter.
5. Lay the scones on a floured baking
   sheet. Bake them for 15 minutes or until
   they are just beginning to brown. Lift
   them onto wire racks to cool.
6. Beat the butter and chop the
   watercress. Put them into a blender or
   food processor with the lemon rind and
   juice. Liquidize them to a smooth purée.
7. Split the scones in half. Spread them
   with the watercress butter. Either
   sandwich them together or leave them
   open and garnish with watercress leaves,
   if wished.
   Note: To freeze, cool the scones
   completely and pack them into a
   polythene bag. Store them for up to two
   months. Thaw them on a rack at room
   temperature.

American

¾ pound fresh hazel or
cob nuts in their shell; or
6 oz (170g) shelled
hazelnuts
4 cups wholewheat flour
1 teaspoon fine sea salt
1 teaspoon baking soda
2 tablespoons chopped
thyme
1¼ cups buttermilk or
unflavored yogurt
Butter:
¾ cup butter, softened
2 ounces watercress
Grated rind and juice of
½ lemon
Watercress leaves for
garnish

Apple Tea Bread

Imperial (Metric)

2 dessert apples
5 oz (150g) pear and
apple spread
½ pint (285ml) milk
2 oz (55g) butter or
vegetable margarine
12 oz (340g) wholemeal
flour
1 teaspoon bicarbonate of
soda
3 oz (85g) raisins

1. Heat the oven to 350°F/180°C/Gas
   Mark 4
2. Peel, core and chop the apples.
3. Put the pear and apple spread, milk
   and butter or margarine into a saucepan
   and set them on a low heat, stirring
   occasionally, until the fat has melted
   and the pear and apple spread has
   become very soft. Take the pan from the
   heat and let the mixture cool.
4. Put the flour and bicarbonate of

American

2 dessert apples
½ cup pear and apple
spread
1¼ cups milk
¼ cup butter or vegetable
margarine
3 cups wholewheat flour
1 teaspoon baking soda
½ cup raisins

(baking) soda into a mixing bowl. Make a well in the centre and pour in the milk mixture. Using a wooden spoon, beat everything to a thick batter.

5. Mix in the apples and raisins.

6. Pour the batter into a greased, 2 lb (900g) loaf tin. Bake the bread for 1 hour, or until a skewer inserted in the centre comes out clean. Turn the bread onto a wire rack to cool.

7. Serve plain or buttered.

Note: To freeze, cool completely. Seal in a polythene bag. Store for up to 1 month. Thaw on a rack at room temperature.

Walnut and Cherry Cake

Imperial (Metric)

6 oz (170g) dried whole apricots
½ pint (285ml) natural orange juice
4 oz (115g) glacé cherries
4 oz (115g) walnuts
6 oz (170g) wholemeal flour
1 teaspoon bicarbonate of soda
3 fl oz (90ml) corn oil
3 eggs, beaten

1. Put the apricots into a saucepan with the orange juice. Bring them to the boil and take the pan from the heat. Soak the apricots in the juice for 4 hours. Drain them, reserving the juice. Liquidize the apricots with 3 fl oz (90ml) juice.

2. Heat the oven to 350°F/180°C/Gas Mark 4

3. Halve the cherries. Chop the walnuts.

4. Put the flour into a bowl. Toss in the bicarbonate of (baking) soda and the walnuts. Make a well in the centre.

5. Pour in the liquidized apricots and oil. Gradually beat in flour from the sides of the well. Beat in the eggs. Fold in the cherries.

6. Put the mixture into a well-oiled, 8 inch (20cm) diameter cake tin. Bake the cake for 40 minutes, or until a skewer stuck in the centre comes out clean.

Note: To freeze, cool the cake completely. Wrap it in clingfilm and seal it in a polythene bag. Freeze it flat. Store for up to 1 month. Thaw on rack at room temperature.

American

6 ounces dried whole apricots
1¼ cups natural orange juice
¼ pound glacé cherries
¾ cup English walnuts
1½ cups wholewheat flour
1 teaspoon baking soda
⅓ cup corn oil
3 eggs, beaten

SOUPS

Soups are a welcome start to a meal on chilly autumn evenings, even at the beginning of the season when runner beans and marrows are still available. Pumpkin is one of my favourite soup vegetables as it has such a thick, creamy texture and mellow flavour and any soup made from it will be a deliciously appetizing colour.

Take advantage, too , of the short-seasoned sweetcorn to make unblended soups; and green tomatoes and the new season's apples to add a refreshing sharpness.

Celery and Apple Soup

Imperial (Metric)

1¼ lb (565g) celery
3 medium cooking apples
1 oz (30g) butter or vegetable margarine
2 medium onions, finely sliced
1 garlic clove, finely chopped
2¼ pints (1.3 litres) vegetable stock
Freshly ground black pepper
Bouquet garni
2 tablespoons chopped savory
2 oz (55g) cashew nut pieces

1. Finely chop the celery. Set aside 4 tablespoons (¼ cup). Peel, core and chop the apples.
2. Melt the butter or margarine in a saucepan on a low heat. Stir in the celery, apple, onions and garlic. Cover them and cook gently for 10 minutes.
3. Pour in the stock and bring it to the boil. Season with the pepper and add the bouquet garni. Cover and simmer for 15 minutes.
4. Remove the bouquet garni. Liquidize the soup in a blender or food processor. Return it to the cleaned pan. Stir in the savory and reheat it.
5. Lay the cashew nut pieces on a heat-proof plate and toast them under a high grill for about 1 minute until they are lightly browned.
6. Pour the soup into individual bowls. Scatter the reserved celery and the cashew nuts over the top.
Note: To freeze, put the soup into a covered container and store it for up to 2 months. Thaw at room temperature and reheat. Prepare the garnish on the day of serving.

American

1¼ pounds celery
3 medium cooking apples
2 tablespoons butter or vegetable margarine
2 medium onions, thinly sliced
1 garlic clove, thinly chopped
5⅔ cups vegetable stock
Freshly ground black pepper
Bouquet garni
2 tablespoons chopped savory
½ cup cashew nut pieces

Mushroom and Sherry Soup

Imperial (Metric)

12 oz (340g) open
mushrooms
1 oz (30g) butter or
vegetable margarine
2 medium onions, finely
chopped
3 tablespoons wholemeal
flour
2 pints (1.1 litres)
vegetable stock
2 tablespoons chopped
thyme
2 tablespoons chopped
marjoram
1 bay leaf
¼ pint (140ml) dry sherry
6 tablespoons chopped
parsley

1. Finely chop the mushrooms.
2. Melt the butter or margarine in a saucepan on a low heat. Put in the onions and soften them.
3. Raise the heat to moderate. Put in the mushrooms and cook them for 1 minute, stirring.
4. Stir in the flour and then the stock. Bring the stock to the boil, stirring.
5. Add the thyme, marjoram and bay leaf. Simmer, uncovered, for 10 minutes.
6. Add the sherry and the parsley and reheat without boiling. Remove the bay leaf before serving.
Note: To freeze, after simmering, remove the bay leaf. Cool the soup completely. Put it into a rigid container and cover. Store for up to 1 month. Thaw at room temperature. Add the sherry and parsley and reheat gently, without boiling.

American

¾ pound open mushrooms
2 tablespoons butter or
vegetable margarine
2 medium onions, finely
chopped
3 tablespoons wholewheat
flour
5 cups vegetable stock
2 tablespoons chopped
thyme
2 tablespoons chopped
marjoram
1 bay leaf
⅔ cup dry sherry
⅓ cup chopped parsley

Spicy Sweetcorn and Courgette (Zucchini) Soup with Peanuts

Imperial (Metric)

4 corn cobs
1 lb (455g) courgettes
1 red pepper
2 oz (55g) peanuts
4 tablespoons sunflower
oil
2 medium onions, finely
chopped
1 garlic clove, finely
chopped
2 teaspoons paprika
¼ teaspoon chilli powder
1 tablespoon potato flour
2¼ pints (1.3 litres)
vegetable stock

1. Cut the corn from the cobs. Finely dice the courgettes (zucchini). Core, seed and finely chop the pepper.
2. Finely grind the peanuts.
3. Heat the oil in a saucepan on a low heat. Put in the courgettes (zucchini), pepper, onions, garlic, paprika and chilli powder. Cover and cook gently for 10 minutes.
4. Stir in the potato flour and then the stock. Bring to the boil, stirring.
5. Put in the corn and the peanuts. Cover and simmer for about 10 minutes.
Note: To freeze, cool the soup completely. Put into a rigid container and cover. Store for up to 1 month. Thaw at room temperature and reheat in a saucepan.

American

4 corn cobs
1 pound zucchini
1 sweet red pepper
3½ tablespoons cashew
nuts
¼ cup sunflower oil
2 medium onions, finely
chopped
1 garlic clove, finely
chopped
2 teaspoons paprika
¼ teaspoon chili powder
1 tablespoon potato flour
5¾ cups vegetable stock

Marrow and Caraway Soup

3¾ lb (1.7kg) marrow
4 tablespoons sunflower
oil
3 medium onions, finely
chopped
1 garlic clove, finely
chopped
1 tablespoon caraway
seeds
1¼ pints (725ml)
vegetable stock
Sea salt and freshly
ground black pepper
8 fl oz (225ml) natural
yogurt

1. Peel the marrow. Cut it into small pieces, without removing the seeds.
2. Heat the oil in a saucepan on a low heat. Stir in the marrow, onions, garlic and caraway seeds. Cover and cook gently for 10 minutes.
3. Pour in the stock and bring to the boil. Season lightly, cover and simmer for 20 minutes.
4. Put the soup through the medium blade of a vegetable mill.
5. Return the soup to the cleaned pan. Stir in the yogurt. Reheat gently, without boiling.

Note: To freeze, do not add the yogurt and cool completely after sieving. Pour into a rigid container and cover. Store for up to 2 months. Thaw at room temperature, stir in the yogurt and reheat gently, without boiling.

American

3¾ pounds marrow
¼ cup sunflower oil
3 medium onions, finely
chopped
1 garlic clove, finely
chopped
1 tablespoon caraway
seeds
3 cups vegetable stock
Sea salt and freshly
ground black pepper
1 cup unflavored yogurt

Green Pepper and Yogurt Soup

Imperial (Metric)

5 medium green peppers
3 medium onions
4 tablespoons olive or
sunflower oil
1 garlic clove, finely
chopped
1½ tablespoons wholemeal
flour
3 tablespoons tomato
purée
2¼ pints (1.3 litres)
vegetable stock
3 tablespoons chopped
thyme
3 tablespoons chopped
parsley
8 fl oz (225ml) Greek-
style ewe's milk yogurt

1. Finely chop the peppers and onions.
2. Heat the oil in a saucepan on a low heat. Put in the peppers, onions and garlic. Cover them and cook them gently for 10 minutes.
3. Stir in the flour and cook it for 30 seconds. Stir in the tomato purée (paste) and the stock and bring the stock to the boil, stirring.
4. Add the thyme.
5. Simmer, uncovered, for 20 minutes.
6. Stir in the parsley and yogurt and cook for 2 minutes more.

Note: Freeze before adding the parsley and yogurt. Cool the soup completely and put it into a covered container. Store for up to 2 months. Thaw at room temperature. Reheat and add the parsley and yogurt.

American

5 medium sweet green
peppers
3 medium onions
¼ cup olive or sunflower
oil
1 garlic clove, finely
chopped
1½ tablespoons
wholewheat flour
3 tablespoons tomato
paste
5⅔ cups vegetable stock
3 tablespoons chopped
thyme
3 tablespoons chopped
parsley
1 cup Greek-style ewe's
milk yogurt

Curried Pumpkin and Lemon Soup

Imperial (Metric)

Pumpkin (approx 2¼ lb/
1 kg in weight)
1 oz (30g) butter or
vegetable margarine
1 large onion, thinly
sliced
1 garlic clove, finely
chopped
1½ teaspoons hot Madras
curry powder
2¼ pints (1.3 litres)
vegetable stock
Juice and thinly pared
rind of 1 lemon
3 oz (85g) low-fat soft
cheese
2 popadoms

1. Cut the rind, seeds and pith from the pumpkin. Chop the flesh into small, thin pieces.
2. Melt the butter or margarine in a saucepan on a low heat. Mix in the pumpkin, onion, garlic and curry powder. Cover them and cook them gently for 10 minutes.
3. Pour in the stock and bring it to the boil. Add the lemon rind and juice. Cover and simmer for 10 minutes.
4. Remove the lemon rind. Cool the rest slightly.
5. Put the soup into a blender or food processor with the cheese and liquidize until it is smooth.
6. Return the soup to the saucepan and reheat it.
7. Grill the popadoms according to the manufacturer's instructions. Crumble them and use them as a garnish.
Note: Popadoms can be bought from Indian shops, delicatessens and some wholefood shops.
To freeze, cool the soup completely and put it into a covered container. Store it up for 2 months. Thaw at room temperature and reheat gently without boiling.

American

Pumpkin (approx 2¼
pounds in weight)
1 oz (30g) butter or
vegetable margarine
1 large onion, thinly
sliced
1 garlic clove, finely
chopped
1 ½ teaspoons hot
Madras curry powder
5⅔ cups vegetable stock
Juice and thinly pared
rind of 1 lemon
⅔ cup low-fat soft cheese
2 popadoms

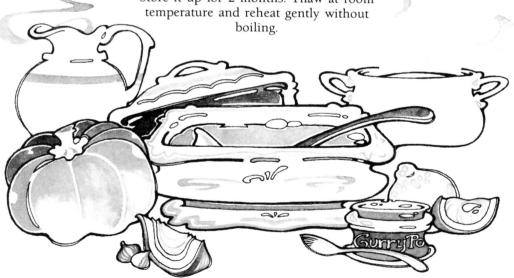

Runner Bean and Mustard Soup

Imperial (Metric)

1½ lb (685g) runner
beans
6 celery sticks
1 large onion
4 tablespoons olive oil
3 tablespoons wholemeal
flour
2 pints (1.14 litres)
vegetable stock
2 teaspoons spiced
granular mustard
¼ pint (140ml) dry white
wine

1. String and thinly slice the beans.
2. Chop the celery and the onion.
3. Heat the oil in a saucepan on a low heat. Put in the celery and onion, cover them and cook them gently for 5 minutes.
4. Stir in the flour and then the stock. Bring the stock to the boil. Stir in the mustard. Put in the beans. Simmer, uncovered, for 15 minutes.
5. Add the wine. Reheat, if necessary, without boiling.

Note: To freeze, do not add the wine. Cool the soup completely. Put it into a covered container. Store it for up to 2 months. Thaw at room temperature. Reheat and then add the wine.

American

1½ pounds runner beans
6 celery stalks
1 large onion
¼ cup olive oil
3 tablespoons wholewheat
flour
5 cups vegetable stock
2 teaspoons spiced
granular mustard
⅔ cup dry white wine

Red and Green Tomato Soup

Imperial (Metric)

1 lb 2 oz (500g) red
tomatoes
1 lb 2 oz (500g) green
tomatoes
1 oz (30g) butter or
vegetable margarine
1 large onion, finely
chopped
1 garlic clove, finely
chopped
1 tablespoon chopped
savory
1 tablespoon chopped
basil
1½ pints (850ml)
vegetable stock
7 fl oz (200ml) dry white
wine
6 slices of red tomato

1. Chop all the tomatoes.
2. Melt the butter or vegetable margarine in a saucepan on a low heat. Put in the onion and garlic, cover it and cook it gently for 5 minutes.
3. Mix in the tomatoes and herbs. Cover again and cook for 10 minutes.
4. Pour in the stock and bring it to the boil. Simmer for 10 minutes.
5. Put the soup through the fine blade of a vegetable mill. Return it to the rinsed pan. Pour in the wine and reheat gently without boiling.
6. Pour the soup into six individual bowls. Float a tomato slice on top of each portion.

Note: To freeze, put the soup through the vegetable mill but do not add the wine. Cool completely. Pack in a rigid container and cover. Store for up to two months. Thaw at room temperature. Add the wine and reheat.

American

1 pound 2 ounces red
tomatoes
1 pound 2 ounces green
tomatoes
2 tablespoons butter or
vegetable margarine
1 large onion, finely
chopped
1 garlic clove, finely
chopped
1 tablespoon chopped
savory
1 tablespoon chopped
basil
3¾ cups vegetable stock
¾ cup dry white wine
6 slices of red tomato

FIRST COURSES

Sweetcorn is a favourite vegetarian first course all the year round, but in the autumn you can buy it fresh and the flavour is so much better. Bake it in the oven, wrapped in foil, or cut it from the cobs and combine it with grated courgettes (zucchini).

Tiny stuffed peppers make a substantial starter to a meal and stir-fried apples one that is hot but light. Don't keep baby onions for pickling alone, try making them into a marinated salad with tangy Feta cheese.

Pomegranates and figs are two exotic fruits that are available only in the autumn, so buy them now to produce cold first courses that are a delight to look at. Then get going with the nut crackers and make a pâté with the fresh kernels. Shelled nuts don't work nearly as well.

Baked Sweetcorn

Imperial (Metric)		American
6 corn cobs 6 oz (170g) butter, softened, or vegetable margarine	1. Heat the oven to 400°F/200°C/ Gas Mark 6 2. Spread the corn cobs with the butter or margarine. Wrap each one individually in kitchen foil. Bake for 20 minutes.	6 corn cobs ¾ cup butter, softened, or vegetable margarine

Flavoured Butters for Baked Sweetcorn

1. Into 6 oz (170g/¾ cup) butter, beat 2 tablespoons each chopped parsley, chervil and chives, plus 1 crushed garlic clove and a little freshly grated black pepper.

2. Into 6 oz (170g/¾ cup) butter, beat 2 tablespoons tomato purée (paste), 2 teaspoons paprika and ¼ teaspoon chilli pepper.

Fresh Figs with Cashew Nut Salad

Imperial (Metric)		American
6 fresh figs 1 garlic clove, crushed with pinch of sea salt Freshly ground black pepper ½ teaspoon ground cumin ½ teaspoon ground coriander 8 fl oz (225ml) Greek-style ewe's milk yogurt 6 oz (170g) cashew nuts 6 tablespoons chopped parsley	1. Cut each fig almost all the way through and open it out. Place it on a small plate. 2. Mix the garlic, pepper and spices into the yogurt. Mix in the cashew nuts. 3. Place a portion of the mixture by each fig. Scatter the parsley over the top of the salad. **Note:** Unsuitable for freezing.	6 fresh figs 1 garlic clove, crushed with pinch of sea salt Freshly ground black pepper ½ teaspoon ground cumin ½ teaspoon ground coriander 1 cup Greek-style ewe's milk yogurt 1⅓ cups cashew nuts ⅓ cup chopped parsley

Fresh Cob Nut Pâté

Imperial (Metric)

1 lb (455g) fresh cob or
hazel nuts, unshelled
3 tablespoons sunflower
oil
2 tablespoons soya flour
¼ pint (140ml) vegetable
stock
1 tablespoon chopped
thyme
1 tablespoon chopped
marjoram
3 tablespoons chopped
chives
3 tablespoons chopped
parsley
Freshly ground black
pepper
Watercress for garnish

1. Shell the nuts and finely grind them.
2. Heat the oil in a saucepan on a medium heat. Stir in the soya flour and stock. Bring to the boil and stir until the mixture is thick.
3. Take the pan from the heat. Mix in the ground nuts, herbs and pepper. Mix well.
4. Press the mixture into an oiled 1 lb (455g/1 pound) loaf tin. Chill it for 2 hours or until it is firm.
5. Turn the pâté onto a serving plate. Garnish it with watercress sprigs.
Note: Unsuitable for freezing.

American

1 pound fresh cob or
hazel nuts, unshelled
3 tablespoons sunflower
oil
2 tablespoons soya flour
⅔ cup vegetable stock
1 tablespoon chopped
thyme
1 tablespoon chopped
marjoram
3 tablespoons chopped
chives
3 tablespoons chopped
parsley
Freshly ground black
pepper
Watercress for garnish

Stuffed Baby Peppers

Imperial (Metric)

6 small green peppers
2 oz (55g) burghul wheat
4 oz (115g) walnuts
8 tomatoes
2 tablespoons sunflower
oil
1 medium onion, finely
chopped
1 garlic clove, finely
chopped
½ pint (285ml) vegetable
stock
1 teaspoon dill seeds
6 tablespoons chopped
parsley
6 black olives

1. Heat the oven to 375°F/190°C/Gas Mark 5.
2. Core and seed the peppers, keeping them whole. If necessary, cut a small slice from the base of each one to enable it to stand upright. Bring a pan of lightly salted water to the boil. Put in the peppers. Cook them for 5 minutes and drain them.
3. Soak the burghul wheat in warm water for 20 minutes. Drain it and squeeze it dry.
4. Finely chop the walnuts. Scald, skin and chop two of the tomatoes. Thinly slice the rest.
5. Heat the oil in a frying pan (skillet) on a low heat. Put in the onion and garlic and soften them.
6. Take the pan from the heat. Mix in the wheat, chopped tomatoes, 4 tablespoons (¼ cup) stock, dill seeds, parsley and walnuts.
7. Fill the peppers with the mixture. Stand the peppers upright in a casserole. Halve and stone (pit) the olives and put

American

6 small sweet green
peppers
⅓ cup burghul wheat
¾ cup English walnuts
8 tomatoes
2 tablespoons sunflower
oil
1 medium onion, finely
chopped
1 garlic clove, finely
chopped
1¼ cups vegetable stock
1 teaspoon dill seeds
⅓ cup chopped parsley
6 black olives

two halves on the top of each pepper. Pour in the remaining stock.

8. Cover the casserole and put it into the oven for 20 minutes.
9. When the peppers are cooked. Put each one onto a small plate and surround it with tomato slices.

Note: To freeze, cool each pepper completely. Pack them upright in a rigid container and cover. Store for up to 1 month. Thaw at room temperature. Reheat by putting the peppers into a casserole and pouring in ½ pint (285ml/1¼ cups) vegetable stock. Cover and put into a hot oven for 15 minutes.

Hot Apple and Cheese Salad

Imperial (Metric)

3 large cooking apples
8 oz (225g) Cheddar cheese
1½ oz (45g) butter or vegetable margarine
1 medium onion, halved and thinly sliced
½ teaspoon ground cloves
3 tablespoons cider vinegar
24 hazelnuts

1. Peel, quarter and core the apples. Thinly slice them lengthways. Cut the cheese into ½ inch (1cm) cubes.
2. Melt the butter or margarine in a frying pan (skillet) on a high heat. Put in the onion and apple slices and stir them around until the onions are just beginning to brown, about 1½ minutes.
3. Scatter in the cloves and then quickly mix in the cheese. Stir and let the cheese heat through but not melt.
4. Pour in the vinegar and let it bubble.
5. Take the pan from the heat and put the salad immediately into six small bowls. Scatter the hazelnuts over the top.

Note: Unsuitable for freezing.

American

3 large cooking apples
½ pound Cheddar cheese
3 tablespoons butter or vegetable margarine
1 medium onion, halved and thinly sliced
½ teaspoon ground cloves
3 tablespoons cider vinegar
24 hazelnuts

Bejewelled Melon

Imperial (Metric)

3 small honeydew melons
10 oz (285g) curd cheese
3 pomegranates

1. Cut the melons in half and scoop out the seeds.
2. Fill the middles with cheese so that it is not piled high but flat with the melon.
3. Press pomegranate seeds into the cheese as closely together as possible.

Note: Unsuitable for freezing

American

3 small honeydew melons
1¼ cups curd cheese
3 pomegranates

Spicy Pots of Courgettes (Zucchini) and Corn

Imperial (Metric)

1 lb (455g) courgettes
3 corn cobs
3 tablespoons sunflower
oil
1 large onion, finely
chopped
1 garlic clove, finely
chopped
1 teaspoon celery seed
2 teaspoons paprika
¼ teaspoon chilli powder
½ teaspoon ground
turmeric
2 tablespoons white wine
vinegar
3 fl oz (90ml) tomato
juice
4 tablespoons chopped
parsley

1. Coarsely grate the courgettes (zucchini). Cut the corn from the cobs.
2. Heat the oil in a saucepan on a low heat. Put in the corn, onion and garlic. Cover them and cook them gently for 10 minutes.
3. Raise the heat to high. Put in the courgettes (zucchini) and spices. Stir for 2 minutes or until the courgettes are just beginning to soften.
4. Divide the vegetables between six individual soufflé dishes.
5. Beat together the vinegar, tomato juice and parsley. Spoon the mixture over the top just before serving.
Note: Unsuitable for freezing

American

1 pound zucchini
3 corn cobs
3 tablespoons sunflower
oil
1 large onion, finely
chopped
1 garlic clove, finely
chopped
1 teaspoon celery seed
2 teaspoons paprika
¼ teaspoon chili powder
½ teaspoon ground
turmeric
2 tablespoons white wine
vinegar
⅓ cup tomato juice
¼ cup chopped parsley

Button Onions with Feta Cheese

Imperial (Metric)

1 lb (455g) button onions
¾ pint (425ml) water
4 tablespoons tomato
purée
¼ pint (140ml) dry white
wine
1 garlic clove, crushed
3 oz (85g) raisins
12 coriander seeds, lightly
crushed
Pinch cayenne pepper
8 oz (225g) Feta cheese
3 tablespoons pine nuts
4 tablespoons chopped
parsley
Wholemeal bread for
serving

1. Bring a large pan of water to the boil. Put in half the onions. Take the pan from the heat. Take the onions from the water one by one and slip off the skins. Repeat with the remaining onions.
2. Put the water, tomato purée (paste), wine, garlic, raisins, coriander seeds and cayenne pepper into a saucepan. Bring them to the boil. Put in the onions. Cover and simmer for 40 minutes or until the onions are tender.
3. Tip the contents of the pan into a bowl and leave them to get quite cold.
4. Dice the cheese. Mix it into the onions. Chill for 1 hour.
5. Divide the onions and cheese between six small bowls. Scatter first the pine nuts and then the parsley over the top.
6. Serve wholemeal (wheat) bread separately.
Note: Unsuitable for freezing.

American

1 pound button onions
2 cups water
¼ cup tomato paste
⅔ cup dry white wine
1 garlic clove, crushed
½ cup raisins
12 coriander seeds, lightly
crushed
Pinch cayenne pepper
½ pound Feta cheese
3 tablespoons pine nuts
¼ cup chopped parsley
Wholewheat bread for
serving

176

Celery, Apple and Blue Cheese Pie (page 180) with Green Cabbage
and Green Tomatoes (page 196).
Overleaf A Hallowe'en Buffet Party (pages 156-9).

Figs and Oranges in White Wine (page 209).

MAIN COURSES

Here are light dishes made with marrow for those sunny, warm days of early autumn, spiced corn dishes for when the evenings begin to draw in and warming dishes of pumpkin and nuts for when the leaves turn gold in the damp autumn mists. Other seasonal specialities are calabrese, button onions and watercress, all of which can be turned into imaginative main dishes for your autumn dinner table.

Cider Nut Roast

Imperial (Metric)		American
3 oz (85g) hazelnuts		*⅔ cup hazelnuts*
3 oz (85g) walnuts		*⅔ cup English walnuts*
2 oz (55g) Brazil nuts		*½ cup Brazil nuts*
8 oz (225g) wholemeal bread		*4 cups wholewheat bread*
4 tablespoons sunflower oil		*¼ cup sunflower oil*
2 medium onions, finely chopped		*2 medium onions, finely chopped*
2 dessert apples, peeled, cored and chopped		*2 dessert apples, peeled, cored and chopped*
6 sage leaves, chopped		*6 sage leaves, chopped*
¼ pint (140ml) dry cider		*⅔ cup dry cider*
2 teaspoons yeast extract		*2 teaspoons yeast extract*
Sauce:		*Sauce:*
1 lb (455g) cooking apples		*1 pound cooking apples*
4 tablespoons dry cider		*¼ cup dry cider*
2 tablespoons honey		*2 tablespoons honey*
Pinch ground cloves		*Pinch ground cloves*

1. Heat the oven to 400°F/200°C/Gas Mark 6.

2. If possible, put the nuts and bread into a large blender or food processor and grind them together. This makes an interesting texture. Alternatively, grind the nuts and make the breadcrumbs separately and then mix them.

3. Heat the oil in a large frying pan (skillet) on a low heat. Put in the onions and apples and cook them until the onions are soft. Mix in the nut and breadcrumb mixture and sage.

4. Pour in the cider and bring it to the boil. Add the yeast extract and mix well. Take the pan from the heat.

5. Put the mixture into a heatproof dish. Bake it for 30 minutes or until the top is brown and crisp.

6. To make the sauce, core and chop the apples, without peeling. Put them into a small casserole with the cider, honey and ground cloves. Cover them and put them into the oven for 30 minutes. Beat them to a rough purée. Serve separately.
Unsuitable for freezing

177

Celery and Nut Rounds with Fig Sauce

Imperial (Metric)

4 oz (115g) hazelnuts
4 oz (115g) Brazil nuts
8 oz (225g) wholemeal
bread
3 tablespoons vegetable oil
1 large onion, finely
chopped
6 celery sticks
6 oz (170g) green split
peas
1 pint (570ml) vegetable
stock
2 tablespoons chopped
thyme
6 sage leaves, chopped
4 tablespoons chopped
chives
4 tablespoons chopped
parsley
2 oz (55g) wholemeal
flour
2 eggs, beaten
Sunflower oil for frying
Parsley sprigs for garnish
Sauce:
8 fresh figs
¼ pint (140ml) dry white
wine
2-inch (5cm) cinnamon
stick
1 tablespoon arrowroot
4 fl oz (125ml) vegetable
stock
1 tablespoon chopped
thyme
4 chopped sage leaves
4 tablespoons chopped
chives

1. Finely grate the nuts. Make the bread into crumbs.
2. Heat the oil in a saucepan on a low heat. Put in the onion and celery and cook until the onion is soft. Stir in the split peas and cook them for 1 minute. Pour in the stock and bring it to the boil. Add the thyme, sage and chives. Cover and simmer for 40 minutes or until the split peas are very soft.
3. Take the pan from the heat. Mix in the nuts and breadcrumbs. Leave the mixture until it is quite cold.
4. To make the sauce, simmer the figs, whole, with the wine and cinnamon for 15 minutes. Drain them, reserving the wine. Discard the cinnamon.
5. Finely chop the figs.
6. Mix the arrowroot with 4 tablespoons of the vegetable stock.
7. Put the figs, wine, herbs and remaining stock into a saucepan and bring them to simmering point. Stir in the arrowroot mixture. Stir for 2 minutes for the sauce to thicken.
8. Add the parsley to the nut mixture.
9. Divide the mixture into 18 portions and make each one into a 2 inch (5cm) round. Pressing the mixture into a biscuit cutter will help do this. Coat the rounds in the flour, dip them in the egg and coat them in the flour again.
10. Heat 3 fl oz (90ml/⅓ cup) oil in a frying pan (skillet) on a medium heat. Put in the rounds and fry them until they are golden brown on each side. Drain them on kitchen paper and keep them warm. Add more oil when necessary.
11. When all the rounds are cooked, pile them onto a serving plate and garnish them with plenty of parsley sprigs. Serve the sauce separately.
Note: To freeze, cool the rounds completely. Lay them all on a baking sheet and freeze them flat. Put them in

American

¾ cup hazelnuts
¾ cup Brazil nuts
½ cup wholewheat bread
3 tablespoons vegetable oil
1 large onion, finely
chopped
6 celery stalks
⅔ cup green split peas
2½ cups vegetable stock
2 tablespoons chopped
thyme
6 sage leaves, chopped
¼ cup chopped chives
¼ cup chopped parsley
½ cup wholewheat flour
2 eggs, beaten
Sunflower oil for frying
Parsley sprigs for garnish
Sauce:
8 fresh figs
⅔ cup dry white wine
2-inch cinnamon stick
1 tablespoon arrowroot
½ cup vegetable stock
1 tablespoon chopped
thyme
4 chopped sage leaves
¼ cup chopped chives

twos into small polythene bags and seal. Store for up to 2 months. The sauce can be frozen for up to 1 month in a covered container. Thaw both at room temperature. Reheat the sauce in a pan on top of the stove. Reheat the rounds by placing them into a preheated, 400°F/200°C/Gas Mark 6 oven for 10-15 minutes.

Carrot-Filled Marrow Rings

Imperial (Metric)

2 small marrows, total weight about 2¼ lb (1kg)
12 oz (340g) carrots
6 oz (170g) buckwheat
¾ pint (424ml) vegetable stock
1 large onion, finely chopped
8 oz (225g) haricot beans, soaked and cooked
1 egg, beaten
6 oz (170g) Cheddar cheese, grated
4 tablespoons chopped chervil
Petals from 8 marigold heads
4 fl oz (125ml) sunflower oil

1. Heat the oven to 400°F/200°C/Gas Mark 6
2. Cut each marrow into 6 rings. Remove the seeds but do not peel. Steam the marrow rings for 10 minutes.
3. Finely grate the carrots. Steam two-thirds of them for 15 minutes.
4. Put the buckwheat into a heavy frying pan (skillet). Set it on a medium heat and stir it for 1 minute. Pour in the stock and bring it to the boil. Put in the onion. Cover and simmer for 20 minutes or until the buckwheat is soft and all the stock has been absorbed.
5. Mash the haricot (navy) beans. Mix in the steamed carrots, buckwheat, egg, two-thirds of the cheese, the chervil and petals from 4 of the marigold heads.
6. Fill the marrow rings with the mixture.
7. Put the oil into a flat, oven-proof dish (or two dishes, depending on their size). Put in the marrow rings. Bake them for 20 minutes.
8. Scatter the remaining grated carrot and then the remaining grated cheese over the top. Return the marrow rings to the oven for a further 5 minutes.
9. Scatter with the remaining marigold petals just before serving.
Note: Unsuitable for freezing.

American

2 small marrows, total weight about 2¼ pounds
¾ pound carrots
¾ cup buckwheat
2 cups vegetable stock
1 large onion, finely chopped
1 cup navy beans, soaked and cooked
1 egg, beaten
1 cup Cheddar cheese, grated
¼ cup chopped chervil
Petals from 8 marigold heads
½ cup sunflower oil

Runner Bean and Macaroni Bake

Imperial (Metric)

1½ lb (685g) runner
beans
12 oz (340g) wholemeal
macaroni
6 oz (170g) hazelnuts
4 tablespoons olive oil
2 medium onions, thinly
sliced
6 oz (170g) cream cheese
or low-fat soft cheese
6 eggs, beaten
2 tablespoons chopped
thyme
1 tablespoon chopped
savory
2 tablespoons tomato
purée
8 oz (225g) tomatoes

1. Heat the oven to 400°F/200°C/Gas Mark 6
2. String and thinly slice the runner beans. Steam them for 15 minutes or until they are just tender.
3. Cook the macaroni in lightly salted boiling water for 12 minutes or until it is just tender. Drain it. Rinse it with cold water and drain it again.
4. Finely grind the hazelnuts.
5. Heat the oil in a frying pan (skillet) on a low heat. Put in the onions and soften them.
6. Put the cheese into a bowl. Gradually beat in the eggs. Mix in the herbs and tomato purée (paste) and then the beans, macaroni, hazelnuts and onion.
7. Put the mixture into an ovenproof dish. Thinly slice the tomatoes and lay them on the top.
8. Put the dish into the oven for 30 minutes or until the egg mixture is set.
Note: Unsuitable for freezing.

American

1½ pounds runner beans
¾ pound wholewheat
macaroni
1⅓ cup hazelnuts
¼ cup olive oil
2 medium onions, thinly
sliced
¾ cup cream cheese or
low-fat soft cheese
6 eggs, beaten
2 tablespoons chopped
thyme
1 tablespoon chopped
savory
2 tablespoons tomato
paste
½ pound tomatoes

Celery, Apple and Blue Cheese Pie

Imperial (Metric)

Shortcrust pastry made
with 12 oz (340g)
wholemeal flour
(see page 24)
1 head celery
2 medium cooking apples
2 medium onions
1 oz (30g) butter or
vegetable margarine
4 sage leaves, chopped
Freshly ground black
pepper
8 oz (225g) soft blue
cheese such as Lymeswold
4 oz (115g) chopped
walnuts

1. Heat the oven to 400°F/200°C/Gas Mark 6.
2. Make the pastry and put it in a cool place while you prepare the filling.
3. Chop the celery. Peel, core and chop the apples. Thinly slice the onions.
4. Melt the butter or margarine in a saucepan on a low heat. Put in the celery, apple and onions. Cover them and cook them gently for 10 minutes. Take them from the heat. Add the sage and season with the pepper. Tip them onto a plate to cool.
5. Finely dice the cheese.
6. Mix the cheese and walnuts with the apples and celery.
7. Roll out two thirds of the pastry and use it to line a 10 inch (25cm) tart tin. Put in the filling. Cover with the

American

Shortcrust pastry made
with 3 cups wholewheat
flour
(see page 24)
1 head celery
2 medium cooking apples
2 medium onions
2 tablespoons butter or
vegetable margarine
4 sage leaves, chopped
Freshly ground black
pepper
½ pound soft blue cheese
such as Lymeswold
¾ cup chopped English
walnuts

180

remaining pastry. Brush the top with the beaten egg.

8. Bake the pie for 30 minutes or until the top is golden.

Note: The pie is best frozen in the tin. Cool it completely first and then seal it in a polythene bag. Store for up to 1 month. To reheat, put frozen into a hot oven for 20 minutes.

Pumpkin, Almond and Egg Bake

Imperial (Metric)		American

1. Heat the oven to 400°F/200°C/Gas Mark 6.

2 lb (900g) pumpkin
6 oz (170g) almonds
8 eggs, beaten
3 tablespoons sunflower oil
1 large onion, thinly sliced
1 garlic clove, finely chopped
¼ nutmeg, grated
4 tablespoons chopped chervil
1 tablespoon chopped thyme
1 tablespoon chopped marjoram
2 tablespoons tomato purée
Sauce:
1 green pepper, cored, seeded and chopped
1 red pepper, cored, seeded and chopped
8 oz (225g) aubergines, chopped
1 lb (455g) tomatoes, chopped
1 medium onion, chopped
3 tablespoons sunflower oil
1 garlic clove, finely chopped

2. Cut the rind, pith and seeds from the pumpkin. Dice the flesh and steam it for 20 minutes or until it is soft. Mash it.

3. Grind the almonds, without blanching.

4. Mix the almonds and eggs into the pumpkin.

5. Heat the oil in a frying pan (skillet) on a low heat. Put in the onion and garlic and soften them. Mix them into the pumpkin together with the herbs and tomato purée (paste).

6. Pour the mixture into a lightly greased, 10-11 inch (25-27cm) square, 2 inch (5cm) deep ovenproof dish. Bake it for 30 minutes or until it is set and the top is beginning to brown. Serve straight from the dish.

7. To make the sauce, heat the oil in a saucepan on a low heat. Put in the onion, garlic, pepper and aubergine (eggplant). Cover and cook gently for 10 minutes. Put in the tomatoes. Cover and simmer for a further 10 minutes. Put the sauce through the fine blade of a vegetable mill or rub it through a sieve. Reheat it and serve it separately.

Note: The bake itself is unsuitable for freezing. The sauce may be cooled and frozen in a covered container. Store for up to 1 month. Thaw at room temperature and reheat.

2 pounds pumpkin
1½ cups almonds
8 eggs, beaten
3 tablespoons sunflower oil
1 large onion, thinly sliced
1 garlic clove, finely chopped
¼ nutmeg, grated
4 tablespoons chopped chervil
1 tablespoon chopped thyme
1 tablespoons marjoram
2 tablespoons tomato paste
Sauce:
1 sweet green pepper, cored, seeded and chopped
1 sweet red pepper, cored, seeded and chopped
½ pound eggplants, chopped
1 pound tomatoes, chopped
1 medium onion, chopped
3 tablespoons sunflower oil
1 garlic clove, finely chopped

Sweetcorn and Eggs with Tortillas

Imperial (Metric)

Tortillas:
4 oz (115g) wholemeal
flour
4 oz (115g) cornmeal
3 oz (85g) vegetable
margarine
½ teaspoon fine sea salt
¼ pint (140ml) water
Sauce:
4 corn cobs
1½ lb (685g) tomatoes
½ medium onion,
chopped
1 garlic clove, crushed
2 green or red chillies
1 tablespoon sunflower oil
2-inch (5cm) cinnamon
stick
Pinch sea salt

Sunflower oil for frying
12 eggs
Garnish:
2 bananas
2 ripe avocados

American

Tortillas:
1 cup wholewheat flour
¾ cup cornmeal
⅓ cup vegetable
margarine
½ teaspoon fine sea salt
⅔ cup water
Sauce:
4 corn cobs
1½ pounds tomatoes
½ medium onion,
chopped
1 garlic clove, crushed
2 green or red chilies
1 tablespoon sunflower oil
2-inch cinnamon stick
Pinch sea salt

Sunflower oil for frying
12 eggs
Garnish:
2 bananas
2 ripe avocados

1. For the tortillas, put the flour and cornmeal into a mixing bowl and toss them together. Rub in the margarine and salt. Make a well in the centre and pour in the water, Mix everything together, adding more water if necessary to make a soft dough. Knead the dough lightly and divide it into 12 pieces. Roll the pieces into thin circles about 5 inches (12.5cm) in diameter.

2. For the sauce, cut all the corn from the cobs. Bring a pan of water to the boil and cook the corn in it for 5 minutes. Drain it.

3. Put the tomatoes, onion and garlic into a blender or food processor. Liquidize them to a purée.

4. Core, seed and finely chop the chillies.

5. Heat the oil in a saucepan on a low heat. Put in the tomato mixture, corn, chillies, cinnamon stick and salt. Bring them gently to the boil. Cover and simmer for 5 minutes. Keep warm.

6. Pour the sunflower oil ¼ inch (6mm) deep into a frying pan (skillet). Heat it on a high heat. Fry each tortilla until it is lightly browned on each side and crisp. Drain them on kitchen paper. Keep them warm.

7. Fry the eggs in the oil, without turning them, and adding more oil to the pan if necessary. Keep them warm.

8. Cut the bananas into thin, diagonal slices. Fry them in about 4 tablespoons oil until they begin to brown.

9. Peel and stone (pit) the avocados. Cut them into thin slices.

10. Spread a portion of the corn and tomato sauce on each of 6 plates. Place a tortilla on top. Put the eggs on the tortilla and another tortilla on top of them. Spread the top tortilla with the remaining sauce. Garnish with the fried banana and avocado slices.

Note: The sauce may be frozen. Cool it, pack it into a rigid container and cover. Store for up to 1 month. Thaw at room temperature and reheat in a saucepan.

Calabrese and Mushrooms with a Pizza Flavour

Imperial (Metric)

2 lb (900g) calabrese
1 lb (455g) open mushrooms
1 red pepper
12 black olives
4 fl oz (125ml) olive oil
½ pint (285ml) vegetable stock
2 medium onions, thinly sliced
1 garlic clove, finely chopped
¼ pint (140ml) dry white wine
2 tablespoons tomato purée
4 tablespoons chopped parsley
2 tablespoons chopped oregano
12 oz (340g) Mozzarella cheese
3 oz (85g) flaked almonds
3 oz (85g) cashew nuts
2 oz (55g) porridge oats

1. Heat the oven to 400°F/200°C/Gas Mark 6.
2. Cut the calabrese into small florets. Thinly slice the mushrooms. Core, seed and finely chop the pepper. Stone (pit) and quarter the olives.
3. Heat 2 tablespoons of the oil in a saucepan on a high heat. Stir the calabrese into the oil. Pour in the stock and bring it to the boil. Cover and cook on a medium heat for 10 minutes or until the calebrese is just tender. Take the pan from the heat.
4. Heat 3 tablespoons of the oil in a frying pan (skillet) on a low heat. Put in the onions, garlic and pepper and cook until the onion is soft. Raise the heat to medium. Put in the mushrooms and stir them for 1 minute. Pour in the wine and bring it to the boil. Add the tomato purée (paste) and boil until the wine is reduced by half. Take the pan from the heat. Mix in the parsley, oregano and olives.
5. Thinly slice the cheese.
6. Mix together the nuts and oats. Add the oil and stir to incorporate it well.
7. Put half the mushrooms into a deep, ovenproof dish. Put in half the cheese, all the calabrese, the remaining cheese and the remaining mushrooms. Top with the nut and oat mixture.
8. Put the dish into the oven for 15 minutes or until the top has browned and the cheese melted.

Note: Unsuitable for freezing.

American

2 pounds calabrese
1 pound open mushrooms
1 sweet red pepper
12 black olives
½ cup olive oil
1¼ cups vegetable stock
2 medium onions, thinly sliced
1 garlic clove, finely chopped
⅔ cup dry white wine
2 tablespoons tomato paste
¼ cup chopped parsley
2 tablespoons chopped oregano
¾ pound Mozzarella cheese
¾ cup slivered almonds
¾ cup cashew nuts
½ cup rolled oats

Mexican Beans and Corn with Totopos and Tomato Rice

Imperial (Metric)

*12 oz (340g) borlotti
beans, soaked
1 large onion, thinly
sliced
1 garlic clove, finely
chopped
Corn tortillas, as in
previous recipe, not
cooked*
Sauce:
*1 lb (455g) tomatoes
1 green pepper
1 red pepper
2 green or red chillies
1 small onion, grated
1 garlic clove, crushed
¼ teaspoon sea salt*

4 corn cobs
Rice:
*3 tablespoons sunflower
oil
1 large onion, thinly
sliced
12 oz (340g) long-grain
brown rice
½ pint (285ml) tomato
juice
1 pint (570ml) vegetable
stock
1 tablespoon chilli powder
½ teaspoon ground cumin
2 tablespoons sunflower
oil
3 fl oz (90ml) soya milk*

1. Cook the beans for 3 hours or until they are very soft, adding the onion and garlic for the final hour. Drain them, reserving the liquid.
2. To make the totopos, cut each tortilla into quarters and leave them for 2 hours to dry slightly. Heat a deep pan of oil to 275°F/190°C. Deep fry the totopos, about 5 at a time, until they are golden brown. Lift them out with a perforated spoon and drain them on kitchen paper.
3. To make the sauce, scald and skin the tomatoes. Purée them in a blender or food processor. Core, seed and very finely chop the peppers and chillies. Mix them into the tomato purée with the onion, garlic and salt. Chill for 2 hours.
4. Cut the corn from the cobs. Cook it in lightly boiling water for 5 minutes. Drain it.
5. For the rice, heat the oil in a saucepan on a low heat. Put in the onion and cook it for 1 minute. Stir in the rice. Pour in the tomato juice and stock. Cover and simmer for 40 minutes or until the rice is soft and all the liquid has been absorbed.
6. To finish the beans, put the chilli powder and cumin into a bowl and stir in 4 tablespoons (¼ cup) of the bean cooking liquid.
7. Heat the oil in a frying pan (skillet) on a medium heat. Put in the beans and mash them until they are almost puréed. Add the corn. Stir in the chilli powder liquid and the soya milk. Cook, stirring, until the beans have thickened, about 30 seconds.
8. To serve, put the rice onto a large serving dish. Place the bean mixture in the centre. Garnish with a few of the totopos and serve the rest separately.
Serve the sauce separately

American

*1½ cups pinto beans,
soaked
1 large onion, thinly
sliced
1 garlic clove, finely
chopped
Corn tortillas, as in
previous recipe, not
cooked*
Sauce:
*1 pound tomatoes
1 sweet green pepper
1 sweet red pepper
2 green or red chilies
1 small onion, grated
1 garlic clove, crushed
¼ teaspoon sea salt*

4 corn cobs
Rice:
*3 tablespoons sunflower
oil
1 large onion, thinly
sliced
1½ cups long-grain brown
rice
1¼ cups tomato juice
2½ cups vegetable stock
1 tablespoon chili powder
½ teaspoon ground cumin
2 tablespoons sunflower
oil
3 fl oz (90ml) soya milk*

Note: Both the beans and the rice may be frozen separately in covered containers. Store for up to 1 month. Reheat the beans by stirring them into 2 tablespoons hot oil in a frying pan (skillet), and the rice in the same way. The totopos and the sauce are unsuitable for freezing.

Autumn Casserole

Imperial (Metric)

12 oz (340g) button onions
4 corn cobs
1 lb (455g) button mushrooms
2 oz (55g) butter or vegetable margarine
2 tablespoons wholemeal flour
2 teaspoons mustard powder
½ pint (285ml) vegetable stock
¼ pint (140ml) dry cider
12 oz (340g) flageolets, soaked and cooked for 1 hour
6 tablespoons chopped parsley
4 tablespoons chopped chervil
3 slices wholemeal bread
French mustard

1. Peel the onions. Cut the corn from the cobs. Trim about ¼ inch (6mm) from the stalk of each mushroom.
2. Melt half the butter or margarine in a flameproof casserole on a low heat. Put in the onions, and cook them, stirring occasionally, until they begin to look transparent. Remove them.
3. Raise the heat to medium. Put in the mushrooms and cook them for 1 minute, stirring. Remove them.
   4. Melt the remaining butter or margarine. Stir in the flour, mustard powder and stock. Bring them to the boil, stirring. Mix in the cider and bring the sauce back to simmering point.
5. Put in the onions, mushrooms, corn, flageolets, parsley and chervil. Cover and simmer for 30 minutes, or until the flageolets are tender.
6. Cut the crusts from the bread. Toast the slices on both sides. Spread them on one side with French mustard. Cut them into cubes.
   7. Turn the casserole into a warm serving dish. Scatter the bread cubes over the top.
   Note: To freeze, cool the casserole completely. Pack it into a rigid container and cover it. Store it for up to 1 month. Thaw at room temperature and reheat gently in a saucepan, stirring frequently. Do not freeze the bread cubes.

American

¾ pound button onions
4 corn cobs
1 pound button mushrooms
¼ cup butter or vegetable margarine
2 tablespoons wholewheat flour
2 teaspoons mustard powdeer
1¼ cups vegetable stock
⅔ cup dry cider
1½ cups flageolets, soaked and cooked for 1 hour
⅓ cup chopped parsley
¼ cup chopped chervil
3 slices wholewheat bread
Frenh mustard

Stuffed Marrow with Spiced Cherry Plum Sauce

Cherry plums are tiny, round crimson plums with sweet yellow flesh and sharp tasting skin. They are usually available for about two weeks in early autumn. If they are unobtainable, use any other variety of red or purple cooking plums.

Imperial (Metric)

2 small marrows, total weight about 2¼ lb (1kg)
Bouquet garni
4 oz (115g) Brazil nuts
4 oz (115g) cashew nuts
4 tablespoons sunflower oil
2 medium onions, finely chopped
8 oz (225g) fresh wholemeal breadcrumbs
6 allspice berries, crushed
6 black peppercorns, crushed
4 fl oz (125ml) dry red wine
16 cherry plums, halved and stoned
Vegetable oil for greasing
Sauce:
1 lb (455g) cherry plums
2 tablespoons sunflower oil
1 medium onion, finely chopped
6 allspice berries, crushed
6 black peppercorns, crushed
4 tablespoons red wine vinegar

1. Peel the marrows. Cut off the tops and, using a long spoon, remove all the seeds from inside. Put a bouquet garni into each marrow. Steam the marrows for 15 minutes, turning them once.
Note: the marrows will probably have to be steamed separately. If a large enough vegetable steamer is not available, use a heatproof colander covered with foil.
Drain the marrows well.
2. Finely grind the nuts.
3. Heat the oven to 350°F/180°C/Gas Mark 4.
4. Heat the oil in a frying pan (skillet) on a low heat. Put in the onions and soften them. Take the pan from the heat. Mix in the nuts, breadcrumbs, spices, wine and cherry plums.
5. Fill the marrows with the mixture. Secure the tops back on with cocktail sticks. Brush the marrows with oil. Lay them in a roasting tin.
6. Bake the marrows for 30 minutes.
7. To make the sauce, halve and stone (pit) the cherry plums. Heat the oil in a saucepan on a low heat. Put in the onion and soften it. Mix in the remaining ingredients and the plums. Cover and simmer for 30 minutes. Rub the sauce through a sieve and reheat before serving separately.
Note: The stuffed marrows are unsuitable for freezing. The sauce may be stored in the freezer in a covered container for up to 2 months and thawed at room temperature.

American

2 small marrows, total weight about 2¼ pounds
Bouquet garni
¾ cup Brazil nuts
¾ cup cashew nuts
¼ cup sunflower oil
2 medium onions, finely chopped
4 cups fresh wholewheat breadcrumbs
6 allspice berries, crushed
6 black peppercorns, crushed
½ cup dry red wine
16 cherry plums, halved and pitted
Vegetable oil for greasing
Sauce:
1 pound cherry plums
2 tablespoons sunflower oil
1 medium onion, finely chopped
6 allspice berries, crushed
6 black peppercorns, crushed
¼ cup red wine vinegar

Stir-Fried Chinese Cabbage with Mixed Nuts and Bean Curd

Imperial (Metric)

1 large Chinese cabbage
1¼ lb (565g) bean curd
1 oz (30g) wholemeal
    flour
Vegetable oil for deep
    frying
8 oz (225g) tin water
    chestnuts
12 oz (340g) carrots
3 fl oz groundnut oil
¼ pint (140ml) vegetable
    stock
8 spring onions
1 garlic clove, finely
    chopped
4 oz (115g) hazelnuts
3 oz (85g) chopped
    walnuts
2 oz (55g) cashew nuts
1 teaspoon ground ginger
4 tablespoons dry sherry
4 tablespoons tamari or
    shoyu sauce

1. Thinly shred the cabbage.
2. Drain the bean curd. Press it gently between 2 pieces of kitchen paper to remove any excess moisture. Cut it into ½ inch (1cm) cubes. Coat them in the flour. Heat a deep pan of oil to 375°F/190°C. Deep fry the cubes of bean curd for about 2 minutes, or until they are golden. Do this in two batches. Drain them on kitchen paper.
3. Drain and thinly slice the water chestnuts.
4. Thinly slice the carrots. Heat half the oil in a large frying pan (skillet) or wok on a high heat. Put in the carrots and stir-fry them for 1 minute. Pour in the stock and bring it to the boil. Cover and cook on a medium heat for 10 minutes. Remove the carrots from the pan, plus any remaining stock.
5. Cut the spring onions (scallions) into 1 inch (2.5 cm) lengths.
6. Heat the remaining oil in the pan on a high heat. Put in the cabbage, water chestnuts, spring onions (scallions) and garlic. Stir-fry them for 2 minutes. Put in the nuts and stir-fry for a further minute. Sprinkle in the ginger.
7. Return the carrots and stock to the pan. Pour in the sherry and tamari or shoyu sauce. Stir-fry for 1 minute more.
Note: Unsuitable for freezing.

American

1 large Chinese cabbage
1¼ pounds bean curd
¼ cup wholewheat flour
Vegetable oil for deep
    frying
½ pound can water
    chestnuts
¾ pound carrots
⅓ cup groundnut oil
⅔ cup vegetable stock
8 scallions
1 garlic clove, finely
    chopped
¾ cup hazelnuts
⅔ cup chopped English
    walnuts
½ cup cashew nuts
1 teaspoon ground ginger
¼ cup dry sherry
¼ cup tamari or shoyu
    sauce

Pumpkin, Rice and Vegetable Gratin

Imperial (Metric)

3 lb (1.4kg) pumpkin
1 lb (455g) carrots
1 head celery
4 tablespoons sunflower
oil
2 medium onions, thinly
sliced
1 garlic clove, finely
chopped
12 oz (340g) long-grain
brown rice
1½ pints (850ml)
vegetable stock
4 teaspoons spiced
granular mustard
1 lb (455g) tomatoes
4 tablespoons chopped
parsley
2 tablespoons chopped
thyme
4 oz (115g) chopped
pecan nuts
8 oz (225g) Mozzarella
cheese
1½ oz (45g) butter or
vegetable margarine
3 tablespoons wholemeal
flour
¾ pint (425ml) milk
1 garlic clove, crushed
6 oz (170g) Cheddar
cheese, grated
2 tablespoons wheatgerm

1. Cut the rind, pith and seeds from the pumpkin. Finely chop the flesh. Steam it for 20 minutes or until it is soft but the pieces are still intact.
2. Finely chop the carrots and celery.
3. Heat the oil in a saucepan on a low heat. Put in the carrots, celery, onions, chopped garlic and rice. Stir them on the heat for 1 minute. Pour in the stock and bring it to the boil. Add half the mustard. Cover and simmer for 40 minutes or until the rice is tender and all the stock has been absorbed.
4. Heat the oven to 400°F/200°C/Gas Mark 6.
5. Scald, skin and chop the tomatoes. Mix them with the pumpkin, herbs and pecan nuts.
6. Put half the rice into a deep ovenproof dish. Put in all the pumpkin and tomatoes. Thinly slice the Mozzarella cheese and lay it on the top. Cover everything with the remaining rice.
7. Melt the butter or margarine in a saucepan on a low heat. Stir in the flour and the milk. Bring the sauce to the boil, stirring. Simmer it for 2 minutes.
8. Take the pan from the heat. Beat in the remaining mustard and the crushed garlic and then about three-quarters of the grated cheese.
9. Pour the sauce over the rice. Scatter the remaining cheese and the wheatgerm over the top.
10. Put the dish in the oven for 20 minutes or until the top has browned.
Note: This can be frozen in the dish if wished. Cool completely. Cover with lid or with clingfilm or put into a polythene bag. Store for up to 1 month. Reheat from frozen, covered with foil, in an oven preheated to 400°F/200°C/Gas Mark 6 for 30 minutes.

American

3 pounds pumpkin
1 pound carrots
1 head celery
¼ cup sunflower oil
2 medium onions, thinly
sliced
1 garlic clove, finely
chopped
1½ cups long-grain brown
rice
3¾ cups vegetable stock
4 teaspoons spiced
granular mustard
1 pound tomatoes
¼ cup chopped parsley
2 tablespoons chopped
thyme
¾ cup chopped pecan
nuts
½ pound Mozzarella
cheese
3 tablespoons butter or
vegetable margarine
3 tablespoons wholewheat
flour
2 cups milk
1 garlic clove, crushed
1½ cups grated Cheddar
cheese
2 tablespoons wheatgerm

Watercress Terrine with Carrot Sauce

Imperial (Metric)

4 oz (115g) watercress
1 oz (30g) butter or
vegetable margarine plus
extra for greasing
12 oz (340g) leeks
8 oz (225g) carrots
4 celery sticks
12 oz (340g) potatoes
1 medium onion, thinly
sliced
4 eggs, beaten
1 garlic clove, crushed
4 fl oz (125ml) soured
cream
4 oz (115g) Cheddar
cheese, grated
Sauce:
8 oz (225g) carrots
1 oz (30g) butter or
vegetable margarine
1 medium onion, thinly
sliced
1 garlic clove, finely
chopped
¼ pint (140ml) tomato
and vegetable juice
½ pint (285ml) vegetable
stock
4 fl oz (125ml) soured
cream

1. Heat the oven to 400°F/200°C/Gas Mark 6.
2. Finely chop the watercress. Melt the butter or margarine in a frying pan (skillet) on a medium heat. Put in the watercress and stir until it wilts. Take the pan from the heat and cool the watercress.
3. Finely chop the leeks. Cut the carrots and celery into matchstick pieces. Boil the leeks for 2 minutes, and the carrots and celery for 5 minutes, all separately. Drain them.
4. Boil the potatoes in their skins with the onion until they are tender. Skin them and mash them with the onion.
5. Put the potatoes, watercress, eggs, garlic and soured cream into a blender or food processor and work them to a smooth, green purée. Mix in the cheese.
6. Grease some greaseproof paper and use it to line a 2 pound (900g) loaf tin.
   Spoon in a little of the watercress mixture to just cover the base of the tin. Put in the leeks and cover them with the watercress mixture. Repeat with the carrots and then the celery, putting the carrots in lengthways and the celery in crossways
7. Cover the tin with greased foil. Bake the terrine for 45 minutes. Turn it out.
8. To make the sauce, finely chop the carrots. Melt the butter or margarine in a saucepan on a low heat. Put in the carrots, onion and garlic. Cover and cook them gently for 10 minutes. Pour in the tomato and vegetable juice and stock. Bring them to the boil. Cover and simmer for 20 minutes. Liquidize everything to a purée in a blender or food processor. Return the sauce to the saucepan and stir in the soured cream. Reheat gently, without boiling.
9. Serve the terrine sliced and the sauce separately.
Note: Unsuitable for freezing.

American

¼ pound watercress
2 tablespoons butter or
vegetable margarine plus
extra for greasing
¾ pound leeks
½ pound carrots
4 celery stalks
¾ pound potatoes
1 medium onion, thinly
sliced
4 eggs, beaten
1 garlic clove, crushed
½ cup sour cream
1 cup grated Cheddar
cheese
Sauce:
½ pound carrots
2 tablespoons butter or
vegetable margarine
1 medium onion, finely
chopped
1 garlic clove, finely
chopped
⅔ cup tomato and
vegetable juice
1¼ cups vegetable stock
½ cup sour cream

189

Pumpkin and Pine Nut Kibbeh

Imperial (Metric)

12 oz (340g) burghul wheat
3 lb (1.4kg) pumpkin
4 tablespoons sunflower oil
2 medium onions, finely chopped
1 garlic clove, finely chopped
2 teaspoons curry powder
2 teaspoons ground cumin
2 teaspoons paprika
¼ teaspoon chilli powder
6 tablespoons chopped fresh coriander or parsley
8 fl oz (225ml) natural yogurt
6 oz (170g) chick peas, soaked and cooked
4 oz (115g) pine nuts
Sauce:
1 garlic clove, crushed
1 teaspoon ground cumin
½ pint (285ml) natural yogurt
½ cucumber, grated

1. Soak the wheat in warm water for 30 minutes. Drain it and squeeze it dry.
2. Remove the rind, seeds and pith from the pumpkin. Cut the flesh into small, thin slices and steam it for 20 minutes or until soft. Mash it.
3. Heat the oven to 400°F/200°C/Gas Mark 6
4. Heat the oil in a frying pan (skillet) on a low heat. Add the onions, garlic and spices and cook them until the onion is soft. Take the pan from the heat and mix the contents into the pumpkin. Mix in 4 tablespoons (¼ cup) of the coriander or parsley.
5. Mix half the pumpkin mixture and all the yogurt into the wheat.
6. Mash the chick peas or purée them in a blender or food processor.
7. Mix the chick peas and the whole pine nuts into the remaining pumpkin.
8. Put half the wheat mixture into a 2 inch (5cm) deep, ovenproof dish. Put in all the pumpkin, chick pea and pine nut mixture. Top with the remaining wheat mixture.
9. Put the dish into the oven for 30 minutes or until the top is brown.
10. Scatter with the remaining coriander or parsley before serving straight from the dish.
11. The sauce can be made while the kibbeh is cooking. Beat the garlic and cumin into the yogurt. Add the cucumber just before serving. Serve separately.

Note: This can be frozen in the dish if wished. Cool completely first and then cover with a lid or clingfilm. Store for up to 1 month. Thaw by covering with foil and putting into a preheated 400°F/200°C/Gas Mark 6 oven for 30 minutes. The sauce is unsuitable for freezing.

American

2 cups burghul wheat
3 pounds pumpkin
¼ cup sunflower oil
2 medium onions, finely chopped
1 garlic clove, finely chopped
2 teaspoons curry powder
2 teaspoons ground cumin
2 teaspoons paprika
¼ teaspoon chili powder
⅓ cup chopped fresh coriander or parsley
1 cup unflavored yogurt
¾ cup garbanzo beans soaked and cooked
¾ cup pine nuts
Sauce:
1 garlic clove, crushed
1 teaspoon ground cumin
1¼ cups unflavored yogurt
½ cucumber, grated

VEGETABLES AND SALADS

Some autumn vegetables overlap with those of summer and winter, others, such as sweetcorn, pumpkin and button onions, are available only for a short time. Imported peppers and courgettes (zucchini) can be bought all the year round, but are really at their best after being ripened by the last of the summer sun. Combine all these vegetables with seasonal herbs such as basil and chervil, add seasonal fruits to salads and all your vegetable dishes will have a true autumn flavour.

Carrots with Chervil

Imperial (Metric)

1½ lb (685g) carrots
1 oz (30g) butter or vegetable margarine
½ pint (285ml) vegetable stock
2 teaspoons Dijon mustard
4 tablespoons chopped chervil

1. Cut the carrots into ¼ inch (6mm) thick slices. Put the butter or margarine and stock into a saucepan, set them on a high heat and bring them to the boil. Stir in the mustard.
2. Put in the carrots and chervil. Cover and cook on a medium heat for 20 minutes, or until the carrots are tender and the stock has been reduced to a glaze.
Note: To freeze, cool completely, pack into a rigid container and cover. Store for up to 1 month. Thaw at room temperature. Reheat by putting into a heatproof dish, covering with foil and putting into a medium oven for 15-20 minutes.

American

1½ pounds carrots
2 tablespoons butter or vegetable margarine
1¼ cups vegetable stock
2 teaspoons Dijon mustard
¼ cup chopped chervil

Runner Beans with Tomatoes

Imperial (Metric)

1½ lb (685g) runner beans
12 oz (340g) tomatoes
4 tablespoons sunflower oil
1 medium onion, finely chopped
1 garlic clove, finely chopped
2 tablespoons chopped fresh basil or 1½ teaspoons dried basil

1. Trim and slice the beans. Scald, skin and chop the tomatoes.
2. Heat the oil in a saucepan on a low heat. Put in the onion and garlic and soften them.
3. Raise the heat and stir in the beans and tomatoes. Let the tomatoes boil and stir in the basil.
4. Cover and cook on a medium heat for 15 minutes.
Note: To freeze, cool completely and pack into a rigid container. Cover. Store for up to 1 month. Thaw at room temperature and reheat in a saucepan.

American

1½ pounds runner beans
¾ pound tomatoes
¼ cup sunflower oil
1 medium onion, finely chopped
1 garlic clove, finely chopped
2 tablespoons chopped fresh basil or 1½ teaspoons dried basil

Marrow with Green Peppercorns

Imperial (Metric)

1 medium-sized marrow
4 tablespoons olive oil
1 large onion, thinly
    sliced
1 garlic clove, finely
    chopped
2 teaspoons pickled green
    peppercorns
6 tablespoons chopped
    parsley

1. Cut the marrow in half lengthways and scoop out the seeds. Peel the two halves and cut each one lengthways again. Cut the quarters into ¼ inch (6mm) thick slices.
2. Heat the oil in a large saucepan on a low heat. Mix in the onion and garlic. Cover them and cook them for 5 minutes.
3. Crush the peppercorns with a pestle and mortar
4. Mix the marrow into the onion and add the peppercorns and parsley.
5. Cover the pan and cook the marrow gently for 15 minutes, turning it several times.
Note: To freeze, cool completely. Pack into a rigid container and cover. Store for up to a month. Thaw at room temperature and reheat quickly in a saucepan.

American

1 medium-sized marrow
¼ cup olive oil
1 large onion, thinly
    sliced
1 garlic clove, finely
    chopped
2 teaspoons pickled green
    peppercorns
⅓ cup chopped parsley

Pumpkin Casserole

Imperial (Metric)

3 lb (1.4kg) pumpkin
4 tablespoons chopped
    parsley
2 tablespoons chopped
    thyme
6 sage leaves, chopped
Sea salt and freshly
ground black pepper
8 fl oz (225ml) vegetable
    stock
1 large onion, thinly
    sliced

1. Heat the oven to 400°F/200°C/Gas Mark 6.
2. Cut the rind, seeds and pith from the pumpkin. Cut the rest into small, thin slices.
3. Mix the herbs together.
4. Layer the pumpkin and herbs in a large casserole, seasoning lightly with salt and liberally with pepper.
5. Put the stock and onion into a saucepan and bring them to the boil. Pour them over the pumpkin.
6. Cover the casserole and put it into the oven for 30 minutes.
Note: To freeze, cool completely. Pack into a rigid container and cover. Store for up to 2 months. To reheat, put frozen into the casserole again. Cover and put into the preheated oven for 30 minutes.

American

3 pounds pumpkin
¼ cup chopped parsley
2 tablespoons chopped
    thyme
6 sage leaves, chopped
Sea salt and freshly
ground black pepper
1 cup vegetable stock
1 large onion, thinly
    sliced

Chinese Leaves and Yellow Pepper Salad

Imperial (Metric)

1 Chinese cabbage
2 yellow peppers
4 tablespoons sunflower oil
2 tablespoons lemon vinegar
1 teaspoon ground turmeric
1 teaspoon honey
1 garlic clove, crushed
Freshly ground black pepper

1. Shred the cabbage. Core, seed and chop the peppers. Put them both into a bowl.
2. Beat the remaining ingredients together to make a dressing. Fold them into the salad.

Note: Lemon vinegar can be bought in some delicatessens and supermarkets. It can also be made by steeping a chopped lemon in a bottle of white wine vinegar for 2 weeks.

American

1 Chinese cabbage
2 sweet yellow peppers
¼ cup sunflower oil
2 tablespoons lemon vinegar
1 teaspoon ground turmeric
1 teaspoon honey
1 garlic clove, crushed
Freshly ground black pepper

Potatoes Roasted with Rosemary

Imperial (Metric)

12 potatoes, about 3 inches (7.5cm) long
3 fl oz (90ml) sunflower oil
1 tablespoon rosemary

1. Heat the oven to 400°F/200°C/Gas Mark 6.
2. Scrub the potatoes and cut them in half lengthways so each one makes two flat pieces.
3. Put the oil into a large baking tin and heat it in the oven for 10 minutes. Take it out and scatter in the rosemary.
4. Turn the potatoes in the oil and then leave them cut side down.
5. Put the potatoes into the oven for 1 hour. The skins should become crisp and the undersides soft and tasty.

Note: Unsuitable for freezing.

American

12 potatoes, about 3 inches long
⅓ cup sunflower oil
1 tablespoon rosemary

Watercress and Apple Salad

Imperial (Metric)

6 oz (170g) watercress
3 tart dessert apples
4 oz (115g) radishes
6 celery sticks
3 oz (85g) raisins
4 tablespoons olive oil
2 tablespoons cider vinegar
1 teaspoon Dijon mustard
1 garlic clove, crushed
Freshly ground black pepper

1. Chop the watercress. Core the apples and cut them into thin, slices lengthways. Thinly slice the radishes. Chop the celery.
2. Mix the watercress, apples, celery and raisins in a salad bowl.
3. Beat together the oil, vinegar, mustard, garlic and pepper.
4. Fold the dressing into the salad.

American

6 ounces watercress
3 tart dessert apples
¼ pound radishes
6 celery stalks
½ cup raisins
¼ cup olive oil
2 tablespoons cider vinegar
1 teaspoon Dijon mustard
1 garlic clove, crushed
Freshly ground black pepper

Stir-Fried Pumpkin Salad

Imperial (Metric)

2 lb (900g) pumpkin
2 tablespoons white wine
vinegar
1 tablespoon tomato purée
1 teaspoon paprika
4 tablespoons sunflower
oil
1 garlic clove, chopped
1 teaspoon caraway seeds

1. Cut the rind, pith and seeds from the pumpkin. Cut the rest into small, thin slices.
2. Mix together the vinegar, tomato purée (paste) and paprika.
3. Put the oil and garlic into a large frying pan (skillet) and heat them on a high heat until the garlic begins to sizzle.
4. Put in the pumpkin and caraway seeds. Stir on the heat for 3 minutes.
5. Pour in the vinegar mixture. Mix it into the pumpkin and let it bubble.
6. Serve as soon as possible.
Note: Unsuitable for freezing.

American

2 pounds pumpkin
2 tablespoons white wine
vinegar
1 tablespoon tomato paste
1 teaspoon paprika
¼ cup sunflower oil
1 garlic clove, chopped
1 teaspoon caraway seeds

Pomegranate and Sesame Salad

Imperial (Metric)

1 small green cabbage
1½ pomegranates
2 tablespoons sesame
seeds
1 teaspoon tahini (sesame
paste)
4 tablespoons olive oil
2 tablespoons cider
vinegar
1 garlic clove, crushed
Freshly ground black
pepper

1. Shred the cabbage and put it into a salad bowl.
2. Take the seeds from the pomegranates and add with the sesame seeds to the cabbage.
3. Put the tahini into a small bowl and gradually work in the oil and then the vinegar. Beat in the garlic and pepper.
4. Fold the dressing into the salad.

American

1 small green cabbage
1½ pomegranates
2 tablespoons sesame
seeds
1 teaspoon tahini (sesame
paste)
¼ cup olive oil
2 tablespoons cider
vinegar
1 garlic clove, crushed
Freshly ground black
pepper

Ratatouille with White Wine

Imperial (Metric)

3 large green peppers
12 oz (340g) mushrooms
4 tablespoons olive oil
1 large onion, quartered
and thinly sliced
1 garlic clove, finely
chopped
¼ pint (140ml) dry white
wine
3 tablespoons tomato
purée

1. Core and seed the peppers and cut them into strips, 1 by ¼ inch (2.5cm by 6mm). Thinly slice the mushrooms.
2. Heat the oil in a frying pan (skillet) on a low heat. Put in the onion and garlic, cover and cook for 5 minutes.
3. Mix in the peppers and cook for 5 minutes more.
4. Add the mushrooms and cook for 5 minutes more.
6. Pour in the wine and bring it to the

American

3 large sweet green
peppers
¾ pound mushrooms
¼ cup olive oil
1 large onion, quartered
and thinly sliced
1 garlic clove, finely
chopped
⅔ cup dry white wine
3 tablespoons tomato
paste

boil. Mix in the tomato purée (paste). Cover and simmer for 5 minutes again. **Note:** To freeze, cool completely, pack into a rigid container and cover. Thaw at room temperature. Reheat gently in a saucepan.

Casserole of Turnips and Baby Onions

Imperial (Metric)

1 lb (455g) white turnips
12 oz (340g) button onions
1 oz (30g) butter or vegetable margarine
8 fl oz (225ml) vegetable stock
Grated rind and juice of ½ lemon
1 teaspoon honey or Barbados sugar
4 tablespoons chopped parsley

1. Heat the oven to 350°F/180°C/Gas Mark 4.
2. Scrub the turnips and cut them into dice the same size as the onions. Peel the onions.
3. Melt the butter or margarine in a flameproof casserole on a high heat. Put in the turnips and onions and stir them until they begin to brown.
4. Pour in the stock and bring it to the boil. Add the lemon rind and juice, honey or sugar and parsley.
5. Cover the casserole and put it into the oven for 45 minutes.

Note: To freeze, cool completely, pack into a rigid container and cover.

American

1 pound white turnips
¾ pound button onions
2 tablespoons butter or vegetable margarine
1 cup vegetable stock
Grated rind and juice of ½ lemon
1 teaspoon honey or Barbados sugar
¼ cup chopped parsley

Mushrooms Baked with Lemon

Imperial (Metric)

2 oz (55g) butter or vegetable margarine
12 large, flat mushrooms
Juice of 1½ lemons
6 tablespoons chopped parsley
Freshly ground black pepper
3 tablespoons wholemeal breadcrumbs

1. Heat the oven to 400°F/200°C/Gas Mark 6.
2. Put the butter or margarine into a large, flat ovenproof dish and put it into the oven to melt.
3. Take the stalks from the mushrooms and reserve them.
4. Put the mushroom caps, black side down, in the butter to coat them. Turn them over. Roll the stalks in the butter and leave them beside the caps. Pour the lemon juice over the mushrooms. Scatter the parsley over them and season with the pepper.
5. Bake the mushrooms for 10 minutes. Scatter them with the crumbs and return them to the oven for a further 5 minutes.

Note: Unsuitable for freezing.

American

¼ cup butter or vegetable margarine
12 large, flat mushrooms
Juice of 1½ lemons
⅓ cup chopped parsley
Freshly ground black pepper
3 tablespoons wholewheat breadcrumbs

Savoury Cabbage and Green Peppers

Imperial (Metric)

1 medium-sized green cabbage
2 large green peppers
1 large cooking apple
1 large onion
4 tablespoons sunflower oil
1 garlic clove, finely chopped
4 tablespoons vegetable stock
4 tablespoons dry cider

1. Shred the cabbage. Core and seed the peppers and cut them into thin strips. Peel, core and slice the apple. Thinly slice the onion.
2. Heat the oil in a saucepan on a high heat. Put in the cabbage, peppers, apple, onion and garlic and stir until they become evenly coated with oil.
3. Pour in the stock and cider and bring them to the boil. Cover and cook on a low heat for 15 minutes, turning the vegetables once. Drain if necessary before serving.
Note: Unsuitable for freezing.

American

1 medium-sized green cabbage
2 large sweet green peppers
1 large cooking apple
1 large onion
¼ cup sunflower oil
1 garlic clove, finely chopped
¼ cup vegetable stock
¼ cup dry cider

Green Cabbage and Green Tomatoes

Imperial (Metric)

1 large green cabbage
12 oz (340g) green tomatoes
1 medium onion
1 oz (30g) butter or vegetable margarine

1. Shred the cabbage. Slice the tomatoes into rounds. Thinly slice the onion.
2. Melt the butter or margarine in a saucepan on a low heat. Put in the onion and soften it.
3. Raise the heat and stir in the cabbage and tomatoes. Stir on the high heat for 1 minute.
4. Lower the heat to a simmer. cover and cook for 20 minutes.
Note: Unsuitable for freezing.

American

1 large green cabbage
¾ pound green tomatoes
1 medium onion
2 tablespoons butter or vegetable margarine

Tomato and Mushroom Salad

Imperial (Metric)

1½ lb (685g) tomatoes
12 oz (340g) button mushrooms
18 green olives
4 oz (115g) sprouted alfalfa
4 tablespoons olive oil
2 tablespoons white wine vinegar
1 garlic clove, crushed
Freshly ground black pepper
2 tablespoons chopped basil or 2 teaspoons dried basil (see note)

1. Chop the tomatoes. Thinly slice the mushrooms. Stone (pit) and quarter the olives. Put them all into a salad bowl with the alfalfa.
2. Beat the oil, vinegar, garlic and pepper together. Fold them into the salad. Mix in the basil.
3. If possible, let the salad stand for 15 minutes before serving to enable the juices and oil to seep into the mushrooms to make them soft and moist.
Note: If using dried basil, make the dressing first, mix the basil into it and leave it to stand for 30 minutes before adding it to the salad.

American

1½ pounds tomatoes
¾ pound button mushrooms
18 green olives
¼ pound sprouted alfalfa
¼ cup olive oil
2 tablespoons white wine vinegar
1 garlic clove, crushed
Freshly ground black pepper
2 tablespoons chopped basil or 2 teaspoons dried basil (see note)

196

Marrow with Mushrooms

Imperial (Metric)

1½ lb (685g) marrow
12 oz (340g) open
   mushrooms
1 oz (30g) butter or
   vegetable margarine
1 large onion, thinly
   sliced
1 garlic clove, finely
   chopped
6 sage leaves, chopped
2 tablespoons Yorkshire
   relish

1. Cut the marrow in half lengthways and scoop out the seeds. Peel the halves and cut them into small, thin pieces.
2. Quarter or halve the mushrooms, depending on their size. If they are very large, cut them into 1 inch (2.5cm) squares.
3. Heat the butter or margarine in a very large frying pan (skillet) or paella pan on a low heat. Put in the onion and garlic and cook them gently until they are just brown.
4. Raise the heat to moderate and mix in the marrow, mushrooms and sage. Cook for 5 minutes, stirring.
5. Pour in the Yorkshire relish. Mix it in and let it bubble.
6. Take the pan from the heat and serve as soon as possible.
Note: Unsuitable for freezing.

American

1½ pounds marrow
¾ pound open mushrooms
2 tablespoons butter or
   vegetable margarine
1 large onion, thinly
   sliced
1 garlic clove, finely
   chopped
6 sage leaves, chopped
2 tablespoons Yorkshire
   relish

Jacket Potatoes with Chervil Filling

Imperial (Metric)

6 large potatoes
3 oz (85g) silken tofu
4 tablespoons chopped
   chervil
Freshly ground black
   pepper

1. Heat the oven 400°F/200°C/Gas Mark 6.
2. Scrub the potatoes and prick them on each side with a fork. Lay them on the oven rack and bake them for 1 hour 15 minutes, or until the skins are crisp and the middles soft.
3. Cut the potatoes in half lengthways. Scoop out the flesh and mash it. Reserve the skins and put them into a large, flat ovenproof dish.
4. Add the tofu, chervil and pepper to the mashed potato and mix well.
5. Put the mashed potato back into the skins and make patterns on the top with a fork.
6. Return the potatoes to the oven for 15 minutes or until the tops are beginning to brown.

American

6 large potatoes
⅓ cup silken tofu
¼ cup chopped chervil
Freshly ground black
   pepper

197

GRAINS AND PASTA

Think of autumn and you might well be reminded of barns full of newly harvested grain. A casserole of barley and vegetables and a dish of wheat cooked with fresh herbs are perhaps the most typically seasonal of the recipes below. The other dishes make use of other autumn produce: plums, corn, runner beans, watercress, apples and mushrooms.

Pasta with Runner Beans

Imperial (Metric)

12 oz (340g) runner beans
12 oz (340g) wholemeal pasta shapes
4 tablespoons olive oil
1 large onion, finely chopped
1 garlic clove, finely chopped
2 tablespoons chopped savory
2 tablespoons grated Parmesan cheese

1. Slice the runner beans.
2. Cook the pasta in lightly salted water for 12 minutes or until it is just tender. Drain it, run cold water through it and drain it again.
3. Heat the oil in a saucepan on a low heat. Put in the onion and garlic and soften them. Raise the heat to high. Stir in the beans and savory. Cover and cook gently for 15 minutes, stirring once. The beans should be just tender.
4. Fold in the pasta and stir gently to heat it through. Mix in the Parmesan cheese.
Note: Unsuitable for freezing.

American

¾ pound runner beans
¾ pound wholewheat pasta shapes
¼ cup olive oil
1 large onion, finely chopped
1 garlic clove, finely chopped
2 tablespoons chopped savory
2 tablespoons grated Parmesan cheese

Pasta with Watercress

Imperial (Metric)

12 oz (340g) small pasta shapes
8 oz (225g) watercress
1 oz (30g) butter or vegetable margarine
4 oz (115g) curd cheese
2 tablespoons tomato purée
2 tablespoons chopped basil or 2 teaspoons dried basil

1. Cook the pasta in lightly salted boiling water for 12 minutes or until it is tender. Drain it, run cold water through it and drain it again.
2. Finely chop the watercress.
3. Melt the butter or margarine in a saucepan on a high heat. Put in the watercress and stir it for 1 minute or until it just begins to wilt. Lower the heat.
4. Stir in the cheese, tomato purée (paste) and basil. When the cheese has melted slightly and become smooth, fold in the pasta. Stir it gently for about 30 seconds to heat it through.
Note: Unsuitable for freezing.

American

2 cups small pasta shapes
½ pound watercress
2 tablespoons butter or vegetable margarine
½ cup curd cheese
2 tablespoons tomato paste
2 tablespoons chopped basil or 2 teaspoons dried basil

Steamed Apple Rice

Imperial (Metric)

2 medium cooking apples
4 tablespoons sunflower
oil
1 large onion, quartered
and thinly sliced
1 garlic clove, finely
chopped
12 oz (340g) long-grain
brown rice
1½ pints (850ml)
vegetable stock
Sea salt and freshly
ground black pepper

1. Peel and core the apples and cut them into thin slices lengthways.
2. Heat the oil in a saucepan on a low heat. Put in the onion and garlic and cook them for 2 minutes.
3. Stir in the rice and apple slices and cook them for 1 minute.
4. Pour in the stock, bring it to the boil and season lightly with salt and liberally with pepper.
5. Cover and cook gently for 45 minutes or until the rice is soft and all the liquid has been absorbed.

Note: To freeze, cool completely, pack into a rigid container and cover. Store for up to 1 month. Thaw at room temperature. Reheat gently in a saucepan in 2 tablespoons sunflower oil.

American

2 medium cooking apples
¼ cup sunflower oil
1 large onion, quartered
and thinly sliced
1 garlic clove, finely
chopped
1½ cups long-grain brown
rice
3¾ cups vegetable stock
Sea salt and freshly
ground black pepper

Rice with Mushrooms, Chervil and Parsley

Imperial (Metric)

8 oz (225g) open
mushrooms
4 tablespoons sunflower
oil
1 large onion, quartered
and thinly sliced
12 oz (340g) long-grain
brown rice
2 tablespoons chopped
chervil
1½ pints (850ml)
vegetable stock
Juice of ½ lemon
Sea salt and freshly
ground black pepper
½ oz (15g) parsley,
chopped

1. Thinly slice the mushrooms.
2. Heat the oil in a saucepan on a low heat. Put in the onion and cook it until it is golden. Stir in the mushrooms and cook them for 1 minute. Stir in the rice and chervil.
3. Pour in the stock and bring it to the boil. Add the lemon juice and season lightly. Cover and simmer for 45 minutes, or until the rice is soft and all the stock has been absorbed.
4. Mix in the parsley just before serving.

Note: To freeze, cool completely, pack into a rigid container and cover. Store for up to 2 months. Thaw at room temperature. Put into a dish and cover with foil. Put into a pre-heated oven (350°F/180°C/Gas Mark 4) for 15 minutes.

American

½ pound open mushrooms
¼ cup sunflower oil
1 large onion, quartered
and thinly sliced
1½ cups long-grain brown
rice
2 tablespoons chopped
chervil
3¾ cups vegetable stock
Juice of ½ lemon
Sea salt and freshly
ground black pepper
1 tablespoon chopped
parsley

Millet with Sweetcorn

Imperial (Metric)

2 corn cobs
4 tablespoons sunflower
oil
1 medium onion, finely
chopped
1 garlic clove, finely
chopped
12 oz (340g) millet
2 teaspoons paprika
¼ - ½ teaspoon chilli
powder, to taste
1½ pints (850ml)
vegetable stock

1. Cut the corn from the cobs.
2. Heat the oil in a saucepan on a low heat. Put in the onion and garlic and soften them. Stir in the millet, corn, paprika and chilli powder.
3. Pour in the stock and bring it to the boil. Cover and simmer for 20 minutes or until the millet is soft and fluffy and all the stock has been absorbed.
Note: To freeze, cool completely, pack into a rigid container and cover. Store for up to 2 months. Thaw at room temperature. Put into a dish and cover with foil. Put into a pre-heated oven (350°F/180°C/Gas Mark 4) for 15 minutes.

American

2 corn cobs
¼ cup sunflower oil
1 medium onion, finely
chopped
1 garlic clove, finely
chopped
1½ cups millet
2 teaspoons paprika
¼-½ teaspoon chili
powder, to taste
3¾ cups vegetable stock

Herby Wheat Casserole

Imperial (Metric)

4 tablespoons sunflower
oil
1 large onion, thinly
sliced
12 oz (340g) whole wheat
grains
6 sorrel leaves, chopped
4 tablespoons chopped
parsley
2 tablespoons chopped
thyme
6 sage leaves, chopped
1½ pints (850ml)
vegetable stock
¼ pint (140ml) dry red
wine
Freshly ground black
pepper
1 bay leaf

1. Heat the oven to 325°F/170°C/Gas Mark 3.
2. Heat the oil in a flameproof casserole on a low heat. Put in the onion and soften it.
3. Stir in the wheat and chopped herbs.
4. Pour in the stock and wine and bring them to the boil. Season with the pepper and add the bay leaf.
5. Cover and put the wheat into the oven for 2 hours. Remove bay leaf before serving.
Note: To freeze, cool completely. Pack into a rigid container and cover. Store for up to 1 month. Thaw at room temperature and reheat by putting into a hot oven (400°F/200°C/Gas Mark 6) for 15 minutes.

American

¼ cup sunflower oil
1 large onion, thinly
sliced
1½ cups whole wheat
grains
6 sorrel leaves, chopped
¼ cup chopped parsley
2 tablespoons chopped
thyme
6 sage leaves, chopped
3¾ cups vegetable stock
⅔ cup dry red wine
Freshly ground black
pepper
1 bay leaf

Barley and Vegetable Bake

Imperial (Metric)

1½ lb (685g) pumpkin
2 medium-sized courgettes
1 red pepper
1 large onion
1 garlic clove
4 tablespoons sunflower
oil
12 oz (340g) pot barley
1 pint (570ml) vegetable
stock
½ pint (285ml) tomato
and vegetable juice

1. Heat the oven to 350°F/180°C/Gas Mark 4.
2. Cut the rind, pith and seeds from the pumpkin and finely chop the flesh. Finely chop the courgettes (zucchini). Core, seed and chop the pepper. Finely chop the onion and garlic.
3. Heat the oil in a flameproof casserole on a low heat. Put in the pumpkin, onion and garlic. Cover and cook them for 10 minutes. Stir in the courgettes (zucchini), pepper and barley.
4. Pour in the stock and tomato and vegetable juice and bring them to the boil.
5. Cover the casserole and put it into the oven for 45 minutes, or until the barley is soft and all the liquid has been absorbed.
Note: To freeze, cool completely. Pack into a rigid container and cover. Store for up to 1 month. Thaw at room temperature. Reheat by putting into a covered casserole and into a hot oven (400°F/200°C/Gas Mark 6) for 15 minutes.

American

1½ pounds pumpkin
2 medium-sized zucchini
1 sweet red pepper
1 large onion
1 garlic clove
¼ cup sunflower oil
1½ cups pot barley
2½ cups vegetable stock
1¼ cups tomato and
vegetable juice

Buckwheat with Plums

Imperial (Metric)

8 oz (225g) cooking
plums
12 oz (340g) buckwheat
1½ pints (850ml)
vegetable stock
¼ teaspoon ground
allspice
1 medium onion, finely
chopped
1 garlic clove, finely
chopped

1. Stone (pit) and quarter the plums. Heat a large, heavy frying pan (skillet) on a medium heat. Put in the buckwheat and stir it until it begins to brown.
2. Pour in the stock and bring it to the boil. Add the plums, allspice, onion and garlic.
3. Cover and simmer gently for 20 minutes or until the buckwheat is soft and all the water has been absorbed.
Note: To freeze, cool completely. Pack into a rigid container and cover. Store for up to 1 month. Thaw at room temperature. Reheat by stirring gently in a saucepan on a low heat.

American

½ pound cooking plums
1½ cups buckwheat
3¾ cups vegetable stock
¼ teaspoon ground
allspice
1 medium onion, finely
chopped
1 garlic clove, finely
chopped

DESSERTS

There are so many fresh fruits available in the Autumn that choosing a dessert should be no problem. There are late varieties of plums and greengages, followed by damsons; the first of the year's cooking apples to combine with blackberries; and, later, pears, both firm and juicy. Pumpkins can make delicious desserts as well as savoury dishes, and figs and pomegranates add an exotic touch.

Brown Rice and Pear Mould

Imperial (Metric)

2 lb (900g) cooking pears
1 pint (570ml) apple juice
4 cardamom pods, bruised
6 coriander seeds
Two 2-inch (5cm)
cinnamon sticks
8 oz (225g) long-grain
brown rice
½ pint (285ml) soya milk
½ pint (285ml) water
4 tablespoons
concentrated apple juice
Agar-agar to set ¾ pint
(425ml) liquid (see
manufacturer's
instructions)
4 tablespoons Calvados
4 squares sugar-free carob
bar
Single cream, optional

American

2 pounds cooking pears
2½ cups apple juice
4 cardamom pods, bruised
6 coriander seeds
Two 2-inch cinnamon
sticks
1 cup long-grain brown
rice
1¼ cups soya milk
1¼ cups water
¼ cup concentrated apple
juice
Agar-agar to set 2 cups
liquid (see manufacturer's
instructions)
¼ cup Calvados
4 squares sugar-free carob
bar
Light cream, optional

1. Peel the pears. Core them and slice them lengthways.
2. Put the apple juice into a saucepan with 2 cardamom pods, all the coriander seeds and one cinnamon stick. Bring it to the boil. Put in the pears and poach them gently for 20 minutes or until they are soft but not falling apart. Drain the pears, reserving the juice. Discard the spices.
3. Put the rice into a saucepan with the soya milk, water, concentrated apple juice, rest of the cardamom pods and other cinnamon stick. Bring it to the boil. Cover and simmer for 45 minutes or until the rice is soft and all the apple juice has been absorbed. Take the pan from the heat.
4. Chop about three-quarters of the pears. Cut the rest into matchstick pieces.
5. Put the reserved juice into a saucepan and bring it to just below boiling point. Stir in the agar-agar until it has dissolved. Take the pan from the heat and mix in the rice and the chopped pears.
6. Put the mixture into a lightly oiled, 2 pint (1.14 litre/5 cup) mould. Leave it in a cool place for 2 hours to set.
7. Lightly toss the reserved pears with the Calvados.
8. Turn the set rice and pears out of the mould. Arrange the pears in Calvados over the top. Grate over the carob bar.
9. Serve the cream separately.
Note: Unsuitable for freezing.

Buckwheat Pancakes (Crêpes) with Damson Sauce

Imperial (Metric)

Pancakes:
½ oz (15g) fresh yeast or
1 tablespoon dried yeast
½ pint (285ml) warm
water
1 teaspoon honey (if using
dried yeast)
4 oz (115g) buckwheat
flour
Pinch fine sea salt
1 egg, separated
2 tablespoons sunflower
oil
Sunflower oil for frying
Sauce:
1½ lb (685g) damsons,
halved and stoned
Grated rind and juice of
1 medium orange
1 oz (30g) butter or
vegetable margarine
4 oz (115g) honey
Pinch ground allspice
1 oz (30g) ground mixed
nuts
For serving:
Soured cream

1. If you are using fresh yeast, crumble it into a bowl and pour in half the water; if dried, dissolve the honey in half the water and stir in the yeast. Leave the yeast in a warm place until it is frothy.

2. Put the flour and salt into a bowl and make a well in the centre. Gradually beat in the egg, the remaining water, oil and yeast mixture. Cover the bowl with a clean tea cloth and leave the batter for 1 hour to rise.

3. For the filling, put the damsons into a saucepan with the orange rind and juice, butter or margarine, honey and allspice.

   Cover and set on a low heat for 15 minutes, or until they can be beaten to a thick purée. Rub the purée through a sieve. Mix in the nuts.

4. Heat 1 tablespoon sunflower oil in an omelette pan on a high heat. Spoon in 3 tablespoons of the batter and tip the pan to spread it evenly. Cook the pancake (crêpe) until it is golden brown on both sides. As the pancakes (crêpes) are cooked, slide them onto a plate standing over a pan of hot water, putting greaseproof paper between them. Add more oil to the pan as necessary.

5. Serve two pancakes (crêpes) at a time on individual plates. Place each one flat, put 2 tablespoons of the filling on one quarter. Fold the pancake (crêpe) into quarters. Spoon a little more filling on top and then a portion of the soured cream. Serve any extra soured cream separately.

Note: To freeze, cool the pancakes (crêpes) completely and stack them with layers of greaseproof paper between them. Seal in a polythene bag and freeze flat. The sauce may be frozen in a covered container. Freeze both for up to 2 months. Thaw at room temperature.

American

Crêpes:
2 tablespoons fresh yeast
or 1 tablespoon dried
yeast
1¼ cups warm water
1 teaspoon honey (if using
dried yeast)
1 cup buckwheat flour
Pinch fine sea salt
1 egg, separated
2 tablespoons sunflower
oil
Sunflower oil for frying
Sauce:
1½ pounds damsons,
halved and pitted
Grated rind and juice of
1 medium orange
2 tablespoons butter or
vegetable margarine
⅓ cup honey
Pinch ground allspice
2 tablespoons ground
mixed nuts
For serving:
Sour cream

Pumpkin and Pecan Pie

Imperial (Metric)

Pastry:
8 oz (225g) wholemeal
flour
1 teaspoon bicarbonate of
soda
Pinch fine sea salt
5 oz (140g) vegetable
margarine
4 tablespoons cold water
Filling:
1 lb (455g) pumpkin
3 oz (85g) pecan nuts
4 oz (115g) Barbados
sugar
1 teaspoon ground
cinnamon
¼ nutmeg, grated
½ teaspoon ground ginger
2 eggs, beaten
½ pint (285ml) soured
cream
Grated rind of 1 lemon
3 tablespoons brandy
Pecan halves for garnish

1. To make the pastry, put the flour into a bowl with the bicarbonate of (baking) soda and salt. Make a well in the centre. Put in the margarine and water. Using a fork, gradually mix in the flour from the sides of the well until a dough is formed. Finally bring the dough together with your fingers. Leave the dough in a cool place while you prepare the filling.
2. Heat the oven to 375°F/190°C/Gas Mark 5.
3. Cut the rind, pith and seeds from the pumpkin. Cut the flesh into cubes. Steam them for 15 minutes or until soft. Rub them through a sieve or the fine blade of a vegetable mill.
4. Finely grind the pecan nuts. Mix them into the pumpkin purée. Add the sugar and spices and gradually beat in first the eggs and then the soured cream. Mix in the lemon rind and brandy.
5. Roll out the pastry and use it to line a 10 inch (25cm) diameter tart tin. Put in the filling.
6. Bake the pie for 50 minutes or until the filling is firm.
7. Cool the pie until it is just warm. Garnish it with the pecan nuts and serve.
Note: Unsuitable for freezing.

American

Pastry:
2 cups wholewheat flour
1 teaspoon baking soda
Pinch fine sea salt
⅔ cup vegetable
margarine
¼ cup cold water
Filling:
1 pound pumpkin
⅔ cup pecan nuts
⅔ cup Barbados sugar
1 teaspoon ground
cinnamon
¼ nutmeg, grated
½ teaspoon ground ginger
2 eggs, beaten
1¼ cups sour cream
Grated rind of 1 lemon
3 tablespoons brandy
Pecan halves for garnish

Blackberry and Apple Cream Pie

Imperial (Metric)

Shortcrust pastry made
with 10 oz (285g)
wholemeal flour (see page
24)
1 lb (455g) cooking
apples
8 oz (225g) blackberries
4 oz (115g) dates
2 bananas
3 oz (85g) honey
¼ pint (140ml) double
cream
1 egg, beaten

1. Heat the oven to 400°F/200°C/Gas Mark 6.
2. Make the pastry. Use about two-thirds to line a 10 inch (25cm) tart tin.
3. Peel, core and chop the apples. Mix them with the blackberries. Chop the dates and bananas and add them to the blackberries and apples.
4. Mix in the honey and the cream.
5. Put the filling into the tart. Cover it with the remaining pastry. Brush the top with beaten egg.

American

Shortcrust pastry made
with 2½ cups wholewheat
flour (see page 24)
1 pound cooking apples
½ pound blackberries
¼ pound dates
2 bananas
¼ cup honey
⅔ cup heavy cream
1 egg, beaten

6. Bake the pie for 30 minutes or until the top is golden brown.

7. Serve hot or warm. No accompaniment is needed.

Note: The pie is best if frozen in the tin. Cool it completely first and then put it into a large polythene bag. Store it for up to 1 month. To reheat, put the pie, frozen, into a preheated 400°F/200°C/Gas Mark 6 oven for 20 minutes.

Greengage Custards

Imperial (Metric)

1½ lb (685g) greengages
½ pint (285ml) water
2 oz (55g) honey
1 blade mace
6 allspice berries
¾ pint (425ml) milk
3 eggs, beaten
¼ teaspoon ground mace
Sauce:
2 tablespoons no-sugar-added apricot jam, sieved
Pinch ground mace
½ pint (285ml) Greek-style natural yogurt
Garnish:
2 pieces preserved stem ginger, chopped

American

1½ pounds greengages
1¼ cups water
2 tablespoons honey
1 blade mace
6 allspice berries
2 cups milk
3 eggs, beaten
¼ teaspoon ground mace
Sauce:
2 tablespoons no-sugar-added apricot jelly, sieved
Pinch ground mace
1¼ cups Greek-style unflavored yogurt
Garnish:
2 pieces preserved stem ginger, chopped

1. Halve and stone (pit) the greengages.
2. Put the water and honey into a wide-based saucepan with the mace and allspice berries. Bring them slowly to the boil, stirring, so the honey dissolves. Boil for 2 minutes.
3. Take the pan from the heat. Put in the greengages, cut side up.
4. Put the pan back on the heat and let the syrup boil over the fruit. Lower the heat, cover and simmer for 15 minutes.
5. Lift out the greengages with a slotted spoon. Either rub them through a sieve or put them through the fine blade of a vegetable mill. Cool the purée completely.
6. Heat the oven to 325°F/170°C/Gas Mark 3.
7. Mix the milk, eggs and ground mace into the greengage purée. Pour the mixture into six individual custard pots or soufflé dishes.
8. Stand the pots in a baking dish with water to come half way up their sides.
9. Bake the custards for 1 hour or until they are set and browned on top.
10. For the sauce, beat the apricot jam (jelly) and the ground mace into the yogurt.
11. When the custards are still warm, spoon a portion of the sauce on the top. Garnish with the chopped ginger. Serve as soon as possible.

Note: Unsuitable for freezing.

Baked Pears with Chilled Walnut Sauce

Imperial (Metric)

6 firm dessert pears
*3 oz (85g) Barbados
sugar*
1 oz (30g) butter
4 tablespoons apple juice
*3 oz (85g) walnuts,
chopped*
*12 fl oz (340ml) Greek-
style natural yogurt,
chilled*
12 walnut halves

1. Heat the oven to 400°F/200°C/Gas Mark 6.
2. Peel the pears. Cut them in half lengthways. Scoop out the seeds. Place the pears, cut side down, in an ovenproof dish. Scatter over half the sugar and dot with butter. Cover the dish with foil.
3. Put the remaining sugar into a saucepan with the apple juice. Set them on a low heat and stir for the sugar to melt. Stir in the chopped walnuts. Take the pan from the heat and cool the contents slightly.
4. Mix the walnuts and syrup into the yogurt. Chill the mixture until the pears are ready.
5. Bake the pears for 20 minutes.
6. To serve, lift the hot pears into warm serving bowls. Top them with the chilled sauce and the walnut halves.
Note: Unsuitable for freezing.

American

6 firm dessert pears
½ cup Barbados sugar
2 tablespoons butter
¼ cup apple juice
*⅔ cup English walnuts,
chopped*
*1½ cups Greek-style
unflavored yogurt, chilled*
12 English walnut halves

Pumpkin and Orange Creams

Imperial (Metric)

1 lb 2 oz (500g) pumpkin
*Grated rind and juice of
1 medium orange*
¼ nutmeg, grated
3 oz (85g) soft honey
2 eggs, separated
*1 lb (455g) low-fat soft
cheese*
4 fl oz (125ml) whisky
*3 fl oz (90ml) double
cream*
Garnish:
Toasted flaked almonds
6 thin orange slices

1. Cut the rind, seeds and pith from the pumpkin. Chop the flesh and steam it for 15 minutes. Rub it through a sieve or put it through the fine blade of a vegetable mill. Beat in the orange rind and juice, nutmeg, honey and egg yolks.
2. Put the mixture into a saucepan. Set the pan on a low heat and stir, without boiling, until the mixture begins to thicken. Take the pan from the heat and let the mixture cool.
3. Put the cheese into a bowl and beat in the whisky. Gradually beat in the pumpkin mixture.
4. Lightly whip the cream. Stiffly whip the egg whites.
5. Fold first the cream and then the egg whites into the pumpkin mixture.
6. Divide the mixture between six dessert glasses. Chill it for 2 hours.

American

*1 pound 2 ounces
pumpkin*
*Grated rind and juice of
1 medium orange*
¼ nutmeg, grated
¼ cup soft honey
2 eggs, separated
2 cups low-fat soft cheese
½ cup whisky
⅓ cup heavy cream
Garnish:
Toasted slivered almonds
6 thin orange slices

7. Scatter the toasted almonds over the creams. Make the orange slices into twists and put them on the top.
Note: Unsuitable for freezing.

Apple-Mousse Tart

Imperial (Metric)

*Shortcrust pastry made
with 8 oz (225g)
wholemeal flour
(see page 24)
1 lb (455g) cooking
apples
¼ pint (140ml) dry cider
3 oz (85g) honey
Agar-agar to set 1 pint
(570ml) liquid (see
manufacturer's
instructions)
2 eggs, separated
10 oz (285g) silken tofu*
Garnish:
*2 dessert apples
¼ pint (140ml) apple
juice
2 tablespoons honey
3 tablespoons chopped
toasted mixed nuts or
hazelnuts*

American

*Shortcrust pastry made
with 2 cups wholewheat
flour (see page 24)
1 pound cooking apples
⅔ cup dry cider
3 tablespoons honey
Agar-agar to set 2½ cups
liquid (see manufacturer's
instructions)
2 eggs, separated
1¼ cups silken tofu*
Garnish:
*2 dessert apples
⅔ cups apple juice
2 tablespoons honey
3 tablespoons chopped
toasted mixed nuts or
hazelnuts*

1. Make the pastry. Use it to line a 10 inch (25cm) tart tin. Bake it blind for 15 minutes. Cool it completely.

2. Quarter, core and chop the apples. Put them into a saucepan with 4 tablespoons (¼ cup) of the cider. Cover them and set on a low heat for 15 minutes or until they are soft and can be beaten to a purée. Take them from the heat and rub them through a sieve.

3. Return the apple purée to a saucepan. Stir in the honey and remaining cider.

4. Bring the apple purée to just below boiling point. Stir in the agar-agar and stir on the heat until it has dissolved.

5. Take the pan from the heat and beat in the egg yolks, one at a time.

6. Leave the mixture until it is lukewarm but not set.

7. Stiffly whip the egg whites. Either rub the tofu through a sieve or cream it in a blender or food processor.

8. Fold first the tofu and then the egg whites into the apple mixture.

9. Pour the mixture into the pastry case. Leave it in a cool place for 2 hours to set.

10. To make the garnish, peel and core the dessert apples and cut them into thin slices lengthways. Put the apple juice and honey into a saucepan. Bring them to the boil. Put in the apple slices and gently poach them until they are transparent but not falling apart. Lift them onto a plate and cool them.

11. Just before serving, scatter the chopped toasted nuts over the apple mousse. Arrange the poached apple slices on top.
Note: Unsuitable for freezing.

Apple and Hazelnut Round

Imperial (Metric)

3 oz (85g) hazelnuts
3 oz (85g) butter or
vegetable margarine
2 tablespoons honey
5 oz (140g) wholemeal
flour
Pinch fine sea salt
1 lb (455g) dessert apples,
Cox's if possible, peeled,
cored and chopped
1 tablespoon no-sugar-
added apricot jam
Grated rind of 1 lemon
2 oz (55g) sultanas
2 oz (55g) raisins
¼ pint (140ml) double
cream, stiffly whipped

1. Heat the oven to 350°F/180°C/Gas Mark 4.
2. Spread the hazelnuts on a baking tray and roast them for 7-8 minutes or until they are a deep, golden brown. Reserve nine. Finely grind the rest.
3. Cream the butter or margarine. Beat in the honey. Mix together the flour, salt and ground nuts. Gradually beat them into the butter or margarine. Knead the mixture lightly with your hands to make a smooth dough. Chill it for 30 minutes.
4. Put the apples into a saucepan with the apricot jam (jelly) and lemon rind. Cover them and set them on a low heat for 10 minutes or until they are soft. Add the sultanas (golden seedless raisins) and raisins. Cover again and cook for 5 minutes. Take the pan from the heat and cool the apple mixture.
5. Divide the dough into two. Roll each piece out on a floured baking sheet to a round of about 8 inches (20cm). They will be very thin. Trim the edges to make them even shaped.
6. Bake the pastry rounds for 10 minutes or until they are firm but not coloured.
7. Cut one of the rounds into eight sections. Leave the pastry on the baking sheets to cool for 5 minutes. Carefully lift them onto wire racks to cool completely.
8. Lay the uncut pastry round on a large serving plate. Cover it with the apple mixture. Lay the sections of the other round on top.
9. Pipe a portion of cream onto each section of the pastry plus one in the middle. Place a reserved hazelnut on top of each.

Note: The apple filling may be frozen in a covered container and stored for up to 2 months. Thaw at room temperature. The pastry rounds are too fragile to be stored in a freezer.

American

⅔ cup hazelnuts
⅓ cup butter or vegetable
margarine
2 tablespoons honey
1¼ cups wholewheat flour
Pinch fine sea salt
1 pound dessert apples,
Cox's if possible, peeled,
cored and chopped
1 tablespoon no-sugar-
added apricot jelly
Grated rind of 1 lemon
⅓ cup golden seedless
raisins
⅓ cup raisins
⅔ cup heavy cream, stiffly
whipped

Figs and Oranges in White Wine

Imperial (Metric)

¾ pint (425ml) medium
sweet white wine
4 oz (115g) honey
12 fresh figs
6 large oranges

1. Put the wine and honey into a saucepan and stir on a low heat for the honey to dissolve. Bring them to simmering point.
2. Put in the whole figs, cover and simmer for 15 minutes. Cool in the liquid.
3. Cut the rind and pith from the oranges. Cut the flesh into skinless segments.
4. Put orange segments into the bottom of six dessert glasses. Put the figs on top. Spoon over a little of the wine syrup. Chill for 30 minutes.
Note: The poached figs can be frozen in the syrup in a rigid, covered container. Store them for up to 2 months. Thaw at room temperature. Arrange them with the oranges in the dishes and chill again.

American

2 cups medium sweet
white wine
⅓ cup honey
12 fresh figs
6 large oranges

Scandinavian-Style Blackberry Tart

Imperial (Metric)

Dough:
5 oz (150g) butter or
margarine
3 tablespoons pear and
apple spread
1 egg, beaten
4 tablespoons single cream
9 oz (250g) wholemeal
flour
1 teaspoon vanilla essence
Filling:
1½ lb (685g) blackberries
4 oz (115g) honey
1 oz (30g) fresh
wholemeal breadcrumbs
For serving:
Either ½ pint (285ml)
double cream, whipped; or
8 oz (225g) silken tofu,
whipped with 2
tablespoons honey or no-
sugar-added jam

1. Heat the oven to 400°F/200°C/Gas Mark 6.
2. Cream the butter or margarine with the pear and apple spread. Beat in the egg, a little at a time. Alternately beat in the cream and flour. Stir in the vanilla essence. With floured hands, spread the dough over the base and sides of a large pie dish.
3. Mix the blackberries with the honey and breadcrumbs. Put them into the dough.
4. Bake the tart for 20 minutes or until the pastry round the edge is golden brown.
5. Serve warm or cold, with the cream or tofu separately.
Note: Unsuitable for freezing.

American

Dough:
⅔ cup butter or
margarine
3 tablespoons pear and
apple spread
1 egg, beaten
¼ cup light cream
2¼ cups wholewheat flour
1 teaspoon vanilla essence
Filling:
1½ pounds blackberries
⅓ cup honey
¼ cup fresh wholewheat
breadcrumbs
For serving:
Either 1¼ cups heavy
cream, whipped; or 1 cup
silken tofu, whipped with
2 tablespoons honey or
no-sugar-added jelly

Filled Choux Buns with Blackberry Sauce

Imperial (Metric)

Sauce:
1½ lb (685g) blackberries
3 tablespoons water
2 tablespoons honey
2-inch (5cm) cinnamon
stick
4 allspice berries
Garnish:
Thinly pared rind of 1
large orange
Choux buns:
7½ fl oz (215ml) water
3 oz (85g) butter or
vegetable margarine
3½ oz (95g) wholemeal
flour
3 eggs, beaten separately
Filling:
8 oz (225g) low-fat soft
cheese
4 tablespoons Greek-tyle
natural yogurt
4 tablespoons no-sugar-
added mixed berry jam

1. Put the blackberries into a saucepan with the water, honey, cinnamon and allspice. Cover them and set on a low heat for 15 minutes, or until the blackberries are soft and juicy. Rub them through a sieve. Keep the sauce hot, or reheat it when needed.
2. Cut the orange rind into small, thin slivers. Cook them in a pan of boiling water for 2 minutes. Drain them.
3. Heat the oven to 400°F/200°C/Gas Mark 6.
4. Put the water and butter or margarine into a saucepan. Bring them to the boil. When they are bubbling, take the pan from the heat. Stir in all the flour at once and beat vigorously for a few seconds to make the mixture smooth. Beat in two eggs, one at a time. Beat in about half the remaining egg. The pastry must be firm enough to keep its shape. Beat until the pastry looks glossy.
5. Pipe the mixture into small balls on a dampened baking sheet; or simply spoon on two-teaspoon amounts and form them into balls with the spoon. Brush the tops with the remaining egg.
6. Put the buns into the oven for 10 minutes. Turn the heat to 425°F/220°C/Gas Mark 7 and cook for a further 15 minutes or until they are firm to the touch. Lift the buns onto wire racks. Prick the side of each with a fine skewer to release the steam. Leave them to cool completely.
8. For the filling, put the cheese into a bowl. Beat in the yogurt and the jam (jelly).
9. Slit the buns crossways and fill them with the cheese mixture.
10. Either divide them between six small bowls or put them all into one large serving dish. Spoon the blackberry sauce

American

Sauce:
1½ pounds blackberries
3 tablespoons water
2 tablespoons honey
2-inch cinnamon stick
4 allspice berries
Garnish:
Thinly pared rind of 1
large orange
Choux buns:
1 cup water
⅓ cup butter or vegetable
margarine
¾ cup wholewheat flour
3 eggs, beaten separately
Filling:
1 cup low-fat soft cheese
¼ cup Greek-style
unflavored yogurt
¼ cup no-sugar-added
berry jelly

over the top. Garnish with the slivers of orange rind.

Note: The cooked buns may be frozen before they are filled. Cool them completely. Freeze them flat on a baking sheet and then pack them into polythene bags. Store for up to 3 months. Thaw by putting them, still frozen, into a hot oven for 10 minutes. To freeze the sauce, pack it into a rigid container and cover. Store for up to 2 months. Thaw at room temperature. The filling is unsuitable for freezing.

Blackberry Ice-Cream

Imperial (Metric)

12 oz (340g) blackberries
3 fl oz (90ml) red grape juice
4 oz (115g) honey
½ pint (285ml) double cream
½ pint (285ml) natural yogurt

1. Put the blackberries into a saucepan with the grape juice and honey. Cover them and set them on a low heat for 15 minutes or until they are soft and juicy. Take them from the heat, rub them through a sieve and cool completely.
2. Lightly whip the cream. Whip in the yogurt and three-quarters of the blackberry purée.
3. Pour the mixture into a freezing tray. Put it into the freezer or into the freezing compartment of the refrigerator (set at the lowest temperature) for 1 hour. Take it out and whip it well. Return the mixture to the freezing tray. Freeze it for a further 1½ hours. Whip it again. Put the mixture into a covered plastic container and freeze it completely.
4. Store in the freezer or in the freezing compartment of the refrigerator (now set at normal) for 24 hours before serving.
5. To serve, scoop out the ice-cream with a scoop that you have dipped in hot water. Put the scoops into chilled individual dishes. Spoon a little of the reserved blackberry purée on top.

Note: The ice-cream may be stored in the freezer for up to 3 months; or in the freezing compartment of the refrigerator for up to 2 weeks or according to the star rating.

American

¾ pound blackberries
⅓ cup red grape juice
⅓ cup honey
1¼ cups heavy cream
1¼ cups unflavored yogurt

Fig Whip with Pomegranate Seeds

Imperial (Metric)

8 fresh figs
¼ pint (140ml) red grape juice
4 tablespoons rose water
3 oz (85g) no-sugar-added strawberry jam
1 lb (455g) silken tofu
2 pomegranates

1. Chop the figs, including the skins. Put them into a saucepan with the grape juice, rose water and jam (jelly). Bring them gently to the boil, cover and simmer for 15 minutes.
2. Rub the contents of the pan through a sieve. You will leave behind the skins but not the seeds of the figs. Cool the purée completely.
3. Put the tofu into a blender or food processor. Whip it until it is smooth. Add the fig purée and blend it in.
4. Turn the mixture into a bowl. Mix in the seeds of the two pomegranates, reserving some for garnish.
5. Chill the whip for 1 hour. Scatter the remaining pomegranate seeds over the top just before serving.
Note: Unsuitable for freezing.

American

8 fresh figs
⅔ cup red grape juice
4 tablespoons rose water
¼ cup no-sugar-added strawberry jelly
2 cups silken tofu
2 pomegranates

Plums in Almond Batter

Imperial (Metric)

1½ lb (685g) plums, stoned and sliced
3 oz (85g) honey, melted and cooled
1 teaspoon ground mixed spice
2 oz (55g) wholemeal flour
Pinch fine sea salt
4 oz (115g) ground almonds
2 eggs
1 egg yolk
1 oz (30g) butter, melted
½ pint (285ml) milk
¼ teaspoon almond essence

1. Put the plums into a bowl and mix them with half the honey and the mixed spice. Put them into the bottom of a 2 inch (5cm) deep, ovenproof dish.
2. Put the flour, salt and almonds into a mixing bowl and toss them together. Make a well in the centre and put in the eggs and egg yolk. Gradually beat in a little of the flour from the sides of the well. Beat in the butter and the remaining honey. Add the milk, a little at a time, adding the almond essence about half way through. Beat until you have a smooth batter. Leave in a cool place for 30 minutes.
3. Heat the oven to 350°F/180°C/Gas Mark 4.
4. Pour the batter over the plums.
5. Bake for 30 minutes until set and golden.
6. Serve warm, with single (light) cream, smetana or yogurt separately.
Note: Unsuitable for freezing.

American

1½ pounds plums, pitted and sliced
3 tablespoons honey, melted and cooled
1 teaspoon ground mixed spice
½ cup wholewheat flour
Pinch fine sea salt
1 cup ground almonds
2 eggs
1 egg yolk
2 tablespoons butter, melted
1¼ cups milk
¼ teaspoon almond essence

Big Plum Layer Cake

Imperial (Metric)

1½ lb plums
¼ pint (140ml) dry red wine
Two 3-inch (7.5cm) cinnamon sticks
4 oz (115g) honey
10 oz (285g) wholemeal flour
1½ teaspoons ground cinnamon
1 teaspoon bicarbonate of soda
10 oz (285g) butter or vegetable margarine
10 oz (285g) pear and apple spread
5 eggs, beaten
Filling:
½ pint (285ml) double cream, whipped
8 oz (225g) curd cheese
2 oz (55g) honey

1. Heat the oven to 350°F/180°C/Gas Mark 4.
2. Stone (pit) and slice the plums.
3. Put the wine, cinnamon and honey into a saucepan. Stir them on a low heat for the honey to melt. Bring them to the boil. Put in the plums. Poach them gently for 10 minutes or until they are soft but still intact. Cool them completely.
4. Toss the flour with the cinnamon and bicarbonate of (baking) soda. Cream the butter or margarine and beat in the pear and apple spread. Alternately beat in the eggs and flour.
5. Line two 10 inch (25cm) flan tins with greased paper.
6. Divide the mixture between the two tins. Bake the cakes for 15 minutes or until they are firm and springy. Turn them onto wire racks to cool.
7. Fold the cream and cheese together. Beat in the honey.
8. Spread half the cream mixture over one of the cakes. Lift the plums from their cooking liquid with a slotted spoon. Lay half on top of the cream mixture. Repeat the layers, arranging the plums on top attractively.

Note: The cakes can be frozen separately. Freeze them flat on baking trays and put them into polythene bags. They will keep for up to 3 months. Thaw them, uncovered, on racks at room temperature. The plums can be cooked and frozen separately in a rigid, covered container, without the cinnamon. Thaw them at room temperature. The cream filling is unsuitable for freezing.

American

1½ pounds plums
⅔ cup dry red wine
Two 3-inch cinnamon sticks
⅓ cup honey
2½ cups wholewheat flour
1½ teaspoons ground cinnamon
1 teaspoon baking soda
1¼ cups butter or vegetable margarine
¾ cup pear and apple spread
5 eggs, beaten
Filling:
1¼ cups heavy cream, whipped
1 cup curd cheese
2 tablespoons honey

213

BAKING

Blackberry bread is an old cottage recipe from the days when blackberries were used as a free substitute for currants. Seeds are harvested from the herb garden in autumn and these make tasty additions to breads and rolls.

Blackberry Bread

Imperial (Metric)

1 oz (30g) fresh yeast or
½ oz (15g) dried yeast
¼ pint (140ml) warm
water
2 tablespoons honey
14 oz (400g) wholemeal
flour
2 oz (55g) bran
½ teaspoon fine sea salt
½ teaspoon ground
cinnamon
⅛ nutmeg, grated
1½ oz (45g) vegetable fat
1 egg, beaten
¼ pint (140ml) milk,
warmed
8 oz (225g) blackberries

American

2 tablespoons fresh yeast
or 1 tablespoon dried
yeast
⅔ cup warm water
2 tablespoons honey
3½ cups wholewheat flour
½ cup bran
½ teaspoon fine sea salt
½ teaspoon ground
cinnamon
⅛ nutmeg, grated
3 tablespoons white
vegetable fat
1 egg, beaten
⅔ cup milk, warmed
½ pound blackberries

1. If you are using fresh yeast, crumble it into a bowl and pout in the water; if dried, pour the water into a bowl, stir in 1 teaspoon honey and sprinkle in the yeast. Leave the yeast in a warm place to froth. Melt and cool the remaining honey.

2. Put the flour, bran, salt and spices into a bowl. Rub in the vegetable fat.

3. Make a well in the centre and pour in the yeast mixture. Mix in a little flour from the sides of the bowl. Put in the egg, milk, honey and blackberries. Mix everything to a moist dough, which should be slippery in consistency. Knead it in the bowl, taking the bottom and sides to the middle. Cover the bowl with a clean tea cloth and leave it in a warm place for 1 hour to rise.

4. Heat the oven to 400°F/200°C/Gas Mark 6.

5. Knead the mixture again with your hands. Divide it between two greased 1 pound (455g) loaf tins.

6. Cover the loaves with the tea cloth and leave them in a warm place for 15 minutes.

7. Bake the loaves for 45 minutes. Turn them onto wire racks to cool.

Note: Serve either for tea or with cheese at the end of a meal.

Beer and Dill Bread

Imperial (Metric)

1 oz (30g) fresh yeast or
½ oz (15g) dried yeast
¾ pint (425ml) bitter beer
1 teaspoon molasses
1½ lb (685g) wholemeal
flour
2 teaspoons fine sea salt
2 teaspoons dill seeds

American

2 tablespoons fresh yeast
or 1 tablespoon dried
yeast
2 cups bitter beer
1 teaspoon molasses
6 cups wholewheat flour
2 teaspoons fine sea salt
2 teaspoons dill seeds

1. Put the yeast into a bowl. Warm ¼ pint (110ml/⅔ cup) beer. Pour it over the yeast. Stir in the molasses. Leave the yeast in a warm place until it froths.
2. Put the flour into a bowl and toss in the salt and the dill seeds.
3. Make a well in the centre. Pour in the yeast mixture and the remaining beer. Mix everything to a dough. Turn it onto a floured work surface and knead it until it is no longer sticky. Return it to the bowl. Make a cross-cut in the top. Cover with a clean tea cloth and leave it for 1 hour to rise.
4. Heat the oven to 400°F/200°C/Gas Mark 6.
5. Knead the dough again. Divide it into two. Shape each piece into a round and lay it on a floured baking sheet. Cover them with the tea cloth and leave them in a warm place for 15 minutes.
6. Bake the loaves for 40 minutes or until they sound hollow when tapped.
7. Lift them into wire racks to cool.
Note: To freeze, cool completely and seal in polythene bags. Store for up to 2 months. Thaw on a rack at room temperature or by putting them into a medium oven for 20 minutes.

Caraway Buns

Imperial (Metric)

1 oz (30g) fresh yeast or
½ oz (15g) dried yeast
8 fl oz (225ml) milk,
warmed
1 teaspoon honey (if using
dried yeast)
1 lb (455g) wholemeal
flour
Pinch fine sea salt
1 tablespoon caraway
seeds
1 oz (30g) butter or
vegetable margarine
1 egg, beaten

1. If you are using fresh yeast, crumble it into a bowl and pour in half the milk; if dried, dissolve the honey in half the milk and sprinkle in the yeast. Leave the yeast in a warm place until it is frothy.
2. Put the flour, salt and caraway seeds into a bowl. Rub in the butter or margarine. Make a well in the centre. Pour in the yeast mixture, remaining milk and egg. Mix everything to a dough. Turn it onto a floured work surface and knead it until it is smooth. Return it to the bowl. Make a cross-cut in the top. Cover it with a clean tea cloth and leave it in a warm place to rise for 1 hour.
3. Heat the oven to 400°F/200°C/Gas Mark 6.
4. Knead the dough again. Divide it into sixteen pieces and make each one into a long-shaped roll. Lay them on a floured baking sheet. Cover the rolls with a clean tea cloth and leave for 15 minutes to prove.
5. Bake the rolls for 20 minutes, or until they are golden brown. Lift them onto a wire rack to cool.

Note: To freeze, cool completely. Seal the rolls in a polythene bag. Store them for up to 3 months. Thaw on a rack at room temperature.

American

2 tablespoons fresh yeast
or 1 tablespoon dried
yeast
1 cup milk, warmed
1 teaspoon honey (if using
dried yeast)
4 cups wholewheat flour
Pinch fine sea salt
1 tablespoon caraway
seeds
2 tablespoons butter or
vegetable margarine
1 egg, beaten

Entertaining in Winter

Winter entertaining always revolves around Christmas. From Bonfire Night to Shrove Tuesday there are no other special days, but the twelve days of Christmas, and possibly a few before as well, stand out like a bright spark in the middle of the darkest time of the year. There is no other time in my calendar when I do so much entertaining and also so much visiting. Carol singers call for mince pies and soup, families that I have not seen since the year before come to tea, I might hold an impromptu buffet party and, of course the highlight must be the Christmas dinner. What a wonderful time of year it is.

Of course, winter does not only mean Christmas. It means dark, cold evenings when guests who have braved the elements need rich, warming foods set off by small touches of freshness all of which can be provided by seasonal fruits and vegetables together with the nuts, pulses, eggs and cheese, that are always available.

The root vegetables of winter have robust flavours and substantial textures and warming colours of oranges and yellows that will always enhance winter dishes. Use them in soups and main dishes and never be ashamed to serve them in their own right for they can be truly delicious. Swede (ruta-baga), parsnips, turnips, carrots and beetroot are the most familiar and for a change try celeriac, Jerusalem artichokes and salsify.

Green vegetables are abundant in winter. There are firm Brussels sprouts, crinkly leaved, vitamin-rich curly kale, and winter cabbages which include the crisp green varieties and the crinkly, loosely packed, more delicate flavoured Savoys. The firmly packed white and red cabbages are the most versatile as they can be both cooked and used in winter salads.

A salad can be just as welcome in the winter as in the summer especially when it accompanies a dish that is rich and substantial. Besides the winter cabbages there are celery, Florence fennel, chicory and sweet peppers to choose from. Mustard and cress is always available and there should always be good supplies of watercress.

Winter's fruits are superb in salads. The apples and pears of autumn last well into the winter months and these are joined in November by oranges from Spain, surely the best for both sweet and savoury dishes. The speciality of the season is the Seville oranges. They are mostly associated with marmalade but can be used in both sweet and savoury dishes in the same way as lemons. Grapefruit are also at their best at this time. Bananas and kiwi fruits, although available all through the year, come into their own in the months when there are no soft fruits to compete with them. Grapes are good, too, especially around Christmas.

In the herb garden, the perennial herbs, sage, thyme, marjoram and savory should always be able to supply you with a few leaves, even in the snow and when your own parsley wilts in the coldest of weather you should still be able to buy glass-house grown bunches in the shops, together with fresh coriander.

The best winter meals are a combination

of all these products plus the nuts, pulses and dried fruits from the store cupboard and fresh eggs and dairy produce. They are colourful, delicious, warming, substantial and refreshing all at the same time and they all help to brighten those dark winter nights.

SPECIAL MENUS

All these menus are designed for the Christmas period, but they are highly adaptable and can really be served at any time during the winter.

The Christmas Eve supper is light and simple - just right for when you want something small but special. Christmas dinner is lavish, but well balanced and the vegetable dishes can be used throughout the season. A section on Christmas would not be complete without the Christmas cake and so there is a light tea to go with it and rum truffles to spoil yourself with.

Whichever day you entertain over the Christmas period or throughout the rest of the winter, you will find the Boxing Day and New Year party recipes ideal for informal gatherings, either at lunch-time or in the evening. Keep the menus as they are or change them around.

Christmas Eve Supper (for 6 people)

Stilton Soup
Stilton Bread
Chicory (Belgian Endive), Grape and Sesame Salad
Mince Pies
Fresh Fruit

Stilton Soup

Imperial (Metric)

12 oz (340g) leeks
3 large celery sticks
2¼ pints (1.3) litres vegetable stock
12 oz (340g) potatoes, peeled and chopped
Bouquet garni
Sea salt and freshly ground black pepper
1 oz (30g) butter
1½ tablespoons wholemeal flour
8 fl oz (225ml) milk
6 oz (170g) Stilton cheese, grated

1. Thinly slice the leeks. Chop the celery.

2. Bring the stock to the boil in a saucepan. Put in the vegetables and bouquet garni. Season, cover and simmer for 20 minutes.

3. Remove bouquet garni. Liquidize the rest in a blender or food processor to make a smooth purée.

4. Melt the butter in a saucepan on a medium heat. Stir in the flour and milk and bring them both to the boil, stirring. Simmer for 2 minutes.

5. Stir in the vegetable purée and reheat without boiling.

6. Add the Stilton and stir, without boiling, for it to melt.

7. Serve as soon as possible.

Note: The soup may be frozen before adding the Stilton. Cool it completely and store it in a covered container for up to 2 months. Thaw at room temperature and gently reheat before adding the Stilton.

American

¾ pound leeks
3 large celery stalks
5½ cups vegetable stock
¾ pound potatoes, peeled and chopped
Bouquet garni
Sea salt and freshly ground black pepper
2 tablespoons butter
1½ tablespoons wholewheat flour
1 cup milk
¾ cup grated Stilton cheese

Stilton Bread

Imperial (Metric)

1 wholemeal French loaf
2 oz (55g) unsalted
butter, softened
3 oz (85g) Stilton cheese
1 garlic clove, crushed
Pinch cayenne pepper
3 tablespoons chopped
parsley

1. Heat the oven to 400°F/200°C/Gas Mark 6.
2. Cut the loaf into twelve diagonal slices.
3. Cream the butter in a bowl. Crumble or grate in the Stilton and cream the two together.
4. Add the garlic, cayenne pepper and parsley and beat to make a smooth paste.
5. Spread the Stilton butter over both sides of the slices of bread. Press the slices together and wrap them in foil.
6. Put the bread into the oven for 30 minutes.
7. Serve it hot, with the soup.
Note: The bread can be prepared, wrapped in foil and frozen before heating. Put it directly into the pre-set oven from frozen and heat it for 45 minutes.

American

1 wholewheat French loaf
¼ cup unsalted butter,
softened
3 ounces Stilton cheese
1 garlic clove crushed
Pinch cayenne pepper
3 tablespoons chopped
parsley

Chicory (Belgian Endive), Grape and Sesame Salad

Imperial (Metric)

6 heads chicory
8 oz (225g) black grapes
2 tablespoons tahini
(sesame paste)
4 tablespoons sesame oil
2 tablespoons white wine
vinegar
1 tablespoon syrup from
jar of preserved stem
ginger
1 garlic clove, crushed
2 tablespoons sesame
seeds

1. Finely chop the chicory (Belgian endive). Halve and seed the grapes. Mix them together and divide them between six small bowls
2. Put the tahini into a bowl and beat in the oil, vinegar, ginger syrup and garlic.
3. Spoon the dressing over the salads.
4. Scatter the sesame seeds over the top.

American

6 heads Belgian endive
½ pound black grapes
2 tablespoons tahini
(sesame paste)
¼ cup sesame oil
2 tablespoons white wine
vinegar
1 tablespoon syrup from a
jar of preserved stem
ginger
1 garlic clove, crushed
2 tablespoons sesame
seeds

Mincemeat

Imperial (Metric)

12 oz (340g) cooking apples
8 oz (225g) figs
2 oz (55g) blanched almonds
4 fl oz (125ml) brandy
8 oz (225g) raisins
8 oz (225g) sultanas
6 oz (170g) currants
2 oz (55g) candied peel in the piece
¼ nutmeg, grated
¼ teaspoon ground mace
1 teaspoon ground mixed spice
1 oz (30g) butter or vegetable margarine, melted

1. Peel, core and chop the apples. Chop the figs.
2. Either put the apples, figs and almonds into a food processor with the brandy and liquidize them to a rough minced mixture before turning them out into a bowl; or mince the apples, figs and almonds together, put them into a bowl and mix in the brandy.
3. Add the raisins, sultanas (golden seedless raisins) and currants.
4. Finely chop the peel and add it to the mixture together with the spices.
5. Mix in the butter or margarine.
6. Put into jars and seal.
Note: Fills about three and a half 1 pound (455g) jars.

American

¾ pound cooking apples
½ pound figs
3 tablespoons blanched almonds
½ cup brandy
1½ cups raisins
1½ cups golden seedless raisins
1 cup currants
2 ounces candied peel in the piece
¼ nutmeg, grated
¼ teaspoon ground mace
1 teaspoon ground mixed spice
2 tablespoons butter or vegetable margarine, melted

Christmas Dinner

Fruit-Filled Melon with Port and Brandy
Cranberry Nut Roast
Chestnut and Celery Bake
Brussels Sprouts with Mixed Nuts and Lemon
Swede (Rutabaga), Carrot and Parsnip Purée
Braised Red Cabbage
Cranberry and Orange Sauce
Alternative to Brandy Butter
Porter Pudding

Fruit-Filled Melon with Port and Brandy

Imperial (Metric)

2 pink grapefruit
2 kiwi fruit
4 oz (115g) black grapes
3 fl oz (90ml) port
3 tablespoons brandy
3 ogen melons

1. Cut the rind and pith from the grapefruit. Cut the flesh into quarters lengthways and thinly slice it.
2. Peel and slice the kiwi fruit.
3. Halve and seed the grapes.
4. Put the prepared fruits into a bowl and mix in the port and brandy. Leave for 2 hours.
5. Halve the melons crossways and scoop out the seeds. Put the halves into individual dishes and fill them with the fruits.

American

2 pink grapefruit
2 kiwi fruit
¼ pound black grapes
⅓ cup port
3 tablespoons brandy
3 ogen melons

221

Cranberry Nut Roast

Imperial (Metric)

8 oz (225g) dark brown
lentils
1 bay leaf
1 large onion, thinly
sliced
4 oz (115g) walnuts
4 oz (115g) hazelnuts
4 oz (115g) Brazil nuts
4 tablespoons dry red
wine
2 tablespoons chopped
parsley
2 tablespoons chopped
thyme
1 tablespoon chopped
marjoram
1 teaspoon chopped
rosemary
Sea salt and freshly
ground black pepper
Stuffing:
4 oz (115g) cranberries
4 tablespoons sunflower
oil
1 large onion, finely
chopped
4 oz (115g) fresh
wholemeal breadcrumbs
2 oz (55g) walnuts,
chopped
1 tablespoon chopped
parsley
½ tablespoon chopped
thyme
½ tablespoon chopped
marjoram
4 tablespoons dry red
wine
Sea salt and freshly
ground black pepper
Finishing:
3 oz (85g) dried
wholemeal breadcrumbs
2 tablespoons sesame
seeds
4 tablespoons sunflower
oil

1. Boil the lentils with the bay leaf and onion for 1 hour or until they are very tender. Drain them, remove the bay leaf and mash the lentils and onion to a purée.
2. Heat the oven to 400°F/200°C/Gas mark 6.
3. Grind or very finely chop the nuts.
4. Mix the nuts into the lentil purée together with the wine, herbs and seasonings.
5. To make the stuffing, finely chop the cranberries. Heat the oil in a frying-pan (skillet) on a low heat. Put in the onion and soften it.
6. Stir in the cranberries and cook them for about 2 minutes so they soften and become lighter in colour. Take the pan from the heat.
7. Mix in the breadcrumbs, walnuts, herbs, wine and seasonings.
8. In a long, flat, ovenproof dish, put in a base of half the lentil and nut mixture. Put all the stuffing on top leaving a space of about ¾ inch (2cm) all round. Cover the stuffing with the remaining nut mixture and form the whole into a long loaf shape.
9. For the coating, mix together the breadcrumbs, sesame seeds and oil. Press the mixture evenly over the surface.
10. Bake the roast for 45 minutes so the crumbs on the outside are crisp and brown.
Note: Unsuitable for freezing.

American

1 cup dark brown lentils
1 bay leaf
1 large onion, thinly
sliced
¾ cup English walnuts
¾ cup hazelnuts
¾ cup Brazil nuts
¼ cup dry red wine
2 tablespoons chopped
parsley
2 tablespoons chopped
thyme
1 tablespoon chopped
marjoram
1 teaspoon chopped
rosemary
Sea salt and freshly
ground black pepper
Stuffing:
¼ pound cranberries
¼ cup sunflower oil
1 large onion, finely
chopped
½ cup fresh wholewheat
breadcrumbs
½ cup chopped English
walnuts
1 tablespoon chopped
parsley
½ tablespoon chopped
thyme
½ tablespoon chopped
marjoram
¼ cup dry red wine
Sea salt and freshly
ground black pepper
Finishing:
⅓ cup dried wholewheat
breadcrumbs
2 tablespoons sesame
seeds
¼ cup sunflower oil

Chestnut and Celery Bake

Imperial (Metric)

4 large celery sticks
1 large onion
3 fl oz (90ml) sunflower oil
1 lb (455g) tinned unsweetened chestnut purée
6 sage leaves, chopped
3 tablespoons dried wholemeal breadcrumbs

1. Heat the oven to 400°F/200°C/Gas Mark 6
2. Finely chop the celery and onion.
3. Heat 2 tablespoons of the oil in a frying pan (skillet) on a low heat. Put in the celery and the onion and cook them for 2 minutes.
4. Take the pan from the heat and mix in the chestnut purée and sage.
5. Put the mixture into a shallow, ovenproof dish. Scatter the breadcrumbs over the top and pour over the remaining oil.
6. Bake for 25 minutes or until the crumbs are well browned.
Note: This is rather like a chestnut stuffing and should be served in the dish to be taken in small amounts to accompany the main dish.
The mixture can be frozen uncooked in a covered container for up to 1 month. Thaw it at room temperature and continue as above.

American

4 large celery stalks
1 large onion
⅓ cup sunflower oil
3 cups canned unsweetened chestnut purée
6 sage leaves, chopped
3 tablespoons dried wholewheat breadcrumbs

Brussels Sprouts with Mixed Nuts and Lemon

Imperial (Metric)

2 lb (900g) Brussels sprouts
1 oz (30g) butter or vegetable margarine
2 oz (55g) chopped mixed nuts
Juice of 1 lemon

1. Trim the Brussels sprouts. Steam them for 20 minutes or until they are just tender.
2. Melt the butter or margarine in a frying pan (skillet) on a high heat. Stir in the nuts. Pour in the lemon juice and let it bubble. Take the pan from the heat.
3. Put the Brussels sprouts into a warm serving dish. Spoon the nuts and lemon over the top.

American

2 pounds Brussels sprouts
2 tablespoons butter or vegetable margarine
½ cup chopped mixed nuts
Juice of 1 lemon

Swede (Rutabaga), Carrot and Parsnip Purée

Imperial (Metric)

10 oz (285g) swede
8 oz (225g) carrots
10 oz (285g) parsnips
3 fl oz (90ml) double cream
Freshly ground black pepper
3 tablespoons chopped parsley

American

10 ounces rutabaga
½ pound carrots
10 ounces parsnips
⅓ cup heavy cream
Freshly ground black pepper
3 tablespoons chopped parsley

1. Scrub the swede (rutabaga), peel it if necessary and cut it into large dice. Slice the carrots. Halve the parsnips. Cut out and discard the cores and roughly chop the rest.
2. Steam the vegetables together for 25 minutes or until they are soft.
3. Put them into a blender or food processor with the cream and season well with the pepper. Liquidize to a smooth purée. You will have to stop the machine several times and stir the vegetables to get an even mixture.
4. Put the purée into a serving dish and scatter the parsley over the top.

Note: This purée can be prepared the day before and put into a heatproof serving dish without the parsley. To reheat, cover the dish with foil and put into a 400°F/200°C/Gas Mark 6 oven for 15 minutes. The purée can also be frozen in a covered container for up to 1 month. Thaw it at room temperature and reheat as above.

Braised Red Cabbage

Imperial (Metric)

1 small red cabbage
1 large cooking apple
1 large onion
1 oz (30g) butter
2 tablespoons red wine vinegar
2 tablespoons water
2 tablespoons redcurrant jelly

American

1 small red cabbage
1 large cooking apple
1 large onion
2 tablespoons butter
2 tablespoons red wine vinegar
2 tablespoons water
2 tablespoons redcurrant jelly

1. Heat the oven to 350°F/180°C/Gas Mark 4
2. Shred the cabbage. Peel, core and slice the apple. Thinly slice the onion.
3. Mix in the cabbage, vinegar, water and redcurrant jelly.
4. Cover the casserole and put it into the oven for 45 minutes.

Note: This reheats well so can easily be made up to two days in advance. Unsuitable for freezing.

Cranberry and Orange Sauce

Imperial (Metric)

2 large oranges
Water
2 oz (55g) honey
1 lb (455g) cranberries
2 oz (55g) raisins
½ teaspoon ground mace
4 tablespoons port

1. Thinly pare the rind from one of the oranges. Cut it into small, thin slivers. Boil them for 2 minutes. Drain them.
2. Squeeze the juice from the oranges. Make it up to ¼ pint (140ml/⅔ cup) with water if necessary.
3. Put the juice into a saucepan with the honey. Set it on a low heat and stir for the honey to dissolve.
4. Put in the cranberries, raisins and mace. Bring them to the boil and simmer for 15 minutes.
5. Cool slightly and stir in the port.
6. Serve warm.

Note: The sauce, without the port, will keep in the refrigerator for up to three weeks or in the freezer for up to 2 months. Cool it completely before putting into a covered container. Thaw at room temperature. Before serving, gently warm it and stir in the port.

American

2 large oranges
Water
2½ tablespoons honey
1 pound cranberries
⅓ cup raisins
½ teaspoon ground mace
4 tablespoons port

Alternative to Brandy Butter

Imperial (Metric)

2 tablespoons pear and apple spread
8 oz (225g) curd or low-fat soft cheese
3 fl oz (90ml) brandy

1. Beat the pear and apple spread into the cheese. If possible use a food processor or blender to make a smoother mixture.
2. Gradually beat in the brandy.

Note: This can be made up to four days in advance and stored in a covered container in the refrigerator. Unsuitable for freezing.

American

2 tablespoons pear and apple spread
1 cup curd or low-fat soft cheese
⅓ cup brandy

Porter Pudding

Imperial (Metric)

2 oz (55g) currants
3 oz (85g) raisins
3 oz (85g) sultanas
2 oz (55g) candied peel
in the piece
2 oz (55g) stoned dates
¼ pint (140ml) Guinness
or other stout
1 oz (30g) almonds
1 small cooking apple
1 medium carrot
1½ oz (45g) fresh
wholemeal breadcrumbs
1½ oz (45g) wholemeal
flour
½ teaspoon baking
powder
Pinch fine sea salt
¼ nutmeg, grated
½ teaspoon ground
cinnamon
2 oz (55g) vegetable
margarine, melted
1 egg, beaten
4 tablespoons brandy
Vegetable margarine for
greasing

1. Put the currants, raisins and sultanas (golden seedless raisins) into a bowl. Finely chop the candied peel and dates. Put them into the bowl with the rest. Mix in the Guinness (stout). Cover and leave for 24 hours.

2. Blanch and shred the almonds. Grate the apple and carrot. Mix these into the soaked fruit.

3. Put the breadcrumbs and flour into a mixing bowl with the baking powder, salt and spices. Mix in the soaked fruit and all its liquid, the melted margarine, egg and brandy.

4. Grease a 1½ pint (850ml/3¾ cup) pudding basin. Put in the mixture, press it down and smooth the top.

5. Cut a ring of greaseproof paper and one of foil. Grease the paper. Lay it on top of the foil, greased side up, and make a pleat down the centre about 1 inch (2.5cm) wide. Cover the basin with the foil outermost. Tie down with string, making a handle for easy lifting.

6. Bring a large saucepan of water to the boil. Lower in the pudding and steam it for 4 hours, topping up the water as and when necessary.

7. Lift out the pudding, cool it completely and replace the foil and greaseproof.

8. On Christmas morning, steam for a further 2 hours.

Note: This type of pudding, made without sugar, is best kept in the refrigerator after the initial steaming. It will keep for up to three weeks.

American

⅓ cup currants
½ cup raisins
½ cup golden seedless
raisins
2 ounces candied peel, in
the piece
2 ounces pitted dates
⅔ cup dark stout
2 tablespoons almonds
1 small cooking apple
1 medium carrot
¾ cup fresh wholewheat
breadcrumbs
⅓ cup wholewheat flour
½ teaspoon baking
powder
Pinch fine sea salt
¼ nutmeg, grated
½ teaspoon ground
cinnamon
¼ cup vegetable
margarine, melted
1 egg, beaten
¼ cup brandy
Vegetable margarine for
greasing

Christmas Day Tea

Cheese Puffs
Cheese, apples and celery
Christmas Cake without Sugar
Rum Truffles

Cheese Puffs

Imperial (Metric)

½ pint (285ml) water
3 oz (85g) butter
½ teaspoon fine sea salt
Freshly ground black
pepper
4 oz (115g) wholemeal
flour
4 eggs, beaten
4 oz (115g) Cheddar
cheese, grated
Glaze:
1 egg, beaten
Filling:
10 oz (285g) curd cheese
1 tablespoon very finely
chopped onion
4 tablespoons chopped
parsley

1. Heat the oven to 400°F/200°C/Gas Mark 6
2. Bring the water to the boil in a saucepan. Add the butter, salt and pepper. Boil until the butter has melted.
3. Take the pan from the heat. Put in all the flour and beat well to make a smooth mixture.
4. Return the pan to the heat. Beat for 1-2 minutes until the mixture pulls away from the sides of the pan without sticking.
5. Take the pan from the heat. Gradually beat in the eggs, a little at a time. Beat until the mixture is smooth.
6. Beat in the cheese.
7. Put the mixture into a piping bag fitted with a medium-sized plain nozzle. Pipe out small bun shapes, about 1½ tablespoons each, leaving a 1 inch (2.5cm) space all round each one.
8. Brush the buns with the beaten egg.
9. Bake the buns for 15 minutes. Lower the heat to 375°F/190°/Gas Mark 5. Continue cooking for a further 10 minutes.
10. Take the buns from the oven and place them on wire racks. Make a small slit in each one to allow the steam to escape. Cool them completely.
11. To make the filling, beat the cheese to make it soft. Beat in the onion and parsley.
12. Just before serving, split the puffs crossways and spread them with a generous amount of filling.
Note: Unsuitable for freezing.

American

1¼ cups water
⅓ cup butter
½ teaspoon fine sea salt
Freshly ground black
pepper
1 cup wholewheat flour
4 eggs, beaten
1 cup grated Cheddar
cheese
Glaze:
1 egg, beaten
Filling:
1¼ cups curd cheese
1 tablespoon very finely
chopped onion
¼ cup chopped parsley

Christmas Cake without Sugar

Imperial (Metric)

8 oz (225g) stoned dates
¼ pint (140ml) rum
¼ pint (140ml) prune
    juice
8 oz (225g) wholemeal
    flour
1 teaspoon ground mixed
    spice
6 oz (170g) vegetable
    margarine
1 medium carrot, finely
    grated
4 eggs, beaten
6 oz (170g) sultanas
6 oz (170g) raisins
4 oz (115g) glacé cherries,
    halved

1. Chop the dates. Soak them in the rum and prune juice for 12 hours. Liquidize them with the rum and juice.
2. Heat the oven to 300°F/160°C/Gas Mark 2. Prepare an 8 inch (20cm) diameter cake tin.
3. Mix the flour with the spice.
4. In a large bowl, cream the margarine and beat in the carrot. Beat in the eggs, alternately with the flour.
5. Beat in the liquidized dried fruits.
6. Fold in the sultanas (golden seedless raisins), raisins and cherries.
7. Put the mixture into the prepared tin.
8. Bake the cake for 1 hour or until a skewer inserted in the centre comes out clean. Cool it in the tin for 5 minutes and turn it onto a wire rack to cool.

Note: Unlike the more conventional types of fruit cake this one is best if made only a few days before it is needed and stored in the refrigerator wrapped in cling film. It can also be frozen for up to 2 months and thawed on a rack at room temperature.

Decorating the Cake

Having made a sugar-free cake, you will probably not wish to coat it in sugar icing. The best answer is to make some almond paste. You can colour it with natural green, red and yellow food colourings, roll it out to a thickness of about ¼ inch (6mm) and stamp it into stars, bells, trees etc. with biscuit cutters. The paste can also be worked to make robins, Father Christmases etc. if wished.

American

½ pound pitted dates
⅔ cup rum
⅔ cup prune juice
2 cups wholewheat flour
1 teaspoon ground mixed
    spice
¾ cup vegetable
    margarine
1 medium carrot, finely
    grated
4 eggs, beaten
1 cup golden seedless
    raisins
1 cup raisins
¼ pound glacé cherries,
    halved

228

Almond Paste

Imperial (Metric)

8 oz (225g) blanched
almonds
4 fl oz (125ml)
concentrated apple juice

1. Finely grind the almonds.
2. Put the almonds into a bowl. Using a wooden spoon, beat in the apple juice.
3. With your hands, work the mixture to a smooth ball.
4. Wrap the paste in cling film and chill it for 30 minutes before using.

To Colour Almond Paste: Do this before chilling. Divide it into three portions. Put each one into a bowl. Add about 1 teaspoon of a different natural food colouring to each and beat to make an even colour. Form the mixture into balls.

Note: When working with the paste, use damp fingers and lightly dampen the rolling pin. This will prevent sticking. The paste is very sticky so no jam (jelly) is necessary in order for it to stick to the cake.

American

2 cups blanched almonds
½ cup concentrated apple
juice

Rum Truffles

Imperial (Metric)

4 oz (115g) raisins
4 fl oz (115ml) rum
8 oz (225g) ground
almonds
5 oz (150g) pear and
apple spread
Ground almonds and
chopped mixed nuts for
coating

1. Put the raisins into a bowl and pour in the rum. Cover with clingfilm and leave for 12 hours. Drain, reserving the rum.
2. Mix the ground almonds and pear and apple spread to a sticky, dark brown paste.
3. Add the raisins and work them in evenly with your fingers.
4. Add as much rum as the mixture will take. It must be moist but should keep its shape when rolling into balls.
5. Form the mixture into balls about ¾ inch (2cm) in diameter.
6. Roll half the balls in ground almonds and the other half in the mixed nuts.
7. Arrange the truffles in boxes lined with coloured napkins
Note: These will keep for up to three weeks. Unsuitable for freezing.

American

⅔ cup raisins
½ cup rum
1⅓ cups ground almonds
⅓ cup pear and apple
spread
Ground almonds and
chopped mixed nuts for
coating

Boxing Day Buffet (for 10 people)

Raised Chestnut Pie
Fennel and Salted Almond Tart
Jacket Potatoes with Apple, Onion and Stilton
Tomato, Avocado and Walnut Salad
Celery Salad with Cinnamon
Fresh Pineapple with Yogurt Jelly
Dried Fruit and Almond Mousse

Raised Chestnut Pie

Imperial (Metric)

1 lb (445g) chestnuts
8 oz (225g) Brussels
sprouts
6oz (175g) carrots
6 oz (170g) leeks
8 oz (225g) parsnips
2 oz ground almonds
4oz (115g) Cheddar
cheese, grated
6 sage leaves, chopped
4 tablespoons chopped
parsley
¼ nutmeg, grated
½ oz (15g) butter or
vegetable margarine
1 tablespoon wholemeal
flour
¼ pint (140ml) milk
1 egg, separated
Shortcrust pastry made
with 1 lb (455g)
wholemeal flour
(see page 24)

1. Slit the tops of the chestnuts. Put them into a saucepan, cover them with water and bring them to the boil. Cover and simmer for 10 minutes. Take the pan from the heat. Take the chestnuts out one by one and skin them.
2. Trim and quarter the Brussels sprouts. Steam them for 15 minutes.
3. Slice the carrots and steam them for 15 minutes.
4. Slice the leeks and steam them for 10 minutes.
5. Halve the parsnips and remove the cores. Steam them for 20 minutes. Mash them and mix in the ground almonds, cheese, leeks, sage, parsley and nutmeg.
6. Melt the butter or margarine in a saucepan on a low heat. Stir in the flour and milk. Bring them to the boil, stirring, and simmer for 20 minutes.
7. Take the pan from the heat. Beat in the egg yolk.
8. Fold in the chestnuts, Brussels sprouts, carrots and leeks.
9. Heat the oven to 400°F/200°C/Gas Mark 6.
10. Roll out the pastry and use three quarters to line a 2 lb (900g) raised pie mould or loaf tin.
11. Put in half the parsnip mixture and spread it out in an even layer. Put in half the vegetables, the remaining

American

1 pound chestnuts
½ pound Brussels sprouts
6 ounces carrots
6 ounces leeks
½ pound parsnips
½ cup ground almonds
1 cup grated Cheddar
cheese
6 sage leaves, chopped
¼ cup chopped parsley
¼ nutmeg, grated
1 tablespoon butter or
vegetable margarine
1 tablespoon wholewheat
flour
⅔ cup milk
1 egg, separated
Shortcrust pastry made
with 4 cups wholewheat
flour
(see page 24)

parsnip mixture and finally the rest of the vegetables.

12. Cover the pie with the remaining pastry. Decorate with the trimmings if wished. Brush the top with the egg white.

13. Bake for 30 minutes, or until the top is golden brown.

14. Cool the pie completely before removing from the mould or tin.

Note: Unsuitable for freezing but the pie will keep for up to two days in the refrigerator after cooling.

Fennel and Salted Almond Tart

Imperial (Metric)

1 lb (445g) Florence fennel
4 oz (115g) almonds
2 tablespoons fine sea salt
4 tablespoons sunflower oil
6 eggs
8 oz (225g) curd cheese
4 sage leaves, chopped
2 tablespoons chopped thyme
2 tablespoons chopped marjoram
Shortcrust pastry made with 8 oz (225g) wholemeal flour
(see page 24)

1. Dice the fennel and steam it for 15 minutes

2. Put the almonds into a shallow pan and cover them with water. Bring them to the boil and drain them. Squeeze them from their skins.

3. Sprinkle the salt onto a double thickness of kitchen paper.

4. Heat the oil in a frying pan (skillet) on a medium heat. Put in the almonds and stir them on the heat until they are golden. Lift them onto the kitchen paper and stir them around to coat them in the salt. Leave them until they are quite cool.

5. Beat the eggs.

6. Cream the cheese in a bowl and gradually beat in the eggs. Mix in the herbs.

7. Roll out the pastry and use it to line a 10 inch (25cm) tart tin. Put the fennel in the bottom of the pastry shell and put the almonds on top. Pour in the egg mixture.

8. Bake the tart at 400°F/200°C/Gas Mark 6 for 30 minutes, or until the filling is set and golden.

9. Serve either hot or cold.

Note: Unsuitable for freezing.

American

1 pound Florence fennel
1 cup almonds
2 tablespoons fine sea salt
¼ cup sunflower oil
6 eggs
1 cup curd cheese
4 sage leaves, chopped
2 tablespoons chopped thyme
2 tablespoons chopped marjoram
Shortcrust pastry made with 2 cups wholewheat flour
(see page 24)

231

Jacket Potatoes with Apple, Onion and Stilton Cheese

Imperial (Metric)

6 large potatoes
3 oz (85g) Stilton cheese
1 medium onion
1 medium cooking apple

1. Heat the oven to 400°F/200°/Gas Mark 6/
2. Scrub the potatoes and prick them on both sides with a fork.
3. Lay the potatoes on the oven rack and bake them for 1 hour 15 minutes so the middles are soft and the skin crisp.
4. Cut them in half. Scoop out and mash the middles. Reserve the skins.
5. Crumble or grate the Stilton, depending on the texture. Finely chop the onion. Peel, core and finely chop the apple. Mix the cheese, apple and onion into the mashed potato. Pile the mixture back into the potato shells. Make patterns on top with a fork.
6. Place the potato shells in a flat, ovenproof dish. Return them to the oven for 15 minutes, or until the tops are beginning to brown.
Note: Unsuitable for freezing.

American

6 large potatoes
3 ounces Stilton cheese
1 medium onion
1 medium cooking apple

Tomato, Avocado and Walnut Salad

Imperial (Metric)

1½ lb (685g) tomatoes
3 ripe avocados
3 oz (85g) walnuts, finely chopped
2 medium oranges
3 tablespoons chopped parsley
3 fl oz (90ml) olive oil
3 tablespoons white wine vinegar
1 garlic clove, crushed
Freshly ground black pepper

1. Thinly slice the tomatoes and arrange them on a serving plate
2. Peel, stone (pit) and chop the avocados and arrange them in the centre.
3. Scatter the walnuts over the avocados.
4. Cut the rind and pith from the oranges. Cut the oranges in half lengthways and thinly slice them. Arrange round the edge of the plate.
5. Scatter the parsley over the avocados and walnuts.
6. Beat the oil, vinegar, garlic and pepper together to make the dressing. Spoon it over the salad.
Note: If the salad is to be left for more than 30 minutes before serving, coat the pieces of avocado in lemon juice to prevent them turning dark.
Unsuitable for freezing.

American

1½ pounds tomatoes
3 ripe avocados
⅔ cup English walnuts, finely chopped
2 medium oranges
3 tablespoons chopped parsley
⅓ cup olive oil
3 tablespoons white wine vinegar
1 garlic clove, crushed
Freshly ground black pepper

Celery Salad with Cinnamon

Imperial (Metric)

1 head celery
2 medium cooking apples
4 tablespoons natural yogurt
2 tablespoons olive oil
1 tablespoon cider vinegar
1 teaspoon ground cinnamon
1 garlic clove, crushed

1. Chop the celery. Core and chop the apples, without peeling. Add them to the celery.
2. Beat the remaining ingredients together.
3. Fold them into the salad.

American

1 head celery
2 medium cooking apples
¼ cup unflavored yogurt
2 tablespoons olive oil
1 tablespoon cider vinegar
1 teaspoon ground cinnamon
1 garlic clove, crushed

Fresh Pineapple with Yogurt Jelly

Imperial (Metric)

1 pint (570ml) pineapple juice
Agar-agar to set 2 pints (1.14 litres) liquid (see manufacturer's instructions)
1 pint (570ml) natural yogurt
2 fresh pineapples
3 tablespoons honey, melted

1. To make the jelly, put the pineapple juice into a saucepan and bring it to just below boiling point. Stir in the agar-agar and stir on the heat until it has dissolved. Take the pan from the heat and cool the juice for 5 minutes
2. Put the yogurt into a bowl and gradually pour in the juice, beating to make the mixture smooth.
3. Pour the jelly into two flat dishes and leave it in a cool place to set completely.
4. Cut the rind and husk from the pineapples. Cut the pineapple flesh into ⅝ inch (1.5cm) slices and cut out the cores. Cut the slices into 1 inch (2.5cm) pieces.
5. Put the pineapple pieces into a bowl, pour on the honey and leave them for 30 minutes.
6. Turn the jelly out of the dishes and cut it into 1 inch (2.5cm) squares.
7. Just before serving, carefully mix the jelly squares into the pineapple.
Note: Unsuitable for freezing.

American

2½ cups pineapple juice
Agar-agar to set 5 cups liquid (see manufacturer's instructions)
2½ cups unflavored yogurt
2 fresh pineapples
3 tablespoons honey, melted

Dried Fruit and Almond Mousse

Imperial (Metric)

6 oz (170g) dried whole
    apricots
4 oz (115g) prunes
¾ pint (425ml) natural
    orange juice
2 oz (55g) ground
    almonds
3 eggs, separated
Agar-agar to set 1½ pints
    (850ml) liquid
    (see manufacturer's
    instructions)
½ pint (285ml) natural
    yogurt
½ pint (285ml) double
    cream
2 tablespoons flaked
    almonds, toasted

1. Put the apricots and prunes into a
bowl with ½ pint (285ml/1¼ cups)
orange juice and soak them for 8 hours.
2. Drain the fruits, reserving the juice.
Liquidize them in a blender or food
processor with ¼ pint (140ml/⅔ cup) of
the juice.
3. Put the fruit purée into a saucepan
and stir in the almonds. Beat in the egg
yolks, one at a time. Stir the mixture on
a low heat until it begins to thicken,
without letting it boil. Take the pan
from the heat.
4. Put the remaining juice from the
fruits, together with the remaining
orange juice into a saucepan and bring
them to just below boiling point. Stir in
the agar-agar and stir on the heat until it
has dissolved. Take the pan from the
heat.
5. Let the mixture come off the boil and
stir it into the fruit. Cool to room
temperature.
6. Stiffly whip the egg whites.
7. Fold first the yogurt and then the egg
whites into the fruit.
8. Pour the mousse into a serving dish
and leave it in a cool place until it has
set completely, about 3 hours.
9. Stiffly whip the cream and pipe it on
top of the mousse. Scatter the toasted
flaked (slivered) almonds over the top.
Note: The cream may be omitted if
wished and the almonds used alone.
Unsuitable for freezing.

American

6 ounces dried whole
    apricots
¼ pound prunes
2 cups natural orange
    juice
½ cup ground almonds
3 eggs, separated
Agar-agar to set 3¾ cups
    liquid
    (see manufacturer's
    instructions)
1¼ cups unflavored
    yogurt
1¼ cups heavy cream
2 tablespoons slivered
    almonds, toasted

New Year's Eve Party (for 16 people)

Savoury Croquettes
Flageolet, Egg and Cheese Salad
Butter (Lima) Bean and Corn Salad
Blue Cheshire Salad
Olive and Tomato Scone Rounds
Burghul, Orange and Nut Salad
Fruit and Sherry Jelly
Spiced Apple Flans

Savoury Croquettes

Imperial (Metric)

1½ oz (45g) butter
1 large onion, chopped
12 oz (340g) mushrooms,
finely chopped
6 tablespoons flour
¾ pint (425ml) milk
6 oz (170g) Feta cheese,
grated
6 oz (170g) walnuts,
chopped
6 oz (170g) fresh
wholemeal breadcrumbs
3 sage leaves, chopped
2 tablespoons chopped
thyme
Coating:
2 oz (55g) wholemeal
flour
2 eggs, beaten
3 oz (85g) dried
wholemeal breadcrumbs
Vegetable oil for deep
frying

1. Melt the butter in a saucepan on a low heat. Put in the onion and soften it.
2. Raise the heat to medium. Put in the mushrooms and cook them for 2 minutes.
3. Stir in the flour and milk. Bring them to the boil, stirring. Simmer for 2 minutes.
4. Take the pan from the heat. Add the Feta cheese and the walnuts.
5. Put in the breadcrumbs and herbs and mix well. Leave the mixture until it is quite cold.
6. Form the mixture into 32 small balls. Coat them in flour, then in beaten egg and then in the breadcrumbs.
7. Heat a deep pan of oil to 375°F/180°C.
8. Deep fry the croquettes, about five at a time, for about 2 minutes, or until golden brown. Drain them on kitchen paper.

Note: The croquettes are best served hot. Cook them in advance and cool them on plates lined with kitchen paper. Just before serving, heat them through in a medium oven for 15 minutes. They can be made a day in advance, deep fried and stored in the refrigerator.
To freeze, coat them but do not deep fry them. Freeze them on trays and store them in polythene bags for up to 1 month. Thaw at room temperature and deep fry as above.

American

3 tablespoons butter
1 large onion, chopped
¾ pound mushrooms,
finely chopped
⅓ cup flour
2 cups milk
6 ounces Feta cheese,
grated
1⅓ cups chopped English
walnuts
3 cups fresh wholewheat
breadcrumbs
3 sage leaves, chopped
2 tablespoons chopped
thyme
Coating:
½ cup wholewheat flour
2 eggs, beaten
¾ cup dried wholewheat
breadcrumbs
Vegetable oil for deep
frying

Flageolet, Egg and Cheese Salad

Imperial (Metric)

8 oz (225g) flageolets,
soaked and cooked
1 oz (30g) parsley,
chopped
½ small onion, very finely
chopped
4 tablespoons olive oil
2 tablespoons white wine
vinegar
5 oz (150g) Cheddar
cheese, grated
6 eggs, hard-boiled

1. Mix the beans with the parsley and onion
2. Beat together the oil and vinegar. Fold them into the beans.
3. Mix in the cheese.
4. Put the bean and cheese mixture onto a large serving plate
5. Garnish with the halved or quartered eggs.

Note: Unsuitable for freezing.

American

1¼ cups flageolets, soaked
and cooked
1 cup chopped parsley
½ small onion, very finely
chopped
¼ cup olive oil
2 tablespoons white wine
vinegar
1¼ cups grated Cheddar
cheese
6 hard-cooked eggs

Butter (Lima) Bean and Corn Salad

Imperial (Metric)

8 oz (225g) butter beans,
soaked and cooked
12 oz (340g) tin
sweetcorn
2 red peppers
1 green pepper
4 tablespoons chopped
parsley
4 tablespoons olive oil
2 tablespoons white wine
vinegar
1 tablespoon tomato purée
½ teaspoon paprika
¼ teaspoon Tabasco sauce
1 garlic clove, crushed

1. Put the butter (Lima) beans into a bowl with the drained sweetcorn.
2. Core and seed the peppers and cut them into thin strips
3. Add the peppers and the parsley to the beans.
4. Beat together the remaining ingredients to make the dressing. Fold them into the salad.

Note: Unsuitable for freezing.

American

1⅓ cups Lima beans,
soaked and cooked
¾ pound can sweetcorn
2 sweet red peppers
1 sweet green pepper
¼ cup chopped parsley
¼ cup olive oil
2 tablespoons white wine
vinegar
1 tablespoon tomato paste
½ teaspoon paprika
¼ teaspoon Tabasco sauce
1 garlic clove, crushed

Blue Cheshire Salad

Imperial (Metric)

8 oz (225g) Blue Cheshire
cheese
1 small head celery
2 medium green peppers
2 crisp dessert apples
2 tablespoons mayonnaise
4 tablespoons natural
yogurt

1. Cut the cheese into ⅜ inch (1cm) dice.
2. Cut the celery across the stalks into thin slices.
3. Core and seed the peppers and cut them into 1 inch (2.5cm) strips.
4. Core and chop the apples.
5. Mix the celery, peppers and apples together.
6. Beat together the mayonnaise and yogurt and mix them into the salad.

American

½ pound Blue Cheshire
cheese
1 small head celery
2 medium sweet green
peppers
2 crisp dessert apples
2 tablespoons mayonnaise
¼ cup unflavored yogurt

7. Arrange the salad round the edge of a serving plate and pile the cubes of cheese in the centre.
Note: Unsuitable for freezing. Stilton cheese may be used if Blue Cheshire is not available.

Olive and Tomato Scone Rounds

Imperial (Metric)

1 1lb (455g) wholemeal flour
1 teaspoon fine sea salt
1 teaspoon bicarbonate of soda
3 oz (85g) vegetable margarine
20 black olives
2 teaspoons dried thyme
½ pint (285ml) natural yogurt
2 tablespoons tomato purée
1 egg, beaten

1. Heat the oven to 400°F/200°C/Gas Mark 6.
2. Put the flour into a bowl with the salt and bicarbonate of (baking) soda. Rub in the margarine.
3. Stone (pit) and finely chop the olives and add them to the flour with the thyme, tossing them in with your fingers to distribute them evenly.
4. Beat the yogurt with the tomato purée (paste).
5. Make a well in the centre of the flour and pour in the yogurt mixture. Mix everything to a smooth dough.
6. Divide the dough into two and roll each piece into a 7 inch (18cm) round.
7. Put the rounds into 7 inch (18cm) skillets or cake tins. Score the tops into twelve wedges.
8. Brush with beaten egg.
9. Bake the scones for 20 minutes or until golden and risen.
Note: The scones are best served warm. The dough can be prepared a few hours in advance and cooked at the last minute. Or the rounds can be cooked the day before, cooled on wire racks and reheated on baking trays in hot oven for 10 minutes.
To freeze, seal each one in a polythene bag and store for up to two months. Reheat from frozen by placing on a baking tray and putting into a hot oven for 15 minutes.

American

4 cups wholewheat flour
1 teaspoon fine sea salt
1 teaspoon baking soda
⅓ cup vegetable margarine
20 black olives
2 teaspoons dried thyme
1¼ cups unflavored yogurt
2 tablespoons tomato paste
1 egg, beaten

Burghul, Orange and Nut Salad

Imperial (Metric)

1 lb (455g) burghul wheat
3 large oranges
8 oz (225g) almonds
4 oz (115g) raisins
1 oz (30g) parsley,
chopped
4 fl oz (125ml) olive oil
Juice of 2 lemons
1 garlic clove, crushed
2 teaspoons ground
turmeric

1. Soak the wheat in warm water for 20 minutes. Drain it and squeeze it dry. Put it into a bowl.
2. Cut the rind and pith from the oranges. Reserve one and chop the other two.
3. Add the chopped oranges, almonds, raisins and parsley to the wheat.
4. Beat together the remaining ingredients and fold them into the salad. Leave the salad for 20 minutes.
5. Just before serving, transfer the salad to a large plate or serving bowl. Garnish it with the remaining orange, either sliced or cut into wedges.
Note: Unsuitable for freezing.

American

2⅔ cups burghul wheat
3 large oranges
2 cups almonds
⅔ cup raisins
1 cup chopped parsley
½ cup olive oil
Juice of 2 lemons
1 garlic clove, crushed
2 teaspoons ground
turmeric

Fruit and Sherry Jelly

Imperial (Metric)

Four 8 oz (225g) tins
fruit cocktail in natural
juice
Approx. 1 pint (570ml)
sweet sherry
Agar-agar to set 1½ pints
(850ml) liquid

1. Drain the fruits, reserving the juice. Put the fruits into a glass serving bowl.
2. Measure the juice. Make it up to 1½ pints (850ml/3¾ cups) with the sherry.
3. Put the juice and sherry into a saucepan and bring them to just below simmering point. Sprinkle in the agar-agar. Stir rapidly over a low heat, without letting the liquid boil, for the agar-agar to dissolve.
4. Take the pan from the heat and cool the mixture without letting it set.
5. Pour the cooled jelly over the fruits. Leave it in a cool place for 3 hours to set.
Note: Whipped cream, soured cream, Greek-style yogurt or creamed smetana can be served separately as an accompaniment.

American

Four ½ pound cans fruit
cocktail in natural juice
Approx. 2½ cups sweet
sherry
Agar-agar to set 3¾ cups
liquid

Spiced Apple Flans

These amounts will make two flans. For cooking you will need two 7 inch (18cm) diameter flan moulds, the centres of which should be raised to make, on turning out, sponge flan bases with dipped centres for filling.

Imperial (Metric)

8 oz (225g) butter
8 oz (225g) honey
8 oz (225g) wholemeal flour
2 teaspoons bicarbonate of soda
2 teaspoons ground mixed spice
4 eggs, beaten
2 oz (55g) raisins
2 oz (55g) sultanas
Filling:
2 lb (900g) cooking apples
2 oz (55g) butter
1 teaspoon ground mixed spice
2 tablespoons honey
Topping:
½ pint (285ml) double cream
2 teaspoons poppy seeds

1. Heat the oven to 350°F/180°C/Gas Mark 4.
2. Cream the butter in a bowl.
3. Gradually beat in the honey.
4. Toss the flour with the bicarbonate of (baking) soda and mixed spice.
5. Beat the flour into the butter and honey, alternately with the eggs.
6. Mix in the raisins and sultanas (golden seedless raisins).
7. Divide the mixture between two buttered, 7 inch (18cm) flan moulds.
8. Bake the flan cases for 20 minutes or until firm and just beginning to colour. Cool them on wire racks.
9. Core and finely chop the apples, without peeling.
10. Melt the butter in a saucepan on a low heat. Mix in the apples, spice and honey. Cover and cook for 15 minutes or until the apples can be beaten to a purée.
11. Rub the purée through a sieve. Cool completely.
12. Whip the cream.
13. Fill the flan bases with apple purée. Cover the purée with whipped cream.
14. Scatter the poppy seeds over the top.
Note: Both the flan bases and the apple purée can be frozen for up to two months. Wrap the flan cases individually in clingfilm and store the apple purée in a covered container. Thaw both at room temperature.

American

1 cup butter
⅔ cup honey
2 cups wholewheat flour
2 teaspoons baking soda
2 teaspoons ground mixed spice
4 eggs, beaten
⅓ cup raisins
⅓ cup golden seedless raisins
Filling:
2 pounds cooking apples
¼ cup butter
1 teaspoon ground mixed spice
2 tablespoons honey
Topping:
1¼ cups heavy cream
2 teaspoons poppy seeds

SOUPS

Guests who have come a long way on a winter's night will be warmed and welcomed with a bowl of hot soup whether it is rich and creamy or light and unblended. Sherry, brandy and wine give extra warming qualities and yogurt, cream and smetana a touch of richness. Vegetables, from the humble carrot to the old-fashioned and unusual salsify, form the base.

Cream of Seville Orange Soup

Imperial (Metric)

6 oz (170g) haricot beans
2 medium onions
1 oz (30g) butter
2 tablespoons wholemeal flour
2 pints (1.14ml) vegetable stock
Grated rind and juice of 1 Seville orange
Bouquet garni
½ pint (285ml) Greek-style natural yogurt
6 thin slices Seville orange, pips removed

1. Soak the haricot (navy) beans, cook them until they are tender and drain them.
2. Finely chop the onions.
3. Melt the butter in a saucepan on a low heat. Put in the onions and soften them. Stir in the flour and then the stock. Bring them to the boil, stirring. Add the Seville orange rind and juice and the bouquet garni. Simmer, uncovered, for 15 minutes. Remove the bouquet garni.
4. Liquidize the soup in a blender or food processor. Add the yogurt and the haricot (navy) beans and liquidize again to make a smooth, creamy soup.
5. Reheat the soup if necessary, without boiling.
6. Serve in individual bowls with a slice of Seville orange floating in each one.
Note: To freeze, liquidize the soup with the beans but not with the yogurt. Freeze it in a covered container and store it for up to 1 month. Thaw at room temperature. Put the yogurt into a bowl and stir in the soup. Reheat it without boiling.

American

⅔ cup navy beans
2 medium onions
2 tablespoons butter
2 tablespoons wholewheat flour
5 cups vegetable stock
Grated rind and juice of 1 Seville orange
Bouquet garni
1¼ cups Greek-style unflavored yogurt
6 thin slices Seville orange, pips removed

Parsnip, Leek and Chestnut Soup (page 243).
Overleaf Christmas Eve Supper (pages 219-21).

Spiced Lentil and Coconut Cobbler (page 258).

Carrot and Artichoke Soup with Tomato

Imperial (Metric)

12 oz (340g) carrots
12 oz (340g) Jerusalem
artichokes
1 oz (30g) butter
1 large onion, thinly
sliced
2¼ pints (1.3 litres)
vegetable stock
2 tablespoons tomato
purée
Bouquet garni
6 firm tomatoes
3 fl oz (90ml) soured
cream

1. Thinly slice the carrots.
2. Peel the artichokes whilst holding them in cold water. Thinly slice them.
3. Melt the butter in a saucepan on a low heat. Mix in the vegetables, cover them and cook them gently for 10 minutes.
4. Add the stock and tomato purée (paste). Bring them to the boil and add the bouquet garni.
5. Cover and simmer for 25 minutes.
6. Remove the bouquet garni. Either liquidize the soup in a blender or food processor or rub it through a vegetable mill. Reheat it.
7. Scald, skin and chop the tomatoes. Put them into the bottom of six soup bowls.
8. Pour the soup over the tomatoes. Top with a tablespoon of soured cream.
Note: The soup can be frozen after liquidizing. Store it in a covered, rigid container for up to 2 months. Thaw at room temperature and reheat as above.

American

¾ pound carrots
¾ pound Jerusalem
artichokes
2 tablespoons butter
1 large onion, thinly
sliced
5½ cups vegetable stock
2 tablespoons tomato
paste
Bouquet garni
6 firm tomatoes
⅓ cup sour cream

Salsify and Lemon Soup

1½ lb (685g) salsify
1 oz (30g) butter
1 large onion, finely
chopped
2¼ pints (1.3 litres)
vegetable stock
Sea salt and freshly
ground black pepper
Bouquet garni including
three thinly pared strips
lemon rind
Juice of up to 1 lemon
3 fl oz (90ml) natural
yogurt

1. Peel the salsify whilst holding it under cold water. Chop it into thin slices.
2. Melt the butter in a saucepan on a low heat. Mix in the salsify and onion. Cover them and cook them gently for 10 minutes.
3. Pour in the stock and bring it to the boil. Season lightly and add the bouquet garni and lemon rind.
4. Cover and simmer for 20 minutes.
5. Remove the bouquet garni and lemon rind and either liquidize the soup in a blender or food processor or put it through the fine blade of a vegetable mill.
6. Return the soup to the saucepan. Add the juice of half the lemon. Taste and add more lemon juice if required.
7. Reheat the soup and pour it into bowls.
8. Swirl a spoonful of yogurt into each bowl.
Note: To freeze, cool completely after adding the lemon juice. Store in a covered rigid container for up to 2 months. Thaw at room temperature.

American

1½ pounds salsify
2 tablespoons butter
1 large onion, finely
chopped
5½ cups vegetable stock
Sea salt and freshly
ground black pepper
Bouquet garni including
three thinly pared strips
lemon rind
Juice of up to 1 lemon
⅓ cup unflavored yogurt

Tomato Soup with Brandy

Imperial (Metric)

2½ lb (1.4 kg) ripe
tomatoes
1 oz (30g) butter
1 large onion, finely
chopped
1½ pints (850ml)
vegetable stock
6 tablespoons chopped
fresh mixed herbs
3 fl oz (90ml) brandy
3 fl oz (90ml) soured
cream

1. Scald, skin and chop the tomatoes.
2. Melt the butter in a saucepan on a low heat. Mix in the onion, cover and cook gently for 5 minutes.
3. Add the tomatoes, cover again and cook for 10 minutes.
4. Mash the tomatoes to a purée using a potato masher or a fish slice.
5. Pour in the stock.
6. Bring the stock to the boil. Add the herbs. Cover and simmer for 15 minutes.
7. Take the pan from the heat and add the brandy.

American

2½ pounds ripe tomatoes
2 tablespoons butter
1 large onion, finely
chopped
3¾ cups vegetable stock
⅓ cup chopped fresh
mixed herbs
⅓ cup brandy
⅓ cup sour cream

242

8. Pour the soup into warmed individual bowls and float a tablespoon of soured cream on each one.

Note: Do not boil again after adding the brandy. If you wish to make the soup in advance, leave it after simmering and then reheat and add the brandy just before serving.

The soup may also be frozen after simmering and cooling. Store in a covered rigid container for up to 2 months. Thaw at room temperature, reheat and add the brandy.

Parsnip, Leek and Chestnut Soup

Imperial (Metric)

1 lb (455g) parsnips
1¼ lb (570g) leeks
1 lb (455g) chestnuts
1 oz (30g) butter
2¼ pints (1.3 litres) vegetable stock
Bouquet garni
½ pint (285ml) creamed smetana

1. Dice the parsnips, removing the cores.
2. Cut 4 oz (115g) of the leeks into matchstick pieces. Thinly slice the rest.
3. Slit the tops of the chestnuts. Put the chestnuts into a saucepan and cover them with water. Bring them to the boil and simmer them for 10 minutes. Skin them.
4. Melt the butter in a saucepan on a low heat. Put in the parsnips and sliced leeks. Cover them and cook them for 10 minutes.
5. Add the chestnuts.
6. Pour in the stock and bring it to the boil. Add the bouquet garni. Cover and simmer for 20 minutes.
7. Remove the bouquet garni. Liquidize the rest in a blender or food processor or put it through the fine blade of a vegetable mill.
8. Return the soup to the saucepan. Stir in the smetana and reheat.
9. Boil the reserved pieces of leek for 1 minute. Drain them and use them as a garnish.

Note: The soup may be frozen before the smetana is added. Cool it and store it in a covered container for up to two months. Thaw at room temperature and reheat. The leek garnish is best freshly prepared.

American

1 pound parsnips
1¼ pounds leeks
1 pound chestnuts
2 tablespoons butter
5½ cups vegetable stock
Bouquet garni
1¼ cups creamed smetana

243

Stilton, Onion and Watercress Soup

Imperial (Metric)

2 medium onions
1 oz (30g) butter
2 tablespoons wholemeal
flour
2¼ pints (1.3 litres)
vegetable stock
4 oz (115g) watercress
6 oz (170g) Stilton cheese,
grated or crumbled

1. Finely chop the onions.
2. Melt the butter in a saucepan on a low heat. Put in the onions and soften them.
3. Stir in the flour and stock. Bring them to the boil, stirring. Simmer, uncovered, for 15 minutes.
4. Chop the watercress. Reserve 6 tablespoons. Add the rest to the soup and simmer for 2 minutes.
5. Put the Stilton into a bowl. Remove the soup from the heat and gradually stir about a quarter of it into the Stilton, creaming it as much as possible. Stir the mixture back into the saucepan.
6. Reheat gently but do not boil.
7. Serve with the remaining watercress floating on the top.
Note: Unsuitable for freezing.

American

2 medium onions
2 tablespoons butter
2 tablespoons wholewheat
flour
5½ cups vegetable stock
¼ pound watercress
¾ cup grated or crumbled
Stilton cheese

Fennel and Red Wine Soup

Imperial (Metric)

1 lb (455g) Florence
fennel
1 medium onion
1 oz (30g) butter
1 garlic clove, chopped
1½ tablespoons wholemeal
flour
2 pints (1.14 litres)
vegetable stock
Leaves of fennel bulbs,
chopped
8 fl oz (225ml) dry red
wine
4 tablespoons chopped
parsley

1. Finely chop the fennel and onion.
2. Melt the butter in a heavy saucepan on a low heat. Stir in the fennel, onion and garlic. Cover and cook gently for 10 minutes.
3. Stir in the flour and stock and bring them to the boil, stirring.
4. Add the chopped fennel leaves.
5. Simmer, uncovered, for 15 minutes.
6. Add the wine and reheat without boiling.
7. Serve with parsley floating on top.
Note: The soup can be frozen before the wine is added. Store in a covered container for up to 2 months. Thaw at room temperature, reheat and add the wine.

American

1 pound Florence fennel
1 medium onion
2 tablespoons butter
1 garlic clove, chopped
1½ tablespoons
wholewheat flour
5 cups vegetables stock
Leaves of fennel bulbs,
chopped
1 cup red wine
¼ cup chopped parsley

FIRST COURSES

When your main course is rich and warming, the first course should be light and fresh. Use all the fresh vegetables and fruits that you have available for small but delectable salads; and where the food is richer serve an accompanying yogurt sauce or salad garnish.

Mustard and Cress Soufflés

Imperial (Metric)

1 oz (30g) butter
1 oz (30g) dried wholemeal breadcrumbs
¼ pint (140ml) milk
Bouquet garni
1 slice onion
1 blade mace
4 black peppercorns
1 tablespoon wholemeal flour
2 teaspoons Dijon mustard
4 eggs, separated
4 oz (115g) cottage cheese
2 boxes mustard and cress
Garnish:
1 lb (455g) tomatoes
2 boxes mustard and cress
4 tablespoons olive oil
2 tablespoons white wine vinegar
1 garlic clove, crushed
Freshly ground black pepper

1. Use half the butter to grease six individual soufflé dishes. Coat the inside of the dishes with the dried crumbs.
2. Heat the oven to 375°F/190°C/Gas Mark 5.
3. Put the milk into a saucepan with the bouquet garni, onion, mace and peppercorns. Set it on a low heat and leave it to infuse it for 10 minutes. Strain it.
4. Melt the remaining butter in the saucepan on a medium heat. Stir in the flour and then the flavoured milk. Bring them to the boil, stirring. Simmer for 2 minutes.
5. Take the pan from the heat. Beat in the mustard and then the egg yolks, one at a time.
6. Beat in the cheese. Cut in the mustard and cress and mix it in well.
7. Stiffly whip the egg whites and fold them into the mixture with a metal spoon.
8. Transfer the mixture to the prepared dishes.
9. Lay the dishes on a baking sheet. Bake the soufflés for 20 minutes or until they are risen and golden.
10. While the soufflés are cooking, thinly slice the tomatoes. Arrange tomato slices on each of six small plates. Scatter mustard and cress over the top. Beat the remaining ingredients together to make the dressing and spoon them over the tomatoes and cress.
11. When the soufflés are done, stand a dish on each plate by the salad.
Note: Unsuitable for freezing.

American

2 tablespoons butter
¼ cup dried wholewheat breadcrumbs
⅔ cup milk
Bouquet garni
1 slice onion
1 blade mace
4 black peppercorns
1 tablespoon wholewheat flour
2 teaspoons Dijon mustard
4 eggs, separated
½ cup cottage cheese
2 boxes mustard and cress
Garnish:
1 pound tomatoes
2 boxes mustard and cress
¼ cup olive oil
2 tablespoons white wine vinegar
1 garlic clove, crushed
Freshly ground black pepper

Celeriac and Almond Salad

Imperial (Metric)

1 lb (455g) celeriac
½ teaspoon fine sea salt
Juice of ½ lemon
2 teaspoons Dijon
mustard
4 tablespoons olive oil
4 tablespoons natural
yogurt
4 oz (115g) almonds
6 satsumas
6 small parsley sprigs

1. Peel the celeriac. Cut it into small, matchstick pieces. Put it into a bowl. Toss in the salt and lemon juice. Leave it to stand for 30 minutes.
2. Put the mustard into a bowl and gradually work in first the oil and then the yogurt.
3. Mix the almonds and then the dressing into the celeriac.
4. Divide the salad between six small plates.
5. Garnish the salads with the satsuma segments and top with parsley sprigs.
Note: Unsuitable for freezing.

American

1 pound celeriac
½ teaspoon fine sea salt
Juice of ½ lemon
2 teaspoons Dijon
mustard
¼ cup olive oil
¼ cup unflavored yogurt
1 cup almonds
6 satsumas
6 small parsley sprigs

Hot Grapefruit with Stilton

Imperial (Metric)

3 large grapefruit
1 garlic clove, finely
chopped
3 tablespoons olive oil
3 tablespoons chopped
parsley
1 tablespoon white wine
vinegar
Freshly ground black
pepper
8 oz (225g) Stilton cheese,
grated or crumbled

1. Cut the grapefruit in half. Cut out all the segments and discard the pith. Put the shells into small, heatproof dishes.
2. Heat the garlic in the oil on a moderate heat, without letting it brown.
3. Put in the grapefruit segments, parsley and vinegar and bring them to the boil. Remove from the heat and spoon them into the shells. Season with pepper.
4. Scatter the cheese over the top.
5. Put the shells under a high grill for the cheese to melt. Serve as soon as possible.
Note: Unsuitable for freezing.

American

3 large grapefruit
1 garlic clove, finely
chopped
3 tablespoons olive oil
3 tablespoons chopped
parsley
1 tablespoon white wine
vinegar
Freshly ground black
pepper
2 cups grated or crumbled
Stilton cheese

Pineapple with Green Pepper Cheese

Imperial (Metric)

1 large pineapple
12 oz (340g) curd cheese
1 garlic clove, crushed
3 medium green peppers,
cored and seeded
Freshly ground black
pepper

1. Cut the husk from the pineapple. Cut the flesh into six thick slices and stamp out the cores. Place each slice on a small plate.
2. Cream the cheese and garlic together in a bowl.
3. Chop two peppers very finely and mix them into the cheese.
4. Pile the mixture on top of the pineapple slices.

American

1 large pineapple
1½ cups curd cheese
1 garlic clove, crushed
3 medium sweet green
peppers, cored and seeded
Freshly ground black
pepper

5. Cut the remaining pepper into thin strips and use them as garnish.
Note: Unsuitable for freezing.

Fennel with Cashew Nuts

Imperial (Metric)

Three 8 oz (225g) fennel bulbs
2 oranges
1 oz (30g) butter
1 garlic clove, chopped
Juice of 1 orange
5 oz (150g) cashew nuts
2 tablespoons chopped fennel leaves

1. Trim the fennel bulbs. Cut them into quarters lengthways.
2. Cut the rind and pith from the other two. Cut them into quarters lengthways and thinly slice them.
3. Melt the butter in a frying pan (skillet) on a high heat. Put in the pieces of fennel and the garlic clove. Turn the fennel on the heat for about 1 minute or until it is beginning to brown.
4. Pour in the orange juice. Cover and cook on a low heat for 10 minutes.
5. Raise the heat to high again. Add the sliced oranges and the cashew nuts. Cook, uncovered, for 1 minute, or until the juices are reduced to a glaze.
6. Put two pieces of fennel on each of six small plates. Surround them with the oranges and cashew nuts. Scatter the chopped fennel over the fennel bulbs. Serve hot.
Note: Unsuitable for freezing.

American

Three ½ pound fennel bulbs
2 oranges
2 tablespoons butter
1 garlic clove, chopped
Juice of 1 orange
1 cup cashew nuts
2 tablespoons chopped fennel leaves

Chicory (Belgian Endive), Grape and Walnut Salad

Imperial (Metric)

1 lb (455g) chicory
8 oz (225g) green grapes
4 oz (115g) walnuts, chopped
2 tablespoons sesame seeds
4 tablespoons sesame oil
2 tablespoons white wine vinegar
1 garlic clove, crushed
Freshly ground black pepper
30 walnut halves

1. Chop the chicory (Belgian endive). Halve and seed the grapes.
2. Mix together the chicory (Belgian endive), grapes, chopped walnuts and sesame seeds.
3. Beat the oil, vinegar, garlic and pepper together and fold them into the salad.
4. Divide the salad between six small bowls.
5. Garnish with the walnut halves.
Note: Unsuitable for freezing.

American

1 pound Belgian endive
½ pound green grapes
¾ cup chopped English walnuts
2 tablespoons sesame seeds
¼ cup sesame oil
2 tablespoons white wine vinegar
1 garlic clove, crushed
Freshly ground black pepper
30 English walnut halves

247

Deep-Fried Aubergines (Eggplants) with Yogurt and Sesame Dressing

Imperial (Metric)

3 medium aubergines
1 tablespoon fine sea salt
2 oz (55g) wholemeal
flour, seasoned
8 fl oz (225ml) natural
yogurt
1½ teaspoons ground
cumin
1½ teaspoons ground
coriander
2 teaspoons dried mint
2 tablespoons chopped
fresh coriander
2 tablespoons sesame
seeds
Vegetable oil for frying
12 parsley sprigs

1. Cut the aubergines (eggplants) into thin slices lengthways. Cut each slice in half lengthways. Put the pieces into a colander. Sprinkle them with the salt and leave them for 20 minutes to drain. Rinse them under cold water and dry them with kitchen paper.
2. Coat the pieces of aubergine (eggplant) in the seasoned flour.
3. Mix together the yogurt, ground cumin and coriander, herbs and sesame seeds.
4. Heat a deep pan of oil to 375°F/190°C.
5. Deep fry the aubergine (eggplant) slices for 1 minute only, turning them once during cooking. Do this in about 5 batches. Drain them on kitchen paper and keep them warm.
6. Deep fry the parsley sprigs.
7. Arrange the aubergines (eggplants) on six small plates. Spoon the yogurt mixture over the top. Garnish with the deep-fried parsley.
Note: Unsuitable for freezing.

American

3 medium eggplants
1 tablespoon fine sea salt
2 oz (55g) wholewheat
flour, seasoned
1 cup unflavored yogurt
1½ teaspoons ground
cumin
1½ teaspoons ground
coriander
2 teaspoons dried mint
2 tablespoons chopped
fresh coriander
2 tablespoons sesame
seeds
Vegetable oil for frying
12 parsley sprigs

Avocado with Mushroom Salad

Imperial (Metric)

7 fl oz (200ml) natural
yogurt
3 tablespoons olive oil
½ teaspoon ground ginger
Grated rind of ½ lemon
1 garlic clove, crushed
12 oz (340g) button
mushrooms, thinly sliced
3 small avocados

1. In a large bowl, mix together the yogurt, oil, ginger, lemon rind and garlic.
2. Fold in the mushrooms and leave them for 30 minutes.
3. Peel, halve and stone (pit) the avocados. Turn them cut side down and make five lengthways slits down their length from about ½ inch (1 cm) from the pointed end and right the way through the round end. Carefully spread the avocado halves into fan shapes.
4. Lay each avocado half on an individual plate. Put a portion of the mushroom salad around the bottom of the rounded end.
Note: Unsuitable for freezing.

American

¾ cup unflavored yogurt
3 tablespoons olive oil
½ teaspoon ground ginger
Grated rind of ½ lemon
1 garlic clove, crushed
¾ pound button
mushrooms, thinly sliced
3 small avocados

MAIN DISHES

Pies, cobblers, casseroles and dishes of roots and nuts — what could be more appropriate for winter meals? Add the freshness of stir-fried vegetables and the bitter-sweet flavour of Seville oranges, eggs, cheese, chestnuts and green winter vegetables and you have menus enough to last throughout the season.

Artichoke and Sage Derby Crumble

Imperial (Metric)

2 tablespoons white wine vinegar
1½ lb (685g) Jerusalem artichokes
6 eggs, hard-boiled
1½ oz (45g) butter or vegetable margarine
3 tablespoons wholemeal flour
1 tablespoon mustard powder
7 fl oz (200ml) vegetable stock
¼ pint (140ml) dry white wine
Juice of 1 lemon
4 tablespoons chopped parsley
8 oz (225g) Sage Derby cheese, grated
Crumble Topping:
4 oz (115g) porridge oats
2 oz (55g) pine nuts
2 oz (55g) chopped hazelnuts
4 tablespoons sunflower oil

1. Heat the oven to 400°C/200°F/Gas Mark 6.
2. Fill a large bowl with water. Add the vinegar. Peel the artichokes, dipping them frequently into the water. Drop them into the water when peeled. This keeps them white.
3. Boil the artichokes for 10 minutes. Drain and slice them.
4. Chop the eggs.
5. Melt the butter or margarine in a saucepan on a medium heat. Stir in the flour and mustard powder. Stir in the stock and bring it to the boil, stirring until the sauce thickens. Stir in the wine, lemon juice and parsley.
6. Take the pan from the heat and mix the artichokes and eggs into the sauce.
7. Put one third of the mixture into a large, ovenproof dish. Scatter in half the cheese. Repeat the layers, finishing with the final third of the artichokes.
8. Mix the ingredients for the crumble topping in a bowl, making sure that the oil is evenly mixed in. Scatter the topping over the artichokes.
9. Bake the crumble for 25 minutes or until the top is lightly browned.
Note: The artichoke mixture can be frozen without the eggs. Store in a covered container for up to 1 month. Thaw at room temperature, add the eggs and layer with the cheese. Top with the crumble mixture and cook as above.

American

2 tablespoons white wine vinegar
1½ pounds Jerusalem artichokes
6 hard-cooked eggs
3 tablespoons butter or vegetable margarine
3 tablespoons wholewheat flour
1 tablespoon mustard powder
¾ cup vegetable stock
⅔ cup dry white wine
Juice of 1 lemon
4 tablespoons chopped parsley
2 cups grated Sage Derby cheese
Crumble Topping:
1 cup rolled oats
½ cup pine nuts
½ cup chopped hazelnuts
¼ cup sunflower oil

Deep-Fried Kale and Cheese Balls with Tomato and Orange Sauce

Imperial (Metric)

1 lb (455g) curly kale
1 oz (30g) butter
½ pint (285ml) water
10 oz (285g) millet
1 medium onion, finely
chopped
1½ pints (850ml)
vegetable stock
¼ nutmeg, grated
8 oz (225g) Double
Gloucester cheese
2 oz (55g) wholemeal
flour
2 eggs, beaten
Vegetable oil for deep
frying
Sauce:
1½ lb (685g) tomatoes
3 medium onions
3 fl oz (90ml) sunflower
oil
2 garlic cloves, finely
chopped
Grated rind and juice of
1 orange
3 tablespoons tomato
purée
1 tablespoon dried thyme

1. Strip the kale from the stalks. Melt the butter in a saucepan on a high heat. Stir in the kale. Pour in the water and bring it to the boil. Cover and cook on a medium heat for 10 minutes. Drain the kale and finely chop it.

2. Put the millet, onion and stock into a saucepan and bring them to the boil. Cover and simmer for 20 minutes or until the millet is soft and all the stock has been absorbed.

3. In a bowl, mix the kale into the millet. Add the nutmeg.

4. Cut the cheese into ⅝ inch (1.5cm) cubes.

5. Make the millet mixture into 36 small balls, each with a cube of cheese in the centre.

6. Roll the balls in the flour, then in beaten egg and a second time in the flour.

7. Heat a deep pan of oil to 375°F/190°C. Fry the balls, about eight at a time, for 2 minutes, or until they are golden brown. Drain them on kitchen paper.

8. For the sauce, scald skin and chop the tomatoes. Finely chop the onions. Heat the oil in a saucepan on a low heat. Put in the onions and garlic and soften them. Add the tomatoes, orange rind and juice, tomato purée (paste) and thyme. Cover and simmer gently for 15 minutes. Serve separately.

Note: The sauce can be frozen in a covered container for up to 1 month. Thaw it at room temperature. The kale balls are not suitable for freezing.

American

1 pound curly kale
2 tablespoons butter
1¼ cups water
2½ cups millet
1 medium onion, finely
chopped
3¾ cups vegetable stock
¼ nutmeg, grated
½ pound Double
Gloucester cheese
½ cup wholewheat flour
2 eggs, beaten
Vegetable oil for deep
frying
Sauce:
1½ pounds tomatoes
3 medium onions
⅓ cup sunflower oil
2 garlic cloves, finely
chopped
Grated rind and juice of
1 orange
3 tablespoons tomato
paste
1 tablespoon dried thyme

Spiced Green Lentils with Brussels Sprout Stir-Fry

Imperial (Metric)

8 oz (225g) green lentils
4 fl oz (125ml) sunflower
oil
2 medium onions, thinly
sliced
2 garlic cloves, finely
chopped
2 teaspoons paprika
1 teaspoon ground mixed
spice
12 oz (340g) millet
2½ pints (1.5 litres)
vegetable stock
1½ lb (685g) Brussels
sprouts
4 oz (115g) pine nuts
Juice of 1 lemon

1. Put the lentils into a saucepan and cover them with water. Bring them to the boil. Take them from the heat and leave them to soak for 1 hour. Drain them.

2. Heat half the oil in a saucepan on a low heat. Put in the onions and one of the garlic cloves and soften them. Stir in half the paprika and mixed spice, the lentils and the millet. Stir on the heat for 1 minute. Pour in the stock and bring it to the boil. Cover and simmer for 45 minutes or until both lentils and millet are soft.

3. While the lentils and millet are cooking, trim and thinly slice the Brussels sprouts. Heat the remaining oil in a large frying pan (skillet) or wok on a high heat. Put in the Brussels sprouts, pine nuts and remaining garlic. Stir-fry for 3 minutes or until the Brussels sprouts are beginning to wilt. Add the remaining spices. Pour in the lemon juice and bring it to the boil. Remove the pan from the heat.

4. Just before serving, mix the Brussels sprouts and pine nuts into the lentils and millet.

Note: The lentil and millet mixture is suitable for freezing. Store it in a covered container for up to 6 weeks. Thaw at room temperature and reheat in a saucepan. The Brussels sprout stir-fry is not suitable for cooking in advance or for freezing.

American

1 cup green lentils
½ cup sunflower oil
2 medium onions, thinly
sliced
2 garlic cloves, finely
chopped
2 teaspoons paprika
1 teaspoon ground mixed
spice
1½ cups millet
6⅓ cups vegetable stock
1½ pounds Brussels
sprouts
¾ cup pine nuts
Juice of 1 lemon

Winter Pie

Imperial (Metric)

Pastry:
1 lb (455g) wholemeal
flour
6 oz (170g) Cheddar
cheese, grated
½ teaspoon fine sea salt
2 teaspoons mustard
powder
1 teaspoon paprika
8 oz (225g) vegetable
margarine
Cold water to mix
1 egg, beaten
Filling:
12 oz (340g) black-eyed
beans, soaked
12 oz (340g) chestnuts
1 lb (455g) swede
12 oz (340g) carrots
1 large onion
1 oz (30g) vegetable
margarine
3 tablespoons wholemeal
flour
½ pint (275ml) vegetable
stock
½ pint (275ml) tomato
and vegetable juice
¼ nutmeg, grated

1. To make the pastry, put the flour into a bowl with the cheese, salt, mustard powder and paprika. Rub them together lightly with your fingertips. Rub in the margarine. Mix everything to a dough with cold water. Leave it in a cold place while you prepare the filling.
2. Cook the beans until they are tender.
3. Slit the tops of the chestnuts. Put them into a saucepan and cover them with cold water. Bring them to the boil and simmer them for 5 minutes. Skin them.
4. Heat the oven to 400°F/200°C/Gas Mark 6.
5. Finely grate the swede (rutabaga) and carrots. Finely chop the onion.
6. Melt the margarine in a large saucepan on a high heat. Put in the swede (rutabaga), carrots and onion and stir them around on the heat for 5 minutes or until they are beginning to soften.
7. Lower the heat to moderate. Stir in the flour and then the stock and tomato and vegetable juice. Bring them to the boil, stirring. Simmer for 2 minutes and take the pan from the heat.
8. Grate in the nutmeg. Put in the beans and chestnuts and mix well. Cool the mixture slightly.
9. Roll out about two thirds of the pastry and line a 10 inch (25cm) square, 2 inch deep (5cm) deep ovenproof dish. Put in the filling. Cover it with the remaining pastry. Seal the edges and brush the top with the beaten egg.
10. Bake the pie for 30 minutes or until it is golden brown. serve it hot.
Note: Freeze in the dish. Cool the pie completely and seal it in a polythene bag. Store for up to 1 month. If the dish can be put directly into the oven from the freezer, the pie can be reheated by

American

Pastry:
4 cups wholewheat flour
1½ cups grated Cheddar
cheese
½ teaspoon fine sea salt
2 teaspoons mustard
powder
1 teaspoon paprika
1 cup vegetable margarine
Cold water to mix
1 egg, beaten
Filling:
1½ cups black-eyed beans,
soaked
¾ pound chestnuts
1 pound rutabaga
¾ pound carrots
1 large onion
2 tablespoons vegetable
margarine
3 tablespoons wholewheat
flour
1¼ cups vegetable stock
1¼ cups tomato and
vegetable juice
¼ nutmeg, grated

being placed in a moderate oven for 45 minutes; if not, thaw the pie at room temperature and reheat in a hot oven for 20-30 minutes.

Root Vegetable and Nut Layer

Imperial (Metric)

12 oz (340g) split red lentils
1½ pints (850ml) vegetable stock
2 bay leaves
Freshly ground black pepper
8 oz (225g) swede
8 oz (225g) carrots
4 tablespoons sunflower oil
1 medium onion, finely chopped
1 garlic clove, finely chopped
4 celery sticks, chopped
1 green pepper, cored, seeded and chopped
¼ nutmeg, grated
2 tablespoons chopped parsley
3 oz (85g) hazelnuts, chopped
4 tablespoons dried wholemeal breadcrumbs
Sauce:
1 lb (455g) tomatoes
2 tablespoons sunflower oil
1 medium onion, chopped
¼ pint (140ml) dry white wine
1 sprig each parsley, thyme and marjoram
4 tablespoons chopped parsley

1. Put the lentils into a saucepan with the stock and bay leaves. Season with the pepper. Bring them to the boil. Cover and simmer gently for 30 minutes.
2. While the lentils are cooking, grate the swede (rutabaga) and carrots. Add them to the lentils. Continue cooking for a further 10-15 minutes, stirring frequently and beating the lentils to a thick purée. Take the pan from the heat.
3. Heat the oven to 400°F/200°C/Gas Mark 6. Oil a deep, ovenproof dish.
4. Heat the oil in a frying pan (skillet) on a low heat. Put in the onion, garlic, celery and green pepper. Cook until the onion is soft. Mix them into the lentils.
5. Add the nutmeg and parsley.
6. Put half the mixture into the dish. Scatter the nuts over the top and put in the remaining mixture. Smooth the top amd scatter it with the crumbs.
7. Bake for 30 minutes or until the top has browned.
8. To make the sauce, chop the tomatoes. Heat the oil in a saucepan on a low heat. Put in the onion, tomatoes, wine and herb sprigs. Bring them to the boil. Cover and simmer for 15 minutes.
9. Rub the contents of the pan through a sieve.
10. Return the sauce to the cleaned pan. Add the parsley and reheat. Serve separately.
Note: Unsuitable for freezing.

American

1½ cups split red lentils
3¾ cups vegetable stock
2 bay leaves
Freshly ground black pepper
½ pound rutabaga
½ pound carrots
¼ cup sunflower oil
1 medium onion, finely chopped
1 garlic clove, finely chopped
4 celery stalks, chopped
1 sweet green pepper, cored, seeded and chopped
¼ nutmeg, grated
2 tablespoons chopped parsley
⅔ cup chopped hazelnuts
¼ cup dried wholewheat breadcrumbs
Sauce:
1 pound tomatoes
2 tablespoons sunflower oil
1 medium onion, chopped
⅔ cup dry white wine
1 sprig each parsley, thyme and marjoram
¼ cup chopped parsley

Pinto (Borlotti) Beans and Walnuts in Choux Pastry

Imperial (Metric)

*12 oz (340g) borlotti
beans
4 oz (115g) shelled
walnuts
12 oz (340g) tomatoes
8 oz (225g) open
mushrooms
3 tablespoons sunflower
oil
1 large onion, finely
chopped
2 tablespoons chopped
thyme
1 tablespoon chopped
marjoram
2 sage leaves, chopped
¼ pint (140ml) dry red
wine
Choux Paste:
3 oz (85g) butter
8 fl oz (225ml) water
4 oz (115g) wholemeal
flour
3 eggs, beaten
Garnish:
4 tablespoons chopped
parsley*

1. Soak the beans, cook them until they are tender and drain them.
2. Chop the walnuts.
3. Scald, skin and chop the tomatoes. Chop the mushrooms.
4. Heat the oil in a frying pan (skillet) on a low heat. Put in the onion and soften it.
5. Raise the heat to medium. Put in the mushrooms and stir them for 2 minutes.
6. Put in the tomatoes, herbs and wine and bring them to the boil.
7. Put in the beans. Cover and simmer for 20 minutes.
8. Mix in the walnuts.
9. Heat the oven to 400°F/200°C/Gas Mark 6.
10. For the choux paste, put the butter and water into a saucepan and set them on a high heat until the butter has melted and the mixture is boiling. Stir in the flour all at once. Take the pan from the heat and beat the mixture until it is smooth. Leave it to cool for 5 minutes. Gradually beat in the eggs and then beat until the mixture is smooth and glossy.
11. Put the bean and walnut filling into a large, ovenproof dish. Cover the edges with the choux paste.
12. Bake for 30 minutes or until the pastry is crisp and risen.
13. Scatter the filling with parsley before serving.

Note: Unsuitable for freezing.

American

*2 cups pinto beans
¾ cup shelled English
walnuts
¾ pound tomatoes
½ pound open mushrooms
3 tablespoons sunflower
oil
1 large onion, finely
chopped
2 tablespoons chopped
thyme
1 tablespoon chopped
marjoram
2 sage leaves, chopped
⅔ cup dry red wine
Choux Paste:
⅓ cup butter
1 cup water
1 cup wholewheat flour
3 eggs, beaten
Garnish:
4 tablespoons chopped
parsley*

Eggs Baked with Aubergine (Eggplant) and Avocado

Imperial (Metric)

1 lb (455g) aubergines
1 tablespoon sea salt
2 large, ripe avocados
1½ lb (685g) tomatoes
4 tablespoons olive oil
2 medium onions, finely
chopped
2 garlic cloves, chopped
12 eggs
1½ oz (45g) Parmesan
cheese, grated
4 tablespoons chopped
parsley

1. Heat the oven to 400°F/200°C/Gas Mark 6.
2. Dice the aubergines (eggplants). Put them into a colander and sprinkle them with the salt. Leave them to drain for 20 minutes. Rinse them under cold water and dry them with kitchen paper.
3. Peel, stone (pit) and mash the avocados.
4. Scald, skin and chop the tomatoes.
5. Heat the oil in a saucepan on a low heat. Put in the onions and garlic and soften them. Add the diced aubergine (eggplant) and cook for 2 minutes. Add the tomatoes, cover and cook for 10 minutes.
6. Cool the mixture a little and mix in the mashed avocado.
7. Divide the mixture between two lightly greased, 10 inch (25cm) diameter ovenproof dishes.
8. Using the back of a tablespoon, make six indentations in the mixture in each dish. Carefully break an egg into each one.
9. Scatter the Parmesan cheese over the eggs.
10. Cover with lightly oiled foil.
11. Bake for 20 minutes so the eggs are just set.
12. Scatter the parsley over the top and serve straight from the dish.
Note: Unsuitable for freezing.

American

1 pound eggplants
1 tablespoon sea salt
2 large, ripe avocados
1½ pounds tomatoes
¼ cup olive oil
2 medium onions, finely
chopped
2 garlic cloves, chopped
12 eggs
⅓ cup grated Parmesan
cheese
¼ cup chopped parsley

Savoy and Almond Mould

Imperial (Metric)

1 large Savoy cabbage
8 oz (225g) almonds
4 oz (115g) burghul
wheat
8 oz (225g) tomatoes
4 tablespoons sunflower
oil
1 large onion, finely
chopped
1 garlic clove, finely
chopped
2 teaspoons ground cumin
1 teaspoon ground
coriander
½ teaspoon ground
cinnamon
Grated rind of 1 lemon
2 oz (55g) currants
2 eggs, beaten
Sauce:
1 oz (30g) butter
1 medium onion, finely
chopped
1 tablespoon wholemeal
flour
1 pint (570ml) vegetable
stock
Juice and thinly pared
rind of 1 lemon
3 egg yolks
8 oz (225g) tomatoes
4 tablespoons chopped
parsley

1. Trim the stalk from the cabbage. Bring a large pan of water to the boil. Put in the cabbage, whole, and boil it for 4 minutes. Drain it.

2. Wring out a piece of muslin or a worn out tea cloth in hot water. Use it to line a 2½ pint (1.4 litre/6⅓ cup) pudding basin. Line the cloth with cabbage leaves with their stalks pointing upwards. Reserve the next five leaves for the cover.

3. Blanch and shred the almonds.

4. Soak the wheat in warm water for 20 minutes, drain it and squeeze it dry.

5. Scald, skin and chop the tomatoes.

6. Heat the oil in a frying pan (skillet) on a low heat. Put in the onion and garlic and soften them. Mix in the spices and cook for a further minute.

7. In a large bowl, mix together the almonds, wheat, tomatoes, onion and garlic, lemon rind and currants. Chop 8 oz (225g/½ pound) of the remaining cabbage and mix it into the rest. Bind with the beaten eggs.

8. Put the mixture into the lined basin and cover it with the reserved leaves. Bring the sides of the muslin or cloth over the top.

9. Bring a large pan of water to the boil. Lower in the basin and steam for 1 hour.

10. Turn the mould onto a flat dish for serving.

11. Make the sauce while the mould is steaming. Melt the butter in a saucepan on a low heat. Add the onion and soften it. Stir in the flour and stock. Bring them to the boil. Cover and simmer for 10 minutes. Add half the lemon juice and all the rind. Cover and simmer for a further 10 minutes. Taste the sauce. Add more lemon juice to taste if required.

12. Strain the sauce, return it to the cleaned pan and gently reheat it.

American

1 large Savoy cabbage
2 cups almonds
½ cup burghul wheat
½ pound tomatoes
¼ cup sunflower oil
1 large onion, finely
chopped
1 garlic clove, finely
chopped
2 teaspoons ground cumin
1 teaspoon ground
coriander
½ teaspoon ground
cinnamon
Grated rind of 1 lemon
⅓ cup currants
2 eggs, beaten
Sauce:
2 tablespoons butter
1 medium onion, finely
chopped
1 tablespoon wholewheat
flour
2½ cups vegetable stock
Juice and thinly pared
rind of 1 lemon
3 egg yolks
½ pound tomatoes
¼ cup chopped parsley

13. Beat the egg yolks in a bowl. Gradually add about ¼ pint (140ml/ ⅔ cup) of the warm sauce. Stir it back into the rest. Stir on a low heat to thicken the sauce slightly but do not let it boil. Remove the sauce from the heat.
14. Scald, skin, seed and finely chop the tomatoes. Mix them into the sauce with the parsley.
15. Serve the sauce separately.
Note: Unsuitable for freezing.

Celeriac Soufflé with Soft Cheese and Brie

Imperial (Metric)

1½ lb (685g) celeriac
1 medium onion
½ oz (15g) butter or
vegetable margarine plus
extra for greasing
1½ tablespoons wholemeal
flour
¼ pint (140ml) milk
12 oz (340g) low-fat soft
cheese
4 tablespoons chopped
parsley
6 eggs, separated
4 oz (115g) Brie, diced
4 tablespoons dried
wholemeal breadcrumbs

1. Heat the oven to 400°F/200°C/Gas Mark 6.
2. Peel and dice the celeriac. Thinly slice the onion. Steam them together for 20 minutes or until tender. Rub them through a sieve or vegetable mill or purée them in a blender or food processor.
3. Melt the butter or margarine in a saucepan on a medium heat. Stir in the flour and milk. Bring to the boil, stirring until you have a thick sauce. Remove it from the heat.
4. Beat the soft cheese into the sauce, a little at a time.
5. Mix in the celeriac purée and parsley.
6. Beat in the egg yolks, one at a time. Mix in the diced Brie.
7. Butter and crumb a large, flat, ovenproof dish.
8. Stiffly whip the egg whites. Fold them into the celeriac and cheese mixture.
9. Pile the mixture into the prepared dish.
10. Bake the soufflé for 40 minutes or until it is set and risen.
Note: The soufflé is best served as soon as possible after it comes from the oven. Unsuitable for freezing.

American

1½ pounds celeriac
1 medium onion
1 tablespoon butter or
vegetable margarine plus
extra for greasing
1½ tablespoons
wholewheat flour
⅔ cup milk
1½ cups low-fat soft
cheese
4 tablespoons chopped
parsley
6 eggs, separated
¼ pound Brie, diced
4 tablespoons dried
wholewheat breadcrumbs

Spiced Lentil and Coconut Cobbler

Imperial (Metric)

2 large onions
1 large cooking apple
4 tablespoons sunflower oil
2 garlic cloves, finely chopped
2 teaspoons ground cumin
2 teaspoons ground coriander
2 teaspoons hot Madras curry powder
12 oz (340g) split red lentils
6 cardamom pods, crushed
2-inch (5cm) cinnamon stick
1½ oz (45g) flaked coconut
1½ pints (850ml) vegetable stock
Cobbler Topping:
12 oz (340g) wholemeal flour
1 teaspoon sea salt
1 teaspoon bicarbonate of soda
1 teaspoon ground coriander
1 teaspoon ground cumin
4 oz (115g) vegetable margarine
7 fl oz (200ml) soured cream

1. Finely chop the onions. Core and chop the apple, without peeling.
2. Heat the oil in a heavy saucepan on a low heat. Put in the onion and garlic and cook them for 2 minutes. Stir in the apple, cumin, coriander and curry powder. Cook gently until the onion is soft.
3. Stir in the lentils and cardamom pods. Add the cinnamon stick and coconut.
4. Pour in the stock and bring it to the boil.
5. Cover and cook gently for 35 minutes, or until most of the stock has been absorbed and the lentils are soft.
6. Heat the oven to 400°F/200°C/Gas Mark 6.
7. For the cobbler, put the flour into a bowl. Add the salt, bicarbonate of (baking) soda and spices and toss them in with your fingers. Rub in the margarine. Bind the mixture together with the soured cream. Knead it lightly to make a smooth ball of dough. Divide the dough into twelve equal-sized pieces and form each one into a round scone shape.
8. When the lentils are cooked, put them into a large, 2½ inch (6cm) deep, ovenproof dish. Remove the cinnamon stick. Place the scones on top.
9. Bake the cobbler for 20 minutes or until the scone topping is golden brown.
10. Serve straight from the dish.
Note: The lentil mixture may be frozen seperately in a covered container and stored for up to 2 months. Freeze the scones, uncooked. Thaw both at room temperature and cook as above.

American

2 large onions
1 large cooking apple
¼ cup sunflower oil
2 garlic cloves, finely chopped
2 teaspoons ground cumin
2 teaspoons ground coriander
2 teaspoons hot Madras curry powder
3 cups split red lentils
6 cardamom pods, crushed
2-inch cinnamon stick
½ cup slivered coconut
3¾ cups vegetable stock
Cobbler Topping:
3 cups wholewheat flour
1 teaspoon sea salt
1 teaspoon baking soda
1 teaspoon ground coriander
1 teaspoon ground cumin
½ cup vegetable margarine
¾ cup sour cream

Chestnut Casserole with Orange

Imperial (Metric)

1 lb (445g) chestnuts
8 celery sticks
1 lb (455g) leeks
1 oz (30g) butter or vegetable margarine
1 tablespoon wholemeal flour
1 pint (570ml) vegetable stock
¼ pint (140ml) dry red wine
Grated rind and juice of 1 medium orange
Freshly ground black pepper
Bouquet of thyme, marjoram and sage
6 eggs, hard-boiled
Thinly pared rind of 1 medium orange
For Serving:
2¼ lb (1.1kg) potatoes
1 small onion, thinly sliced
1½ oz (45g) butter
3 fl oz (90ml) milk
2 tablespoons chopped parsley

1. Nick the tops of the chestnuts. Put them into a pan of cold water. Bring them to the boil. Take the pan from the heat and skin the chestnuts, leaving them in the water until you are ready for them.

2. Chop the celery and slice the leeks.

3. Melt the butter or margarine in a large saucepan or flameproof casserole on a low heat. Mix in the celery and leeks. Cover and cook them gently for 10 minutes.

4. Stir in the flour and then the stock. Bring it to the boil, stirring. Simmer for 1 minute and add the wine, orange rind and juice and pepper.

5. Put in the chestnuts and bouquet garni. Cover and simmer for 15 minutes.

6. Put in the eggs and simmer for 5 minutes more.

7. Cut the thinly pared orange rind into thin slivers. Boil them for 2 minutes and drain them.

8. While the chestnuts are cooking, peel the potatoes and boil them with the onion. Drain them and mash them with the onion, butter and milk.

9. Arrange the potato round the edge of a serving dish. Put the chestnut casserole inside.

10. Scatter the orange rind slivers over the chestnuts and the parsley over the potatoes.

Note: The chestnut casserole can be frozen before the eggs are added. Store it in a covered container for up to 1 month. Thaw at room temperature. Reheat, add the eggs and simmer for 10 minutes. The potatoes are best if they are freshly prepared.

American

1 pound chestnuts
8 celery stalks
1 pound leeks
2 tablespoons butter or vegetable margarine
1 tablespoon wholewheat flour
2½ cups vegetable stock
⅔ cup dry red wine
Grated rind and juice of 1 medium orange
Freshly ground black pepper
Bouquet of thyme, marjoram and sage
6 hard-cooked eggs.
Thinly pared rind of 1 medium orange
For Serving:
2¼ pounds potatoes
1 small onion, thinly sliced
3 tablespoons butter
⅓ cup milk
2 tablespoons chopped parsley

Nut Roast with Celery and Apricot Stuffing

Imperial (Metric)

Stuffing:
4 large celery sticks
2 oz (55g) dried whole apricots
4 tablespoons sunflower oil
1 large onion, finely chopped
4 oz (115g) fresh wholemeal breadcrumbs
2 oz (55g) walnuts, chopped
4 tablespoons chopped parsley
2 tablespoons chopped thyme
1 tablespoon chopped marjoram
4 tablespoons dry white wine
Pinch ground mace
Sea salt and freshly ground black pepper
Nut Roast Mixture:
8 oz (225g) black-eyed beans, soaked
1 bay leaf
1 large onion, thinly sliced
4 oz (115g) Brazil nuts
4 oz (115g) hazelnuts
4 oz (115g) almonds
4 tablespoons dry white wine
2 tablespoons tomato purée
4 tablespoons chopped parsley
2 tablespoons chopped thyme
2 tablespoons chopped marjoram
Sea salt and freshly ground black pepper

1. For the stuffing, finely chop the celery and the apricots. Heat the oil in a saucepan on a low heat. Put in the celery and onion and cook them until the onion is soft. Take the pan from the heat. Mix in the breadcrumbs, apricots, nuts, herbs and wine. Season with the mace, salt and pepper. Cool completely.
2. Heat the oven to 350°C/180°C/Gas Mark 4.
3. For the main mixture, cook the beans in water with the bay leaf and onion for 45 minutes, or until they are soft. Drain them and mash them with the onion.
4. Grind the nuts. Mix them into the mashed beans.
5. Add the wine, tomato purée (paste), herbs and seasonings. Mix well.
6. Lay half the mixture in a long, flat ovenproof dish in a rectangle shape. Put all the stuffing on top, leaving a space of about ¾ inch (2cm) all round. Cover the stuffing with the remaining nut mixture and, using a flat knife or spatula, form the mixture into a long, loaf shape.
7. For the coating, mix together the breadcrumbs, sesame seeds and oil and press the mixture evenly over the surface.
8. Bake the roast for 45 minutes so the crumbs on the outside are crisp and brown.
9. For the sauce, melt the butter or margarine in a saucepan on a low heat. Put in the celery and onion. Cover them and cook them gently for 10 minutes. Stir in the flour and stock. Bring them to the boil, stirring. Simmer for 10 minutes, uncovered. Stir in the wine and herbs. Reheat but do not boil. Serve the sauce hot, separately.

Note: The roast may be frozen in the dish before cooking and stored for up to

American

Stuffing:
4 large celery stalks
2 ounces dried whole apricots
¼ cup sunflower oil
1 large onion, finely chopped
2 cups fresh wholewheat breadcrumbs
½ cup English walnuts, chopped
¼ cup chopped parsley
2 tablespoons chopped thyme
1 tablespoon chopped marjoram
¼ cup dry white wine
Pinch ground mace
Sea salt and freshly ground black pepper
Nut Roast Mixture:
1⅓ cups black-eyed beans, soaked
1 bay leaf
1 large onion, thinly sliced
¾ cup Brazil nuts
¾ cup hazelnuts
¾ cup almonds
¼ cup dry white wine
2 tablespoons tomato paste
¼ cup chopped parsley
2 tablespoons chopped thyme
2 tablespoons chopped marjoram
Sea salt and freshly ground black pepper

Finishing:
3 oz (85g) dried wholemeal breadcrumbs
2 tablespoons sesame seeds
4 tablespoons sunflower oil
Sauce:
1 oz (30g) butter or vegetable margarine
4 celery sticks
1 large onion
3 tablespoons wholemeal flour
½ pint (285ml) vegetable stock
¼ pint (140ml) dry white wine
4 tablespoons chopped parsley
1 tablespoon chopped thyme

1 month. If the dish can be taken from the freezer to oven, the roast can be put directly into a hot oven for 1 hour. If the dish will not survive this, thaw the roast at room temperature first and cook as above. The sauce can be frozen before the wine is added and stored for up to one month. Thaw at room temperature and reheat before adding the wine.

Finishing:
¾ cup dried wholewheat breadcrumbs
2 tablespoons sesame seeds
¼ cup sunflower oil
Sauce:
2 tablespoons butter or vegetable margarine
4 celery stalks
1 large onion
3 tablespoons wholewheat flour
1¼ cups vegetable stock
⅔ cup dry white wine
¼ cup chopped parsley
1 tablespoon chopped thyme

Cream of Chick Peas (Garbanzo Beans) with Seville Orange

Imperial (Metric)

12 oz (340g) chick peas
12 oz (340g) mushrooms
2 red peppers
2 medium onions
4 tablespoons olive oil
1 garlic clove, chopped
4 oz (115g) salted peanuts
½ pint (285ml) soured cream
Grated rind and juice of 1 Seville orange

1. Soak the chick peas (garbanzo beans), cook them until they are tender and drain them.

2. Thinly slice the mushrooms. Core, seed and dice the peppers. Finely chop the onions.

3. Heat the oil in a frying pan (skillet) on a low heat. Put in the onions and garlic and soften them. Add the peppers and mushrooms. Cover and cook on a low heat for 5 minutes.

4. Stir in the chick peas (garbanzo beans) and peanuts. Add the soured cream and orange rind and juice. Cover and simmer for 5 minutes.

Note: To freeze, pack into a rigid container and cover. Store for up to 1 month. Thaw at room temperature and reheat gently in a saucepan.

American

1½ cups garbanzo beans
¾ pound mushrooms
2 sweet red peppers
2 medium onions
¼ cup olive oil
1 garlic clove, chopped
¾ cup peanuts
1¼ cups sour cream
Grated rind and juice of 1 Seville orange

Nutlets with Lemon-Flavoured Chicory (Belgian Endive)

Imperial (Metric)

4 oz (115g) Brazil nuts
2 oz (55g) walnuts
2 oz (55g) hazelnuts
2 oz wholemeal flour
1 teaspoon bicarbonate of
soda
2 oz (55g) vegetable
margarine
2 oz (55g) fresh
wholemeal breadcrumbs
¼ nutmeg, grated
¼ teaspoon ground
allspice
2 teaspoons chopped
savory
2 tablespoons chopped
parsley
2 eggs, beaten
6 heads chicory
Juice of 1 lemon
Sea salt and freshly
ground black pepper
1½ oz (45g) butter or
vegetable margarine

1. Grind the nuts.
2. Put the flour and bicarbonate of (baking) soda into a bowl and rub in the margarine.
3. Mix in the breadcrumbs, nuts, spices and herbs. Bind the mixture together with the beaten eggs.
4. Form the mixture into small balls each about ¾ inch (2cm) in diameter.
5. To cook, bring a large pan of water to the boil. Drop in the nutlets and poach them for 10 minutes or until they are cooked through. Lift them out with a perforated spoon and drain them a second time in a colander. Keep them warm.
6. When cutting the chicory (Belgian endive), make the first cut on the diagonal to make a piece about ½ inch (1cm) thick. Give the chicory (Belgian endive) a quarter turn and slice again. Continue slicing and turning until all the chicory is cut.
7. Put the chicory into a bowl and with your hands toss in the lemon juice and seasonings.
8. Melt the butter or margarine in a large frying pan (skillet) on a high heat. Put in the chicory (Belgian endive) and stir-fry it for three minutes.
9. Mix in the nutlets and serve as soon as possible.

Note: The nutlets can be made in advance and kept warm but the chicory (Belgian endive) must be prepared only at the last minute otherwise it will become too limp. The nutlets can be frozen before cooking. Freeze them on a tray and pack them into polythene bags. Thaw at room temperature and cook as above.

American

¾ cup Brazil nuts
½ cup English walnuts
½ cup hazelnuts
½ cup wholewheat flour
1 teaspoon baking soda
½ cup vegetable
margarine
1 cup fresh wholewheat
breadcrumbs
¼ nutmeg, grated
¼ teaspoon ground
allspice
2 teaspoons chopped
savory
2 tablespoons chopped
parsley
2 eggs, beaten
6 heads Belgian endive
Juice of 1 lemon
Sea salt and freshly
ground pepper
3 tablespoons butter or
vegetable margarine

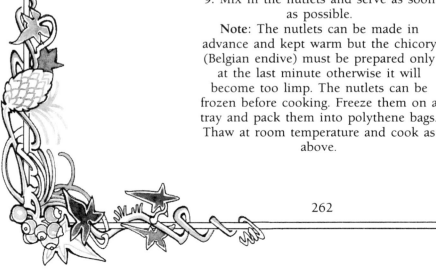

VEGETABLES AND SALADS

Winter vegetables are full of flavour and goodness and deserve to be treated well and given a special place on the table. Here are two unusual ways with jacket potatoes, a stuffed crinkly cabbage, a creamy purée of artichokes with cheese and many more.

Salads are just as welcome in the winter as in the summer and contrast well with warming winter main courses.

Brussels Sprouts with Almond Flakes (Slivers)

Imperial (Metric)

1½ lb (685g) Brussels
sprouts
1½ oz (45g) butter
2 oz (55g) flaked almonds
3 tablespoons chopped
parsley

1. Trim the Brussels sprouts and steam them for 20 minutes or until they are tender.
2. Melt the butter in a frying pan (skillet) on a medium heat. Put in the almond flakes (slivers) and stir them on the heat until they are an even golden brown.
3. Put the Brussels sprouts into a warmed serving dish. Scatter first the parsley and then the browned almond flakes (slivers) over the top.
Note: Unsuitable for freezing.

American

1½ pounds Brussels
sprouts
3 tablespoons butter
½ cup slivered almonds
3 tablespoons chopped
parsley

Stir-Braised Kale with Onion

Imperial (Metric)

1 lb (455g) curly kale
4 tablespoons sunflower
oil
1 large onion, thinly
sliced
¼ pint (140ml) vegetable
stock
2 tablespoons tomato
purée

1. Tear the kale from its tough stalks and then into small pieces about 1 inch (2.5cm) square.
2. Heat the oil in a large frying pan (skillet) on a low heat. Stir in the onion and soften it.
3. Mix together the stock and tomato purée (paste).
4. When the onion is soft, raise the heat to medium and carefully fold in the kale. There will seem to be rather a lot at this point but it will cook down.
5. When the kale is well coated with oil, pour in the stock mixture and bring it to the boil.
6. Cover the pan and keep it on a medium heat for 20 minutes.
Note: Unsuitable for freezing.

American

1 pound curly kale
¼ cup sunflower oil
1 large onion, thinly
sliced
⅔ cup vegetable stock
2 tablespoons tomato
paste

263

White Cabbage and Carrots with Thyme

Imperial (Metric)

1 small white cabbage
12 oz (340g) carrots
1½ oz (45g) butter
2 tablespoons chopped
thyme

1. Finely shred the cabbage. Cut the carrots into matchstick pieces.
2. Melt the butter in a saucepan on a high heat. Mix in the vegetables and thyme.
3. Cover and cook on a very low heat for 12 minutes so the vegetables are glossy and slightly crisp.

Note: Unsuitable for freezing.

American

1 small white cabbage
¾ pound carrots
3 tablespoons butter
2 tablespoons chopped
thyme

Julienne of Parsnip and Potato

Imperial (Metric)

1 lb (455g) parsnips
1 lb (455g) potatoes
1½ oz (45g) butter
Sea salt and freshly
ground black pepper

1. Heat the oven to 400°F/200°C/Gas Mark 6.
2. Scrub the parsnips. Cut them in half lengthways and remove the cores. Cut them into matchstick pieces.
3. Peel the potatoes and cut them into matchstick pieces.
4. Mix together the parsnips and potatoes.
5. Use half the butter to grease thickly an 8 inch (20cm) diameter skillet or shallow cake tin. Press in the parsnips and potatoes. Season the top only to prevent them from sticking.
6. Thickly butter a piece of foil to fit over the top with about 1 inch (2.5cm) overlap. Press this down on top of the vegetables. Cover it with a fitting lid or ovenproof plate.
7. Put the skillet on top of the stove on a medium heat for about 5 minutes or until you can smell the butter beginning to brown. Then put it into the oven for 45 minutes.
8. Remove the lid and foil. The vegetables will have set together to make a flat 'cake'. Loosen the edges and base with a rounded knife or palette knife. Turn it out onto a flat plate.

Note: Unsuitable for freezing.

American

1 pound parsnips
1 pound potatoes
3 tablespoons butter
Sea salt and freshly
ground black pepper

Potatoes Baked with Sage and Apples

Imperial (Metric)

6 large potatoes
1 large cooking apple
1½ oz (45g) butter
10 sage leaves, chopped

1. Heat the oven to 400°F/200°C/Gas Mark 6.
2. Scrub the potatoes and cut them in half lengthways to give two fairly flat pieces.
3. Peel and core the apple and thinly slice it lengthways.
4. Spread a little butter on the cut surfaces of each potato half and use the rest to grease a flat, ovenproof dish.
5. Arrange the apple slices on six of the potato halves. Scatter them with sage. Put the other potato halves on top so you have an 'apple sandwich'.
6. Put the potatoes into the prepared dish. Bake them for 1 hour 15 minutes, checking from time to time to make sure that the apple slices do not become exposed. Keeping them covered will enable them to melt deliciously into the potatoes as they cook.

Note: Unsuitable for freezing.

American

6 large potatoes
1 large cooking apple
3 tablespoons butter
10 sage leaves, chopped

Baked Onions with Herb Butter

Imperial (Metric)

6 large onions
6 oz (170g) unsalted butter, softened
Grated rind of ½ lemon
1 tablespoon lemon juice
3 tablespoons chopped parsley
1 tablespoon chopped thyme
1 tablespoon chopped marjoram

1. Heat the oven to 400°F/200°C/Gas Mark 6.
2. Leave the onions as they are, without trimming or peeling. Stand them on the oven rack and leave them for 1 hour 30 minutes.
3. Put the butter into a bowl and beat in the lemon rind and juice and chopped herbs. Form the butter into a roll and wrap it in greaseproof paper. Chill it for 1 hour or until it is firm.
4. Take the onions from the oven. Put them, unpeeled, onto a serving plate. Cut a cross in the top of each one. Cut the butter into pats and insert one into each onion. Serve the rest of the butter separately.

Note: Unsuitable for freezing.

American

6 large onions
¾ cup unsalted butter, softened
Grated rind of ½ lemon
1 tablespoon lemon juice
3 tablespoons chopped parsley
1 tablespoon chopped thyme
1 tablespoon chopped marjoram

Pineapple and Cress Salad

Imperial (Metric)

½ medium pineapple
8 oz (225g) watercress
2 boxes mustard and cress
3 tablespoons chopped
fresh coriander
½ teaspoon ground
coriander
1 garlic clove, crushed
4 tablespoons olive oil
Juice of ½ lemon
Grated rind of 1 large
orange

1. Cut the husk and core from the pineapple. Dice the flesh.
2. Chop the watercress.
3. Put the pineapple and watercress into a salad bowl and cut in the mustard and cress.
4. Add the fresh coriander.
5. Put the ground coriander and garlic into a small bowl and beat in the oil and lemon juice. Mix in the orange rind.
6. Fold the dressing into the salad.

Note: If fresh coriander is not available use 6 tablespoons (⅓ cup) chopped fresh parsley. Unsuitable for freezing.

American

½ medium pineapple
½ pound watercress
2 boxes mustard and cress
3 tablespoons chopped
fresh coriander
½ teaspoon ground
coriander
1 garlic clove, crushed
¼ cup olive oil
Juice of ½ lemon
Grated rind of 1 large
orange

Savoy Cabbage Stuffed with Apples and Yogurt

Imperial (Metric)

1 large Savoy cabbage
1 large cooking apple
3 tablespoons sunflower
oil
1 large onion, finely
chopped
3 fl oz (90ml) natural
yogurt
¼ pint (140ml) vegetable
stock

1. Heat the oven to 350°F/180°C/Gas Mark 4.
2. Remove the outer leaves from the cabbage and trim the stalk. Cut the main part of the cabbage in half lengthways.
3. Using a small, sharp knife, scoop out the inner leaves of the cabbage, leaving two shells about ¼ inch (6mm) thick. Shred the scooped out parts.
4. Peel, core and finely chop the apple.
5. Heat the oil in a large, wide-based casserole on a low heat. Put in the onion and soften it.
6. Take the casserole from the heat and mix in the shredded cabbage, the apple and the yogurt.
7. Press all the mixture into the cabbage shells and pack the shells into the casserole.
8. Pour round the stock and bring it to the boil on a high heat. Cover the casserole and put it into the oven for 30 minutes.

Note: Unsuitable for freezing.

American

1 large Savoy cabbage
1 large cooking apple
3 tablespoons sunflower
oil
1 large onion, finely
chopped
⅓ cup unflavored yogurt
⅔ cup vegetable stock

266

Cabbage with Lemon and Nutmeg

Imperial (Metric)

1 large green winter cabbage
4 tablespoons sunflower oil
Juice of 1 lemon
¼ nutmeg, grated

1. Finely shred the cabbage.
2. Heat the oil in a saucepan on a medium heat. Stir in the cabbage.
3. Add the lemon juice and nutmeg.
4. Cover the pan tightly and cook on a very low heat for 10 minutes. The cabbage should be a light, translucent green and slightly crisp.

Note. Unsuitable for freezing.

American

1 large green winter cabbage
¼ cup sunflower oil
Juice of 1 lemon
¼ nutmeg, grated

Brussels Sprouts and Leeks Braised with Orange

Imperial (Metric)

12 oz (340g) Brussels sprouts
12 oz (340g) leeks
1 oz (30g) butter
¼ pint (140ml) vegetable stock
Grated rind and juice of 1 large orange
1 teaspoon Dijon mustard

1. Heat the oven to 350°F/180°C/Gas Mark 4.
2. Trim the Brussels sprouts. Thinly slice the leeks.
3. Melt the butter in a flameproof casserole on a low heat. Stir in the leeks, cover and cook them gently for 5 minutes.
4. Put in the Brussels sprouts.
5. Pour in the stock and bring it to the boil.
6. Add the orange rind and juice and mustard.
7. Cover the casserole and put it into the oven for 1 hour.

Note: Unsuitable for freezing.

American

¾ pound Brussels sprouts
¾ pound leeks
2 tablespoons butter
⅔ cup vegetable stock
Grated rind and juice of 1 large orange
1 teaspoon Dijon mustard

Cut and Breadcrumbed Jacket Potatoes

Imperial (Metric)

12 even-sized potatoes
3 oz (85g) butter
*4 tablespoons dried
wholemeal breadcrumbs*

1. Heat the oven to 400°F/200°C/Gas Mark 6.
2. Scrub the potatoes but do not peel them. Make cuts in them about 1/8 inch (3mm) apart and at least three quarters of the way through.
3. Put the butter into a baking dish and melt it in the oven.
4. Roll the potatoes in the butter, leaving them cut side up. Bake them for 1 hour, basting them several times.
5. Scatter the crumbs over the potatoes, baste them again and return them to the oven for 15 minutes.
Note: Unsuitable for freezing.

American

12 even-sized potatoes.
⅓ cup butter
*4 tablespoons dried
wholewheat breadcrumbs*

Fennel, Cabbage and Grape Salad

Imperial (Metric)

*8 oz (225g) Florence
fennel*
½ small white cabbage
6 oz (170g) green grapes
*3 fl oz (90ml) natural
yogurt*
1 garlic clove, crushed
*1 teaspoon granular white
wine mustard*

1. Chop the fennel. Shred the cabbage. Halve and seed the grapes. Put them all into a salad bowl.
2. Beat the remaining ingredients together to make the dressing and fold them into the salad.
Note: Unsuitable for freezing.

American

½ pound Florence fennel
½ small white cabbage
6 ounces green grapes
⅓ cup unflavored yogurt
1 garlic clove, crushed
*1 teaspoon granular white
wine mustard*

Spiced Baked Beetroot

Imperial (Metric)

1½ lb (685g) beetroot
4 allspice berries
4 juniper berries
4 black peppercorns
*¼ pint (140ml) dry red
wine*

1. Heat the oven to 400°F/200°C/Gas Mark 6.
2. Peel the beetroot and quarter them. Put them into a casserole.
3. Crush the spices and peppercorns together and scatter them over the beetroot.
4. Pour in the wine.
5. Cover the casserole and put it into the oven for 1 hour. Serve hot.
Note: Unsuitable for freezing.

American

1½ pounds beetroot
4 allspice berries
4 juniper berries
4 black peppercorns
⅔ cup dry red wine

Turnips with Cheese and Mustard

Imperial (Metric)

1½ lb (685g) white
turnips
7 fl oz (200ml) vegetable
stock
½ oz (15g) butter
1 teaspoon mustard
powder
4 oz (115g) Cheddar
cheese, grated

1. Cut the turnips into quarters.
2. Put the stock and butter into a saucepan and set them on a medium heat. When the butter has melted fold in the turnips and sprinkle in the mustard powder.
3. Cover the pan and cook on a low heat for 15 minutes, or until the turnips are tender and glazed and all the liquid has evaporated. If there is still some liquid in the pan after 15 minutes, remove the lid and cook on a high heat for it to reduce.
4. Take the pan from the heat. Scatter the cheese on top of the turnips. Cover and leave for 2 minutes for the cheese to melt.
Note: The cheese can be omitted if wished. Unsuitable for freezing.

American

1½ pounds white turnips
¾ cup vegetable stock
1 tablespoon butter
1 teaspoon mustard
powder
1 cup grated Cheddar
cheese

Chicory (Belgian Endive), Orange and Walnut Salad

Imperial (Metric)

6 heads chicory
4 tablespoons walnut oil
2 tablespoons red wine
vinegar
1 garlic clove, crushed
Pinch cayenne pepper
3 oz (85g) walnuts,
chopped
3 large oranges
3 tablespoons chopped
parsley

1. Trim the chicory (Belgian endive) heads. Cut them in half lengthways and thinly slice them. Arrange them in the centre of a large serving plate.
2. Beat together the oil, vinegar, garlic and pepper and spoon the resulting dressing over the chicory (Belgian endive).
3. Scatter the walnuts over the top.
4. Cut the rind and pith from the oranges. Cut the oranges in half lengthways and thinly slice them. Arrange the slices round the chicory (Belgian endive).
5. Scatter the parsley over the orange slices.
Note: If walnut oil is unavailable, use olive oil. Unsuitable for freezing.

American

6 heads Belgian endive
¼ cup walnut oil
2 tablespoons red wine
vinegar
1 garlic clove, crushed
Pinch cayenne pepper
⅔ cup chopped English
walnuts
3 large oranges
3 tablespoons chopped
parsley

Purée of Artichokes with Cheese

Imperial (Metric)

1½ lb (685g) Jerusalem artichokes
2 medium onions
3 fl oz (90ml) milk
1 teaspoon mustard powder
Sea salt and freshly ground black pepper
4 oz (115g) Cheddar cheese, grated

1. Peel the artichokes, holding them in cold water.
2. Peel, quarter and thinly slice the onions.
3. Bring a saucepan of lightly salted water to the boil. Put in the artichokes and onions. Cover and simmer for 25 minutes, or until the artichokes are quite tender.
4. Heat the oven to 400°F/200°C/Gas Mark 6.
5. Drain the artichokes and onions and mash them together. Mix in the milk and mustard powder and season well.
6. Put the mixture into an ovenproof dish. Cover it with the cheese.
7. Put the dish into the oven for 15 minutes or until the cheese has melted and is beginning to brown.
Note: Unsuitable for freezing.

American

1½ pounds Jerusalem artichokes
2 medium onions
⅓ cup milk
1 teaspoon mustard powder
Sea salt and freshly ground black pepper
1 cup Cheddar cheese, grated

Celeriac and Celery Salad

Imperial (Metric)

12 oz (340g) celeriac
¼ teaspoon fine sea salt
Juice of 1 large orange
6 large celery sticks
4 tablespoons natural yogurt
4 tablespoons mayonnaise
1 teaspoon mustard powder
2 tablespoons chopped celery leaves

1. Cut the celeriac into ⅜ inch (1cm) dice. Put it into a bowl. Sprinkle it with the salt and orange juice and leave it for 1 hour.
2. Dice the celery and add it to the celeriac.
3. Mix together the yogurt, mayonnaise and mustard powder. Fold the resulting dressing into the salad.
4. Put the salad into a serving bowl and scatter the celery leaves over the top.
Note: Orange slices or satsuma segments can be used as an additional garnish. Unsuitable for freezing.

American

¾ pound celeriac
¼ teaspoon fine sea salt
Juice of 1 large orange
6 large celery stalks
¼ cup unflavored yogurt
¼ cup mayonnaise
1 teaspoon mustard powder
2 tablespoons chopped celery leaves

Hot Red Cabbage Salad

Imperial (Metric)

1 small red cabbage
1 large onion
1 large cooking apple
4 tablespoons olive oil
2 tablespoons red wine
vinegar
2 teaspoons molasses

1. Shred the cabbage. Thinly slice the onion. Peel, core and slice the apple.
2. Heat the oil in a large frying pan (skillet) or paella pan on a medium heat. Put in the cabbage, onion and apple. Stir-fry them for 4 minutes, or until they are just beginning to wilt.
3. Pour in the vinegar and add the molasses. Bring them to the boil and serve immediately.
Note: Unsuitable for freezing.

American

1 small red cabbage
1 large onion
1 large cooking apple
¼ cup olive oil
2 tablespoons red wine
vinegar
2 teaspoons molasses

Braised Grated Swede (Rutabaga) with Thyme

Imperial (Metric)

1½ lb (685g) swede
1 oz (30g) butter
1 large onion, finely
chopped
2 tablespoons chopped
thyme
Freshly ground black
pepper
7 fl oz (200ml) vegetable
stock

1. Heat the oven to 350°F/180°C/Gas Mark 4.
2. Grate the swede (rutabaga).
3. Melt the butter in a flameproof casserole on a low heat. Put in the onion and soften it.
4. Stir in the swede (rutabaga) and thyme. Season with the pepper.
5. Pour in the stock and bring it to the boil
6. Cover the casserole and put it into the oven for 45 minutes.
Note: Unsuitable for freezing.

American

1½ pounds rutabaga
2 tablespoons butter
1 large onion, finely
chopped
2 tablespoons chopped
thyme
Freshly ground black
pepper
¾ cup vegetable stock

Bean Sprout and Ginger Salad

Imperial (Metric)

6 oz (170g) mung bean
sprouts
4 oz (115g) watercress
8 oz (225g) carrots
4 tablespoons sesame oil
Juice of 1 lemon
1 teaspoon clear honey
1 tablespoon tamari or
shoyu sauce
½ teaspoon ground ginger
1 garlic clove, crushed

1. Put the bean sprouts into a bowl.
2. Chop the watercress. Coarsely grate the carrots. Add them to the bean sprouts.
3. Beat the remaining ingredients together to make the dressing and fold it into the salad.
Note: If sesame oil is not available, use sunflower oil. Unsuitable for freezing.

American

6 ounces mung bean
sprouts
¼ pound watercress
½ pound carrots
¼ cup sesame oil
Juice of 1 lemon
1 teaspoon clear honey
1 tablespoon tamari or
shoyu sauce
½ teaspoon ground ginger
1 garlic clove, crushed

GRAINS

Grains combine well with winter vegetables and fruits to make tasty accompaniments for vegetarian main courses. Combine rice with winter roots or cabbage or with light fresh oranges, burghul wheat with curry flavours, barley more unusually with fennel and richly-flavoured buckwheat with succulent aubergines (eggplants). Try a creamy carrot sauce for pasta, or raid the pickle cupboard to make a spicy walnut coating.

Savoy and Rice Casserole

Imperial (Metric)

1 medium Savoy cabbage
4 tablespoons sunflower oil
1 large onion, thinly sliced
12 oz (340g) long-grain brown rice
2 teaspoons strong granular mustard
1½ pints (850ml) vegetable stock
Pinch sea salt

1. Heat the oven to 350°F/180°C/Gas Mark 4.
2. Finely shred the cabbage.
3. Heat the oil in a large, flameproof casserole on a low heat. Put in the onion and soften it.
4. Stir in the rice and mustard. When they are well mixed with the onion, add the cabbage.
5. Pour in the stock and bring it to the boil. Season lightly with the salt.
6. Cover the casserole and put it into the oven for 45 minutes. Take it from the oven and leave it to stand, covered, for 10 minutes before serving.
Note: Unsuitable for freezing.

American

1 medium Savoy cabbage
¼ cup sunflower oil
1 large onion, thinly sliced
1½ cups long-grain brown rice
2 teaspoons strong granular mustard
3¾ cups vegetable stock
Pinch sea salt

Pasta with Fresh and Pickled Walnuts

Imperial (Metric)

12 oz (340g) pasta shapes
4 tablespoons olive oil
1 large onion, finely chopped
1 garlic clove, finely chopped
4 oz (115g) walnuts
4 pickled walnuts
4 tablespoons chopped parsley

1. Cook the pasta in lightly salted boiling water for 12 minutes, or until tender. Drain.
2. Heat the oil in a saucepan on a low heat. Put in the onion and garlic and soften them.
3. Grind the fresh walnuts. Finely chop the pickled walnuts. Mix them into the onion and garlic.
4. Fold in the pasta and half the parsley. Reheat the pasta if necessary.
5. Serve with the remaining parsley scattered on top.
Note: Unsuitable for freezing.

American

¾ pound pasta shapes
¼ cup olive oil
1 large onion, finely chopped
1 garlic clove, finely chopped
¾ cup English walnuts
4 pickled English walnuts
¼ cup chopped parsley

Orange Pilaf

Imperial (Metric)

2 medium oranges
4 tablespoons sunflower
oil
1 large onion, thinly
sliced
1 garlic clove, finely
chopped
12 oz (340g) long-grain
brown rice
2 teaspoons ground cumin
1½ pints (850ml)
vegetable stock
4 oz (115g) pine nuts

1. Squeeze the juice from one of the oranges. Cut the rind and pith from the others, cut them into quarters lengthways and thinly slice them.
2. Heat the oil in a saucepan on a low heat. Put in the onion and garlic and soften them.
3. Stir in the rice and cumin.
4. Pour in the stock and bring it to the boil. Add the orange juice.
5. Cover and simmer for 30 minutes.
6. Add the pine nuts, cover again and cook for a further 15 minutes.
7. Take the pan from the heat. Mix in the sliced oranges and leave the rice standing for 5 minutes, covered, before serving.
Note: The pine nuts can be omitted if the rice is to be served with a nut-based dish.
Freeze before adding the oranges. Cool completely, pack into a rigid container, cover and store for up to 1 month. Thaw at room temperature and reheat gently in a saucepan before adding the oranges.

American

2 medium oranges
¼ cup sunflower oil
1 large onion, thinly
sliced
1 garlic clove, finely
chopped
1½ cups long-grain brown
rice
2 teaspoons ground cumin
3¾ cups vegetable stock
¾ cup pine nuts

Winter Rice

Imperial (Metric)

8 oz (225g) carrots
8 oz (225g) swede
8 oz (225g) parsnips
1 large onion
4 tablespoons sunflower
oil
12 oz (340g) long-grain
brown rice
½ pint (285ml) tomato
and vegetable juice
1 pint (570ml) vegetable
stock
Freshly ground black
pepper
4 tablespoons chopped
parsley

1. Dice the vegetables.
2. Heat the oil in a saucepan on a low heat. Stir in the vegetables, cover and cook on a low heat for 10 minutes.
3. Stir in the rice. Pour in the tomato and vegetable juice and stock and bring them to the boil. Season with the pepper. Cover and simmer for 45 minutes or until the rice is tender and all the liquid has been absorbed.
4. Mix in the parsley just before serving.
Note: To freeze, cool completely, pack into a rigid container and cover. Store for up to 1 month. Thaw at room temperature and reheat gently in a saucepan.

American

½ pound carrots
½ pound rutabaga
½ pound parsnips
1 large onion
¼ cup sunflower oil
1½ cups long-grain brown
rice
1⅓ cups tomato and
vegetable juice
2½ cups vegetable stock
Freshly ground black
pepper
¼ cup chopped parsley

Cream of Carrot Sauce for Pasta

This will go with any shape of pasta that is to be served as an accompaniment to a meal. Cook the pasta (you will need 12oz (340g) for six people), drain it and put it into a shallow serving plate. Spoon the sauce over the top.

Imperial (Metric)

1 lb (455g) carrots
1 medium onion
1 pint (570ml) vegetable stock
1 garlic clove, crushed
2 tablespoons tomato purée
3 fl oz (90ml) soured cream

1. Thinly slice the carrots and onion.
2. Bring the stock to the boil in a saucepan. Add the carrots, onion and garlic. Cover and simmer for 20 minutes, or until the vegetables are quite tender.
3. Liquidize the vegetables and any remaining stock in a blender or food processor.
4. Add the tomato purée (paste) and soured cream and blend again.
5. Reheat gently if necessary.

Note: The sauce can be frozen before adding the tomato purée (paste) and soured cream. Cool it completely and store in a covered rigid container for up to 2 months. Thaw at room temperature, reheat gently in a saucepan and stir in the tomato purée (paste) and soured cream.

American

1 pound carrots
1 medium onion
2½ cups vegetable stock
1 garlic clove, crushed
2 tablespoons tomato paste
⅓ cup sour cream

274

Buckwheat with Aubergines (Eggplants)

Imperial (Metric)

12 oz (340g) aubergines
1 tablespoon sea salt
12 oz (340g) buckwheat
1 egg, beaten
1½ pints (850ml)
    vegetable stock
2 tablespoons tomato
    purée
4 tablespoons olive oil
1 large onion, thinly
    sliced
1 garlic clove, finely
    chopped

1. Dice the aubergines (eggplants). Put them into a colander and sprinkle them with the salt. Leave them to drain for 30 minutes. Rinse them under cold water and dry them with kitchen paper.
2. Put the buckwheat into a large frying pan (skillet) and set it on a medium heat. Stir it until it begins to brown and smell nutty.
3. Add the egg, stirring briskly so that it coats all the buckwheat grains.
4. When the egg has set round the grains, pour in the stock. Bring it to the boil and stir in the tomato purée (paste).
5. Cover and simmer for 20 minutes or until the buckwheat is soft and fluffy and all the stock has been absorbed.
6. Heat the oil in another pan on a low heat. Put in the aubergines (eggplants), onion and garlic and cook them, stirring occasionally, for 4 minutes. Mix them into the buckwheat just before serving.
Note: Unsuitable for freezing.

American

¾ pound eggplants
1 tablespoon sea salt
2 cups buckwheat
1 egg, beaten
3¾ cups vegetable stock
2 tablespoons tomato
    paste
¼ cup olive oil
1 large onion, thinly
    sliced
1 garlic clove, finely
    chopped

Curried Burghul with Ginger

Imperial (Metric)

1 oz (30g) fresh ginger
    root
4 tablespoons sunflower
    oil
1 medium onion, thinly
    sliced
1 garlic clove, finely
    chopped
8 oz (225g) open
    mushrooms
12 oz (340g) burghul
    wheat
2 teaspoons curry powder
1½ pints (850ml)
    vegetable stock
Juice of ½ lemon

1. Peel and grate the ginger root.
2. Heat the oil in a saucepan on a low heat. Add the onion and garlic and cook them for 2 minutes.
3. Thinly slice the mushrooms, add them to the onion and cook for 2 minutes more.
4. Stir in the burghul and curry powder.
5. Pour in the stock and bring it to the boil.
6. Add the ginger and lemon juice.
7. Cover and simmer for 20 minutes or until all the stock is absorbed and the burghul is soft and fluffy.
Note: To freeze, cool completely, pack into a rigid container and cover. Store for up to 1 month. Thaw at room temperature and reheat gently in a saucepan.

American

1 ounce fresh ginger root
¼ cup sunflower oil
1 medium onion, thinly
    sliced
1 garlic clove, finely
    chopped
½ pound open mushrooms
2 cups burghul wheat
2 teaspoons curry powder
3¾ cups vegetable stock
Juice of ½ lemon

DESSERTS

Hot Marmalade Soufflé

Imperial (Metric)

Butter and breadcrumbs
for preparing 8-inch
(20cm) soufflé dish
½ pint (285ml) milk
2-inch (5cm) cinnamon
stick
1 blade mace
1 oz (30g) butter
2 tablespoons wholemeal
flour
Grated rind and juice of
1 Seville orange
2 oz (55g) honey
4 eggs, separated
4 oz (115g) no-sugar-
added marmalade

1. Butter an 8-inch (20cm) soufflé dish. Butter a piece of greaseproof paper twice the height of the dish and just longer than the circumference. Scatter both the dish and the paper with dried wholemeal (wholewheat) breadcrumbs. Tie the paper round the dish. Cover a cardboard tube with greaseproof paper and butter it.

2. Heat the oven to 190°C/375°F/Gas Mark 5.

3. Put the milk into a saucepan with the cinnamon and mace. Leave it on a low heat for 10 minutes. Take the pan from the heat and remove the cinnamon and mace.

4. Melt the butter in a saucepan on a low heat. Stir in the flour and flavoured milk. Bring them to the boil, stirring. Simmer for 2 minutes. Take the pan from the heat.

5. Beat the orange rind and juice and the honey into the milk. Beat in the egg yolks, one at a time.

6. Stiffly beat the egg whites. Fold them into the yolk mixture.

7. Put the prepared cardboard tube into the centre of the soufflé dish. Fill it with the marmalade. Pour the soufflé mixture around the tube.

8. Put the soufflé into the oven. Turn the heat to 400°F/200°C/Gas Mark 6. Cook the soufflé for 30 minutes.

9. Remove the tube just before serving.

Note: A cardboard tube from a roll of kitchen paper is most suitable as its height prevents the soufflé from rising over the top.

Unsuitable for freezing.

American

Butter and breadcrumbs
for preparing 8-inch
soufflé dish
1¼ cups milk
2-inch cinnamon stick
1 blade mace
2 tablespoons butter
2 tablespoons wholewheat
flour
Grated rind and juice of
1 Seville orange
2½ tablespoons honey
4 eggs, separated
⅔ cup no-sugar-added
marmalade

276

Cranberry Shortcake Mousse

Imperial (Metric)

Shortcake:
3 oz (85g) cranberries
1½ oz (45g) walnuts
6 oz (170g) wholemeal
flour
2 oz (55g) Barbados
sugar
1 teaspoon bicarbonate of
soda
1 oz (30g) butter or
vegetable margarine
2 eggs, beaten
Mousse:
1 lb (455g) cranberries
½ pint (285ml) water
4 oz (115g) honey
Agar-agar to set 1½ pints
(850ml) liquid (see
manufacturer's
instructions)
2 tablespoons cherry
brandy
2 eggs, separated
¼ pint (140ml) Greek-
style natural yogurt
Decoration:
¼ pint (140ml) double
cream
Walnut halves

1. Heat the oven to 400°F/200°C/Gas Mark 6.
2. Chop the cranberries and walnuts.
3. Put the flour, sugar and bicarbonate of (baking) soda into a bowl. Rub in the butter or margarine.
4. Mix in the cranberries and walnuts.
5. Bind the mixture together with the beaten eggs.
6. Press the mixture into the base of a lightly greased 8-inch (20cm) diameter spring form tin. Bake it for 20 minutes, or until firm. Cool it completely in the tin.
7. With the base still in the tin, line the sides of the tin with oiled greaseproof paper.
8. For the mousse, put the cranberries into a saucepan with the water. Bring them to the boil on a medium heat. Simmer them for 20 minutes, crushing them occasionally.
9. Rub them through a sieve.
10. Return the cranberry purée to the rinsed pan. Set it on a low heat. Add the honey and stir for it to dissolve.
11. Bring the mixture to just below boiling point. Sprinkle in the agar-agar and stir for it to dissolve. Take the pan from the heat. Stir in the cherry brandy. Beat in the egg yolks, one at a time. Leave the mixture until it is on the point of setting.
12. Stiffly whip the egg whites.
13. Fold first the yogurt and then the egg whites into the mixture.
14. Pour the mixture into the tin on top of the shortcake. Leave it in a cool place for 2 hours to set.
15. Remove the shortcake and mousse from the tin.
16. The top may be garnished simply with walnut halves or with piped portions of whipped cream plus the walnuts.
Note: Unsuitable for freezing.

American

Shortcake:
3 ounces cranberries
4 tablespoons English
walnuts
1½ cups wholewheat flour
¼ cup Barbados sugar
1 teaspoon baking soda
2 tablespoons butter or
vegetable margarine
2 eggs, beaten
Mousse:
1 pound cranberries
1¼ cups water
⅓ cup honey
Agar-agar to set 3 cups
liquid (see manufacturer's
instructions)
2 tablespoons cherry
brandy
2 eggs, separated
⅔ cup Greek-style
unflavored yogurt
Decoration:
⅔ cup heavy cream
English walnut halves

Apple and Yogurt Layer Cake

Imperial (Metric)

8 oz (225g) wholemeal
flour
2 teaspoons bicarbonate
of soda
2 teaspoons ground
cinnamon
4 fl oz (125ml) corn oil
4 fl oz (125ml) natural
apple juice
8 oz (225g) pear and
apple spread
4 eggs, beaten
Filling:
1 lb (455g) cooking
apples
2-inch (5cm) cinnamon
stick
6 cloves
4 tablespoons natural
apple juice
2 tablespoons pear and
apple spread
½ pint (285ml) Greek-
style natural yogurt
Chopped mixed nuts, to
garnish

1. Heat the oven to 350°F/180°C/Gas Mark 4. Oil two 8-inch (20cm) diameter shallow cake tins
2. Put the flour into a bowl. Toss in the bicarbonate of (baking) soda and cinnamon. Make a well in the centre.
3. Put the oil, apple juice and pear and apple spread into a saucepan. Set them on a low heat and stir until the spread has softened considerably and is beginning to melt. Cool the mixture slightly and beat it into the flour.
4. Beat in the eggs to make a thick batter-like consistency. (Alternatively, all the ingredients can be put directly into a food mixer or food processor without the oil, juice and spread being heated.)
5. Divide the mixture between the two tins.
6. Bake the cakes for 20 minutes or until they are firm and springy and have shrunk slightly from the sides of the tins.
7. Turn the cakes onto wire racks and cool them completely.
8. Peel, core and chop the apples. Put them into a saucepan with the cinnamon, cloves, apple juice and pear and apple spread. Cover them and set them on a low heat for 15 minutes, or until they can be beaten to a purée.
9. Remove the cinnamon stick. Rub the purée through a sieve. Cool it completely.
10. Mix half the apple purée with half the yogurt. Sandwich the cakes together with this mixture. Spread the remaining apple purée over the top. Spoon the remaining yogurt on top. Either swirl it into the apple purée with the knife, or carefully spread it to cover the purée. Sprinkle the mixed nuts over the top.
Note: The cakes can be frozen separately. Wrap each one in clingfilm, freeze it flat and store for up to 2

American

2 cups wholewheat flour
2 teaspoons baking soda
2 teaspoons ground
cinnamon
½ cup corn oil
½ cup natural apple juice
1⅓ cups pear and apple
spread
4 eggs, beaten
Filling:
1 pound cooking apples
2-inch cinnamon stick
6 cloves
¼ cup natural apple juice
2 tablespoons pear and
apple spread
1¼ cups Greek-style
unflavored yogurt
Chopped mixed nuts, to
garnish

months. The apple purée can also be frozen separately, in a covered container for up to 2 months. Thaw both at room temperature before assembling the layers. The yogurt should be used fresh.

Mulled Wine Granita

Imperial (Metric)

1¼ pints (720ml) full-bodied red wine
4 oz (115g) honey
1 orange
1 lemon
2 teaspoons cloves
2-inch (5cm) cinnamon stick

1. Put the wine into a saucepan with the honey.
2. Cut the orange and lemon into thick slices and add them to the wine with the cloves and cinnamon.
3. Set the saucepan on a low heat and stir until the honey has dissolved.
4. Cover the pan and infuse the wine, without letting it boil, for 20 minutes.
5. Strain the wine, pressing down hard on the orange and lemon to extract as much juice as possible.
6. Cool the wine completely and chill it.
7. Either pour the wine into an ice-cream machine and leave it until it becomes frozen to a soft purée; or freeze it in a tray in the coldest part of the freezer or in the ice compartment of the refrigerator, set at the coldest temperature, for 3 hours, stirring every 30 minutes.
8. Serve immediately, directly from the freezer, in chilled glasses, garnished with thin twists of orange peel.
Note: Do not leave the granita standing at room temperature or even in the refrigerator for it melts very quickly. If you wish to make it for storing, do not use an ice-cream machine and do not stir it whilst it is freezing. Freeze it solid and then thaw for about 1 hour in the refrigerator, stirring frequently.

American

3 cups full-bodied red wine
⅓ cup honey
1 orange
1 lemon
2 teaspoons cloves
2-inch cinnamon stick

Christmas Cake Ice-Cream

Imperial (Metric)

*8 oz (225g) sugar-free
Christmas Cake (see page
228)
4 fl oz (125ml) rum
½ pint (285ml) double
cream
½ pint (285ml) Greek-
style natural yogurt*

1. Chop the Christmas cake. Put it into a bowl and pour in the rum. Leave it to soak overnight.
2. Mash the Christmas cake with the rum.
3. Stiffly whip the cream. Fold in the yogurt and the cake and rum.
4. Put the mixture into a freezing tray. Put it into the coldest part of the freezing compartment of the refrigerator (set at the lowest temperature). Freeze for 2 hours.
5. Take out the ice-cream and whip it to break up the ice particles. Put it into a plastic container and cover. Freeze for a further 4 hours.

Note: Once the ice-cream has completely frozen, it can be stored in any part of the freezer for up to 3 months; or in the freezing part of the refrigerator, set at normal temperature, for up to 2 weeks or according to the star rating.

American

*½ pound sugar-free
Christmas Cake (see page
228)
½ cup rum
1¼ cups heavy cream
1¼ cups Greek-style
unflavored yogurt*

Cold Crumble of Pineapple, Orange and Dried Fruits

Imperial (Metric)

*6 oz (170g) dried whole
apricots
6 oz (170g) prunes
½ pint (285ml) dry white
wine
¼ pint (140ml) natural
orange juice
1 pineapple
2 oranges
¾ pint (425ml) Greek-
style natural yogurt
3 oz (85g) crunchy oat
cereal*

1. Soak the apricots and prunes in the wine and orange juice for 8 hours. Drain them, reserving the juice. Halve and stone (pit) the prunes. Return the dried fruits to the juice.
2. Cut the husk from the pineapple. Slice and then dice the flesh, removing the core.
4. Cut the rind and pith from both oranges. Cut the oranges into quarters lengthways and thinly slice them.
5. Add the pineapple and oranges to the dried fruits.
6. Put the mixed fruits into a serving bowl. Cover them with the yogurt and scatter the crunchy cereal over the top.

Note: Unsuitable for freezing.

American

*6 ounces dried whole
apricots
6 ounces prunes
1⅓ cups dry white wine
⅔ cup natural orange
juice
1 pineapple
2 oranges
1½ cups Greek-style
unflavored yogurt
¾ cup crunchy oat cereal*

280

Cream of Christmas Puddings

This is an excellent, last minute alternative to the traditional Christmas pudding either on Christmas Day or at any time over the festive season.

Imperial (Metric)

4 oz (115g) sultanas
4 oz (115g) raisins
4 dried figs, chopped
2 oz (55g) candied peel, chopped
¼ pint (140ml) brandy
3 oz glacé cherries
2 oz (55g) flaked almonds
12 oz (340g) low-fat soft cheese
Grated rind of 1 medium orange

1. Soak the sultanas (golden seedless raisins), raisins figs and peel in the brandy overnight. Drain them, reserving the brandy.
2. Halve the cherries.
3. Toast the almonds.
4. Beat the cheese in a bowl to soften it. Mix in the sultanas (golden seedless raisins), raisins, peel, figs, cherries and almonds, the grated orange rind and 3 tablespoons of the brandy.
5. Lightly oil a 1½ pint (850ml/3¾ cup) pudding basin. Put in the mixture, press it down and smooth the top.
6. Chill the pudding for 2 hours.
7. Turn out the pudding and garnish with a sprig of holly.

Note: Unsuitable for freezing.

American

⅔ cup golden seedless raisins
⅔ cup raisins
4 dried figs, chopped
2 ounces candied peel, chopped
⅔ cup brandy
3 ounces glacé cherries
½ cup slivered almonds
1½ cups low-fat soft cheese
Grated rind of 1 medium orange

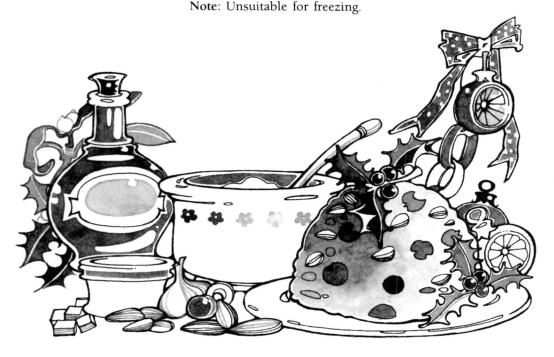

Banana Mould Filled with Oranges and Kiwi Fruits

Imperial (Metric)

*Thinly pared rind and
juice of 1 lemon
8 fl oz (225ml) water
2 oz (55g) honey
Agar-agar to set 2 pints
(1.14 litres) liquid (see
manufacturer's
instructions)
6 bananas
½ pint (285ml) double
cream*
Filling:
*2 medium oranges
3 kiwi fruit
2 tablespoons clear honey*

1. Put the thinly pared rind into a saucepan with the water. Bring it to the boil. Take the pan from the heat and leave to infuse for 30 minutes.
2. Strain the liquid. Return it to the pan. Add the lemon juice and honey.
3. Stir on a low heat for the honey to dissolve.
4. Bring the syrup to just below boiling point. Sprinkle in the agar-agar and stir for it to dissolve.
5. Put the syrup into a bowl and leave it until it is on the point of setting.
6. Mash the bananas.
7. Stiffly whip the cream. Mix in the bananas.
8. Whisk the jelly until it is frothy. Fold in the bananas and cream.
9. Pour the mixture into a 2 pint (1.14litre/5 cup) ring mould and leave it in a cool place to set.
10. For the filling, thinly pare the rind from one of the oranges. Cut it into thin slivers.
11. Cut the remaining pith from the orange and the rind and pith from the other. Cut the oranges into quarters lengthways and thinly slice them.
12. Cut the peel from the kiwi fruits. Cut the fruits in half and thinly slice them. Mix them in a bowl with the oranges.
13. Spoon the honey over the fruits and leave them for 30 minutes.
14. Boil the slivered orange rind for 2 minutes, drain and reserve it.
15. Turn the banana jelly out of the ring mould. Fill the centre with the oranges and kiwi fruits. Garnish with the slivers of orange rind.
Note: Unsuitable for freezing.

American

*Thinly pared rind and
juice of 1 lemon
1 cup water
3 tablespoons honey
Agar-agar to set 2½ cups
liquid (see manufacturer's
instructions)
6 bananas
2⅓ cups heavy cream*
Filling:
*2 medium oranges
3 kiwi fruit
2 tablespoons clear honey*

Mincemeat and Curd Tart with Apple Cream

Imperial (Metric)

Pastry:
8 oz (115g) wholemeal
flour
Pinch sea salt
5 oz (150g) butter,
softened
2 egg yolks
1 tablespoon honey
Filling:
12 oz (340g) curd cheese
4 oz (115g) dark
Barbados sugar
3 eggs, beaten
1 lb (455g) mincemeat
(see page 221)
Apple Cream:
2 medium cooking apples
2 tablespoons honey
2 tablespoons water
½ pint (285ml) double
cream

1. Heat the oven to 375°F/190°C/Gas Mark 6.
2. For the pastry, put the flour and salt onto a work surface and make a well in the centre. Put in the butter, egg yolks and honey and working with your fingertips, gradually bring flour from the sides of the well into the butter, until all the ingredients are well incorporated into a smooth dough. Cover the dough with a clean tea cloth and leave it to rest for 30 minutes.
3. For the filling, cream the cheese in a bowl. Beat in the sugar and then the eggs, a little at a time.
4. Line a 10 inch (25cm) tart tin with the pastry.
5. Spread the mincemeat in the bottom.
6. Pour in the cheese mixture.
7. Bake the tart for 30 minutes so the filling is set and lightly browned.
8. Cool it in the tin before removing and serving.
9. For the apple cream, core and chop the apples without peeling. Put them into a saucepan with the honey and water. Cover them and cook them gently for 15 minutes or until they are soft. Rub them through a sieve and cool them completely. Stiffly whip the cream and fold in the apple purée. Serve separately.

Note: The tart will rise in the oven but sinks gradually as it cools. Unsuitable for freezing.

American

Pastry:
2 cups wholewheat flour
Pinch sea salt
1⅓ cups butter, softened
2 egg yolks
1 tablespoon honey
Filling:
1½ cups curd cheese
2 cups dark Barbados
sugar
3 eggs, beaten
1 pound mincemeat (see
page 221)
Apple Cream:
2 medium cooking apples
2 tablespoons honey
2 tablespoons water
1¼ cups heavy cream

Index